JONATHAN HASLAM

Near and Distant Neighbors

Jonathan Haslam is the George F. Kennan Professor at the School of Historical Studies, Institute for Advanced Study, Princeton. He is also a fellow of Corpus Christi College, Cambridge, and a professor emeritus of Cambridge University.

NEAR AND
DISTANT NEIGHBORS

NEAR AND DISTANT NEIGHBORS

A New History of Soviet Intelligence

JONATHAN HASLAM

FARRAR, STRAUS AND GIROUX • NEW YORK

Farrar, Straus and Giroux
120 Broadway, New York 10271

Published in 2015 by Farrar, Straus and Giroux
First paperback edition, 2016

The Library of Congress has cataloged the hardcover edition as follows:
Haslam, Jonathan.
    Near and distant neighbors : a new history of Soviet intelligence /
Jonathan Haslam. — First edition.
        pages   cm
    Includes bibliographical references and index.
    ISBN 978-0-374-21990-1 (hardback) — ISBN 978-0-374-71040-8 (e-book)
    1. Intelligence service—Soviet Union—History.   2. Secret service—Soviet
Union—History.   3. Military intelligence—Soviet Union—History.   4. Espionage,
Soviet—History.   5. Cryptography—Soviet Union—History.   6. Soviet Union—
Politics and government.   7. Soviet Union—Foreign relations.   I. Title.

    JN6529.I6 H37 2015
    327.1247009'04—dc23

                                                                    2014046634

Paperback ISBN: 978-0-374-53627-5

Designed by Abby Kagan

Our books may be purchased in bulk for promotional, educational, or business
use. Please contact your local bookseller or the Macmillan Corporate and Premium
Sales Department at 1-800-221-7945, extension 5442, or by e-mail at Macmillan
SpecialMarkets@macmillan.com.

www.fsgbooks.com
www.twitter.com/fsgbooks • www.facebook.com/fsgbooks

P1

Intelligence is for us sacred, a matter of ideals.

—Stalin

Fear has large eyes.

—Russian proverb

CONTENTS

RUSSIAN INTELLIGENCE IDIOM (SOVIET PERIOD)

Agenturíst: operative responsible for running agents

Aktívnaya razvédka/aktívka (active intelligence): terrorism and sabotage

Aktívnye meropriyátiya (active measures): black propaganda, dirty tricks, etc.

Boevýe shífry: working ciphers

Bol'shói Dom (literally, the "Big House"): Comintern; later the Lubyanka

Chertvyórtyi: the Fourth Directorate of the Staff/General Staff, later GRU

Dezá (dezinformátsiya): disinformation

Enkavedíst: employee of the NKVD (GUGB), state security

Ente-eróvsev: scientific and technical intelligence operative

Gámma: ciphering sequence/one-time pad

Gebíst: state security operative

Geberóvskii: state security operative

Gereúshnik: GRU operative

Kagebíst/kagebéshnik: KGB operative

Kirpích (literally, "brick"): watchman on delegations abroad

Komitétchik (literally, "committee man"): KGB operative

Kontóra (literally, "office"): KGB First Main Directorate at Yasenevo

Krokíst: counterintelligence operative, state security (OGPU)

Krýsha (literally, "roof"): cover

Lástochnik (swallow): female operative employed for seduction

Lesá (the woods): KGB school, later the First Main Directorate at Yasenevo

Lózung: a crib for breaking open a cipher

Marshrútnyi agént: employee of state security handling communications

Nevidímyi front (invisible front): secret intelligence

Óboroten (literally, "shapeshifter"): turncoat/traitor

Omsóvets: operative in Comintern's department for international communications

Opér: abbreviation for either Operatívnyi sotrúdnik/ofitsér or Operabótnik

Operabótnik: KGB operative

Operatívnyi sotrúdnik/ofitsér: GRU operative

Opertékhnik: a technical operative

Operupolnomóchennyi: one responsible for a particular operation

Osobísty: GRU officers

Osóbye meropriyátiya (special measures): assassination and other tasks approved only by the Politburo

Osóbye zadáchi (special tasks): assassination and other tasks approved only by the Politburo

Osvedomítel': information operative

Pe-eróvets: political intelligence operative

Podkrýshnik: operative under deep cover

Razvédupr' (*Razvedyvatel'noe upravlenie*): a generic term for military intelligence

Rezident: chief of a secret intelligence station

Rezidentura: secret intelligence station

Sapogí (boots): KGB term for GRU counterparts

S"em (literally, "removal"): seizure of a traitor

Shifrográmma: ciphered telegram

Svád'ba (literally, "wedding"): seizure of a traitor

Tsereúshnik: CIA officer

Verbóvshchik: operative specialising in recruitment

Vorón ("raven"): male operative employed for seduction

Zagrantóchka: overseas post

EUROPE, 1920

ICELAND

Atlantic Ocean

NORWAY

SWEDEN

FINLAND

Helsinki

Leningrad

Stockholm

Tallinn/Reval

ESTONIA

Moscow

DENMARK

LATVIA

Riga

LITHUANIA

Kaunas

EAST PRUSSIA

SOVIET RUSSIA

IRELAND

GREAT BRITAIN

London

NETHERLANDS

Berlin

Warsaw

BELGIUM

GERMANY

POLAND

Paris

LUXEMBOURG

Prague

CZECHOSLOVAKIA

FRANCE

Vienna

SWITZERLAND

AUSTRIA

HUNGARY

ROMANIA

PORTUGAL

Madrid

SPAIN

ITALY

Rome

YUGOSLAVIA

BULGARIA

ALBANIA

GREECE

TURKEY

Mediterranean Sea

0 Miles 200 400

0 Kilometers 400

© 2015 Jeffrey L. Ward

EUROPE, 1941

ICELAND

Atlantic Ocean

SWEDEN

FINLAND

NORWAY

Helsinki

Leningrad

Stockholm

Moscow

IRELAND

GREAT
BRITAIN

Cambridge

USSR

London

Berlin

Warsaw

GERMANY

GERMAN
OCCUPIED
TERRITORY

Paris

Prague

FRANCE
(GERMAN OCCUPIED)

Budapest

Bern

SWITZERLAND

HUNGARY

ROMANIA

Belgrade

PORTUGAL

Madrid

ITALY

YUGOSLAVIA

BULGARIA

Rome

SPAIN

ALBANIA

TURKEY

GREECE

Mediterranean Sea

0 Miles   200   400

0 Kilometers   400

© 2015 Jeffrey L. Ward

EUROPE, 1955

ICELAND

FINLAND

NORWAY

SWEDEN

DENMARK

IRELAND

UNITED KINGDOM

NETHERLANDS

EAST GERMANY

POLAND

USSR

BELGIUM

WEST GERMANY

LUXEMBOURG

CZECHOSLOVAKIA

FRANCE

WEST AUSTRIA

HUNGARY

EAST AUSTRIA

ROMANIA

SWITZERLAND

YUGOSLAVIA

ITALY

BULGARIA

PORTUGAL

SPAIN

ALBANIA

GREECE

TURKEY

Atlantic Ocean

Mediterranean Sea

Western Bloc

Eastern Bloc

Neutral

0 Miles 200 400

0 Kilometers 400

© 2015 Jeffrey L. Ward

PREFACE

The role of secret intelligence in the history of international relations has long been a neglected one. To the undaunted icebreakers in Britain and the United States who nevertheless forged ahead into these uncharted and inhospitable waters, we owe a debt of gratitude.[1] Their drive for greater openness slowly yielded results on both sides of the Atlantic. Subsequent research on the history of the Western intelligence services has since been made possible by the greater freedom of information such sustained lobbying produced.

In the East, however, even the most optimistic held out no hope that access to similar information could ever be obtained. What did appear invariably originated with defectors from the KGB (such as Oleg Gordievsky) working with the Western intelligence services, and came on trust. Yet even when defectors offered as complete an overview of the KGB as they could manage, their knowledge inevitably fell short given the tight compartmentalisation of official secrets; filling in gaps of knowledge with rumour and guesswork only complicated matters further. And the KGB was not everything. It may have been the largest intelligence service in the world, but it was heavily weighted in favour of its domestic role, a role never played by its military counterpart, the GRU, the second-largest intelligence service in the world. The KGB without the GRU is thus only half the story. Yet there are no GRU memoirs of any consequence; certainly nothing comparable to those from the KGB.

As a result, thus far nothing comprehensive has been produced that takes in *all* the branches of Soviet intelligence: the KGB *and* the GRU, human intelligence *and* communications intelligence, foreign intelligence *and* counterintelligence operations. Since history is about perspective as well as information, the gaps in knowledge matter a great deal.

To be precise, the most detailed new revelations, notably two weighty volumes coauthored by Christopher Andrew and Lieutenant Colonel Vasili Mitrokhin, focus on the KGB and almost exclusively on the years of the Cold War (1947–1989).[2] One of the KGB's erstwhile archivists, Mitrokhin had devoted more than a decade and, indeed, risked his life making detailed notes from the files of the First Main Directorate (foreign intelligence) as they were transferred from the Lubyanka, off Gorky Street, to the bright and shiny new headquarters at Yasenevo in "the woods." In so doing, he smashed the dam of secrecy that had held firm over seven decades.

Without a doubt, the two books together represent a stunning achievement. They also caused a veritable sensation as Soviet agents, hitherto hidden, were exposed to the intrusive glare of uninvited publicity. Most but not all of these files have now been opened to public inspection at the Archives Centre, Churchill College, Cambridge University. Their availability has unquestionably transformed our knowledge of the inner workings of the KGB in its foreign operations.

The undoubted strengths of Mitrokhin's revelations notwithstanding, they are not entirely without problems: most important, the fact that the British government, which authorised release of the files, exercised its censorship over what has been made publicly available. Nine files on Britain and twenty-nine files on the United States (eight hundred pages of "dense typescript") remain closed.[3]

Doubtless as a result of restrictions on access imposed by the British, the Russians appear the sole initiators of operations. But are we really to assume that Moscow was alone in taking the initiative, whereas the West only reacted? We know from other operations in the Third World, for instance, that CIA and MI6 hardly sat on their hands. Yet the dirty linen hung out to dry is solely Russian. How can one write a balanced account of a long-standing conflict with more than half the sources deliberately removed?

The dilemma faced by the historian of the contemporary world is here highlighted in its most extreme form: surely only the most naïve would suppose that what has been so assiduously hidden from us is less significant than that which has been so frankly revealed. The honest historian of the recent past is thus at the mercy of those in power—and their priorities are not necessarily our priorities. The truth is that a balanced view of the past is not seen as in the national interest of the authoritative agencies on either side. Their job is to protect those interests come what may. We have therefore to rely upon unauthorised indiscretions and revelations from defectors harried by their former employers.

Other problems arise not only as a result of agency, but also from force of circumstance. The Mitrokhin Archive covers human intelligence only. The crucial sphere of Russian cryptography is neglected because Mitrokhin had no access. This may seem enough for some. The reader is naturally more readily captivated by derring-do. Spies, after all, are somehow accessible, even glamorous, to the seeker after sensation sceptical of the grubby reality immortalised by the former MI5/MI6 officer David Cornwall (John le Carré).

Only the intrepid reader will want to take a step further, beyond secret agents and into another dimension: the back rooms where the pencil has proven infinitely mightier than the sword. Yet it is by looking here, too, that evidence will be found as to the intentions of the adversary.

Neglect of Moscow's activities in this sphere was justified by the focus on human intelligence. Whereas the Americans elevated decryption of enemy communications to the highest calling in intelligence, one that required exceptional prowess in diverse fields (engineering, mathematics, linguistics, statistics, even the realm of the imagination), the Russians traditionally adhered to a different order of priorities. Nonetheless, Soviet cryptography should never be underestimated. It, too, has to be investigated.

With respect to human intelligence, the Russians were always stronger in counterintelligence than in foreign intelligence. Some of the best operations abroad directed at the main adversary were initiated by former counterintelligence operatives who were therefore all the better equipped to outwit their foreign counterparts. Yet this aspect is not fully reflected in Andrew and Mitrokhin. Also, because operatives in counterintelligence were least likely to defect, their side of the story receives less coverage.

Finally, the extensive history of the second-largest intelligence organisation in the world, Soviet military intelligence (the GRU), lay entirely beyond Mitrokhin's grasp and, therefore, has yet to reach the public eye.

Thus, although the shelves have been richly replenished by Andrew and Mitrokhin, we still have a published record that remains tantalisingly incomplete. This has important consequences. On the basis of the materials made public, we are at best able to say that a particular individual was or was not an agent of the KGB or that the KGB did or did not launch a particular operation (unless, of course, it concerns operations against the United States); the available materials do not enable us to say that a potential agent might not instead have worked for the GRU or that a particular operation was run by the GRU.

Furthermore, even with respect to the KGB, some operations (specific assassinations, permission for which had to come from the Politburo) could be too sensitive to be found in the files within reach of Mitrokhin. They were retained in the requisite operational department, as were personal files, including certain material relating to the notorious Cambridge spy Kim Philby. So the fact that Mitrokhin found nothing on the attempt on the life of the Pope, to give one obvious example, proves absolutely nothing as to Soviet complicity or innocence. Absence of evidence is not evidence of absence.

Had these been our only sources from Moscow, intrepid explorers in the foothills might have lost hope and turned back. Thankfully, however, an impressive array of new archival documents has been published in Russian, including an important series brought to light by the former Gorbachev aide Aleksandr Yakovlev.

Of equal importance, changes in Russian society, almost entirely negative for freedom of information as a whole, have ironically rendered the history of Soviet intelligence more accessible than one would have expected. The control of newspapers and television media by the state, which has stifled freedom of expression in Russia, did not forestall officially authorised releases of documents on secret intelligence.

Under Putin's first term as president, the security organs were evidently encouraged to advertise their vital role in Russia's past (and, by implication, its present) by rummaging in the archives for evidence of patriotic deeds. They then began steadily releasing the information they had uncovered, under carefully controlled conditions, through certain selected newspapers and journals: most notably *Nezavisimoe voennoe obozrenie, Voenno-promyshlennyi kur'er, Kommersant vlast', Rossiiskaya gazeta, Krasnaya zvezda, Bratishka ru, Voinskoe bratstvo,* and *Sovershenno sekretno.*

Books and television documentaries have also contributed to our knowledge of human intelligence operations. We have, for instance, the entire story of the spy Colonel Pen'kovskii's entrapment, rendered all the more vivid in a film made at the time by KGB counterintelligence.[4] Similar documentaries under the rubric "Secrets of Intelligence," about General Polyakov, for example, or lesser spies such as Ogorodnik, fill in much of the detail hitherto denied to us. Also, the memoirs of operatives now no longer in the service—such as the two Olegs, Gordievsky and Kalugin, but also others available only in Russian—enliven our sense of what this secret world was really like from the inside.

Of course these, as with all intelligence sources, have to be handled with care. In many instances information provided is extremely difficult to cross-check. Also, one must never forget the sobering fact that just because a source is unique, that does not make it entirely reliable, regardless of provenance. Unfortunately, on March 12, 2014, the Interdepartmental Committee on the Defence of State Secrets took a decisive step backwards in deciding to institute a thirty-year delay on the release of everything relating to the history of the security services from 1917 to 1991.[5]

Since foreign intelligence operations are by their very nature interactive, access to restricted CIA and MI5 archives now open has provided correctives to random revelations from Moscow. With respect to communications intelligence (codes and ciphers), the U.S. National Security Agency (NSA) appears to have made available on its website most of (three thousand) but not all the decrypted intercepts of Soviet wartime communications: code-named Venona.[6] This was the late senator Daniel Patrick Moynihan's achievement in the face of stiff bureaucratic opposition. Further progress was apparently halted, however, because the Russians threatened to retaliate were the remaining decrypts published.[7]

The myopia of officialdom came home to me when, having found MI5 and MI6 documents within the archive of the Communist International (Comintern) in Moscow in 1993, I protested to a figure in authority from the British Cabinet Office that, to my dismay, the Russians were now revealing British intelligence documents that Her Majesty's Government was still unwilling to release. Why could we not read these here? Her sharp retort was that London "would not be dictated to by Russian policy!" Information is, after all, power.

Lack of openness by officials renders the historian's task all the more difficult—and this comes at a cost, because the history of intelligence matters. Without knowing what secret information has been decrypted, it is impossible to assess the data upon which statesmen based their decisions at key moments in international relations. Had the Russians been as scrupulously secretive as our own side—we know, for example, the syllabus for cryptographic training in the Soviet Union but, ironically, not our own—any attempt to write about Soviet decryption would have been impossible. Thankfully, in this instance Russia has proven more enlightened than the West.

My intention in this book is to build upon the foundations of existing knowledge and extend them further in order to present the history of Soviet intelligence in all its several parts both thematically and chronologically. The result is about as comprehensive as can be contained within one volume, given prevailing restrictions. It should take you, the reader, farther down the road than hitherto, to a more thorough understanding of how the East-West struggle was fought underground, with implications as to why the Soviet régime lost, and no less important, towards a greater understanding of the mentality of those who rule Russia today.

The organisation of this work follows chronological lines interrupted only by the need to fill in events that occur simultaneously on different levels. We begin with an alarming element of continuity between the present day and the Soviet period: the use of targeted assassination, and the conduct of "active intelligence," as in the seizure of the Crimea and the operation to detach Eastern Ukraine effected by special forces from the summer of 2014. We raise in starkest form the question of how much present-day Russian intelligence differs from its Soviet predecessors.

But how did the Soviet setup come into being? The first chapter traces the emergence of the Cheka, its foreign and domestic components, and the development of its rival institution, the Fourth Directorate of the army staff. It highlights the successes of the domestic counterintelligence sections and the relative weakness of those responsible for foreign operations.

These two elements, rivalry between the military and civilian intelligence services and the imbalance of effectiveness between intelligence and counterintelligence, play a key role in the events of chapter 2, which covers the 1930s. The eventual outcome unfolded in two parts and in sequence: the takeover of foreign operations by counterintelligence and the subsequent subordination of military intelligence to civilian intelligence.

The impact of the first takeover, with foreign operations in the hands of counterintelligence, resulted in dramatic successes, particularly against Britain (the recruitment of the so-called Cambridge Five), but also against Japan and the United States. However, military intelligence was the only branch that had had a proper analytical section, and that section was summarily abolished. The joint supervision of civilian with military intelligence could have led to greater effectiveness in other ways but for the resistance it engendered and the fact that both institutions (now called the GUGB of the NKVD and the Fourth) were broken by Stalin's Terror.

The Terror also jeopardised the development of Soviet decryption. As chapter 3 illustrates, the cryptographic effort always trailed behind human intelligence in terms of priorities. The failure to develop decryption was not a momentary neglect. It was a standing feature of the Stalin régime from beginning to end. The consequences were to be felt well into the Cold War.

The Terror thus crippled the capabilities of Soviet intelligence across the board. It created, as chapter 4 demonstrates, certain areas of relative weakness that proved critical to the security of the Soviet Union: one thinks most notably of the abject failure to penetrate the upper reaches of the Nazi Party in Germany. The underlying problem here, however, was Stalin's failure to take Hitler at face value, which was not an intelligence failure at all.

The consequences of Stalin's mismanagement of foreign, defence, and intelligence affairs came to be felt when Hitler decided in late 1940 to attack the Soviet Union. Operation Barbarossa took place in June of the following year. The ground lost to German forces had to be reconquered more than once—because in 1942 Stalin again neglected sound intelligence. This resulted in the greater part of the losses suffered by the Soviet people in World War II, which, by the end of the conflict, totalled twenty-seven million. This brings us through chapter 5.

The story then moves into the Cold War era. Here the West held considerable potential advantage at the outset in the form of mechanised decryption of Soviet secret communications. But this advantage was lost in 1948, just at the point that it would have made all the difference. In the world of human intelligence, notably that of the Cambridge Five, it was the Russians who held the best if not in fact all the cards. The astute exploitation of this crucial advantage made all the difference in the early Cold War.

Chapter 7 focuses on the consequences flowing from the loss of Stalin's human intelligence assets both in the United States and Britain. It became ever more difficult to recruit agents following Khrushchev's denunciation of Stalin, the god of the international Communist movement. In these circumstances, it was counterintelligence that took and held the lead. Meanwhile, military intelligence and cryptography hastened to catch up and reduce the growing Anglo-American advantage in orbital satellites and high-technology interception of ground communications. Image intelligence mattered because Khrushchev's much-vaunted superiority in strategic missiles was just a bluff.

Only in Germany did the Russians seize and hold the higher ground, not least due to the contributions of the allied East German services; and even here the Berlin Tunnel dreamt up by MI6 and financed by the Americans briefly made deep inroads into the security of Soviet forces occupying the centre of Europe. Operations in Britain and France, based on strong anti-American sentiment, proved crucial assets. Yet the great bluff of Soviet strategic superiority broke under satellite surveillance from the United States and the treachery of Pen'kovskii. The attempt to compensate for what was now revealed to be U.S. superiority by installing theatre-range nuclear missiles in Cuba was then destroyed by a combination of U.S. intelligence and political resolve.

One underlying vulnerability of the Soviet system was loss of faith, a loss initially delayed at home through timely populism, but immediately damaging abroad. In the end it meant that recruitment of agents could be based almost exclusively upon material incentives. It also meant that as time went on and stagnation took hold at home, Soviet citizens and operatives increasingly fell victim to hostile recruitment.

The Americans, too, had succumbed to disillusion as a consequence of the failed war in Vietnam, and the Russians took every opportunity to undermine their U.S. counterparts from within: hence the betrayal of CIA by Aldrich Ames and the FBI by Robert Hanssen. Of course none of this availed Moscow, except in the short term, as the Soviet Union's ultimate collapse was due to forces far larger than secret intelligence could muster or block. It nevertheless seemed that at the very time that Gorbachev was allowing the Soviet Union to be elbowed out of Eastern Europe, his secret services were more successful than ever. Should we be surprised? One of my Soviet friends was forever reminding me that of those graduating from his alma mater, the main training school for international relations (MGIMO), the KGB took the best and the brightest.

The end of the Soviet experiment thus left those services and the men who gave their lives to them with a deep-seated and justified feeling of having been cheated on the very eve of their most momentous successes. We should therefore not be surprised that they look to their history as an inspiration for the future—and with the country led by a former operative, every expectation is of greater achievements ahead. There is no sign that President Putin has much incentive to hold back—rather, the reverse.

To my relief, no intelligence service offered or gave me any assistance. Some individuals, since retired, were kind enough to alert me to errors of fact, but all the mistakes are entirely my own. Without the World Wide Web, the task of tracking down this mass of obscure Russian sources would have been impossible; the writing of history has thus been immeasurably strengthened by technological change. I have met a few of the cast, including Sergei Kondrashyov and Vadim Kirpichenko, but I could never claim to be the recipient of secrets. My previous, brief connexion with Trinity College has in no way subverted my objectivity towards other old members who appear in these pages. Those I have to thank include first and foremost my wife and in-house critic, Karina Urbach; Allen Packwood and the Archives Centre at Churchill College, Cambridge; and the following, for guidance at various stages on points of fact, a broader understanding of events, or just critical comment: "Nigel West" (Rupert Allason), the late Baroness Park, Stefan Halper, Phillip Knightley, Gordon Barrass, the late Chapman Pincher, and Zara Steiner.

Lastly, may I record a debt of thanks to my editor, Eric Chinski; Peng Shepherd; and the unfailing support of my agent, Andrew Wylie, and his team in London and New York.

—JONATHAN HASLAM, Institute for Advanced Study,
Princeton, August 2015

NEAR AND
DISTANT NEIGHBORS

INTRODUCTION

> The Secret Intelligence Service has existed for 150 years.*
> We, for 10. That is their advantage. But we have our advan-
> tages: a clear goal, our incorruptibility, sense of purpose; but
> above all, devotion to the cause of socialism.
> —ARTUR ARTUZOV, head of counterintelligence OGPU, 1927[1]

As recently as July 2010, the United States expelled eleven Russian spies who had been operating deep under cover for up to a decade. The leak was discovered to have come from Colonel Aleksandr Poteev, whose daughter was living in the United States. Poteev had been deputy head of S Directorate, responsible for agents under deep cover ("illegals") at the SVR, the KGB's successor for foreign intelligence.

A senior official from the Kremlin warned, "We know who he is and where he is. He committed treachery either for money or he simply got caught for something. But you cannot doubt the fact that a Mercader [Trotsky's assassin] has already been sent after him. The fate of such a person is unenviable. He will drag this along behind him throughout his entire life and each day he will live in fear of retribution."[2]

Was this just an idle boast? Four years earlier, on November 23, 2006, Aleksandr Litvinenko, a Russian citizen formerly an officer in Soviet intelligence (FSB), died in agony from an obscure cause (poisoning by radioactive polonium-210) at University College Hospital in

---

*Of course, Artuzov is wrong: one could say either sixteen (for MI6) or three hun-
dred fifty years (for the first such service).

London. Litvinenko had taken tea at the Millenium Hotel, Grosvenor Square, with two other Russians, one also a former officer of the FSB, Andrei Lugovoi. Lugovoi and his compatriot Dmitrii Kovtun left a trail of polonium across London, leading to a frantic search for others who might also have been poisoned by fortuitous contact.

Litvinenko's previous boss, Lieutenant Colonel Aleksandr Gusak, branded him "an out-and-out traitor" on the grounds that he had betrayed Russian agents to British intelligence. For this he would have faced the death penalty in Soviet times. Indeed, one of those exposed had offered to assassinate him.[3] Litvinenko's widow, Marina, later confirmed that her husband had indeed received tens of thousands of pounds from MI5 and MI6 for services rendered.[4]

Litvinenko and others had originally found a patron in a rising oligarch, the late Boris Berezovsky, the victim of an attempted assassination in July 1994. The former head of Moscow counterintelligence claims that Litvinenko, flanked by others, approached him about forming an assassination squad to wipe out organised crime to protect figures such as Berezovsky. He ejected them from his office, brusquely dismissing the proposal with the comment that Russia was not Brazil, at one time a country of death squads run by policemen.[5]

In 1997, Litvinenko became deputy to Gusak, then head of the seventh department of the directorate, responsible for investigating and prosecuting criminal organisations. Here, Litvinenko and his colleagues engaged in kidnapping, assault, and "protection."[6] Litvinenko was safe, however, only so long as his benefactor Berezovsky remained close to power. Once Vladimir Putin took over, having been funded by Berezovsky on extravagant expectations of political influence, Putin turned against the oligarchs as potential usurpers. More astute than some and with much to lose, Berezovsky fled into exile. Meanwhile, Litvinenko was imprisoned, and on release, he followed his erstwhile patron to London.

If, at this point, Litvinenko did indeed identify to MI6 former fellow officers involved in his nefarious practices, those officers would have been exposed to blackmail, vengeance, and penetration by MI5 or MI6. Worse still, some were by then operating in Britain: in 2003, Putin had given the FSB, formerly the Second Main Directorate of the KGB with no experience of foreign operations, unprecedented permission to operate abroad. This measure is said to have infuriated the SVR, formerly the First Main Directorate and uniquely responsible. So when the FSB apparently bungled the Litvinenko murder, a certain amount of schadenfreude was evident at the SVR.[7]

In Britain, the Crown Prosecution Service sought to bring the accused, Lugovoi, to trial. But the Russian government vociferously refused to consider extradition; Lugovoi had, in the meantime, managed to secure a seat in the Russian parliament, thus forestalling any question of extradition. The two countries remain at an impasse, and the British government, fearing revelations about the behaviour of the secret services, prohibited the release of information that could throw light directly on Litvinenko's assassination. Now, however, a public enquiry has been opened in Britain to determine responsibility for the murder. This enquiry can oblige the British government to divulge classified information and resolve the matter, though the final report is to be censored.

The significance of these stunning events is extraordinary. Russia paid a price in the deterioration of relations with a leading European power and in damage to its public image. This surely outweighed the meagre advantage gained by defending the assassination of a minor former intelligence officer who had turned coat.

Yet this was by no means the first time Moscow chose to affirm its unrestricted sovereignty by sacrificing international relations at the altar of vengeance, allowing a cascade of pent-up emotions to overwhelm the normal constraints of reason. The most striking precedent was set nearly a century ago, under Stalin. At the time, the revolution was a very recent memory. Only the Reds were fully aware of how close they had come to defeat at the hands of the Whites. The obsession with a possible reversal of fortune, even after victory had been secured, was therefore completely natural.

The tsarist counterrevolutionary organisation in Paris, ROVS, counted twenty thousand active members. Its leader was the notoriously psychopathic Lieutenant General Aleksandr Kutyepov. He had ordered his men to step up terrorist activity within the Soviet Union; their attacks were aimed at the Party and the secret police (OGPU). The Kremlin decided to dispose of him once and for all. Next in line of fire was his deputy, Major General Nikolai Skoblin, but here the idea was to turn him and his wife, the celebrated opera singer Nadezhda Plevitskaya, which they did within a matter of months.

Operation Zamorskie sprang into action. At around 11:00 a.m. on January 26, 1930, while on his weekly walk to church, Kutyepov was bundled into a car at the corner of rue Oudinot and rue Rousselet. He was never seen again. On holiday in the South of France at the time, Deputy Commissar for Foreign Affairs Nikolai Krestinsky suddenly found the climate change from mild to malevolent. "The situation may become serious," the Soviet ambassador in Paris warned. "[Prime Minister André] Tardieu is in London, [Foreign Minister Aristide] Briand has returned for only a few days. The government is in fact headless. It is possible that anti-Soviet forces will try to use this anarchy to create an atmosphere conducive to a breach of relations." The Soviet mission was effectively in a state of siege. Yet, in Moscow, the leadership reacted with indignation rather than fear. Its official mouthpiece, *Izvestiya*, aggressively asked whether the French government "prefers the maintenance of diplomatic relations with the government of the Soviet Union to co-operation with white guard emigrés?"[8]

The Russians vigorously rebutted all allegations, though few believed them. Not until September 22, 1965, did the Soviet military newspaper *Krasnaya zvezda* refer to Sergei Puzitskii, former deputy head of counterintelligence, as having "brilliantly carried out the operation to arrest Kutyepov." The operation had been organised by Yakov Serebryanskii, who headed the "Special Group Uniquely Designated," which was separate from and not subordinate to the foreign department of the OGPU (formerly the Cheka). The unit was also known as "Yasha's Group," after "uncle" Yasha, "Yasha" being the Russian diminutive of Yakov. This unit was directly controlled by Vyacheslav Menzhinsky, head of the secret police and successor to his friend and fellow Pole Feliks Dzerzhinsky, the former religious fanatic who had created the Cheka. When Serebryanskii reached Moscow on March 30, 1930, he was awarded the Order of the Red Banner for his achievement.[9]

Massively overweight with wide, drooping shoulders and roving eyes, Menzhinsky, the son of a Polish admiral, gave every impression of being seriously unwell. Indeed, he had chronic asthma, and after a car accident, he was plagued by a severe spinal problem that meant he could barely sit and spent most of his days stretched out on a sofa. He disappeared on sick leave for weeks on end.[10] But Menzhinsky was a gifted intellectual given to paradox who had found his true métier representing Soviet Russia in Berlin after peace was signed at Brest-Litovsk in March 1918. It was here that he developed a strong taste for covert action.[11] After his young wife died under the knife on the operating table, however, the life went out of him:[12] he was "not a man but the shadow of one," Trotsky opined.[13] As a result, Menzhinsky's two deputies, Meer Trilisser (for foreign operations) and Artur Artuzov (for domestic matters), gradually took over.

In response to the Kutyepov assassination and Soviet subversion of its empire overseas, the French government embargoed trade with the Soviet Union, debated a breach in diplomatic relations, and sought to rally the other great powers to its cause. The timing could scarcely have been worse for the Russians. At that very moment the die-hard anti-communist Adolf Hitler was hustling his way into power in Germany. Moscow needed allies, not more enemies.

Decades separate Kutyepov from Litvinenko, yet both cases offer a litmus test of Moscow's commitment to Western values. Today, Russia approximates a democracy. The KGB abroad has been replaced by the SVR. The massive and traumatic changes unleashed by the breakup of the Soviet Union in 1991–1992 nevertheless appear to have left something fundamental unchanged in Russia. These continuities are evidence of a deeper determinant that predates the Bolshevik revolution and explains its extraordinary vigour: a primitive political culture originating in a medieval despotism. It was buttressed by a sense of identity antithetical to the West. Fyodor Dostoevsky, for instance, was far from alone in despising Western rationalism. The Slavophile and Eurasian movements shared these prejudices to the full.

Ironically, the October Revolution's internationalism proved the greatest asset for Soviet intelligence. The degree to which the services were manned in the field by non-Russians (the greater number being Jews and Poles) for the first two decades highlights the international nature of the Communist cause. They could recruit for not merely a Russian but also a worldwide revolutionary movement. No other intelligence service relied so extensively on identifying and turning waverers in the enemy camp, on playing the Pied Piper of the Promised Land and turning credulous believers into ruthless agents who followed wherever they were led and did whatever they were told to do, without hesitation. "In intelligence," Stalin counselled, "one must have several hundred who are friendly (i.e., more than the agents) and ready to fulfill whatever task is set them." This was written towards the end of 1952.

The Cambridge Five could not have been far from his thoughts, as two of them, Guy Burgess and Donald Maclean, had defected just over a year before. Such friends were appreciated by Stalin as "the highest class of intelligence."[14] Yet no other service had so many of their own shot from behind by their own comrades. This brutal paradox brings us to the heart of the history of the world's two largest secret services: the civilian KGB and the military GRU, the "near" and "distant" neighbours of the Foreign Ministry.

The birth of Soviet intelligence was entirely unanticipated by the evil genius behind the revolution, Lenin—"Ilyich" to his comrades. The Russia he returned to after years in exile was a brutish place, the backwater of Europe, a Eurasian hodgepodge without the benefits of the Renaissance, the Reformation, or, to any sustained degree, the Enlightenment. Nor could it claim to have a proud Asiatic past like the civilisations of India and China. And, crucially, Russia was behind the industrialised world, as Lenin openly complained, defeated in war even by the hated Japanese (1904), themselves Asian newcomers to the states system. But Lenin and Trotsky were by no means alone in the hope that once the revolution triumphed in Germany, they would move bag and baggage to civilised Berlin, the rightful seat of socialist revolution. This would lead directly to the dawning of a new order, the communism envisaged by Marx and Engels, built on the back of European culture, not barricaded against it in rank defiance.

After the civil war was won, Trotsky, the second great figure of the Bolshevik revolution, delivered a dramatic declaration of war on the capitalist world:

> From provincial Moscow, from half-Asiatic Russia, we will embark on the expansionist path of the European revolution. It will lead us to a world revolution. Remember the millions of the German petite bourgeoisie, awaiting the moment for revenge. In them we will find a reserve army and bring up our cavalry with this army to the Rhine to advance further in the form of a revolutionary proletarian war. We will repeat the French revolution, but in the reverse geographical direction: the revolutionary armies will advance not from the west to the east, but from the east to the west. The decisive moment has come. You can almost literally hear the footsteps of history.[15]

Even Stalin, hitherto the dour sceptic, urged Lenin in the heady summer of 1920 to recognise that

> we have already entered the field of direct conflict with the Entente [Britain and France], that the policy of tacking to the wind has already lost its overwhelming significance, that we can and must now conduct an offensive policy (not to be confused with a policy of collision), if we wish to hold the initiative to ourselves in foreign affairs that we recently attained. Thus we need to set as the agenda for Comintern [Communist International] the matter of organising an uprising in Italy and in such states that have not yet bolstered themselves such as Hungary, Czechoslovakia (Romania must be smashed) ... In short, we need to weigh anchor and take to sea while imperialism has yet to get ship shape ...[16]

In the autumn chill of 1923, Stalin crowed about moving "the centre of revolution from Moscow to Berlin."[17] Yet these idle boasts bore little in common with the cruel reality: the much-promised uprising in Germany collapsed ignominiously in November 1923, just as it had in March 1921. And this left the Bolsheviks with a recalcitrant, backward country peopled overwhelmingly by illiterate peasants facing the choice of giving up entirely or going it alone.

It was this unrelieved, desperate sense of isolation, and a damned inheritance from a benighted past, that more than anything ensured Stalin's victory in the struggle for power. Stalin, at times the unblinkered realist, saw the Soviet Union as "this country of the Middle Ages."[18] Under him, it very soon began reverting to the savagery of arbitrary rule, a "kingdom of darkness," as the author of *Life and Fate*, Vasilii Grossman, called it. The consequences for the future were critical. No Westernised Bolshevik (notably Nikolai Bukharin even more than Trotsky) could feel comfortable in such conditions. "Let's not forget that Russia is an Asiatic country," a senior Soviet diplomat (likely as not the anglophile Deputy Commissar for Foreign Affairs Maxim Litvinov) commented at the time, "the way of Genghis Khan and Stalin suits it better than the European civilisation of Leon Davidovitch [Trotsky]."[19]

Because Russia stood substantially alone, secret intelligence operations became critical not just for the furtherance of a receding revolution but also as a vital safeguard for national security—hence the Cheka's insignia of sword and shield. Russia had no army worthy of the name and relied instead upon extensive disinformation spread by the intelligence services to fool adversaries as to its true military capabilities.

The tsarist legacy of unenlightened autocracy had an impact upon Soviet secret intelligence that is easily underestimated. Not that there existed a continuity of personnel. Quite the opposite—the Bolsheviks had to start from scratch. But life underground and in exile, poisoned by pervasive conspiracy, left its ugly scars. It reached its frightening apogee in the person of Stalin and the paranoid condition that drove him to suffocate the Soviet people in an unrelenting embrace. His most devoted follower, Vyacheslav Molotov, was not much different, according to Molotov's grandson Nikonov.[20]

The crucial secret intelligence deficit was in code making and code-breaking, and the technologies that could render them paramount, all of which had flourished under the tsars. This led Moscow to rely more than anything upon human intelligence. Stalin had anyway placed more emphasis on morale than materiel, particularly in war: "technology does not decide everything," he scoffed at the die-hard modernisers.[21] The ultimate irony is that a dictator so relentless in his distrust of others was left with no choice but to place confidence in agents he had never met. It was the technological backwardness of Russia that made this inevitable.

The KGB's predecessors were always known as the "near neighbours" of the Commissariat of Foreign Affairs because the Lubyanka, where they were housed, neighboured the Commissariat, which was a short walk away at Kuznetsky Most. From 1953 the Foreign Ministry occupied a brutish Stalinist gothic skyscraper on the other side of the city at Smolenskaya, but the term *near neighbours* nonetheless stuck.

Military intelligence, which became known as the Fourth, or Raz-vedupr (from 1942, the GRU), was always a long reach from Kuznetsky Most. As of the summer of 1919, it could be found in Arbat, at 19 Bol'shoi Znamenskii Pereulok, a large, reddish-brown house that belonged to the millionaire Ryabushkin. There, the offices occupied two buildings surrounding a courtyard. The entrance lay to the back; the benches opposite the entrance, used for occasional meetings, were incessantly patrolled by secret policemen under civilian cover, typecast in canvas coats. Those at the Fourth called it "the little chocolate house." This complex also encompassed the main building of the Commissariat of Military and Naval Affairs, which included the army staff and the army's political directorate. The contrast between this low level of visibility and the prominence of the Lubyanka is striking, as was the difference between the crammed and dilapidated offices of the military as against the red-carpeted grandeur lavished on their civilian rivals.

In 1968, after pressing chief of the General Staff Matvei Zakharov and Defence Minister Andrei Grechko for more space on one purpose-built integrated site—he himself had the third floor of the General Staff building in Arbat—GRU director Pyotr Ivashutin reluctantly accepted a compromise. Located well out of the centre by the Khodynka airfield from which he once flew sorties, it became known as the "Steklyashka" (Glass House). Later, the defector Vladimir Rezun ("Suvorov") introduced it to the reading public as the "Akvarium" (Aquarium). Located at 76 Khoroshevskoe Chaussée, the new GRU headquarters had been designed as a hospital and only latterly retrofitted for a less therapeutic role. Those at headquarters referred to it not as the Aquarium but as *Polezhaevskii ob"ekt* ("the Polezhaevskii place"), Polezhaevskaya being the nearest station on the Metro.[22]

Thus, military intelligence remained "distant neighbours"—indeed, they were ever more distant and ever larger, too. Not to be outdone, the ever-expanding foreign directorate of the "near neighbours" burst out of the crowded Lubyanka, which had already been enlarged to its limits, and moved to an extensive new complex far away in "the woods," to purpose-built premises south of Moscow at Yasenevo on June 20, 1972.

The terminology stuck. It highlighted the fact that both organisations were instruments of the country's foreign policy dictated from the Kremlin and by the Party, but implemented by diplomats who relied upon the neighbours' specialist expertise. Not all were entirely grateful. Neighbours do not always get on with one another. Rivalry was never far away. Indeed, at one extreme, quondam Commissar for Foreign Affairs Georgii Chicherin keenly felt that the KGB's predecessor was one of two "internal enemies" (along with the Communist International).[23]

I. STARTING FROM SCRATCH

The beginnings of the Soviet secret services are inextricably identified with the Cheka, a name that soon struck fear into the hearts of most Russians.

The Cheka was rooted in the Bolshevik revolution. The collapse of the imperial autocracy in March 1917, after an unpopular war and food shortages, had rapidly led to widespread social disorder. Those in office but not in power had reason to fear revolution from below. The coup d'état that launched Lenin and the Bolsheviks and their allies into government on November 7 then gave birth on December 20 to an "Extraordinary Committee," or Cheka, for short, initially to combat counterrevolution and sabotage; soon it had unquestionably become the secret police of the revolution.

Yet it was only after Lenin transferred the government from cosmopolitan Petrograd to provincial Moscow in March 1918 (when the revolution was threatened with annihilation both from within the country and from without) that the Cheka truly became notorious. The Bolsheviks had just signed a peace treaty with the Germans at Brest-Litovsk, but the capital remained vulnerable. Barely a week earlier, an advance party of British marines had landed in Arkhangelsk, on the White Sea. The connexions between internal unrest and external intervention were real and growing.

Signing a peace treaty with the Kaiser's Germany in the midst of the world war, on March 3, 1918, proved highly controversial—it split the ruling coalition between Bolsheviks and left Socialist Revolutionaries who targeted their former allies for assassination. It also came at a high price: territorial losses and financial indemnities for the Bolsheviks. More important perhaps, it alienated the British government. London rightly expected that the loss of the Eastern Front against Berlin would be catastrophic for the war effort on the Western Front. Bringing down the Bolsheviks was therefore seen as a sure way to restore the Eastern Front and ensure final victory over Germany.

The evacuation to Moscow thus rescued the régime from potential attack, on land and by sea. It also meant turning its back on Peter the Great's Palladian window on the world for the Byzantine grandeur of the Kremlin, secreted deep in the heart of old Russia. The move represented a bold leap into the unknown; it symbolised a decisive step backwards into a darker and more brutal past. Here in Moscow, the Cheka was established in former insurance offices at the Lubyanka, overlooking the main street, Tverskaya (later Gorky), not far from the Commissariat of Foreign Affairs at Kuznetsky Most and from the Kremlin itself, on Red Square.

The Cheka quickly established itself as a crucial instrument of power for those struggling to establish themselves as successors to Lenin. In the decade that followed its formation, this shield of the revolution was directed primarily against the counterrevolution from abroad—those who had fled the country in the wake of retreating Allied armies that had tried and failed in their attempt to conquer Bolshevik Russia. For the main enemy was less the foreign powers, alarmed by the spectre of socialist revolution, than the angry and impatient exiles, who dreamed of return yet had absolutely no idea how to secure it.

The end of the First World War saw two great myths. The new rulers of Russia were convinced that its revolution could go global and transform a states system dominated by great powers founded on free market capitalism into a world without borders, ruled by the working class. Thus normal interstate relations with capitalist governments were not paramount; instead, subverting the West through covert action was seen as essential to the survival of the new Soviet régime. This myth seemed all the more plausible because world war had dislocated relations between the great powers and undermined social and economic stability across the face of Europe.

The second myth, held by the leading Great Powers, most notably France, the British Empire, and, momentarily, the United States, was that the agreements negotiated to end the First World War—most notably the Treaty of Versailles (June 28, 1919)—would forge a stable peace. This would be done by subjugating Germany for the indefinite future; an international outcast, it would be stripped of its ability to wage war and economically crippled through the payment of reparations. Yet this policy was bought at a high price by the victors. Persistent German resistance to subjugation meant that the West was not united in facing down the threat to the capitalist order from the Soviet Union. It enabled the Bolsheviks to find breathing room in a hostile world, first for survival and then eventually for expansion.

The KRO

Naturally, Moscow's first priority as it tried its hardest to incite an international uprising was to protect the revolution at home. Thus counterintelligence (run by the KRO, the *krokisty*), the shield of the revolution, was the Cheka's most vital function. The sword (intelligence abroad), wielded by the Cheka's foreign department (INO), was of lesser importance.

At the head of the *krokisty* was a unique figure, who made all the difference to the future of Soviet intelligence, Artur Artuzov. Born to an Italian Swiss father (Fraucci), Artuzov did not even have a Soviet passport. He was introduced to the Cheka by his uncle Misha, Dr. Mikhail Kedrov, Lenin's comrade-in-arms. Kedrov was the first head of the all-powerful Special Department, the shock troops who policed the emergent Red Army. Kedrov soon burned out as a Chekist, however, and eased himself back into the world of medicine.[1]

Artuzov was made of stronger stuff: small but solid, with a large head and the body of a weightlifter, he was ill-fitted to evening dress but well suited to a military uniform and long boots. His face was distinctive: a large mouth bordered by a small goatee, lively dark grey eyes that narrowly bridged a solid, stubbed nose, sheltering under a shock of black hair that turned snow white within a decade.

A good tenor, a winter sportsman, and a man with varied cultural interests, Artuzov was also even-tempered, ruthless, ascetic, self-critical, and given to ironical observations. These qualities helped ensure his good rapport with and great respect for his immediate superior, Menzhinsky. Most important, he was brilliant at talent spotting. Artuzov also had great integrity. Yet, oddly for so accomplished an intelligence officer, he retained a touching innocence under his thick hide. Indeed, he could be trusting to the point of naïveté.[2] He denounced the first Show Trial (of industrial specialists) in 1930, only to be roundly rebuked by his chief, Genrikh Yagoda, for sticking his nose in other people's business.[3] As Artuzov discovered, not everyone was as committed to principle as he, and this would prove decisive in his eventual fate; Stalin preferred ruthlessness.

At home, the KRO faced a challenge to Soviet power as a result of Lenin's retreat, in March 1921, from war communism. This was known as the New Economic Policy (NEP). The countryside, home to the overwhelming majority of the population, reverted to capitalism. The cities thereafter stood as isolated outposts of state socialism, leaving over 85 percent of the people effectively beyond range of the government's grasp.

The KRO's report for 1923–1924 highlighted the core alliance between the richer peasantry who owned some property (even just a horse) and the monarchist counterrevolutionaries headquartered abroad. This alliance had four important causes: first, "the re-establishment of the peasant economy near enough to a former, prerevolutionary state"; second, "the weakness of Soviet power (and Party apparatus) in the countryside," where "the murder of agricultural correspondents [volunteer Party reporters] . . . testifies to desperate resistance" by the kulak to growing Soviet penetration; third, "the formation of massive groups of former people [i.e., those identified with the old régime], without the means to sustain themselves." Fourth, "the return of significant groups of emigrés from the impoverished White emigration, unable to adapt to Soviet conditions."[4]

Immigration controls had broken down. It was estimated that eleven thousand people a month were crossing porous borders illegally. Soviet Russia was immense, sprawling across 8,176,000 square miles; it would take many years to seal itself off. Moreover, budget shortages meant that the growing number of former enemies returning to Russia were no longer processed in holding camps. The OGPU (so named in 1923) believed that those who wished to subvert Soviet power had some reason to vest their hopes in the Red Army. Artuzov's report added that "The New Economic Policy, the improvement in the material well-being of the intelligentsia, 'the rule of law,' and the possibility of 'legal' status, *the blending in of former White officers amidst Russian society,* have provided fertile soil for the renewal of counterrevolutionary activity."[5]

Within, the spirit of revolt awaited its opportunity, inflamed rather than dampened by greedy entrepreneurs accumulating surpluses for profit. Capitalism had every expectation of thriving in rural Russia—after all, the masses there had been told to enrich themselves. At the same time, they felt oppressed by taxes and resented the fact that, under the Bolsheviks, few goods were available to buy from the cities. The very magnitude of peasant Russia and its overwhelming ignorance was a source of recurrent anxiety. Artuzov outlined one issue in especially stark terms: "*There is every intention of using the strengthening of anti-semitism among the peasant masses to raise discontent against Soviet power by underscoring the connexion between communism and the Jews, and the influence of the latter on the USSR's politics*" (italics in the original).[6]

Foreign intelligence services, notably the British, evidently hoped that this economic drought would make enough tinder to spark a forest fire. "Between August 9 and 23, of the current year [1924]," Artuzov reported, "English intelligence in Reval [Tallinn] made an offer to a range of royalists to take up actively hostile work against the USSR, certain of which were offered quite hefty sums of up to £5,000 sterling to organise the blowing up of bridges on any [railway] lines, the fouling of the water supply, [sabotage] of electric lighting, trams, telephones, telegraphs etc." By October similar offers were being made in Helsinki, and with even greater persistence.[7]

Abroad, Soviet representatives were never safe from counter-revolutionary terrorism. On the eve of the first postwar international economic conference, to be held at Genoa in April 1922, word came in that the notorious terrorist Boris Savinkov was preparing to assassinate Soviet delegates; as a result of this warning, the plot was foiled.[8] Vatslav Vorovskii, the Soviet envoy to the Lausanne conference in Switzerland settling the status of the Dardanelles, the straits that separated Europe from Asia, was not so lucky. On May 10, 1923, to the horror of his fellow diners, including Deputy Commissar for Foreign Affairs Maxim Litvinov, Vorovskii was gunned down by counterrevolutionary bullets in the restaurant of the Hotel Cecil. The attack was orchestrated by Arkadii Polunin and carried out by Maurice Conradi, whose family had been wiped out by the Bolsheviks.

On February 5, 1926, Teodor Nette, a diplomatic courier, was shot on the Moscow–Riga train. On June 7, 1927, Pyotr Voikov, the Soviet ambassador to Poland and a key player in the slaughter of the Russian royal family, was assassinated by an emigré, Boris Koverd, on the platform of Warsaw station. On September 2 another emigré, Traikovich, attempted to kill a Soviet diplomatic courier, Shlesser, but was killed by Shlesser's companion, Gusev. At the end of 1927, V. Ukolov, an INO member under cover at the Soviet consulate in Beijing, was murdered along with five others in Hangzhou. On May 4, 1928, another attempt was made, this time against trade representative A. S. Lizarev. For the rest of the decade, Soviet diplomatic personnel nervously asked themselves who would be next.

At this turbulent time, a dramatic contrast emerged between the KRO, which enjoyed some striking successes, and its less impressive counterpart, the INO. Initially, the *krokisty* were hamstrung by an instinctive reluctance to borrow from time-honoured tsarist practices, in particular the use of agents provocateurs secreted within counterrevolutionary structures. Yet pragmatism—and the KRO's successes in turning Polish intelligence officers through ideological persuasion—brought a change of heart. Thus in January 1921, Feliks Dzerzhinsky made conversion the norm rather than an exception. The *ABC of Counterintelligence*, which highlights the importance of the psychological approach, appeared as a working manual four years later, in 1925.[9] The *ABC* was written by Artuzov, under whose inspired leadership the KRO launched a series of highly successful dummy counterrevolutionary organisations—most prominently the "Trust," which was operational between November 1922 and April 1927.

The Trust had its roots in advice that Vladimir Dzhunkovskii gave to secret police heads Dzerzhinsky and Menzhinsky personally. Dzhunkovskii had previously served as tsarist minister of the interior and commander of what amounted to the palace's own Praetorian Guard, a force 12,700 men strong known as the Special Police Corps. There, he learned about police penetration of the revolutionary movement, efforts that included the use of agents provocateurs such as Evgenii Azef, who rose, astonishingly, to head the Socialist Revolutionary Party's combat division, and was behind a number of high-profile assassinations. The other leading provocateur was Sergei Zubatov, who tried to develop anticapitalist trade unions loyal to the tsar. Dzhunkovskii believed these practices to be unconstitutional, and strongly disapproved of them; as a result, he was sacked by the tsar for being too principled. His principles, however, did not stop him from offering advice that later would prove very valuable to the Bolsheviks when they were in power.[10]

The history of the Trust begins in November 1921, when Artuzov intercepted a fascinating letter from Yuri Artamonov to the Supreme Royal Council (VMS) in exile. Artamonov worked as an interpreter at the passport office (MI6 station) of the British legation in Reval, Estonia. The letter revealed a determination to establish a subversive presence within Soviet Russia with the help of a certain Aleksandr Yakushev. Yakushev, an aristocrat and civil servant under the tsar, later worked for the Foreign Trade Commissariat. He had been en route to Norway and Sweden when he encountered Artamonov in Reval; Artamonov had been Yakushev's pupil at the Imperial Alexandrovsk Lycée. Artamonov loathed the Bolsheviks and talked Yakushev into cooperation.

Artamonov proved to be a source of inspiration to Dzerzhinsky and Menzhinsky: "Yakushev is an outstanding professional. Intelligent. He knows everything and everyone. He thinks just as we do. He is exactly what we need. He asserts that his opinion is the opinion of the best people in Russia . . . After the fall of the Bolsheviks the professionals will come to power. The government will be created not from emigrés but from those who are in Russia. Yakushev said that the best people in Russia not only get together, counterrevolutionary organisations exist and are active in the country." Yakushev was dismissive of the emigré community: "In the future," he wrote, "they are welcome in Russia, but to import a government from abroad is out of the question. The emigrés do not know Russia. They need to come and stay and adapt to the new conditions."[11]

When Yakushev returned to Moscow, he was promptly arrested by the Cheka. Dzerzhinsky knew him personally; they had worked together in 1920, when Dzerzhinsky was commissar of transport. Yakushev quickly admitted everything, and Artuzov then spent many hours trying to convince him that his patriotic duty was to cooperate. Yaku-shev, eager to escape further incarceration, finally gave in. Together with Artuzov, he set up the Monarchist Organisation of Central Russia (MOTsR), which the Cheka nicknamed the Trust.

Artuzov summed up the purposes and procedures of the Trust: first, as a means of monitoring the royalists, "to create the appearance of an existing royalist organisation in the USSR, in order to concentrate the attention of all foreign royalists on this supposed organisation." Second, to keep up to date on which states were financing the royalists. Third, to find out which foreign embassies within Soviet Russia were in touch with the emigrés. Fourth, to provide disinformation specially compiled by the military to mislead the enemy about Soviet capabilities. Fifth, to convince emigrés "that they cannot take an active role in general: a change of régime as with any other revolution can take place only from within the country. The emigrés can return only after a change of régime."[12]

It now remained to be seen whether this bright idea could be turned into practice. Gaining credibility was essential to the whole enterprise. So, on November 14, 1922, Yakushev, who had been released from prison, left for Berlin to make contact with the Supreme Royal Council (VMS). The following year, he met General Peter Wrangel in Berlin, then with the Organisation of the Russian Army (ORA) in Paris. The fact that these various emigré groups were scheming at one another's expense created the opportunity to divide them further. After Yakushev's visit, General Kutyepov, who was technically Wrangel's junior, sent personal emissaries—his own niece, in fact: Maria Zakharchenko-Shul'ts—into Russia to verify the legitimacy of the Trust.

Maria was beautiful, passionate, and much married. With flashing grey eyes and a fearless spirit, she craved danger above all. As fanatical advocates of terrorist methods against the Bolsheviks, Maria and her latest husband, Georgii Radkovich, proved hard to please: convincing them that the Trust was real became top priority.[13] The ploy succeeded. When Wrangel then sent in his own man to check out the Trust, he did so without consulting Yakushev. To reinforce the message that everything must be done through the Trust, the envoy was promptly arrested; he disappeared without a trace. The result was growing friction between Kutyepov, now a firm believer in the Trust, and Wrangel, a resolute sceptic. In June 1924, Moscow decided it was time to deepen this cleavage.[14]

Another character, Eduard Ottovich Upelin'sh, otherwise known as Opperput, from Latvia, had by this time become embroiled in Polish intelligence; he was tied to the terrorist Boris Savinkov, who was at that point operating across the Byelorussian frontier. Opperput was caught, and it was Menzhinsky himself who turned him. Opperput was soon installed in the Trust.

The centre of emigré operations against the Bolsheviks, ROVS, was created on September 1, 1924, by Kutyepov, with help from Wrangel and the main pretender to the Romanov throne, Grand Prince Nikolai Nikolaevich. ROVS received financial and logistical support largely from France and its allies in Eastern Europe. ROVS knew it could count on the Finnish and Polish General Staffs, in particular—indeed, their communications were carried by diplomatic bag to and from Moscow.[15]

Whereas Wrangel and others continued to be intensely suspicious of the Trust,[16] Kutyepov clung desperately to the firm belief that it was genuine. Nevertheless, every attempt to lure Kutyepov onto Soviet soil failed.[17] Operations parallel to the Trust also took place elsewhere: "D-7" until 1929, "C-4" until 1932, and "Zamorskoe" until 1934. These supplied disinformation to the Eastern European intelligence services and Britain's secret service MI6.[18]

The INO

The resolution forming the INO on December 20, 1920, defined the organisation's top priority: the "exposure of counterrevolutionary organisations on the territory of foreign states engaged in subversive activity against our country."[19] The instructions subsequently issued to the INO, on November 28, 1922, were more explicit in defining the department's role in terms of both Soviet Russia and Comintern: that of "unmasking on the territory of all states counterrevolutionary groups engaged in both active and passive activity directed against the interests of the RSFSR [Soviet Russia] and also against the international revolutionary movement."[20]

In sharp contrast to the KRO, headed successfully by Artuzov, the lacklustre INO had a mixed record. Its first acting head was Yakov Davtyan, a bit of a dandy and a highly strung soul who also happened to be a protégé of Lenin's close collaborator and lover Inessa Armand.

This connexion explains Davtyan's sudden rise to prominence, despite the fact that he had no experience whatsoever and demonstrated no evident inspiration for this line of work. Dzerzhinsky, however, soon managed to squeeze him out, playing upon his inordinate self-importance by depriving him of real power, and thereby prompting him to resign not once but twice.[21]

Davtyan's removal enabled Dzerzhinsky to put in his own man. A Jew and a native of Astrakhan, Meer Trilisser had known Dzerzhinsky since the 1905 revolution and was four years his senior in Party service. Trilisser looked like the typical harmless Russian intellectual: skinny and bespectacled, he sported a little toothbrush moustache. But in his case, appearances were deceptive. Trilisser's leading role, for example, in the famous Sveaborg naval uprising of 1906 resulted in his imprisonment and exile to Siberia for five years. There, mindful of the future, he devoted his energies to studying English and German.[22] Under his leadership, the INO grew steadily. From 70 men in 1922, it attained a total of 122 in 1930, of whom 62 served abroad.[23] Diplomats proved to be the main beneficiaries of INO intelligence. Nevertheless, Commissar for Foreign Affairs Georgii Chicherin's relations with the "neighbours" Menzhinsky and Trilisser were no better than tolerable. He was naturally irritated by the OGPU's habit of spying on him and his subordinates. The secret police, for its part, saw the commissariat as "the class enemy" and were liable to believe any nonsense said about it.[24]

Chicherin's intolerance was easily explained by the fact that foreign intelligence was not only weak but focused more on stirring up and organising revolution than on spying on Soviet Russia's rivals. Indeed, the INO was so feeble that for the first half of the decade, the main rezidentury (secret intelligence stations) in Europe were jointly run with military intelligence. The largest by far was in Germany, which was momentarily aligned with Russia against Anglo-French predominance and, more important, was seen as the locus of a future revolution.

In Germany, the Soviet intelligence setup was known as the Berlin Command Centre (Berlinskii rukovodyashchii tsentr). The centre had two purposes: first and foremost, aiding and abetting the German revolution, an attempt that proved disastrous when the Hamburg uprising collapsed in November 1923; second, managing espionage across Western and Central Europe, a task that took higher priority after the revolution failed.

Gathering intelligence on the German state took a backseat. Indeed, the authorities in Berlin never worried about Soviet espionage. They took revolutionary propaganda much more seriously—and even this threat seemed manageable. Before long, the centre for Soviet intelligence was reduced to two normal rezidentury, of the INO and military intelligence (the Fourth), because joint operations proved impossible to manage from Moscow.[25] Such rezidentury consisted of the main rezident and his or her assistant, plus a rezident and a rezident in reserve, an information officer (*osvedomitel'*), a recruiter (*verbovshchik*), an agent for communications (*marshrutnyi agent*), a keeper of safe houses (apartments), and a courier.

Poland, newly reborn as a state and now dominant in Eastern Europe, was racked by both ethnic and class-based unrest. Its leadership was split as to whether Moscow or Berlin constituted the greater menace. Poland was also threatened by the Treaty of Rapallo, signed by Moscow and Berlin on April 16, 1922, which symbolised a united front against a revival of the Polish empire and implicitly envisaged the dismemberment of a hated rival. In return for secret training grounds and poison gas and armaments factories in Russia, the Bolsheviks received the latest military technology from the Germans, who made full use of the opportunity for intelligence gathering. On the Soviet side, all the arrangements were also handled by military intelligence. Germany and Russia, by this point, could be described as the best of enemies. The most powerful national targets of Soviet intelligence, however, remained out of reach: Britain, France, and, looming offshore as a potential superpower, the United States, which appeared to be growing ever wealthier.

The Fourth/Razvedupr

In the 1920s, military intelligence seemed more promising than its civilian counterpart, both larger and more substantial. Relations with the Cheka (and its successors, the GPU and OGPU) were of course invariably fraught, especially since its key backers, the single-minded fanatic Dzerzhinsky and the untiring conspirator Stalin, were determined not to let this powerful instrument fall entirely into the hands of the military, whom they saw as inherently untrustworthy.[26] The Bolsheviks could never have won the civil war without the military, but it was hardly reassuring that one hundred sixty of the army's most senior officers had once loyally served Tsar Nicholas II.

Mistrust was pervasive particularly so long as Trotsky remained people's commissar for military and naval affairs. The Party was too busy watching this Bolshevik Napoléon to realise that a far more dangerous threat lay right in front of them: that swarthy, curly-haired, pipe-smoking, seemingly egalitarian picture of congeniality, Stalin. Under Stalin, personal loyalty was valued infinitely more than efficiency. As a result, political machinations at the top invariably interfered with best practice. The adverse consequences for Soviet intelligence were keenly felt.

Like its rival, the Cheka, military intelligence could not focus exclusively on enemy states. It, too, had to devise a way to neutralise the threat of counterrevolution from abroad. Formally entitled the Razvedupravlenie (or Razvedupr, for short), it was known from within as the Fourth, as it was the Fourth (superceded in 1939 by the Fifth) Department of the Red Army staff. The term *General Staff* was rejected for ideological reasons until 1935.[27]

Even before the brilliantly disastrous march on Warsaw, Trotsky lamented "the complete bankruptcy of human intelligence on the Western front."[28] Recognition of this sad truth should have instilled greater caution; instead, the Red Army's retreat from Warsaw in August 1920 unexpectedly highlighted what Trotsky already knew: Moscow's intelligence was not up to the standard. Worse still, the Second Department of the Polish General Staff had intercepted and decrypted most of its signals: 410 in all, including those transmitted between Trotsky and Mikhail Tukhachevsky.[29]

The fate of Central Europe and thereby the revolutionary advance worldwide thus turned on the inadequacies of Soviet encryption. Yet the Bolsheviks knew only the half of it. In September, the Politburo drew stark conclusions: "We went to Warsaw blindly and suffered a catastrophe. Bearing in mind the complex international situation in which we find ourselves, the question of our intelligence service must be made the appropriate priority. Only a serious, properly constituted intelligence service will save us from blindly meeting the unexpected."[30] Finally, Yan Lentsman from Latvia took over. Lentsman at last gave structure to the protean organisation, a structure that essentially lasted until the Fourth was subordinated to the INO in 1934.

The proliferation of Latvian personnel ("Letts") is easily explained. They were unusual revolutionaries and determined warriors, more Western in outlook than Russians, because of the polyglot society from which they emerged. In Latvia, German traditionally predominated in the towns and Russian in the countryside. Displaced from their homeland, the Lettish Bolsheviks were both fanatical and efficient; as such, they were more than willing to do Dzerzhinsky's dirty work. They were "special people," as Stalin called them many years later; people capable, he believed, of throwing a counterrevolutionary terrorist such as the hated Savinkov out a window—Stalin never believed the report that Savinkov had leapt out the window at the Lubyanka.[31] Also, since both civilian and military intelligence services were instruments of a revolution that still defined itself as worldwide, the fact that they were heavily populated with non-Russians was seen not as strange but as perfectly normal. Only when Moscow decided that global revolution was no longer its top priority did this become a problem.

Yet for years, especially early on, the internationalist revolutionary impulse burst through every attempt to constrain it. Both the aims and practices of Soviet intelligence were shaped by its reverberations. Despite the fact that 1921 was the triumphal year of diplomatic recognition for the Soviet régime, the Bolsheviks nonetheless saw themselves as engaged in "war" with their neighbours. Indeed, a resolution of the Fourth dated April 7, 1921, stated that "The class character of the war that Soviet Russia is conducting with the white guard states surrounding it necessitates placing on the agenda the work of human intelligence on class principles in relation to states possessing a developed working class." This by no means excluded "employment of elements alien to us depending on the local situation and timing." Indeed, this was precisely the direction the Fourth was increasingly taking. Yet the "class character" of human intelligence expressed itself "in the choice of agents on the basis of Party membership and class origins" and "in the widest cooperation with Communist organisations fighting states alongside us."

Thus, Lentsman concluded that the network of agents in every country "must consist of people chosen by the communist organisations of these countries." Of course, everything was conditional upon "producing results that satisfy our organs whether politically or militarily." At a further meeting on August 6, this time with representatives from the Comintern and the Cheka, it was decided that local Communist parties should be approached only through a Comintern representative "obliged to render the Cheka and Razvedupr [the Fourth] and its representatives every assistance." But, as events were soon to show, such decisions were more frequently honoured in the breach than in the observance.[32]

Jan Berzin

It was under Lentsman that Berzin (Pēteris Ķuzis), one of Lentsman's two deputies and later a name inseparable from that of the Fourth, took charge of the human intelligence network. But it was under Lentsman's immediate successor, Arvid Zeibot, a clever Lett and a talented administrator who took control on April 15, 1921, that a unit focused on research and analysis was developed. It would serve Moscow well until wantonly destroyed in 1935.

Though he possessed superb organisational ability, Zeibot had no interest or experience in military matters, and he repeatedly asked to be able to step down. Since Berzin already ran the agent network abroad, and actively enjoyed the challenge, it made sense for him to take over the entire operation; by the time he did, on April 1, 1924, the organisation had been promoted to become a full directorate.[33] Henceforth, the head of the Fourth and of its successors was referred to as the director. Though he was only in his thirties, Berzin was more often known as "the old man." Stocky, tight-lipped, prematurely bald with piercing blue eyes, his fine features cast in stone, he was destined to become a legend in his own lifetime. Berzin was fearless, he had been "schooled in hate" at a seminary, and he had been cast onto death row as a teenager—and yet he displayed a degree of humanity all too rare elsewhere under the Soviet régime.[34]

In fact, Berzin believed intelligence officers needed "a cool head, a warm heart, and nerves of steel."[35] Though he was tough when it came to defending his turf from rivals, Berzin was at the same time diligently attentive to subordinates. One recalled that when he sent an officer abroad, Berzin "always underlined his complete confidence in him . . . that in the event of failure he would support him and stick up for him."[36] Telegrams were invariably personal, never dictatorial. "He often wrote them himself and, despite the fact that [the officers] had code names assigned to them, addressed them individually by their known name."[37]

By the end of October 1926, the conflicts of interest generated by the clash between the needs of Soviet intelligence operatives and the needs of local Communist parties in the countries where those operatives were working had become alarmingly apparent. When the Fourth's rezident in Prague was arrested, along with two Czech agents, it resulted in a chain reaction that rippled through the local Communist Party and led to the detention of several of its leaders. Faced with a severe rebuke from the Kremlin, Berzin innocently claimed that he had no idea that he was not allowed to use local Communists as agents. Duly chastised, on January 8, 1927, he sent out a circular to all rezidentury, reminding them to isolate espionage activity from Party organisations.[38]

It was casual neglect of conspiratorial rules and instinctive empathy towards his men that eventually got Berzin into trouble: poor recruitment, followed by tolerance of poor performance, led to dire consequences. Those consequences, however, were delayed so long as Berzin benefited from the patronage of Iosif Unshlikht. Unshlikht, a Polish Jew and so, like Berzin, an outsider, had headed the all-encompassing Special Department (military counterintelligence) until May 1922. Before becoming deputy chairman of the powerful Revolutionary Military Council, Unshlikht had worked directly under Dzerzhinsky. He was, in short, a dominant figure in security matters—close to Lenin and high up in the Party hierarchy.

Sustained by Unshlikht's support until the latter's sudden demotion in June 1930, Berzin presided over more men and commanded greater resources than the Cheka, even after the drastic budgetary cuts of the early to mid-twenties. The Fourth also enjoyed more exalted status than its civilian counterpart. With Unshlikht as his protector, or "roof," as the Russians say, Berzin ensured that the service "jealously guarded its independence."[39] The prestige of the Fourth was due in part to the fact that it was tied to the Party more closely than was the Cheka or the OGPU—and this was, after all, a one-party state. After 1929, it became one man's (Stalin's) state. And that made all the difference.

Comintern

The Fourth had the closest ties with the Communist International (Comintern). Founded in March 1919, Comintern had the unique responsibility to turn the Bolshevik revolution into a worldwide phenomenon. When, at a meeting on August 14, 1923, it was agreed that the intelligence agencies should work entirely independently of Comintern, the Fourth, predictably, proved the most reluctant. Director Berzin argued that it was impossible for his operatives to do their job without the apartments and the addresses of local comrades.[40]

Comintern, its ranks bursting with native speakers of foreign languages, exported a steady stream of fanatical recruits to the Fourth. This process of reinforcement gained momentum after Stalin systematically replaced Comintern's most imaginative members with men slavish to orders from Moscow, a process known as bolshevisation. Within a decade, the Fourth would be subjected to the same treatment as Comintern—with the same damaging consequences.

One notable talent was Richard Sorge ("Ika"), who began running secret errands abroad for Comintern's executive in order to escape the purge of those linked to Stalin's opponent Nikolai Bukharin, brusquely ousted as president of Comintern. Sorge was of Russian German descent, and fluent in both languages. He cut a dashing figure: young, bold, well-built, good-looking—a thrusting forehead over a long nose; a full head of dark hair; a hard face offset by sensual lips—elegantly dressed, oozing easy charm.[41] A "he-man" in the words of his lover Agnes Smedley, Sorge acted the dominant male among women but was too uninhibited in his sexual appetites for his more straitlaced Russian colleagues, who strongly disapproved even of the German habit of bathing in the nude.[42] Though married—his wife was in the United States—Sorge openly carried on his relationship with Smedley while working in Shanghai.[43]

Sorge was, however, by no means the perfect operative. He was hot-blooded, and had already made a reputation for himself as impulsive and high-handed, interfering on his own initiative in the political affairs of more than one party belonging to Comintern.[44] Moreover, Abeltyn ("Basov"), his immediate sponsor early in September 1929, was responsible for the most spectacular mess Berzin had ever presided over (see page 58).[45]

These adventurous buccaneers of the Fourth were inspired amateurs rather than fully trained professionals—this was true even of those tapped from the plentiful reservoir of Comintern's most clandestine department, the OMS, or *omsovtsy*. After May 2, 1921, this office operated under the purview of Osip Pyatnitsky (Iosel' Tarshis), a self-educated Jew and close colleague of Berzin's, whose life had been spent in conspiracy underground. After September 1926 the OMS was run by Aleksandr Abramov ("Mirov"), a Jew educated in Germany, anxious to please Stalin at all costs, though Pyatnitsky remained Sorge's ultimate patron. The OMS ran its own network, indistinguishable from an intelligence service: shipping armaments, agents, couriers, funds, and propaganda across the globe, using its own cryptography and, until May 1927, taking advantage of official trade missions and embassies for cover.[46]

In its first decade, the Fourth also acted in a spirit of independence that undercut its rivals. The Chekists were overburdened: responsible for a massive length of border from Leningrad to Vladivostok, it was no surprise that they were stretched paper thin. Several years of frontier conflicts with Poland and Romania made war more likely. The Lubyanka wanted to keep complications to a minimum. Dzerzhinsky was thus exasperated to learn early in 1925 that the Fourth had been independently running terrorist operations—known euphemistically as "active intelligence"—across the frontier with Poland on a regular basis.[47] Dzerzhinsky's attention was alerted to these covert operations on January 5 of that year when Polish forces attacked across the border in the region of Volynsk to take and destroy the frontier forces' command post.[48]

Dzerzhinsky railed against "the irresponsible activities of the Razvedupr, dragging us into conflict with neighbouring states." He demanded an investigation. The Politburo responded with a commission on "active intelligence" chaired by Valerii Kuibyshev. If there were to be armed bands operating with Soviet support, Dzerzhinsky insisted, "these groups should not have as their goal intelligence and other assignments on behalf of the USSR's military institutions." They should fight only "for their own military goals," subordinated to the local Communist Party. On March 14, both Unshlikht and Mikhail Frunze (briefly commissar for military and naval affairs), who were ultimately responsible for the whole business, agreed to end "active intelligence," a serious retreat. The proposal was accepted and the border area finally cleared in the course of the following year.[49]

Tension with Britain peaked after a breach in diplomatic relations in May 1927. The situation further deteriorated after the murder of the Soviet ambassador in Warsaw on June 7, which prompted Kliment Voroshilov, the new commissar for military and naval affairs, to propose to the Politburo the establishment of sabotage organisations within hostile states. With the war of independence at an end but Catholics still oppressed by the Protestant ascendancy in the northern counties, Ireland emerged as a possible theatre of operations.[50] On June 23 the proposal was accepted with the provision that this be done with "maximum caution." A committee chaired by Party secretary Stanislav Kosior was set up; it was composed of Pyatnitsky (Comintern), Yagoda (OGPU), and Berzin (the Fourth), and tasked with reporting back on implementation within a fortnight.[51]

It is not clear exactly what resulted from the proposal, but we do know that operations against Poland were selectively revived in 1928, after Dzerzhinsky's death.[52] The fact that the *aktivka* had continued for so long without being subject to any oversight from the Party illustrated the uniquely privileged position enjoyed by the Fourth. But that was about to change. Friction with the Commissariat of Foreign Affairs over such measures was inevitable. "It is impermissible to write about the adventures of the [O]GPU's foreign agents," Chicherin cautioned his as-yet-unknown successor. "The Razvedupr [Fourth] is considerably worse [than the OGPU] (especially during the period of comrade Unshlikht's 'active intelligence.')"[53]

The mid-1920s also saw clashes over the Fourth's excessive reliance on local Communists, not just for recruiting operatives but also as supportive agents in the field. This practice was, as already noted, formally banned. Yet Valter Krivitsky (né Samuel Ginsberg), who defected amid a successful career in the service, recalls having recruited around 80 percent of his agents from local parties. Although the Fourth's officers were "forbidden to meet [helpers from local parties] in any circumstances," Krivitsky acknowledges that "in practice it was found almost impossible to enforce this rule."[54]

Initially less worried about ideological commitment, the INO opportunistically recruited from the flotsam and jetsam drifting aimlessly through postwar Europe. Though recruitment was light touch, tradecraft was taken seriously. In stark contrast, the fanaticism at the Fourth meant that enthusiastic amateurism all too frequently overrode strict security procedures. It takes no effort to imagine which fitted Stalin's needs more perfectly, and therefore who would win out in the end.

The INO and the Fourth were preeminently human intelligence operations. Soviet code/cipher making and breaking, formally the domain of the Cheka/OGPU, could not compete. Having lost key personnel to the counterrevolution, cryptanalysts were forced to start from scratch; they worked with scant resources and lacked innovation. The INO made up the deficit by bribing foreign cipher clerks and breaking into embassy safes where keys to enemy codes and ciphers were stored. Given the yawning gap between the ability to crack codes and the ever-greater demand for access to the secrets of others, the burden on the INO soon became excessive.

One promising institutional innovation was the special office for disinformation founded by Artuzov and subsequently taken up by Unshlikht. On January 11, 1923, the production of disinformation (*deza*) about Russia's domestic and foreign policy "and also the state of its armed forces and the measures taken for the defence of the republic" was centralised.[55] Faking Politburo minutes, departmental memoranda, and false orders of battle topped the list of priorities. These practices peaked under Nikita Khrushchev with the formation of A Directorate (disinformation) in the KGB buttressed by the Information Department of the Central Committee, which ballooned as the International Information Department into the 1980s.

One of Artuzov's assistants, Vladimir Styrne (Stirne Voldemārs), yet another Lett, recorded that "we have provided the staff of every state in Central Europe" with false military data. These fabrications also reached the General Staffs of the British, French, Japanese, and German armed forces. As a result, the Red Army acquired a phantom capability that went unquestioned.[56] The Russians took pride in the fact that 95 percent of the information upon which Russia's foreign enemies based their military estimates of Soviet capabilities came from disinformation.[57]

Yet there was a downside: by prompting exaggerated foreign military estimates of Soviet capabilities, Moscow misrepresented itself as a more serious threat than hitherto supposed. This inflated threat then justified the Poles' inflated military expenditure (one-quarter of the state budget). As the decade proceeded, the Kremlin found it necessary to deflate its purported military power in order to soothe the anxieties of neighbouring states.

With respect to threat assessment and operations abroad, Soviet foreign intelligence was crucially dependent upon the human factor. And, even here, it had to scrounge for resources often quickly snapped up by the more successful counterintelligence department.

Great Britain as Bête Noire

The First World War had turned Great Britain into an empire with power unrivalled except at sea by the United States—that is, when it chose to act and turned a blind eye to pressing imperial preoccupations. However incompetently and indecisively, the die-hard anti-Bolshevik secretary of state for war Winston Churchill had spearheaded military intervention against the Bolshevik "baboons" in 1919. Little did the British know how close they had come to taking Petrograd in March 1919, and overthrowing the Bolsheviks.[58] Thereafter a tendency prevailed to exaggerate the capacity of the Bolsheviks to succeed in spreading their creed worldwide that lasted throughout the interwar period. Having failed by orthodox means (which carried with them the risk of unleashing revolutionary war across the continent), London turned to indirect methods—on the one hand through commerce, according to the classic liberal belief that trade binds mankind together; and on the other, through secret service operations—to dislodge the uncertain foundations of Soviet power.

Here, MI6—by no means as old as the Russians believed, though its predecessors had their origins in the sixteenth century—was fortuitously blessed by a strong Russian contingent. The blessing, however, also proved to be a curse because of a crucial weakness: most of if not all members of the Russian contingent were the offspring of British businessmen dispossessed by the Bolshevik Revolution. They could scarcely be counted on to make an objective assessment of the prospects for such a loathed régime. Their continued and uncritical purchase of dubious official documents fabricated for this undiscriminating market inadvertently provided welcome dividends for the Soviet Union's needy foreign exchange reserves.

The Russians, of course, noticed how active the British were. Not only did MI6 carry out espionage on its own account, but it could also rely on help from foreign countries similarly preoccupied by the Bolshevik threat. The KRO report for 1923–1924 noted, "So, for example, the intelligence services of Estonia, Finland, Latvia and Lithuania, and, to a certain extent, those of Poland, and recently the Swedes and Norwegians, work especially and exclusively for England. The Poles and the Romanians work for the French. The Germans for the time being work alone."[59] In turn, the Polish, Estonian, and Finnish governments backed the Trust, even providing its members diplomatic asylum in the event of failure.[60]

The brunt of MI6 subversion and intelligence gathering was carried out via passport control officers at British legations in Reval (now Tallinn, Estonia), Riga (Latvia), Helsinki (Finland), and Stockholm (Sweden). The KRO had already recruited Ado Birk under a false flag (American) by the time he was sent to serve in the Estonian mission to Russia (1922–1926). In June 1923, Birk made contact with the British legation in Reval, where Colonel Ronald Meiklejohn, assisted by an emigré named Zhidkov, was MI6 station chief. Zhidkov opened communication with the Trust.[61] It was also through the Trust, and via Captain Ernest Boyce at the MI6 station in Helsinki, that the former secret service employee Sidney Reilly, notorious as the "Ace of Spies" and hitherto much feared by the Bolsheviks, crossed the Finnish border on September 25, 1925, only to be lured to his death. Reilly was executed on November 3.[62] His corpse lies to this day under a courtyard within the Lubyanka.[63]

Moscow and London reached an uneasy truce after mutual diplomatic recognition was achieved in March 1921, and ambassadors were even exchanged in 1924, during Ramsay MacDonald's short-lived Labour government. But relations rapidly deteriorated under the strain of accelerated Comintern activity within the British Empire, including, importantly, in the treaty ports of China. China mattered greatly. It was Britain's second-largest trading partner and the second-largest recipient of British investment. Stanley Baldwin's die-hard Conservative government (1924–1929) swept to power on the back of the Zinoviev Letter, which purported to be an instruction from Comintern to instigate mutiny in the armed forces. Pressure from the backbenches in Parliament forced a breach in diplomatic relations on May 26, 1927.[64]

This unusual step, invariably a precursor to war, was preceded shortly before by a police raid on the premises of the Soviet trade delegation in

London. The delegation shared a building with the innocuous-sounding Anglo-Russian Co-operative Society (ARCOS), a Soviet trading company. British counterintelligence, MI5, had traced a network operated by the Russians back to this address. It involved William Ewer, the foreign editor of the Labour Party's *Daily Herald*, who was intermittently in receipt of classified information from the Metropolitan police force at Scotland Yard and other departments of government, through agents within those institutions working purely for money.[65] Arcos was also the centre of an international network of seamen controlled by Comintern. But Special Branch of Scotland Yard had double agents on the inside: two Letts, Karl Korbs and Peter Miller. MI5 had also inserted its own double, Anatoly Timokhin, recruited in Murmansk during British occupation in 1918.[66]

The litany of disasters that year, 1927, was disturbing: as prelude, in March an INO network was exposed by the police in Warsaw. The cataclysm, however, occurred in China, where the Soviet leadership had counted on transforming the bourgeois nationalist revolution into a full-fledged Communist takeover. On April 6 the embassy in Beijing, which sheltered an ample archive of secret Soviet operations, was raided by the northern warlord Zhang Zuolin, with the encouragement and assistance of the British from behind the scenes. The compound was massive—effectively an embassy tacked onto a military camp. Through interconnecting doors, troops managed, with little difficulty, to break into the diplomatic sections and into the extensive quarters occupied by the military attaché and the Fourth's rezident, V. S. Oginskii, while the rezident's staff raced to burn as many documents as possible.

The raid's most embarrassing finding was that Chinese Communists, including Li Dazhao, one of the Party cofounders, were living and working on-site in blatant defiance of diplomatic convention. Armaments and truckloads of propaganda were also discovered. The secret documents rescued from the ensuing conflagration included Oginskii's situational reports; his correspondence with Moscow; lists of agents and payments; documents purloined from other embassies; details on the supply of armaments to the Nationalist armies; lists of Soviet advisors to those armies, along with their noms de guerre; reports from the same, including from the Soviet military commanders Vasilii Blyukher and Mikhail Borodin; the Chinese Communist Party's regional committee records; and the secret addresses of Communists.[67]

The *North China Daily News* published seven pages of less sensitive though still embarrassing documents, in translation. This was followed by extracts in the *Straits Times* that included techniques of agent recruitment—recruitment under a false flag, for example, which would make the target believe he or she worked for a government other than the one recruiting. More damaging raids ensued: on consulates in Shanghai, Tianjin (Tientsin), and then in Guangzhou (Canton).

Meanwhile, in France the officially prohibited practice of using members of the Party for intelligence also endangered the network. On April 9 the rezident's assistant, Uzdanskii, and an agent named Bern-shtein, an emigré, were arrested in the act of receiving classified documents from two employees of armaments factories. The assistant to the secretary of the Paris branch of the Communist Party was implicated. This led to a raid on a Politburo member, Jean Cremet, a former docker who, astonishingly, in blatant defiance of explicit instructions from the Kremlin, headed the Fourth's illegal rezidentura. One hundred members of the network were detained, though only eight were indicted. Cremet escaped to the Soviet Union and was sentenced in absentia.[68] Meanwhile, in Vienna, Austrian Foreign Ministry employees supplying classified information to Moscow were also detained.[69]

The Politburo was determined to fight back, and on May 28, two days after Britain broke off diplomatic relations, it took hold of the problem by legislating use of illegals as the norm. This meant that intelligence officers would have to operate under deep cover, without the benefit of diplomatic immunity. Personnel from the INO, the Fourth, Comintern, the Red International of Trades Unions (Profintern), and the International Workers' Aid (MOPR) were all forbidden from belonging to embassies or permanent trade delegations. Ciphered communications concerning especially secret matters would be transmitted only through encrypted letters sent via the diplomatic bag—never via telegraph or radio. All such communications would be signed by code names, and a special oversight committee was set up, consisting of Stanislav Kosior (a secretary of the Party), Pyatnitsky, and Yagoda.[70]

The trouble was that, effectively, the Politburo decision was not implemented either in full or immediately. During a review of the Fourth's rezidents abroad, conducted under the chairmanship of Nikolai Kubyak, a member of the Party's organisational bureau, it was decided to leave many legal rezidents in place.

Bad news arrived on the domestic front, too. The exceptionally successful Trust ended in catastrophic failure after the Russians decided to close it down in February 1927. When Opperput responded by changing sides, Kutyepov understood the Trust to have been a sham, and hastened to Finland to determine the truth. Opperput, Zakharchenko, and Voznesenskii ("Georgii Peters") were trained for terrorist operations and dispatched by Kutyepov and Captain Ross from MI6. They crossed the Finnish border on May 31, 1927.[71]

On the night of June 3, the terrorists tried to break into OGPU accommodation at No. 3/6, one of the smaller Lubyanka buildings, with eight pounds of British-made explosives. They fled westwards towards the Polish frontier, until they were eventually caught and shot in the region of Smolensk. On June 7, three others (Viktor Larionov, Sergei Solov'ev, and Vladimir Monomakhov) threw two bombs into the Central Party club in Leningrad during a seminar on historical materialism. They wounded thirty-five people and managed to make it to the Finnish border that August. Solov'ev, however, was shot. Others (Nikolai Stroev, Vladimir Samoilov, Aleksandr Bolmasov, Aleksandr Sol'skii, and Aleksandr von Aderkas) were tried and executed on September 23. In July 1928, Radkevich and Dmitrii Monomakhov made another attempt and, with the help of Romanian secret police, crossed over the frontier into the Soviet Union. In Moscow they lobbed a bomb into the checkpoint at the Lubyanka. They were also eventually hunted down and executed.[72]

According to a report from the INO of July 19, 1928:

> On returning to Paris, Kutyepov planned a series of terrorist incidents in the USSR and presented his plan for review by the staff which accepted the plan with certain changes. Basic to the plan were:
> a) The assassination of Stalin
> b) Blowing up military plants
> c) The assassination of OGPU leaders in Moscow
> d) Simultaneously, the assassination of those in command of military districts—in the south, the east, the north, and west of the USSR.[73]

After years of triumph Artuzov's efforts had ultimately ended in failure. Sacked in November 1927, he was forced to work his way back up the ladder, in the role of second deputy assistant of the Secret

Operations Directorate of the OGPU under someone soon to become notorious as Stalin's hatchet man, Yagoda. It was a demotion that sorely tested Artuzov's capacity for tact.

Yagoda (Yenon Gershonovich Iegoda) had apprenticed as an engraver with Yakov Sverdlov's brother, and had married his daughter. Until his untimely death in 1918, Sverdlov had worked successfully as Lenin's powerful assistant, turning into reality ideas his boss had not fully thought through. It was this connexion that secured Yagoda's rapid rise to power, initially as secretary to Menzhinsky, whom he treated with great deference. But Yagoda was in fact Stalin's creature. Menzhinsky's poor physical condition meant that he was more figurehead than boss. This suited Stalin perfectly. Yagoda, in turn, was deferential towards superiors but "crude and uncivilised" towards subordinates.[74]

"Small, nimble, obliging, with an energetic and weird face," Yagoda was also "hard, dry, laconic." He sported a small, unkempt moustache yet dressed fastidiously in uniform. Most important, Yagoda was, like Stalin, a man of the apparat, with significant organisational skill. He even micromanaged the staging of executions.[75] Gardening was said to have been a hobby of his: plants, after all, could not answer back, with or without their heads. He also led a secret erotic life. Those searching his apartment after his arrest in 1937 found 1,008 antiques, 18 women's fur coats, 53 cashmere scarves, 11 pornographic reels of film, 3,904 pornographic photographs, and 549 books—including Trotskyist works.[76]

The Threat of War Discounted

Until the breach with Britain, the rezidentury of both INO and the Fourth invariably made extensive use of Soviet embassies and trade missions. Although the convenience of cover afforded by diplomatic immunity was obvious, it was bought at a high price. The local police had only to watch comings and goings to identify suspects. After August 1927, however, measures were taken, at least in principle, to begin moving the rezidentury under deep cover. But reform moved agonisingly slowly. Old habits proved hard to abandon.[77]

The Fourth alone had shown its mettle, but rather more through analysis—the INO had no such capacity—than agents. Indeed, at the Fourth in 1924 the proportion of operational officers to analysts was one to four.[78] INO operations against neighbouring Poland's military potential were regarded as highly effective, however. They enabled Moscow to reproduce its order of battle.

Polish intentions were another matter. Determining what exactly these were took high priority. Although relations with the Russians had reached an impasse, British intolerance of higher taxes and need for trade—and therefore peace in Europe—meant that direct war with the Soviet Union was not an option. Poland had previously been closely allied to France against the prospect of German revival and Bolshevik expansionism. The British now sought to bring Germany back into the European concert and, simultaneously, further isolate the Soviet Union. They accomplished this by means of the Locarno Pact on December 1, 1925. The pact guaranteed the western borders of Germany and, in return, French and Belgian security, but it left the frontiers to the east dangerously exposed. An inevitable effect of the pact was that Poland lost confidence in France as its protector. This was to British advantage. Marshal Józef Piłsudski, leading the old aristocracy (the *szlachta*) that dreamed of empire at the expense of the Soviet Ukraine, seized power one weekend in May 1926 with tacit British backing. War by Polish proxy, supported from London, suddenly no longer seemed such a remote possibility. Rumours of war began circulating through the Soviet Union that autumn.

The threat assessment of Poland that was drawn up in Moscow led to a direct clash between the INO and the Fourth. It was a difference of opinion that directly reflected INO weakness—in particular its costly lack of an analytical department. At the Fourth, priorities were very different. Here the information-statistical department was headed by Aleksandr Nikonov, who doubled as one of two assistants to Berzin. Reports went to Unshlikht; the contentious chief of staff Mikhail Tukhachevsky; the dullard commissar Voroshilov; and the tireless Dzerzhinsky, with an extra copy for Nikolai Bukharin (at Comintern). During the sustained crisis with London at the end of June 1926, Nikonov concluded that Poland was uninterested in provoking war and that "this year there are no serious bases for fearing a breach in peaceful relations with Poland." Dzerzhinsky, however, disagreed, and on July 11 he wrote to Stalin insisting that his fellow Poles, whom of course he felt he knew best, were, on the contrary, bent on a war of conquest.[79]

The intervention prompted further discussion, drawing in leaders of the Commissariat of Foreign Affairs in addition to Trilisser and Unshlikht. They brokered a compromise made possible by Dzerzhinsky's premature death brought on by extreme stress. The OGPU's long-time leader collapsed at home on July 20 from heart failure at the age of forty-nine; his advanced arteriosclerosis was worthy of a man in his seventies.

Though increasingly likely, war was still by no means certain. A new memorandum from Nikonov, at the end of July, argued that "There is no likelihood of a direct danger of war for the USSR on the part of Poland and the Baltic states at the present moment and for the near future (at least until the spring of 1927)." More detailed assessments of Polish capabilities followed. Poland's inherent weaknesses, including poor military industries, lack of reserves, and restricted military budgets, indicated no great threat to the Soviet Union at the end of January 1927. Berzin predicted that "you can expect no immediate preparation for war in the forthcoming year, 1927."[80]

The breach of diplomatic relations by Britain in May was, as already noted, followed by the assassination of the Soviet envoy to Poland, Voikov. Stalin was taking a holiday in Sochi, on the Black Sea, when he heard news of the murder. The following day, he telegraphed Molotov in Moscow: "The murder of Voikov gives grounds for the complete liquidation of monarchist and white guard cells in every part of the USSR by all revolutionary measures. It requires of us that we strengthen our own rear."[81] The Politburo took action immediately.

But Stalin also sought to use this event and accompanying acts of terrorism by Opperput to justify repression of legitimate political opposition. "The course towards terror taken by London's agents," Stalin wrote to Molotov on June 17, "changes the situation fundamentally." On his view, Opperput's actions pointed in the direction of open preparation for war. Yet instead of arguing for mobilisation, he insisted on measures designed to strengthen the rear and put down "opposition" speedily. "Without this, the slogan of reinforcing the rear is an empty phrase."[82] When Menzhinsky showed every sign of dragging his feet, Stalin wrote to him: "My personal opinion: 1) London's agents have nestled in among us deeper than it seems; they are still lurking around."[83] The legend of MI6 invincibility died hard, especially when it suited Stalin's ulterior motives.

For the time being, the threat of war could safely be dismissed as a convenient instrument wielded in the inner-party struggle between Stalin and Trotsky. However, just as the Soviet Union was industrially and technologically unprepared for a conflict with the major European powers, its secret intelligence was not ready, either. This was not least because its primary focus was less upon rival foreign powers than on the enemy within. Also, Stalin's decision to force the countryside into a "socialist" mode of production in October 1929 increased discontent to the point of open revolt. The enemy within thus became ever more a threat to Soviet power. This had serious implications for the allocation of already-scarce resources to intelligence.

That year, 1929, was momentous for the fortunes of the Soviet Union both economically and politically. Having regretfully concluded that the long-hoped-for revolution in Germany, the ultimate salvation of the October Revolution in Russia, was out of reach in the distant future, and that most probably it could be secured only through a mighty Red Army, Stalin and his allies decided that they had no other choice but to go it alone. Thereafter, central planning in industry and agriculture determined the form and speed of the country's accelerating economic growth. Politically, Stalin had simultaneously and ruthlessly eliminated all effective opposition within the ruling Party.

Nineteen twenty-nine was a turning point not only for the Soviet Union: the crash of the Wall Street stock market that October undercut the apparently secure foundations of Western prosperity which characterised most of the postwar decade and provided the best buffer against the spread of Bolshevism. The net effect of growing and widespread impoverishment was by the same token to undermine democracy, discredit free trade in favor of protectionism, reinforce the United States' isolationism, and spirit fascism into power across the European continent on the back of mass discontent.

Whereas Moscow found Italian fascism a not uncongenial interlocutor entirely compatible with core Soviet interests, its German incarnation turned out to be a very different animal, as the following decade demonstrated. The key question was whether Stalin would grasp that Hitler's *Mein Kampf* and its declared intention to colonise the hinterland of Eastern Europe was no idle threat but a plan of action.

Here the problem was complicated by the fact that the primary purpose of the Soviet intelligence services was above all to gather information from Russian counterrevolutionaries in order to undermine them from within. Foreign powers were secondary targets, and political intelligence within Germany, a country Stalin had never set foot in, had always been a particularly weak point. When, for instance, the INO became a fully independent department within the OGPU on July 30, 1927, its purpose was defined as penetration of enemy intelligence responsible for subversion within the Soviet Union; exposure of saboteurs crossing into the Soviet Union; and the analysis of sabotage techniques.[84] The restricted nature of this brief said much about Stalin's immediate priorities.

Moreover, Lenin's tactic in dealing with the capitalist powers was to set one against the other: "exploiting inter-imperialist contradictions," in Soviet jargon. This meant not favouring one state over another for any length of time but instead keeping all options open, even in close relations with Weimar Germany. To conduct policy on this basis through the series of accelerating diplomatic crises that the Great Depression unleashed placed too heavy a responsibility on intelligence services working under a dictator with no firsthand experience of the countries with which he was dealing.

Stalin's existing sources of information were unlikely to yield what was needed with respect to Hitler's immediate intentions. A great deal, however, hinged upon his waking up to a major threat to Soviet security and redirecting his services accordingly. Only with hindsight, perhaps, does that threat seem so blindingly obvious; most European statesmen in Europe were just as mistakenly complacent about Hitler. Stalin had his own special reasons for his blindness: his main rival, Trotsky, now in exile, pointed vociferously to the threat posed by fascism in Germany.[85] This undoubtedly played a role in clouding Stalin's judgement, for to admit that the threat was real meant admitting Trotsky's judgement was better than his own.

2. BUT <u>WHO</u> WAS THE MAIN ENEMY?

The main enemy was not, as one might have supposed, a state, but the counterrevolutionary movement headquartered abroad. The Trust was a vital holding operation, a prophylactic for Whites and foreign powers eager to pounce. It was crucial to sustain counterrevolutionary hopes while simultaneously nullifying any possibility of their being realised. Artuzov drew comfort from the fact that, because of the Trust, Kutyepov had decided against sending fighters into the USSR from the remnants of the White armies that fled after the civil war. Making the case that the Soviet régime was softening, allowing greater freedom of criticism, ending OGPU terror, and so forth, the Trust "protested energetically against activation of the White movement (terrorism, sabotage), warning against a repeat of the Red terror from the Communists and of the chance, by these means, of losing all possibility of legal activity."[1]

As we have seen, once Kutyepov realised, in March 1927, that he had been fooled, he decided to unleash a terror campaign against Soviet officials within and outside Russia. A former supporter recalls that for Kutyepov "terror was an end in itself and he presupposed that terrorist acts carried out by the Kutyepovites would, as he told me, produce a detonation in Russia."[2] Indeed, between 1927 and 1930, Kutyepov produced "several lucky acts of force on Russian territory," though at the cost of "most of the participants."[3] His intended abduction was designed not merely to dispose of a minor irritation and take over the emigré leadership; it was also provoked by a renewed sense of urgency in Moscow. Peasant uprisings had begun to threaten the precarious armistice that had been established in the countryside in March 1921. The stability of the entire system was at stake, even before the collectivisation of agriculture began with the onset of winter in 1929.

It therefore made some sense for the Soviet leadership to treat counterrevolutionary organisations abroad as a more immediate threat than foreign governments. Germany was Russia's only ally, but it was now undergoing a fundamental upheaval as a result of the Great Depression. Everyone expected the extreme left to blast its way into power. Instead, it was the turn of the extreme right, with a deadly combination of violent intimidation, virulent populism, and astute manipulation of the country's leading statesmen. Also, without direct personal experience of other societies, Stalin—and he was not alone—took a long time to make full sense of what the emergent Nazi Party actually portended. One could argue, in fact, that it remained a complete mystery to the very end because the Nazis were always an amorphous movement not based on any one class. None of this made sense to a dogmatic Marxist-Leninist. The assumption that followed was that, lacking homogeneity, the movement would ultimately shatter under bombardment in war.

The eve of Hitler's rise to power gave few clues as to what was about to happen. Moscow was hopelessly distracted by the bogey of France, now viscerally anti-Bolshevik as a result of Comintern backing the revolt in distant Indochina. INO reports in 1932 indicated France's willingness to bail out the German economy in return for cooperation against Russia, and when a Roman Catholic, Frantz von Papen, himself a former spy, became chancellor that year, intelligence reported that he had offered the French an anti-Soviet alliance. Both the French and the Germans were encouraged by the emerging threat to the Russians from the Japanese to the east.[4] The German ambassador to the USSR, Herbert von Dirksen, reported "great anxiety" in Moscow, facing the possibility of "a complete change of policy towards the Soviet Union."[5] Not until the end of 1932 did the rezidentura in Berlin belatedly consider it essential to focus reporting on the Nazis.[6]

To the extent that Stalin paid any attention to the Nazis, their hostility to France, Britain, and the United States was entirely welcome. "The new German Government," *Pravda* editorialised, "will also have to take into account that nationalist wave which has been caused by the worsening, in conditions of crisis, of the burden of the Versailles system and which will lead many millions of the petite bourgeoisie of the towns, the peasantry and even individual workers into Hitler's camp. These millions have voted in the presidential and Prussian elections not so much for Hitler as against France and Poland."[7] Blocking Hitler's progress by allowing the German Communist Party to align with pro-Western social democrats was therefore entirely out of the question.[8]

Changes at the Top

Once it became evident that foreign intelligence at the INO was not as effective as it might have been, Stalin decided to transfer the best talent from counterintelligence to rejuvenate it. This process was made easier as a result of the injudicious involvement of INO leaders in Kremlin squabbles.

On July 30, 1927, Trilisser, now deputy head of the OGPU, finally managed to release the INO from supervision by the Secret Operations Directorate, which was led by the hated Yagoda. Trilisser, himself rumoured to be sympathetic to the right wing of the Party (now banished by Stalin), took the first opportunity to attack Yagoda for the very same sin. This was done behind Yagoda's back at a local Party meeting in Moscow. Artuzov, however, stood up and spontaneously defended Yagoda's right to be held to account only by the Central Committee, given his position at the top of the OGPU.[9]

Yagoda's rebellious subordinate had acted on the foolhardy assumption that Party democracy was still a going concern. On October 27, 1929, Trilisser was summarily dismissed. The rules of hierarchy had to be respected at all costs. At a stroke, Trilisser's closest protégés found themselves enforcing grain collections on starving peasants or working in cultural relations with foreigners—jobs for which they were equally unsuited.

Artuzov Moves Up

Artuzov was made deputy head of the INO. His overriding task was to implement the Politburo's directive, of January 30, 1930, that sought to secrete rezidentury under deep cover. Artuzov had undoubtedly been welcomed on board because of his superb record as an inspired innovator. No less important, however, was the fact that he had stood up for Yagoda. On August 1, 1931, Artuzov was handed full leadership of the INO.

The INO was now to be professionalised. A first step, in 1932, was the establishment of special courses for operatives: twenty-five would be taken in on recommendation from the Party for two years' training. In addition, those already in service could receive extra training for three- to six-month stints.[10] These innovations were essential because Artuzov made illegals the highest priority.

Although provision had been made for illegal rezidentury as far back as 1920, up to the time of the Arcos Raid, in 1927, only in France and the United States had they been properly instituted—of necessity in Washington because the United States had steadfastly refused Moscow diplomatic recognition.[11] An illegal rezidentura was then established in London in 1929, headed, from a safe distance, by Boris Bazarov. For mutual security, these rezidentury communicated with one another as well as with Moscow.[12] With the first postwar crisis breaking on the Japanese occupation, from September 1931, of Manchuria, a territory that neighboured the Soviet Far East, the new requirement came just in time. Yagoda gave Artuzov full rein. "At work I always dared to take the offensive," he boasted, whereas Yagoda, a cautious man, would hang back.[13] Meanwhile, the ailing Menzhinsky, having been released from work on Politburo instructions for six months in the autumn of 1929, had repeatedly begged the leadership for permission to resign but had been refused.[14] He died in office five years later.

Parparov Penetrates the German Foreign Ministry

One of the first illegals to make an impact was Fyodor Karpovich (originally Faivel' Kalmanovich) Parparov, a handsome Jew with an abundance of charm and intelligence. Born in Velizh, Vitebsk, on

November 23, 1893, Parparov began working as an apprentice to a wood exporter in Riga at the age of fourteen, which did not prevent his graduating from high school. He then became a clerk in a Petrograd bank, before joining the Red Army as a political commissar. After he was demobilised in 1920, he became deputy head of a directorate at the Commissariat of Supply in the Russian Republic, while studying law in his spare time. A degree under his belt, in 1925 he moved over to Foreign Trade, where he was trained to proficiency in German. He was then rapidly sent to the massive trade mission in Berlin, where he was recruited by the INO. Four years later he was recalled to be trained as an illegal.

In 1930 he returned to Berlin with wife and child; to create his legend, he formally disavowed his Soviet citizenship, became temporarily stateless, and then succeeded in obtaining a Romanian passport. Parparov set up an export company and opened branches across Europe and beyond—into North Africa, Turkey, Iran, and Afghanistan. Making contacts useful to Moscow was by no means easy, however, given that his associations were largely if not wholly with ambitious young entrepreneurs rather than those within the state apparatus. He now also posed as a journalist.

Driven by desperation, Parparov placed an advertisement in the personal column of a Berlin newspaper in the summer of 1931: "A young entrepreneur seeks a female partner with whom to pass the time and to help with journalistic work. Complete confidentiality is guaranteed." Within a fortnight he received a reply that went far beyond any reasonable expectation: "I would like to get to know you if you are as modest as promised. I am from the best of Berlin society to whom I will willingly introduce you once we have become acquainted with one another. I am married but very often I am alone as I am too honest [sic]. You must decide for yourself whether you wish to get to know me. As soon as you respond, you will know who I am. Naturally, confidentiality is essential." Parparov rang the telephone number enclosed and arranged an encounter.[15] It was a fortuitous discovery of a source he could never have encountered through any other means.

They met in a café. She turned out to be a pretty thirty-year-old who described her husband as hard-hearted, dry, and miserly—he even refused her a fur coat—and 100 percent devoted to his work as a senior official in the Auswärtiges Amt (Ausamt), the German Foreign

Ministry. Her striking candour, her evident loneliness, her personal financial straits, and her husband's parsimony—all assured Parparov that she was the genuine article.

But the Centre remained sceptical. It seemed too good to be true. She was nonetheless given a code name, "Marta." "In relation to Marta be cautious, continue with the warm up but do not make a move to recruit until you have taken the precaution of verification. Show no interest in her husband and his work, to the documents in his possession. Give Marta the impression that you are interested in her above all as a woman and also as a possible assistant in your activities as a journalist."

Soon, however, conversation fell into larger political questions, and Marta found herself attracted to Parparov and his outlook, which differed so markedly from those of her husband and his colleagues. She also believed that Parparov valued her judgement for his work as a journalist. "She is a little more than 30 years old," he wrote to the Centre.

> She was born in one of the cities on the Rhine into the family of a businessman of significance. She completed studies at the Conservatoire, and then took courses in music with the idea of perfecting her skills. She loves making music at home. After her father's death, Marta, her mother, and her sister spent the summer months in the resorts in Southern Germany. There she became acquainted with her future husband, already no longer a young diplomat, a typical Prussian civil servant. People who know Marta characterise her as a lover of life, a sociable person who loves to amuse herself but always conducts herself like a lady. She knows her own worth and has a good reputation.

Moscow eventually permitted recruitment under a false flag, the Japanese, for which she was paid. A camera was purchased with the story that Marta had taken up photography; in fact, she used it to copy documents. Throughout most of the thirties, Marta was in a position to provide the Russians with direct information from the very top of the Ausamt and copies of original documents that enabled Moscow's cryptanalysts to break open the German diplomatic one-time pads (ciphers used only once).

There was only one hiccup, at the beginning of 1938, after the defection of Krivitsky, who knew Parparov. On May 27 Parparov was arrested, imprisoned, and badly beaten until his release by Beria in June 1939. Meanwhile, Marta was persuaded (with some difficulty) to continue cooperation with the INO, even though, because his writing hand had been smashed by his torturers, Parparov's letters to her had to be typed—which made her deeply suspicious. Nonetheless, she was eventually persuaded to continue her work and has remained unidentified to this day.

The Zarubins

Berlin housed one legal OGPU rezidentura of ten men. Under Artuzov's guiding hand, the Russians opened two additional, illegal rezidentury: the lesser run by Vasilii Zarubin from 1933 to 1937, which operated alongside the legal structure, and the other, under Abram Slutsky, an Artuzov deputy, with a wide remit as main rezident for Western and Central Europe as a whole.[16]

Zarubin represented the new breed of intelligence operatives, with no direct experience of the revolution, men who began their careers as the Soviet Union was consolidating itself under Stalin. Nicknamed "Vasia," he had arched eyebrows that gave him a sad look, though he was in fact a rather likeable man.[17] He was a good tennis player, of medium height, solidly built, with thinning blond hair; though he was a veteran of World War I, he still had the look of a schoolboy.[18] The myopic son of a train conductor, he was nonetheless a natural linguist. After working successfully in the Soviet Far East against contraband, he had been drafted into the INO in 1925, running an illegal rezidentura first in Denmark and later in Sweden, before transferring to France in 1929.[19]

Zarubin thereafter worked as a team with his wife, Liza (née Rosenzweig), who was Jewish, petite, pretty, elegant, and refined. She came from the right side of the tracks, and her upbringing made up for his chronic lack of education.[20] Even more outgoing than Vasilii, Liza was fluent in English, German (her father's language), French, and Romanian. (She was born in northern Bukovina.)[21] On graduating from Chernovitskii University in 1920, she moved on to the Sorbonne and then to Vienna, before working as an interpreter for the Soviet mission in Austria. By March 1925 the INO had taken her on board—the Soviet service was an equal opportunity employer in its early days.

But behind her seductive looks and surface charm lurked fervent conviction and great courage. Liza was appointed assistant head of illegal operations at the INO in 1928. Contact with the former Socialist Revolutionary terrorist Yakov Blyumkin was inevitable. A friendship—perhaps something more—developed. Blyumkin, still much in sympathy with the opposition, was appointed illegal rezident in Istanbul, a pivotal post that took in the entire Near East. Within two days of his arrival, he encountered Trotsky's son Lev Sedov in the street. They met regularly thereafter. On April 16, Blyumkin spent four hours at Trotsky's apartment. The conversation inspired him to behave recklessly, providing funds and acting as a link with the opposition in Russia. Blyumkin's contact ran through Sedov to avoid compromising Trotsky by virtue of association with an OGPU illegal. Such folly was very much in his nature. Yet he had overlooked the fact that his protector Dzerzhinsky was no longer there to cover for him.

On arriving in the Soviet Union, Blyumkin was supposed to deliver Trotsky's letters (written in invisible ink on the pages of two books) to his daughter, his daughter-in-law, or his son-in-law. "Your main task above all is to make contact," Sedov emphasised. But, chronically anxious, Blyumkin hesitated, growing ever more nervous at the risks of following through. After seeing both Karl Radek and Ivar Smilga, Blyumkin shared his worries with his great friend Liza. She advised him to go straight to the Party's Central Control Commission or the OGPU and come clean about his "mistakes." On October 15 he wrote to Trilisser, but then, later that day, after further conversation with Liza, he went straight to the Lubyanka to confess all.[22] It did not save him. No doubt to Liza's silent horror, Blyumkin was condemned to death on November 3, 1929: the first victim within the Party to lose his life as a result of Stalin's very personal vendetta against Trotsky.[23]

Operation Tarantella

Artuzov may not himself have invented the Trust, but he did turn it into a legend, though its demise ultimately proved impossible to avert. Operations on a similar scale were now contemplated to neutralise Moscow's main foreign adversary, the British Empire, through disinformation on a grand scale. This led to the birth of Operation Tarantella in the summer of 1930. Artuzov's Italian roots no doubt made this an amusing choice of title: the tarantella is by legend a Neapolitan dance designed to drive men mad.[24] The operation's broad aim was to convince London that the industrialisation of the Soviet Union was a huge success. That this soon began to work is apparent from the switch in the focus of MI6 in 1932 from predominantly military intelligence (including the counterfeits produced by the army staff in Moscow) to planned industrialisation and the foreign and domestic policies of the Soviet government.[25]

Aside from media manipulation and carefully orchestrated foreign tourist visits, one target was Viktor Bogomolets, a key figure in MI6 operations against the Soviet Union based in southeastern Europe, known as HV/109.[26] Bogomolets had also been asked in 1930 to make contact with Polish intelligence through the MI6 resident (Ilychyov) for authorisation of British operations into the Soviet Union from Polish soil. Two years later the British began to make use of Prague in like manner.[27]

Bogomolets had been working for the British since serving on General Anton Denikin's staff in the Crimea during the last phase of the Russian Civil War. Afterwards, he moved to Constantinople, then on to Bucharest under the regional head of station, Captain Harold Gibson. Gibson worked from Prague with and through the Romanian and allied Polish services against the Bolsheviks. Artuzov had had his eye on Bogomolets for a considerable time.

Every detail of Bogomolets's operations in the region was mustered from multiple sources before Artuzov had him in his sights. Crucial to the scam was the former tsarist general Boris Lago-Kolpakov, a secret INO agent ("A/243") who had known Bogomolets since Constantinople. When the Bolsheviks created an amnesty at the end of 1921, Lago approached the Soviet embassy in Prague for permission to return.

Instead, the Cheka recruited him. Yet, lacking any real training, the luckless Lago was rapidly identified as a Soviet agent by General Peter Wrangel's people. After arrest and a month's imprisonment for attempting an illegal frontier crossing, Lago made it to Bucharest. Here, after initial success in recruiting a few agents, he had the cruel misfortune to run into Bogomolets, who, knowing what Lago was up to, promptly betrayed him to the Romanian security service, the Sigurantsa. Imprisoned for

five years, Lago was then released as the result of a general amnesty in
1929.

Following a further encounter with Bogomolets, Lago offered his
services to MI6, which despatched him to Vienna. En route via Berlin,
he reported to the Soviet embassy there for a full debriefing. The instructions from the Lubyanka were to break with Bogomolets. He did
not do so. Instead, Lago sustained his cover and published sensationalist memoirs in an emigré newspaper recounting his experiences at the
INO. Now, under Artuzov's more agile and imaginative direction,
the INO immediately reinstated Lago in the service, where he quickly
found a role to play in Operation Tarantella. He travelled to the Soviet
Union in 1931, made contact with oppositional elements in Odessa,
and, en route, briefed MI6.

Tarantella began amid an acute crisis. The peasantry constituted
two-thirds of the country. Stubborn resistance to the forced collectivisation of agriculture had led to massacre or deportation by boxcar to
the barren hinterland. The compliant were passively herded like cattle
into "cooperative" farming, the notorious *kolkhozy*. The Politburo took
the view that "The foolhardy resistance of the kulaks [propertied peas-
ants] to the collective farm movement of toiling peasants, already
growing at the end of 1929 and taking the form of setting fires and acts
of terror against collective farm leaders, necessitated the application by
Soviet power of mass arrests and severe kinds of repression in the form
of the mass deportation of kulaks and their henchmen to northern and
distant regions."[28] Artuzov had to play a part in this brutal operation.

Abroad, such calamitous conditions inevitably inspired certain fan-
tasies within MI6: of recruiting opponents of the régime on a significant scale and even of finding a Party functionary opposed to Stalin
willing to assassinate him or some other leading figure. On his way out
of Russia, Lago headed for Riga to brief Bogomolets and meet Gibson.

Having fastened the bait and cast his line, Artuzov now sought to
reel in a mouthwatering catch. His deputy from August 1931, Abram
Slutsky, was still working from the trade mission in Berlin, overseeing
operations in Europe as a whole.[29] Round faced, with a broad nose, a
wide mouth, and startling eyebrows, Slutsky is described as "likeable"
and "a mild-mannered man," "part dutiful N.K.V.D. official and in part
sentimentally attached to the past as a Communist revolutionary,"[30]

though not devoid of initiative. On February 18, 1934, he suggested recruiting Bogomolets. On March 4 the young Matus Shteinberg ("Max") appeared in Bogomolets's apartment in Paris. Here he revealed every operation that Bogomolets had been associated with, which had long been an open book to Moscow. The game was up. Bogomolets understood the futility of MI6 operations.

Shamefully exposed, Bogomolets nonetheless bravely resisted Soviet blackmail: a week later, he honourably reported everything to Gibson. It did him no good. Bogomolets was summarily dismissed. The damage done to Britain went far beyond him, however. Tarantella involved the spreading of disinformation to MI6 on a substantial range of important topics, from the development of the Soviet defence industry to Kremlin high politics and the quantity of Soviet gold held in reserve.[31]

Moscow wanted London to believe that the Soviet Union was far stronger than it actually was and that its industrialisation had been a complete success. This was the message also carried by fellow-travelling foreign correspondents such as the Englishman Walter Duranty at the *New York Times*, whose want of perspicacity and integrity did not exactly enhance the newspaper's reputation as a journal of record. He won a Pulitzer Prize (1932) for his writing on the Ukraine, despite the fact that he continued to insist, against the evidence, that "there is no famine."[32] Stalin himself took a direct and no doubt gratifying interest in Tarantella, which revealed Gibson's subversive operations and intelligence gathering to be the victim of yet another theatrical performance.

MI6 sought to penetrate the Soviet Union by various means, having given up on maintaining a station within the embassy. One such means was through firms conducting trade on Soviet territory, which could provide "natural cover." Here one company in particular offered an obvious opportunity, as the Russians desperately needed foreign technology and know-how to make the Five-Year Plans for industrialisation a success, not least for armaments production. This was the Metropolitan-Vickers Electrical Company (Metrovick), originally a British subsidiary of the American Westinghouse corporation. Economic Section VI of MI6 was interested in industrial intelligence that could throw light on the development of foreign military capabilities. For this purpose, in 1931 it spawned the Industrial Intelligence Centre (IIC) under Major

Desmond Morton, which necessarily exploited the global presence of major British companies.[33]

At the end of 1931, Menzhinsky received news that the leading global companies supplying equipment had agreed on October 16, 1930, to "pool their information for the purposes of the cartel"[34] and that MI6 was involved.[35] The Russians had obtained the minutes of a meeting of the International Price Arrangements Committee held in Zurich on June 5–6, 1931, between the Germans (Siemens-Schuckert, AEG, Pittler), the Swiss (Brown, Boveri & Cie), the British (Metrovick), and the Americans (General Electric). At the meeting the Metrovick representative was Charles Richards, the London manager, who was also working for the IIC of MI6, having served in military intelligence during the war of intervention to overthrow the Bolsheviks (May 1918–November 1919).

In pursuit of intelligence on Soviet capabilities, Richards made use of Allan Monkhouse, Metrovick's manager in the Soviet Union, and Leslie Thornton, both of whom were Russian-speakers and had also been in military service during the war of intervention. They paid large sums of money to Russian employees for secret information about growing Soviet defence capabilities. Richards was also interested in more general classified information that could be obtained. When arrested and questioned, Thornton confessed, and Monkhouse confirmed Thornton's statements about Richards's role in events.

The Soviet task was made all the easier because, although Thornton had sent his diary back to London before the end of 1932, the Russians had already photographed its contents. The only problem for them was that Stalin ensured that the indictment against the British was focused, no doubt for popular consumption, on sabotage rather than espionage. This made it all the easier for London to deny everything and for Foreign Secretary Sir John Simon to claim no connexion between these events and MI6. But the Soviet spy Kim Philby later sent the Russians a copy of an internal MI6 memorandum, "Penetrating Russia," which commented that "natural cover served us well in Russia in the past— indeed, right up to the Metropolitan-Vickers affair, which was due entirely to our own carelessness."[36] And since Show Trials appeared to have become a Soviet habit, everyone easily fell into thinking that the whole affair had simply been fabricated.

Naum Eitingon

Hitler's accession to power at the end of January 1933 completely altered the complex of international relations in Europe. Few anticipated the tragedy that lay ahead, but, as events unfolded, the most fearful predictions proved true. Stalin initially hoped for the best and, indeed, won momentary support from those alarmed at this new and unexpectedly disturbing course of events. Reliable intelligence was in short supply as the Nazis imposed their own institutions on existing foundations. The strategy of constructing networks of illegals now made even better sense than before. To buttress this vital process, Artuzov installed Naum Eitingon as head of the first section of the INO, the illegals, in April 1933.

Eitingon, like Zarubin one of the new breed, emerges as a saturnine figure closely associated with the darkest dimension of foreign intelligence, "a fat and disagreeable man" who "substituted arrogance for lack of intelligence," according to one who knew him and obviously disliked him. Defamation notwithstanding, he was also something of a ladies' man.[37] Eitingon was born in the small town of Shklov, Mogilev, on December 6, 1899. Shklov, even today, is 88 percent Jewish. Located in the borderlands between Russia and Poland, it suffered a succession of rampages: from the Cossacks, to the Swedes, to Napoléon. Despite being the son of a Jewish office worker in a local paper factory, Eitingon came from the merchant class.[38] His father died when he was only thirteen, leaving his mother with two daughters and another, younger son. For a while his grandfather, a lawyer, looked after them. When his grandfather died, Eitingon moved to Mogilev proper and was sent to a commercial college. After graduation, he taught statistics.

During the February Revolution, Eitingon was, like many of the young, attracted very briefly to the left Socialist Revolutionaries; their rhetoric was the most radical, and they were actively engaged in terrorism as the heirs of the Narodniki. But, after October, he joined the Bolsheviks, who proved more consistently radical in their deeds. Eitingon had dark brown eyes and sported a mop of thick black hair. He was reserved, but given to irony; courageous and also determined—all in all, a leader, a man of action. He fought in Gomel during the civil war. In May 1920 he took charge of the special department charged with defeating the counterrevolution, which was soon rolled up and incorporated into the Cheka. From there he was sent for training to the Eastern Faculty of the Red Army military academy.

Eitingon caught Dzerzhinsky's eye as a fellow fanatic. Assigned to Shanghai, he arrived at the end of 1925, but was tossed about in the backwash of the failed Chinese Revolution. He briefly served as rezident in Beijing, before Chinese troops raided and destroyed the Soviet consulate. From there he was sent to run the rezidentura in Kharbin, Manchuria. There, the preoccupation was as much with the Japanese as it was with the Chinese and the massive number of Whites in the vicinity. Soon, disaster struck again: on May 27, 1929, the local warlord raided the Soviet consulate. Legal operations were promptly closed down, and Eitingon was immediately repatriated.

The Chinese experience was a baptism by fire. Eitingon's next assignment was Istanbul, where he replaced Yakov Minsker as rezident; his posting ran parallel to the illegal rezidentura under the ill-fated Blyumkin. The latter's replacement turned out to be a disaster, former head of the INO's Eastern Sector Georgii Agabekov, who defected in June 1930 and published sensationalist revelations about the OGPU. Having been identified, Eitingon saw his life as a legal come to an abrupt end. On his return, he adopted the nom de guerre Leonid Naumov.

Brief service as deputy to "Yasha" Serebryankii, followed by an even briefer stay in the United States recruiting Chinese and Japanese migrants, led Eitingon to request a return to the INO at the end of 1931. He spent several months heading the newly activated eighth department (scientific and technical intelligence) and was then given missions to France and Belgium. It was at this point that Artuzov put him in charge of illegal operations based on Eitingon's considerable experience overseas. This was no desk job, and it suited him well: he spent the next couple of years on the road—in the United States, China, Iran, and Germany—orchestrating illegal operations. As a result, in 1936 he was promoted to the rank of major (equivalent to the rank of colonel in the Red Army).[39]

The INO that Artuzov now led had long coveted the resources and status of its rival, the Fourth, and had persistently sought to seduce the latter's better officers into its own ranks. Artuzov's star had never burned more brightly, but how long would it last in this perilous system? In fact, an incident soon threatened to undercut his position. Hitler had been working to destroy the Rapallo relationship with Moscow (based on military collaboration) that had been devised as a threat to Poland; at the same time, in a populist act of defiance, he immediately broke out of the restrictions on military training and innovation imposed by the Versailles treaty.

Hitherto, the brunt of Nazi propaganda had been directed against Poland in eastern Europe. Now, increasingly, it was directed at the Soviet Union and international communism in general. The head of the USSR's international information department, Karl Radek, himself a Pole, suggested to Stalin that they sound out Warsaw about aligning against Berlin. After all, France was groping its way towards an effective alliance against Germany, and it was to be expected that allies in eastern Europe, such as Poland and Czechoslovakia, would move in concert.

When the Radek mission was discussed at a specially enlarged meeting of the Politburo, Artuzov insisted that the Poles were merely flirting with the Russians and would eventually embrace the Germans. But Radek insisted that the Polish move towards the Soviet Union was "an about-turn and not a manoeuvre vis-à-vis the USSR."[40] Radek was convinced he was right. From April 30 to May 3, Colonel Bogusław Miedziński, chief editor of the semiofficial *Gazeta Polska*, had come over to Moscow as an unofficial emissary. These talks were continued by Radek, who visited Poland from July 6 to 22, ostensibly to see his mother. The small change the Russians tossed at the Poles was Lithuania, still technically at war with Poland since the latter's annexation of Vilnius in 1920.[41]

Taken in by Radek's brilliance, plausible logic, and personal knowledge of native Poland—he had, after all, been right about the folly of the 1920 counteroffensive—Stalin reacted with unconcealed hostility to Artuzov's scepticism, and as the year proceeded, he relentlessly belittled Artuzov in front of others. This should have made Artuzov nervous, but when, on January 30, 1934, Poland and Germany put their names to a nonaggression declaration, Artuzov was dramatically vindicated, and Stalin's attitude towards him completely turned around—at least for the time being.[42]

The Fourth Loses Its Way

An ideal opportunity for the INO to establish ascendancy over the Fourth fortuitously presented itself. Police forces across Europe had for some time exchanged intelligence on Soviet activities. By the end of the 1920s, a turning point had been reached: the free trade in anti-Bolshevik counterintelligence had finally fulfilled its potential. As a result, Moscow now faced what it called the "police international." Almost overnight, the end of sloppy practices made possible by national police services, acting alone or at most in tandem, threw the operations of the Fourth into jeopardy.

The Fourth had undoubtedly racked up some impressive achievements. From 1930, the Bulgarian Ivan Vinarov ("Mart"), working as a general rezident based in Austria, recruited an extensive network that encompassed the entire French alliance system throughout eastern Europe. But slipups were inevitable. A gifted amateur, Vinarov was ignorant of other cultures, which put him at risk of exposure. On one memorable occasion, he met his agents in a kosher restaurant. The customers were invariably Orthodox Jews, whose heads have to remain covered. When he and the agents handed their hats to the maître d'hôtel, eyes turned in hostile curiosity, while the waiters reacted with bafflement and indignation. Several spies drawing attention to themselves, innocent of the culture of others—surely this was an object lesson in the importance of appropriate training.

Vinarov's main task was to penetrate the secret radio-telegraphic departments of the post offices in national capitals throughout the Balkans to obtain copies of ciphered traffic sent by foreign embassies. A trading company was set up to disguise illicit movement across frontiers. This venture, Operation Telegraph, proved extraordinarily productive until January 1933, when a number of agents were arrested in Bucharest, though the authorities never worked out entirely what they were up to.[43] Vinarov went on to become a senior figure in the security structure of postwar Bulgaria.

Not all operations conducted without regard to rules of procedure worked out so well. As recently as 1927, confronted with operational shortcomings and outright failures, Berzin could excuse himself with the lame plea that "our intelligence is still young: it is only 5–6 years old."[44] But half a dozen years on, that hardly sufficed as a convincing argument. His luck had finally run out.

In Vienna, the local rezident was a fellow Lett, Konstantin Basov (Yan Abeltyn'), who had served under the director as his assistant for human intelligence. In Baden, on the outskirts of the capital, Basov set up an illegal radio station to transmit agent reports to Moscow. In December 1931, he and four comrades were detained by the police after holding a meeting in a café. The meeting had gone ahead despite reports to Moscow that Basov was being tailed. Basov's assistant, Vasilii Didushok, succeeded in getting him out of custody due to the efforts of Colonel von Bredow of the Abwehr, who claimed that those detained were working for the Reichswehr. Yet, while under arrest, Basov had lost his nerve and had already confessed to being the Soviet rezident. Not only that, he broke all the rules by giving his real identity as Abeltyn'.[45]

The Lettish authorities had close contacts with the Austrian police. On June 4, 1933, three agents arrested in Riga had variously come to the attention of the Austrian police and Lettish counterintelligence. As a consequence of the collapse of this network, Julius Trossin, a courier, was identified by the Germans. This came as a great blow to Moscow. His circuit ran through the rezidentury in Germany, Romania, Finland, Estonia, Great Britain, and the United States; his arrest exposed the entire network.

Soon after, the Fourth's recruiting agent in Germany was arrested. The consequences cascaded and arrests multiplied as Trossin was linked to various illegal rezidentury across Europe. That October saw the detention of the rezident Maria Yul'evna Shul'-Tyltyn', her assistants Arvid Jacobson, Yukho Vyakh'ya, and Frans Klemetti, and others in Finland—a massive trawl that yielded a catch of twenty-seven in the net.

The problem was not just that agents had cracked under interrogation. More troubling was that the Fourth had frozen like a bewildered rabbit gripped by fear in the face of oncoming traffic, whereas one might have expected it to have acted speedily to avert total disaster. The next to fall was the rezident in Paris. On December 19, 1933, Veniamin Berkovich was arrested along with his wife; his assistant, Shvarts; his communications officer, Lidiya Shtal'; and a number of other agents, including a cipher specialist at the naval ministry. Soon after, the police swooped down in Britain, Germany, and the United States.[46]

Shambles in Shanghai: The Noulens Affair

The Fourth's calamities were astounding, unprecedented in scale within the service, and irrevocably accumulative: the rot had set in. In Berzin's defence, he had lost in Bronisław Bortnowski a trusted deputy charged with agent operations. Bortnowski's replacement, Ruben Tairov, did not have the appropriate experience; in fact, his only asset was loyalty to the Party hierarchy. Disasters in China and Europe soon demonstrated Tairov's unsuitability, but it took Berzin until February 1932 to get him replaced. By then, the damage had been done. The worst consequences were to rise to the surface well after his departure. And the director himself was by no means blameless.

In order to run deep-cover operations, Berzin had to set up companies that could both generate a profit to fund the rezidentury and provide operatives with apparently legitimate need for travel. Aleksandr Ulanovskii ("Sherif") was recruited by the Fourth in October 1929, and on the basis of very little real experience (one year with the rival service in Germany) Tairov sent him to Shanghai as the new rezident. He was seriously out of his depth.

Ulanovskii was a simple man who, though formerly an anarchist/ Socialist Revolutionary, believed utterly in the Bolshevik revolution. Whittaker Chambers, who knew him as "Ulrich," describes him rather unkindly as "monkey-like" in looks as well as in manner, "in the droop of his arms and the roll of his walk . . . his brown eyes that were most monkey-like, alternately mischievous and wistful."[47] His strong point was psychological: he had the ability, unusual for a Russian, to see matters from another's point of view. But, as was the case with Sorge, Ulanovskii found it hard to run intelligence operations without seeking out the like-minded, and that made the necessary separation of these operations from Party activity almost impossible.

Ulanovskii was encouraged to act as a representative for arms manufacturers from Belgium and France. Almost anywhere else this might have proved unproblematic. But China fell squarely within the British sphere of influence, and the British policed the International Settlement in Shanghai. Under Czechoslovakian cover as "Kirshner," Ulanovskii took the customary passage by P&O via Marseilles and the Suez Canal. He duly arrived in Shanghai along with the more junior Sorge and Weingart ("Zeppel"), a radio operator, on January 10, 1930.

It was not long before Weingart was accosted by an Englishman who had been on board. He was quizzed in a persistent manner about Ulanovskii's whereabouts. When he was evasive, the Englishman insisted that Ulanovskii would be discovered and prevented from selling armaments. Taking fright, Moscow instructed Ulanovskii to refrain from any negotiations on arms purchases. He was thus stranded without any plausible cover.[48] Worse was to follow. In mid-February, Ulanovskii recruited a friend from the old days, Rafail ("Folya") Kurgan, who proved completely unstable and a danger to the whole group.

Ulanovskii's luck, it must be said, was also spectacularly bad. In 1927 he had visited Shanghai and Hangzhou with a Soviet front organisation called the Pan-Pacific Trades Union Secretariat; at the time, the Communists were on the verge of seizing the major cities. In Shanghai, the favourite dive for Soviet operatives was the Arcadia Restaurant and Night Club. It was here that Ulanovskii had encountered a German businessman with whom he had unfortunately shared a compartment on the train to Vladivostok from Moscow in 1927. The man had not only seen Ulanovskii with the head of Profintern (the Soviet-created trades union international), Solomon Lozovskii, but had also heard him speak in his own name at the Pan-Pacific conference of trades unions. A second such encounter made it impossible for Ulanovskii to remain in Shanghai.

"Captain Eugene Pik" was born Kozhevnikov in 1898 in Astrakhan. He had also come across the unfortunate Ulanovskii in Hangzhou in 1927. During the first Chinese Revolution, Kozhevnikov had served in the INO with the Soviet military mission under Commander Vasilii Blyukher. When Chinese forces raided the embassy in Beijing on April 6, 1927, all the intelligence operatives moved to Hangzhou—except Kozhevnikov, who instead switched sides. In May he had sent the names of sixty-two Comintern agents to the Shanghai Municipal Police along with the brazen suggestion that they hire him; he also published a series of mildly revelatory articles for the *North China Daily News and Herald*.[49] Kozhevnikov subsequently turned up uninvited at Ulanovskii's apartment claiming to work for Chinese counter-intelligence and revealing that he knew what Kurgan had been up to. It was time for Ulanovskii to leave—in a hurry.[50]

This left Sorge, still under deep cover as a newspaper correspondent, fully responsible for the Shanghai rezidentura, at the heart of

British imperialism in China, and with very limited previous experience. The scandal that threatened him was not of his own making, though the risks he took in handling it were characteristic of him—a feature noticeable also later, during his service in Tokyo. The scandal was prompted by the arrest on June 15, 1931, of Yakov Rudnik (now code-named "Henri") and his wife ("Henrietta"), operating under cover as a Belgian couple, the Noulens. Since 1928 they had been running the China Trading Company on behalf of the OMS, Comintern's logistical organisation.

The timing could scarcely have been worse. Japan was about to launch its occupation of Manchuria, a territory of great value in its own right but also affording the quickest route to invade Russia's maritime provinces. Moscow was itself not unaware of what lay ahead. The OGPU had penetrated the Japanese embassy in Moscow by recruiting an agent working in the office of the military attaché, Yukio Kasahara. In July 1931, Maj.-Gen. Komakichi Harada of the General Staff arrived to discuss the future with Kasahara and the ambassador, Koti Hirota. The documentary record was photographed by the agent and pored over by Stalin. Hirota "considered it essential that Japan embark upon a firm policy towards the Soviet Union, ready to start a war at any moment." The main aim was "not so much to protect Japan from communism as to seize the Soviet Far East and Eastern Siberia."[51] On September 18 the Japanese began their invasion of Manchuria.

An impoverished Ukrainian Jew with natural gifts, Rudnik had joined the Cheka and ran the illegal rezidentura in France for barely a year before he was arrested. He served two years in prison, then went on to work for the OMS in Austria under the code name "Luft." Ignatii Reiss served with him at the embassy in Vienna in 1926. Reiss's wife described Rudnik as "not unattractive-looking but extremely tense, forever moving about and switching from one to another of his three languages apparently without noticing. Although not in the opposition, he often spoke too openly about the way the party was being run." On a trip to Rome he fell in love with and swiftly married a secretary from the Soviet embassy, Tat'yana Moisenko-Velikaya. She had been educated at the Smolny Institute in St. Petersburg, a school for the maidens of the aristocracy.[52] Moisenko-Velikaya now worked for the INO.[53]

Early in February, Sorge had advised Moscow that Rudnik's place was under surveillance. He was warned, but instead of shutting up shop, Rudnik merely moved house.[54] When he and his wife were arrested and indicted in June, Sorge had no need to do anything. After all, the vast stash of secret documents that the Shanghai Municipal Police trumphantly took not from their home, but from the apartment at 49 Nanking Road, threw only Comintern into chaos—it did not in any way directly affect the Fourth. Yet one would not have guessed this, given what followed.

On June 23, Aleksandr Abramov, Pyatnitsky's deputy at the head of OMS, turned to Berzin in desperation. Abramov needed Sorge to do everything he could to secure the Rudniks' release. Comintern would furnish the funds. It was not unusual for the Fourth to route funds to Comintern outlets abroad, particularly in China. But this request went much further. That day, Berzin conveyed the request from the "Big House" (Comintern) to help "those who had fallen ill" (the Rudniks) by hiring a lawyer, arranging for food, and, if necessary, paying for a doctor. This had to be done carefully and through third parties. Sorge had to hide in the shadows. Should that prove impossible, he should stand aside.[55]

Sorge typically did as asked. His sense of himself as an active revolutionary made this choice certain, but the demands grew. Sorge soon agreed to take over management of OMS activities, including liaising with the Chinese Communist Party (CCP). This level of exposure placed him in jeopardy; clearly he was viewed as expendable. Both OMS and the Fourth appeared willing to risk Sorge for the sake of the Rudniks, even though MI6 already had all the information it needed to break up the existing networks and nullify Comintern activities in the region.[56]

Sorge was instructed to arrange safe passage for the CCP leaders Zhou Enlai (China's future foreign minister) and Chen Shaoyu (Wang Ming), so that they could escape possible capture.[57] The irony was that even though Sorge had to carry the extra load for the "friends," thus increasing the danger to himself and to his primary mission, the ill-informed Tairov lambasted him from Moscow for not gathering more secret intelligence.[58] Notwithstanding the Fourth's warnings about sustaining close links with the CCP, pressure continued to carry on as before.[59]

Sorge wrote to Pyatnitsky ("Mikhail"), insisting that with the reestablishment of Comintern's apparatus in Shanghai, Comintern people could handle contacts with the Rudniks and their lawyer. "This is not because we have been unwilling to do [this work] but because our affairs are not going so well that we took the burden of this connexion onto ourselves lightly." Sorge's rezidentura was even burdened with producing a new periodical, *China Forum*, but the Comintern comrades refused to offer any help. Dmitrii Manuilskii, running the organisation after Bukharin's removal, said that Sorge was lazy. Sorge much resented this slur. "I am already, at the very least, compromised quite enough." Could not Smedley (his lover) be asked to edit *China Forum*?[60]

The Rudniks' trial took place in Nanzhing from July 5 to August 19, and was accompanied by a noisy international campaign orchestrated for their immediate release. They were brilliantly and misleadingly portrayed as victims of injustice by Willi Münzenberg, the head of the German Communist Party's illegal apparatus and Comintern's media magician. As the number of arrests rose in October 1932, Sorge, at his wits' end, finally asked to be pulled out. Nothing happened. Moscow gave in at the very last moment, in August 1933. It was a close call. By May, Sorge was already on the Shanghai Municipal Police list of thirteen suspected Soviet agents, as was Smedley.[61] In spite of her tireless self-promotion, Smedley was not in fact an operative, just an asset. Sorge had recommended her in a somewhat backhanded manner to Berzin as "very valuable" though unwell, highly strung, and difficult to handle, suitable for employment anywhere but on the most risky terrain: India or Japan.[62] She remained the object of the deepest suspicion to Stalin.

Stalin Subordinates the Fourth to the INO

Stalin had seen enough. The catalogue of disasters prompted him to gather under one roof the leaders of civilian and military intelligence, a move forestalled on a previous attempt in 1920 due to resistance from the army. But Unshlikht was now no longer there to protect the Fourth.

In Russia, as in the United States, the first floor is the ground floor. Stalin's *ugolok*—literally, "little corner"—stood at the end of one wing on the second floor of the Kremlin. His right-hand man, Molotov, chairman of the Council of People's Commissars, had an office that stood at the end of the other wing. It was in the *ugolok* on April 19, 1934, that Stalin received the director, along with Artuzov and Yagoda, to discuss what had to be done about the Fourth.[63] On May 25, Artuzov was again invited, this time without Berzin, for a final decision.[64] The following day, a resolution in the name of the Politburo was issued on "Questions About the Fourth Directorate of the Red Army Command." The disasters that had occurred the year before represented "the most blatant breach of the basic principles of security." Inter alia the leadership of the Fourth was indicted for insufficient due diligence in choosing its officers and for training them inadequately.

The indictment found fault with the lack of coordination between the Fourth and the INO, as a result of which misunderstandings had arisen. The Fourth was also accused of wasting resources on countries of no strategic significance to Moscow. Berzin was personally attacked for paying insufficient attention to human intelligence operations, and even the Third Department was criticised for not obtaining the technological information needed by the defence industries.

The solution required that the Fourth be subordinated directly to Commissar Voroshilov rather than to the Red Army staff, then headed by Tukhachevsky. Yet Voroshilov was merely a cipher, which prompted the following joke: At celebrations on May 1 and November 7, when Trotsky arrived at Red Square as commissar on a white stallion, everyone yelled, "Look at Comrade Trotsky!" When Voroshilov turned up as commissar, everyone cried, "Look at the horse!"

The Fourth had to reorganise its operations to ensure that small cells worked independently of one another. It had to set up a special school for training, overseen by the OGPU. And its reach was to be severely curtailed. The focus of its operations was to be reduced to "Poland, Germany, Finland, Romania, Britain, Japan, Manchuria, and China." Research on the armed forces of others was to be conducted only through open sources. A committee composed of both the Fourth and the INO was required by the Politburo to coordinate operations.

These drastically punitive proposals did more than break down the Chinese wall that had separated the two services since the mid-1920s. Provision was made for mutual planning, sharing of information to avert failures, exchange of experience (including lessons learned from failed operations and the adoption of joint measures to prevent such failures), and close inspection and supervision of operatives abroad.[65]

What the resolution did not make explicit was that this was no merger between equals, but rather, the humiliating subordination of one rival to the other. Artuzov was ordered to supervise operations on behalf of an alien agency; his daunting assignment was to turn that agency around, as he had done with the INO, but this time without the seniority that made direct access to Stalin possible. So, while he remained head of the INO, Artuzov also became deputy head of the Fourth. He asked to bring with him more than two dozen stalwarts from the INO, and the request was granted. Artuzov immediately took charge of the second section, the most important one, over which Berzin retained only nominal control, and inserted his own people to manage it. Thus, the INO effectively supervised military as well as political intelligence.[66] Artuzov understood that he was to become Stalin's "eyes in the RU [Razvedupr],"[67] but it was most unwise to have said so.

On July 10, 1934, the OGPU (including the INO) was subsumed into the Main Directorate of State Security (GUGB) of the Commissariat of Internal Affairs (NKVD): thereafter, secret policemen became known generically as *gebisty* or *enkavedisty*. These reorganisations so beloved by Stalin did little to change anything substantial, however. The Lubyanka remained the headquarters of the "organs." Also if Stalin's ultimate aim was to keep everyone on his toes, he certainly failed. This was most evident at the Fourth. What the Sorge interlude in China demonstrated so clearly was that, when placed under pressure from Pyatnitsky at Comintern, Berzin had been prepared to bend the rules of tradecraft even at the risk of exposure. The revolutionary wave might have ebbed in Europe, but it still flowed in the Far East, dammed only by the thin crust of European colonisation—and the revolutionary impulse was hard to resist.

An interlude in the United States was unaccountably free of slipups—most likely because the FBI had its eyes elsewhere. Then Ulanovskii was transferred back to Europe. From the safety of Denmark, operations could be run against Germany. But in Copenhagen, Ulanovskii plunged into a new mess just as Berzin's own position was in jeopardy. His subordinate in Copenhagen was George Mink (né Minkovsky); the two had met in the United States, and Mink had just joined the Fourth. Mink was "muscle," having headed the Communist Maritime Workers Industrial Union in New York. He was alternatively known as "Mink the Fink" and "Mink the Butcher" after he led a gang of bruisers backing the Stalinist William Foster's bid for leadership of the U.S. Communist Party; this was an extension of the normal tactics used to terrorise ship owners into meeting union demands.[68]

As an overconfident novice, Mink was a loose cannon on the deck in the intelligence war. Along the Copenhagen dockside, he began recruiting sailors who were Communists. This led to complaints from the Danish Party. From Moscow, Ulanovskii was warned off and advised to send Mink back home. He did not. Unfortunately for him, one of those recruited was a police agent; worse still, Mink assaulted a chambermaid, though it is entirely possible this was set up by the police, as they placed a watch on the safe house and on the address receiving German mail.

When they did finally swoop in, on March 8, 1935, initially in search of Mink, the police happened upon an unexpected windfall. Not only did they pick up Ulanovskii, Mink, and another American, Leon Josephson, but they also captured one of the rezidents from Germany, David Uger; former rezident in Germany Max Maximov, who appeared to be passing through on his way back to Russia; and the assistant head of the first department at the Fourth, D. L'vovich.[69]

So, on March 16, 1935, it was Artuzov who now had to answer not only for his error of judgement in appointing Ulanovskii, but also for mistakes that took place on his watch. "Comrade Ulanovskii has been arrested because he broke the rule forbidding recruitment of Party members," Artuzov informed Voroshilov. "All three Danes recruited by him are Communists. Comrade Ulanovskii hid from us the fact that they are Communists."[70]

"The most notable thing in this business," he added, "is that our employees, who had not done badly in fascist Germany, on arriving in a 'neutral' country disregarded elementary rules of security." The fact that the Danes had found them working not against national interests but against the Germans at least relieved Moscow of a diplomatic row. Nonetheless, Ulanovskii received a four-year sentence.

Still bitter at the serious blow to his authority—that is, losing to others direct control over the Fourth that he had lamentably failed to exercise—Voroshilov took full advantage of this incident to discredit Artuzov. The day after Artuzov reported on the fracas in Copenhagen, Voroshilov vociferously and unscrupulously condemned the fact that "our foreign intelligence limps along on all fours. Artuzov has done little for us in the sense of improving this serious defect. In the next few days I will institute measures to be taken to avert any repetition of instances such as that in Copenhagen."[71]

The knives were out. On April 15, 1935, Uritsky was brought in to replace Berzin, and Voroshilov immediately began pressing him to complain about Artuzov. The underlying message was not hard to read. The fact was that Artuzov and the thirty *enkavedisty* he brought with him were being systematically ostracised within the Fourth. Sometime later Artuzov complained: "I think that you [in the Fourth] have changed your attitude towards the comrades that came in with me, Semyon Petrovich. To what end? I do not understand. I don't want to believe that the wave of certain unhealthy sentiments among many of your comrades towards the Chekists also touches upon you . . . I think the people I brought into the Razvedupr are not bad. They have no military schooling, they have many defects, but they are useful in intelligence and there is no need to get rid of them."[72]

Even Stalin understood that changing the culture of the Fourth was bound to take time. Unfortunately for the Soviet Union, however, not all the changes put through by Artuzov were sensible. Stalin had no respect for research and analysis, and the Fourth's department was large and expensive. It employed significant numbers of ex-tsarist officers. It did not devote its time merely to classified documents but also screened open source material and prepared books for publication.

Back in the autumn of 1932, faced with more intelligence information than he could assimilate, a disastrous famine in sight, and a wife driven to suicide by his cruel indifference, Stalin had reached a peak of intolerance and ordered a halt to "quarterly surveys of foreign countries."[73]

Bearing in mind the Big Boss's preferences, Artuzov abolished research and analysis. Since the INO lacked such a section, Moscow was thereafter blind. Though the Soviet Union had signed a mutual-assistance pact with France against Germany on May 2, 1935, the French shifted to the right under Pierre Laval and failed to follow through with the military collaboration that the Russians had sought. In response, Stalin did nothing to restrain the French Communist Party from wrecking the country's defence capability through waves of strikes. France's ally Czechoslovakia, however, which had also signed a mutual-assistance pact, agreed to exchange secret intelligence. Artuzov, having relinquished his role as head of the INO on May 21, 1935, was fully engaged in trying to establish links with Prague.[74]

When Captain František Moravec, charged with Czechoslovakian military intelligence, opened cooperation with his Russian counterparts in 1936, he was astonished to discover that the Fourth was "having difficulties in establishing contact with important sources of information in the Reich as well as in organising a productive net of lower-level agent-observers" and "they had not organised proper supporting activities, such as the study of the German news media." The Russians made "careful note of our experience with provincial newspapers, published in the smaller German towns, in which numerous indiscretions about military matters could still be found despite the severe Nazi censorship."[75] But no one in the Fourth appeared to have direct experience of Central Europe, or knowledge of foreign languages. Everything was done through interpreters and translators. "The unexpected inefficiency in the military Intelligence service of a régime which had been born and nourished on clandestine undertakings was surprising," Moravec recalled.[76] The Czechs had unwittingly stumbled upon an awkward truth hidden behind the Stalinist façade of all-knowing invincibility.

Ironically, and tragically, to the extent that intelligence was allowed to work as it should have done, the Russians were soon to become far better informed about their future allies than about their immediate adversaries. The performance of Soviet foreign intelligence did not notably improve under Artuzov until the impact of two separate initiatives was felt: first at the INO, then at the Fourth.

The Importance of Whom You Know: The Cambridge Five

It was under Artuzov's overall supervision that the notorious "Cambridge Five" were lured on board—and it was Artuzov who recruited their recruiter. The project started almost by chance. It was the alertness and the ingenuity of the response in the field and at the Lubyanka that turned rare opportunity into stunning achievement. "Kim" Philby, the promising son of a rather eccentric father, was as yet a man only in the making. He was not gifted except in foreign languages, and at Westminster School his progress was faltering; but his mind, once it was made up, had a coldly determined quality to it, and he set his heart on his father's college, Trinity, at Cambridge.[77] As a student, he responded to the Great Depression by irrevocably moving to the left, and served as treasurer to the Socialist Society, a forum for those interested in theoretical aspects of Marxism. The abject failure of the reformist

Labour Party and the apparent indifference of government to the plight of the mass unemployed lacking adequate social provision was to turn a significant number of privileged young men and women in the direction of the Communist cause. At a loss as to what to do upon graduating, he was advised by Maurice Dobb, a lecturer in economics and an early member of the British Communist Party (1922), to go abroad and work for a branch of the MOPR, an international organisation for aid to workers run from Moscow, and also a Comintern front organisation. Philby's destination was Austria, a country drifting fast towards civil war. In fact, it appears he would become a courier for OMS.

Philby proved utterly dependable, cool, and resourceful—though he remained somewhat unsure of himself in other respects. His shy charm was marred only by an intermittent stutter that, oddly enough, proved a source of attraction to the opposite sex. It somehow gave the disarming impression that he was earnestly in search of the right word and thus invited trust. Furthermore, Philby's British passport enabled him to travel through the Balkans without hindrance, and his letter of introduction to the *Daily Telegraph* correspondent Eric Gedye, a former member of British military intelligence but also a passionate antifascist, enabled him to "plunder" six suits from Gedye's wardrobe on behalf of resistance fighters fleeing persecution.[78]

As a consequence of his commitment, Philby was drawn to the attention of Tivadar Mály ("Man"), after being noticed by Viennese comrades. As one who had initially aspired to the priesthood but had then trained for war and volunteered to serve in the army, Mály turned Bolshevik during imprisonment in Russia.[79] He fought in the Red Army from 1918 to 1921, which included imprisonment in Siberia by the Whites for an entire year. Thereafter, he served in the Cheka as an investigator and then secretary of its secret operational unit in the Crimea, and moved to Moscow as assistant to Artuzov at the KRO from 1926. After a spell at the Special Department, he was taken into the INO by Artuzov.[80]

Nicknamed "der Lange" because of his height, he was a handsome, blue-eyed Hungarian, operating underground throughout Central Europe from 1932. Mály was seriously impressed by Philby's steadfastness in adversity and recommended him to Moscow for possible recruitment.[81] Philby knew nothing of this.

To the horror of his mother, Philby returned from Austria married to a divorcée. Lizy (Alice) Feldman, scarcely a radiant beauty, was Austrian, Jewish, and a committed Communist to boot. They had apparently fallen into bed and in love immediately. Philby thus returned to London determined to join the Party and begin life as an activist. They brushed him off at headquarters on King Street, but news of his contact was evidently passed on.

The Star Recruiter: Arnold Deutsch

At that time, according to new rules, the main illegal rezidentura in London was nominally run from Paris (later from Copenhagen), which gave more junior operatives on the ground in Britain a certain freedom of action. Also Philby's recruiter, Arnold Deutsch ("Otto"), a very intelligent Slovakian Jew, was a master of improvisation.[82] Born in Vienna (1904) to a former teacher who had moved recently to the capital, Deutsch gravitated towards the revolutionary left at the age of sixteen.

At university (1923–1928), while reading physics, chemistry, and philosophy, he joined the Party (1924), and finally visited Moscow on a delegation in 1928. On his return he worked as a chemical engineer in a textile factory for just three months before the secretary of the Austrian Party and the head of its Young Communists recommended him for work in Comintern's OMS. In October 1931, as a result of a foul-up (*chepe*, in Russian) by others, who exposed the operation, and having fallen out with a key operative who was bent on bureaucratising the outfit, he had to go underground for a couple of months; then he was withdrawn and, in January 1932, called to Moscow. Even while employed by OMS, he ran occasional errands for the INO in Vienna, so he was not unknown to the Lubyanka's operatives.

After a few months kicking his heels, he was sent off on occasional errands to Greece, Palestine, and Syria, but because he had criticised Abramov, his boss, he was dismissed and disdainfully told to find work in a factory. It was at this point, in August 1932, that Georg Müller of the INO, whom he had encountered in Vienna, recommended him onwards and upwards. Sick with typhoid for three months, Deutsch was finally called in for interview. Taking into account Deutsch's strength of personality, his track record at OMS, and his broad range of foreign languages (fluency in German and English, good French, reading knowledge of Italian and Dutch), and no doubt because he was short of promising illegals, Artuzov propelled him, after barely three months' tradecraft, straight into the field (Paris) in the New Year.[83] Even after transferring to the INO, Deutsch found that falling out with Abramov was to continue to cause him grief, until Abramov was removed from OMS in 1935 and shot in 1937.

Primarily a chemical engineer, Deutsch had a keen interest in human behaviour; though, despite his undoubted Viennese charm, he was not entirely to everyone's taste: the defector Krivitsky ("Grol"), himself a proud man, found him "bumptious," and Mály found him "difficult."[84] He was very much aware of his own worth and suffered from the fact that, working in a strict hierarchy, others saw him as merely technical support, and a little too "pushy," rather than as an authoritative operative deserving of respect.[85] This was surely his only obvious weakness, because he was without question a born recruiter. Deutsch's arrival in Paris was soon followed by Hitler's rise to power in neighbouring Germany, which undoubtedly raised the stakes for all illegal networks, as a crackdown on the KPD was inevitable. Deutsch's role, however, was mainly technical (photography, etc.), but he did, ingeniously, recruit fishermen off the coast of France, Belgium, and the Netherlands, in order to have immediate access to their fleets to use for radio transmission in the event of war. He also recruited two women to the department.[86]

After Paris, the Centre decided in October 1933 to post Deutsch to London with a small team of three recruited in Vienna. This team included the child photographer Edith Tudor Hart (née Suschitzky), who had become acquainted with Philby in Vienna through his bride, Lizy. Deutsch had known Edith since 1926 and abetted in her recruitment to the OGPU three years later. She ran a bookshop in Vienna that served as cover for the courier network that employed Philby.[87] Edith fled, however, after the shop was raided by the police. Married to an Englishman, Alex Tudor Hart, she turned up with him in Britain as part of Deutsch's little team. Something of a risk taker, it was she who ultimately pressed for Philby's recruitment.[88]

Deutsch's arrival in London in April 1934 was followed by that of a more senior operative, Reiss (Nathan Poretsky), who was to supervise operations.[89] Reiss stayed through to July. In contrast to Mály, he was known as "der Dicke" ("Fatty"). He had a round face, black hair, good teeth, and was easy to talk to, naturally gregarious, a social chameleon, and fond of singing. At the same time, however, he was extremely rigorous about tradecraft. Nothing was ever left to chance.[90] Born into a middle-class Jewish family in Poland, he was consumed by the revolution while studying for a degree at Vienna University and ran errands for the Fourth until finally he was called to Moscow, where he served in the OGPU from 1929 to 1932. Beset by doubts about Stalin, Reiss was persuaded to move across to the INO when it became apparent that Berzin was losing his autonomy and that Comintern did not represent a reasonable alternative, since it was subjected to the strictest subordination by the Kremlin. Besides, the challenge of finally penetrating the British establishment was too good to miss.[91]

Building the "Gold Reserve" of Soviet Intelligence

The "important factors" in recruiting Philby represented a combination unique to him: first, "the position of his father" (St. John Philby, advisor to the Saudi king), and second, "his intention to enter the Foreign Office."[92] The latter failed at the first attempt, however. His bid for a job in the Foreign Office was deliberately scuppered by Dennis Robertson, former director of studies, fellow of Trinity, reader in economics, and longtime lover of George ("Dadie") Rylands at King's. Robertson, however, was in some ways very orthodox. He dismissed Philby out of hand as "a radical socialist" and said he was not to be trusted to join the civil service. He therefore refused to grant Philby the necessary reference.[93] Robertson was himself elected a member of the "Apostles" in 1926, before it began filling up with Marxists.

The Apostles constituted a Victorian secret society of high-achieving male undergraduates in Cambridge chosen on the supposition, occasionally borne out, that they were cleverer than everyone else. It had begun at Trinity but extended to King's. Robertson's election no doubt came through the patronage of Maynard Keynes, who had been elected some twenty-three years earlier.[94] Keynes also held a poor opinion of Marxism, though tolerated it in college among the very young. Part of his aversion, other than to the dogma, was the fact that he was married to a Russian emigrée, the ballerina Lydia Lopokova, and not altogether ignorant of what was going on in Moscow. Indeed, he blocked another Apostle, Anthony Blunt, from election to the fellowship of his own college, King's, on the grounds that Blunt infused his work on art with Marxist mumbo jumbo.[95]

The clandestine meeting with Deutsch in Regent's Park altered Philby's entire life, thereafter irrevocably fractured into two. Deutsch is remembered affectionately by Philby as "a man in his middle thirties. He was rather below medium height, and the breadth of his shoulders was accentuated by his general stoutness. He had fair, curly hair, and a broad, clear brow. His blue eyes and wide mouth were highly mobile, hinting at rich possibilities of mischief." He and Philby spoke in German—Deutsch in a now-familiar, melodious Viennese marred only by the distinct discordance of Slovak. Seated on the grass, Deutsch angled himself in one direction and Philby faced the other, to keep a wary eye out for MI5's "watchers," in a conversation that lasted less than an hour.[96] They need not in fact have bothered.

After meeting Philby, Deutsch grasped this unique opportunity to inject a deadly bacillus into the heart of the British establishment.[97] Deutsch had a very quick mind. His capacity to reorient himself in entirely alien milieux was extraordinary, and he came to like his life in Britain. The idea that emerged was to recruit Britain's gilded yet disillusioned youth as they emerged from university. Despite the noted presence of the Russian physicist Pyotr Kapitsa at Cambridge, the easy but false assumption was that the most important university could be found in the capital city—true in Austria, Czechoslovakia, France, and the Soviet Union. That meant London University would be the obvious place to start. This was where Deutsch registered for a degree. It was not until he met the likes of Philby that he realised efforts might better be directed towards the jeunesse dorée from Oxford and Cambridge.

Moreover, the banner under which the youth were to be rallied was not antifascism. Moscow still slandered socialists as "social fascists." Comintern had yet to switch its line to antifascism, a turn anticipated only in September 1934 with the birth of the Popular Front as an idea and not finalised until the summer of the following year.[98] The cause Philby joined was not antifascism as such, but communism *tout court*. Deutsch had no interest in anyone other than die-hard believers in revolutionary socialism who were capable of sustaining a double life regardless of personal cost.

On June 19, Alexander Orlov (né Leiba Feld'bin), the skilled rezident in Copenhagen who had been talent-spotted by Artuzov, was assigned to London to deputise for Reiss. He was to handle the illegals in Britain.[99] Orlov ("Schwed"), having taken English-language courses at Columbia University, had managed to pick up an American accent. (He also had numerous relatives in the United States.) A dapper man with a close-clipped moustache, this veteran of guerrilla fighting in the civil war turned up in Britain under deep cover as a plausible representative of the American Refrigerator Company.[100] In July, with Orlov and Reiss in place, Artuzov ordered the penetration of MI6.[101] This was a long shot but ultimately a successful one.

No doubt prompted by Deutsch, Orlov suggested to Reiss that Philby be used to spin a web: the first strands being Guy Burgess and Donald Maclean.[102] That October Orlov and Reiss recommended that Philby, code-named "Söhnchen" (German for "Sonny"), "should be assigned the task of sounding out all of his Cambridge friends who held the same conviction so that we could use some of them for our work. To tell the truth, we spoke mainly about two of them: Burgess and Maclean. Burgess is the son of very well-off parents. For two years he has been a party member, very clever and reliable but in 'S's [Philby's] opinion somewhat superficial and can occasionally make a slip of the tongue. On the contrary Maclean ["Waise," German for "orphan"] is highly praised by 'S.' "[103]

The contrast between Deutsch's recruitment method and that customarily used by other *gebisty* is striking. It had hitherto been all about money or blackmail. Indeed, at the very time that he, Mály, and Orlov were working on winning over those committed to a common cause against a common enemy, the more down-to-earth Dmitrii Bystrolyotov (of whom more on page 97) crossed palms with banknotes. Bystrolyotov passed through London to secure the recruitment of Captain John King, an Irishman charged with codes and ciphers at the Foreign Office. His services were finally bought in mid-February 1935.[104]

With the exception of Philby, all the Cambridge Five had displayed outstanding academic ability: the louche but brilliant Burgess read part one of the history tripos (degree) with customary panache, and attained an elusive first class in part one in June 1932. This marked him out as the best young historian in his college (Trinity) and meant that he was entitled to proceed directly by special regulation to a research degree that, however, he never completed; he was too busy networking.[105] Within months of his outstanding performance at examination, on November 12, 1932, Burgess was elected to the Apostles and was, very soon, its seventy-first secretary. This enabled him to secure the election on May 20, 1933, of his very rich friend, the enigmatic Victor Rothschild, who had also startled everyone in the first part of the Tripos (natural sciences) and was also fast-tracked to a research degree.[106] The society was now increasingly Marxist in composition and potentially also a network of high value, given the fact that former Apostles could return to dine together once a year as "angels" after they had fulfilled their promise by occupying the commanding heights of society.

Maclean, donnish, tall, and handsome, hailed from Trinity Hall; though never an Apostle, he did take a first in modern languages. The distinguished art historian Blunt, also an Apostle—his place was taken by Burgess—and later a fellow of Trinity, had an inestimable advantage, which he cashed in on for the rest of his life: he was second cousin to the future Queen Elizabeth, then wife to the Duke of York, later George VI. An exception to this glittering public school array was the edgy, puritanical scholarship boy from Glasgow, John Cairncross. In all senses a fish out of water, he nonetheless came out on top in the Foreign Office examinations. Blunt joined the cause early, in 1937, and introduced Deutsch to others, including the wealthy American Michael Straight, another Apostle (elected March 8, 1936).[107]

Reiss did not interview Maclean in October 1934 until background checks had been made. In February 1935 he moved on and handed Maclean, now preparing for examinations to enter the Foreign Office, directly to Orlov.[108] The fact that Donald's mother, Lady Maclean, was a friend of Prime Minister Baldwin, and that the latter took a personal interest in her son's advancement, impressed the Russians. But Maclean had anyway demonstrated his great ability at the examinations. Deutsch disappeared to Moscow for a three-month break. That October, with a friend of Lady Maclean's chairing the interview panel, her golden boy succeeded in entering the service.[109]

By then another member had been recruited by Deutsch and Orlov, in December 1934. Code-named "Mädchen" ("Girl") in a rather obvious reference to his ostentatious homosexuality, Burgess was to prove a prime catch, though this was not instantaneously appreciated in Moscow, where the Lubyanka reacted with alarm.[110] Under the régime installed by Artuzov, all recruitment had to receive prior sanction from the Centre.[111] Anxieties were, however, placated by the great possibilities for penetration, in every sense, that Burgess presented. For the benefit of more prudish comrades, Orlov had to explain "the mysterious laws of sexual attraction in this country" (Britain) so that they could understand the opportunities that lay ahead. Concern remained, however, not least about Burgess's inherent emotional instability and therefore unpredictability in the field: "He is, therefore, prone to panic easily and he is also prone to desperation."[112] This was a very accurate reading and, in the end, would prove his undoing, and Philby's, too.

The Importance of Maclean

Maclean was the most promising. In January 1936 he delivered the first file of secret material to his handler. Thereafter, both quality and quantity increased. In July, when civil war broke out in Spain, he reported the timely revelation that London was intercepting and decrypting Comintern communications at the Government Code and Cypher School (GC&CS). This was Operation Mask, made easier by the recruitment of the Comintern operative Johann Heinrich de Graaf, with access to OMS communications across the globe.[113] Mály, who served as rezident from April to the end of August, valued Maclean so greatly that he wanted him handled independently of anyone else.[114] He got his wish.

Early in 1937 a newcomer entered Maclean's life to help him photograph the documents (including Comintern decrypts) he borrowed from the office. This was Kitty ("Gipsy") Harris, who was in fact Jewish and from Byelorussia, born in Bialystok on May 24, 1899. Her father had fled to Britain with the failure of the revolution in 1905 and migrated to Winnipeg, Canada, three years later. In 1923 the family moved on to Chicago, where, as a union activist, Harris met and married the up-and-coming Communist militant Earl Browder three years later. The two of them carried out secret work for the Profintern in Asia until 1929. They separated two years later. Harris worked as a secretary for the Soviet trade monopoly Amtorg, in New York, where she was recruited by Abram Eingorn ("Taras"), the man in grey: grey eyes, grey hair, grey coat, even grey skin. He was a friend of the ill-fated Beso Lominadze from Odessa; Lominadze was later found guilty of plotting against Stalin and was arrested.[115] Harris then operated as a courier in Germany with Parparov and Zarubin, carrying documents on unprocessed film.

Apart from a bureaucratic hiccup that prevented entry into France—the illegal rezidentura in Berlin mistakenly forged a passport referring to "Chicago, Indiana"—Harris did so well that she went to Moscow for extended training in October 1935. In mid-1938 Maclean was assigned to the embassy in Paris. The two of them left on September 28, at a point of crisis in Moscow's relations with both Britain and France as a result of Russia's exclusion from the negotiations with Germany in Munich that resulted in the dismemberment of Czechoslovakia.[116]

By this time Deutsch had not only witnessed the birth of his son in London (1936), but had also displayed an envious record of productivity. He had now landed recruits in double figures, including the son of a "former minister" and, through him, the son of an MI6 employee.[117] Their code names lie somewhere among the seventeen of those he recruited while coming and going between early April 1934 and late November 1937: "Synok" and "Söhnchen" (Philby), "Medkhen," "Mädchen" (Burgess), "Attila" (and his son), "Otets" (1936), "Ber" (October 1934), "Helper," "Saul" (1936), "James," "Scott" (centrepiece of the Oxford group, apparently Bernard Floud, who later committed suicide), "Socrates," "Molière" (Cairncross), "Poet," "Tony" (Blunt), "Nigel" (Straight), "Chauffeur" (1936), "Molly" (Jenifer Hart?) and "Om." Reiss evidently took credit for recruiting "Waise" (Maclean), and the list did not include the recruits of others, such as "Naslednik." Some of these had been spotted by the Communist Party member and agent Percy Glading ("Got"), who focused on military-industrial targets at the Woolwich Arsenal, of which he was formerly an employee: namely "Attila," "Naslednik," "Otets," "Ber," "Saul," "Chauffeur"; plus two others, "Nelly" (1936) and "Margarit" (1937).[118]

Civil War in Spain

Philby, the original recruit, was initially a grievous disappointment to his handlers, obtaining only tidbits of information from his father's desk and from friends such as Tom Willey at the War Office; finally, Deutsch and Mály suggested posting him to Spain. There, civil war had broken out with a military insurrection from the right on July 18, 1936, in anticipation of revolution from below.

In both France and Spain, Popular Front governments had emerged, in 1935 and 1936 respectively, to block the rise of fascism. These consisted of socialists and their allies, including peasant parties and urban liberals. They were backed by Communist Parties on instruction from Moscow. In Spain they faced an insurrection armed by the two fascist powers, Italy and Germany. On July 25 Prime Minister José Giral asked for assistance.

Stalin was very reluctant to do anything to help. Comintern backing may have seemed enough, as the British were insistent upon instituting a nonintervention agreement, and Moscow still had hopes of an entente with London. Indeed, word had it that until September 6, all action was strictly forbidden.[119] Yet something changed Stalin's mind. On September 14, Uritsky, for the Fourth, and Slutsky, for the INO, put together a plan: Operation X (the letter pronounced "Kha" in Russian) to supply arms for the Popular Front government in Spain. On September 29 this was formally agreed by the Politburo, with Stalin telephoning into the discussion from his distant datcha in Sochi, on the Georgian coastline.[120] Artuzov then supervised the secret supplies of arms, a delicate operation managed by the former Chekist Boris El'man.[121] For this purpose a special unit, Section X, was created within the Fourth.[122]

Stalin had finally taken the plunge only because, were the Spanish government to fall, an alliance with France would be rendered impotent because the French would find themselves flanked on three sides by fascist neighbours.[123] Spain was thus a cause Stalin adopted chiefly for geostrategic reasons. No doubt his support also conveniently undermined Trotskyist accusations that he was a counterrevolutionary. At the same time, however, he avenged himself on Trotsky's former supporters in the Soviet Union, beginning with Grigorii Zinoviev and Lev Kamenev, by indicting them in a show trial and then having them executed for treason.[124]

Would Philby go behind General Franco's lines as a freelance correspondent for intelligence purposes? Orlov had been in Spain, formally attached, since September 16, 1936, to the newly formed Soviet embassy under diplomatic cover. His deputy was Eitingon ("Kotov"), who trained the Republican secret police and saw to the physical liquidation of local Trotskyists centred in Barcelona. They were joined by other talented operatives, such as Naum Belkin, Grigory Siroezhkin, and Lev Vasilevskii. The first deputy head of the INO, Sergei Shpiegel'glas, who had "a sweet little face," also turned up.[125] They filled a vacuum created by local incompetence. The extensive power they accumulated was inevitably wielded to stamp out the Trotskyist and anarcho-syndicalist left in the misplaced belief that this would advance the "moderate" Republican cause.

On returning to England early in 1937, Philby produced an article that impressed Robin Barrington Ward, the deputy editor of the *Times* and a friend of St. John Philby, a regular contributor to the newspaper's columns on the Middle East. Ralph Deakin, the paper's foreign editor, agreed to take Kim on board, and promptly sent him back behind Franco's lines as "special correspondent," despite his evident lack of journalistic experience. He arrived with a recommendation from the German embassy in London and boasting an acquaintance with Ribbentrop, now Hitler's trusted foreign minister.

"The halcyon days are over," Philby reported soon after his arrival.[126] Indeed they were, for him as well. Witnessing the bloody civil war proved a harrowing and a brutalising ordeal for someone from so sheltered a background, a harsh test of his ability to hide his true convictions. "It was a horrifying experience. I tried to suppress all feeling in my articles," he recalled. "I tried to convey only cold fact."[127] The experience altered Philby fundamentally, however, and not altogether for the better. His oldest friend noticed a marked change in manner (now, ironically, he was much more outgoing but "more cynical and worldly wise") and appearance (considerably fatter if not "Falstaffian") after his return.[128] Yet the foreign editor was impressed and, despite the young man's inexperience, intended "to get more good out of the very good Philby."[129]

Deutsch Comes Unstuck

An even greater test then faced Philby. The slick and ruthless Orlov took up the reins as his handler, though they could not meet on neutral ground except in Paris. After a disturbing visit from the police, enquiring about his intentions to remain, on September 15, Deutsch left by boat from Dover to Calais, heading for Paris, in order to bring Philby together with Orlov.[130] By then both Krivitsky and Reiss ("Raymond") had absconded. Reiss was murdered, but Krivitsky, who knew Deutsch, was still at large: returning to Britain was thus perilous. This news was brought to him in Paris by Shpiegel'glas ("Duce"), now deputy head of what was now the seventh department (formerly the INO). Deutsch hastened back to Britain at the beginning of November, to put the network in mothballs for three months. Effectively, however, no one then took charge, and Deutsch's paternalism can be heard in his emotionally charged plea to Shpiegel'glas that the network be brought back into play. "They are all young and have no particular experience in our line of work. For them contact with more senior comrades is very important to give them hope and assurance. Many of them are counting on receiving money from us since they need it to live off . . . Without news from us they must be experiencing disillusionment. They all work from conviction and enthusiasm; the thought might arise among them that they are no longer needed."[131] Deutsch was now on garden leave and destined to be laid off altogether, while others above and around him were being arrested and executed.

Worse news then followed. After being recalled to Moscow, Orlov suddenly defected on July 12, 1938. Even though contact was only intermittent, Orlov's abrupt and unexplained disappearance could not have calmed Philby's nerves.[132] Eitingon took over, saw to the removal of the rezidentura to Barcelona, on the front line, but then left for Moscow in the spring of 1939.[133] There, Deutsch fortuitously sidestepped the axe that descended on almost everyone else. He was quietly devoting himself to learning Russian before disaster nearly struck when the new (temporary) head of the seventh department, Vladimir Dekanozov, destined him for interrogation on December 29, 1938. By luck, Beria abruptly changed his mind, and began to undo some of but not all the damage done under Yezhov. In March 1939 a lieutenant by the name of Kazhdan came to see Deutsch with good news, asking him to work up a brief for renewing operations in Britain.

War Comes to the Rescue

The isolation of the Cambridge Five came to an end. En route to Moscow, Eitingon established contact with Burgess in Paris, and set him up to work with Anatoly Gorskii in London beginning that same month.[134] Republican Spain was by then a tattered remnant. Philby did not return to London until August, as Franco established himself in power. By then the *Times* had Philby marked out as chief war correspondent in the event of hostilities with Germany, which broke out on September 3, 1939.

After the Phoney War, in which no fighting occurred on the Western Front for the rest of the year, Hitler successfully overran every obstacle encountered, from the Pyrennees to the Arctic Circle, including, crucially, France. British nationals were evacuated from Brest after the fall of Paris in the summer of 1940. There Philby encountered the formidable Hester Harriot Marsden-Smedley. She was, ostensibly, the *Daily Express* correspondent in Belgium and Luxembourg. In reality, Marsden-Smedley was far more: from the mid-1930s, MI6 had been recruiting correspondents from major newspapers.

Born the daughter of a major general of the Indian Army in Poona in 1901, Marsden-Smedley was an open-minded memsahib with a "strong personality" and a "contempt for cant." Soon she was sounding out Philby on the situation in Europe and asking him what he had in mind on his return. Philby said he would probably join up.[135] Marsden-Smedley promptly changed tack. Philby thought no more about this apparently accidental encounter, but this generous spirit was not just a correspondent—she also worked for the newly created Section D (sabotage) in MI6. On her arrival, Marsden-Smedley personally recommended Philby to Marjorie Maxse, the head of recruitment at MI6 and another larger-than-life Miss Marple of unalterable conviction.

Meanwhile, in Paris, Maclean's relationship with Harris, which had developed into a full-blown affair, had broken down when he met a beautiful young American woman studying at the Sorbonne, Melinda Marling, whom he married just before Paris fell to the Germans, on June 8, 1940. Maclean, did, however, explain that he was a Soviet spy, and she, of left-wing convictions, took it all in without demur. Harris went on to Bordeaux and thereafter to Moscow, where suspicions about the Cambridge Five were now growing. So she was taken out of active service and redirected towards training novices. Her requests to return to active duty were listened to only after the Soviet Union was invaded. Fitin, now heading the Fifth Department—formerly the Seventh—of the NKGB, or People's Commissariat for State Security, supported her case, describing her as one of those people who should never be cast aside: those who constituted "the gold reserve of Soviet intelligence." She was thus despatched to the United States via Vladivostok, to act as courier for the American and Mexican networks.[136]

In England, Blunt, at one point Burgess's closest friend, was recruited without haste. He seemed unlikely ever to join government, let alone the secret service, so his value was limited. Finally, the prospects for using him as a talent spotter won out. After Burgess introduced Blunt to Deutsch in January 1937, the job was done.[137] In recommending Blunt as a talent spotter, Burgess had assured Deutsch that Blunt was a "born pederast" and the impression given was that "he enjoys great authority among students."[138] The outstanding linguist John Cairncross followed, by a similar path. Having striven to overcome relative social deprivation through a scholarship to private education, Cairncross took his first degree in Glasgow, then studied at the Sorbonne, before advancing to yet another first degree, at Cambridge, where his Francophilia met with Blunt's sympathies.

He came out on top in the civil service examinations and, despite an angular personality that would normally have ruled him out as "unclubbable," was taken on by the Foreign Office in 1936. In March 1937, after Burgess sounded out Cairncross as to his views and advised caution, Mály sought help from James Klugmann (recruited in 1936), then in Paris, who had been the Communist Party organiser in Cambridge and was now secretary of the International Organisation of Students Against War and Fascism, in order to avoid compromising any of the existing Cambridge spies. At the end of May, after two visits by Klugmann to ensure that Cairncross was ready for recruitment, Deutsch came to Paris to meet them both and finalise the arrangement. The Centre congratulated Mály on this "great achievement."[139] Except as a talent scout, Blunt did not really come into his own until wartime, however, when he was taken on at MI5, recommended by his friend Rothschild, also a fellow of Trinity.

A complicated man who had early on rebelled against the burdensome destiny his banking dynasty had defined for him, Rothschild had a somewhat ambivalent attitude to Moscow: the cause might be just, but everything had to be on his terms. Rothschild, who had the "closest of relations" with Blunt and Burgess, effectively provided cover for the Cambridge Five.[140] Several retired operatives of the KGB long insisted that he was recruited as an agent, a suspicion he never really shed, though solid proof is lacking.

Rothschild's position was not eased by the fact that his second wife, Tessa Mayor (Newnham College, Cambridge, 1935), was very close to the Cambridge spies—above all Blunt (till the end of his days), but also Burgess. It was Rothschild who briefed Burgess on Prime Minister Neville Chamberlain's telling last-minute peace efforts with the Nazis in August 1939. It was Rothschild who secured Blunt's admission to MI5. Moreover, in 1940, he also let out his apartment at No. 5 Bentinck Street to Tessa, now assisting him at MI5, and a female friend, who then brought in both Burgess and Blunt to share the rent.[141] Before long it became a venue for parties that lured well-connected and gullible British intelligence officers such as Guy Liddell, who headed anti-Soviet operations. It was not exactly something the Russians would have encouraged, however. Moscow strongly disapproved of independent agents associating so closely with one another, but since the Five had at this point been deserted by their handlers, they could hardly be blamed for sticking together.[142]

At the Lubyanka, with suspicion at its height, intelligence from Britain had been brusquely dismissed as "based on dubious sources, on an agent network acquired at a time when it was led by enemies of the people and therefore extremely dangerous."[143] This network was a powerful Trojan Horse nonetheless: it took in eighteen agents recruited between 1934 and 1937, including twelve connected to the world of foreign policy and six in counterintelligence.[144] Yet it was in danger of being left stranded in the field.

Meanwhile, in Artuzov's other bailiwick, the Fourth, the skeleton of a new network had emerged, spearheaded by an ingenious Hungarian cartographer, Alex (Sándor) Radó, an old acquaintance of Sorge's, yet another man of ability recruited by Artuzov. It was Radó's ring, operating from Switzerland during the war, that provided information on German military preparations—most notably on the eve of the battle of Kursk in 1943—which could then be checked against what was known elsewhere.[145]

Without the inspirational myth of the Soviet Union's "radiant future," which provided a glowing contrast to the gruesome reality of fascist persecution and, notoriously, the single-minded victimisation of German Jews, it is most unlikely Moscow could have secured such a windfall of foreign talent—even by means of blatant bribery or the precarious device of honey traps. After all, such devices, though frequently used, could be effective only for the short term, as Stalin later acknowledged: "You must understand that if you recruit someone on the basis of his appetite for women, money, or belongings, without drawing him over to your own ideological position, then sooner or later this agent will betray you. Betray us."[146] In short, the most effective agents were believers. Blind belief against all odds was, after all, the essential precondition to the October Revolution. Stalin understood this only too well.

Stalin's Machine Infernale

Having signed on to the common cause, like it or not, all agents found that belief in the revolution yoked them to Stalin, who had effectively helped himself to the revolution as a vehicle for the realisation of his own vaulting ambitions. He was, of course, capable of being coolly rational, but he was also a shape-shifter and could, without warning, turn into an ogre reminiscent of Sergei Eisenshtein's *Ivan the Terrible*, a film produced in 1945. His priorities were first and foremost driven by personal obsession. The elimination of the ultraleft in Spain at the hands of Orlov and others, and the subsequent assassination of Trotsky in Mexico (Operation Duck, in August 1940), thus took higher priority than the Nazi threat.

Stalin's fears were not entirely irrational. The anti-Stalinist emigrés who supported Trotsky were organically bound to the régime's palpitating inner core. They saw the revolution as their own and worked relentlessly towards repossessing it. In response to Stalinist oppression, members of the Party had long been accustomed to dissimulation (*dvurushnichestvo*). It thus became next to impossible for the Kremlin to know what they really believed. It was therefore always feared in the Kremlin, not entirely implausibly, that a true revolution in Spain could sweep away the Stalinist model and leave the road open to Trotsky. This was insisted upon by insiders such as Krivitsky, before he defected.[147] Formerly with the Fourth, Krivitsky was the INO's illegal rezident in the Netherlands, with a watching brief for the rest of Western Europe.[148] The man now heading the elimination of Stalin's enemies abroad was the young Pavel Sudoplatov, a favourite of Beria's: "mathematically efficient, energetic and powerful with a tremendous memory for detail and a cool, incisive mind"—of whom, more later.[149]

The destruction of half the intelligence services in the spy frenzy of 1937–1939, a direct result of Stalin's paranoid priorities, left foreign operatives gasping for air and barely able to do their jobs. The problem really began with the appointment of the more headstrong Yezhov, in place of the more cautious Yagoda, as head of the NKVD on October 11, 1936.[150] Stalin had always looked upon the troublesome Polish Communist leaders with a jaundiced eye. He showed ever-growing mistrust of all Poles after Piłsudski reached an understanding with Hitler in 1934. Yagoda's fall was connected to the fate of Yu Makowskii, a Pole who served as rezident in Warsaw. In the safe house he used, more money was found than could be accounted for. Letters from his sisters were also discovered that included references to contacts with high-level Poles.

These facts were deemed sufficiently compromising to warrant Makowskii's arrest at the end of 1935. Yagoda, however, backed him. This proved Party secretary Yezhov's chance to unseat and replace Yagoda. Yezhov insisted that Yagoda was covering up an entire Polish espionage ring of which Makowskii was just a part. So, when Stalin replaced Yagoda with Yezhov, a Polish network had to be uncovered, whether one existed or not. More arrests soon followed. This had consequences for Artuzov, too. He had, since 1920, served under Poles in both counterintelligence and foreign intelligence, both Dzerzhinsky and Menzhinsky. Forced confessions inevitably yielded denunciations directed against him.[151] The Polish Communist Party was to be the only European Party completely dissolved during the Terror.

On January 11, 1937, Artuzov was sacked, so too Otto Shteinbruk, his deputy responsible for intelligence in the West. As news travelled, operatives abroad faced an ugly choice: either give up the cause they had lived for and defect to the enemies of the revolution, or hold out the hope that the revolution would soon right itself. Another option was to turn to Trotsky's Fourth International. Reiss, who had played a leading role in building up the Cambridge group, made contact with the Fourth International in the spring of 1937, warning of assassination attempts.[152]

Shteinbruk was arrested on April 21, and Artuzov was taken at night on May 12–13. Three days later, Fyodor Karin, the deputy responsible for the East, was dragged off to the cells. On July 17, Reiss wrote an angry and foolhardy letter of resignation to the Politburo, committing himself to "free humanity from capitalism and the Soviet Union from Stalinism."[153] The letter proved to be his death warrant. Before he himself defected, Krivitsky is said to have passed on an instruction to the agent Henri Pieck to assassinate Reiss, but Pieck bluntly refused to do so.[154] On August 21, Artuzov was tried in absentia and shot the same day.[155] Reiss's bullet-ridden corpse was found late at night on September 4, along the road to Lausanne.

A speech Stalin had delivered on May 21 to the surviving senior officers of the Fourth showed him to be both paranoid and confused. It was utterly demoralising. Stalin warned them against being too open in their collaboration with the new ally, bourgeois Czechoslovakia. "Intelligence must constantly take into account that there are open enemies and possible enemies. Every ally is a possible enemy and one has to test one's allies. From the intelligence vantage point we cannot have friends. Therefore don't give away any secrets. In collaborating with the Czechs give them material that does not reveal our plans. Look upon the Czechs as the enemies of our enemies. You have to take fully into account the lesson of co-operation with the Germans on the basis of close relations with them after Rapallo."

Berzin had been dismissed as chief of the service, but unknown to this audience, Stalin was about to reinstate him for what would turn out to be the briefest time: "Comrade Berzin is an honest man," Stalin continued, "but he did not take sufficient care and along with his apparatus he fell into the hands of the Germans . . ." This was the man he was about to reinstate as head of the Fourth. A further surprise awaited. Stalin went on: "The Intelligence Directorate network must be liquidated. It would be best to liquidate everything." Personnel could be called in and reassigned, but in Stalin's byzantine mind, there could be no contradiction between dissolving military intelligence, with war just ahead, and simultaneously asserting its importance. "We must create a strong intelligence for ourselves. Good intelligence can delay the onset of war. If the enemy has strong intelligence and our intelligence is powerless, this will provoke war. One should not be blind; one must use one's eyes. It means that we have to have a strong intelligence and counterintelligence."[156] This was no less than a madhouse.

The issue of Stalin's true mental condition is probably never to be resolved with any precision. It is, however, not irrelevant to such an assessment that after Stalin's death, his medical cabinet was found to contain quantities of cocaine. Cocaine's impact on his mind, giving rise to alternating episodes of wild exhilaration and paranoid despair, doubtless enhanced the more extreme and bewildering contradictions in his vindictive and ultimately self-destructive behaviour.[157]

On June 3, Uritsky was demoted to deputise command of the Moscow military district. Six days later Berzin resumed leadership of the Fourth, only to be dismissed once again at the beginning of August 1937. He was arrested and executed at the end of July 1938. What remained of the Fourth was, in May 1939, renamed the Fifth, but stayed in the hands of those so fearful for their lives and for their families that they were effectively incapable of rational, independent judgement; a fact that became only too apparent on the eve of war. Stalin's near-total reliance on vulnerable people as opposed to technology then came into direct collision with his inveterate suspicion of his own operatives.

When the artist Pavel Gromushkin joined foreign intelligence at the height of the Terror, in March 1938, he found himself "literally on another planet or in another dimension"; everything he understood was in a state of disintegration.[158] As a direct consequence of this mindless bloodbath, agents in place (the Cambridge Five, for instance) were intermittently deprived of their handlers at the most crucial phase of the European crisis (1937–1940). Only after the defection of Orlov in July 1938 was Eitingon instructed to make contact with Burgess, and in March 1939, Burgess was handed over to the legal rezident in London, Gorskii.[159] By then, 275 of the 450 operatives that made up what was once the INO had been shot or sent to a camp—over 60 percent.[160]

Stalin was, to say the least, lucky that his prize agents remained devoted to the cause and that even those who dropped out (such as the Oxford academic Goronwy Rees, whom Burgess offered to assassinate) failed to tell on their friends. They were heretics, but they refused to become renegades. It was not, in fact, until 1962 that Philby was betrayed by an old friend, Flora Solomon. After decades of painstaking care, Philby's fatal mistake in Solomon's eyes was not that he had once tried to recruit her for the Soviet cause or that he had for so long been betraying his country to the enemy, but that, while working as Middle Eastern correspondent for the *Observer*, he had insensitively attacked her adopted mother country, Israel. It proved a costly and uncharacteristic instance of self-indulgence on his part. It was Rothschild who reported Solomon's statement to MI5. It appears Philby never forgave him for this.

The consequences of Stalin's dangerous obsession with the intelligence effort were very nearly fatal to all. On the one hand, Stalin's failure to clarify who represented the most lethal threat to the Soviet Union seriously obstructed the Kremlin's intelligence effort. The massive investment in human operations that had just begun to yield serious results when Artuzov took over was then squandered by Stalin because of his paranoid delusions. On the other hand, by underestimating the crucial importance of cryptanalysis, Stalin foolishly deprived himself of the ability to compensate in other ways for what had been lost in human intelligence.

3. CRYPTOGRAPHY: STUNTED BY NEGLECT

Communications on secret matters were encrypted into codes (words) and then into ciphers (random letters or numbers). After the October Revolution, the new Commissariat of Foreign Affairs inherited a printing department and, within it, a number of specialists in codes and ciphers. By the end of April 1918, a designated section had come into being, though it existed in name only. Then, on November 13, Lenin ordered the creation of a cipher section in the General Staff to meet an urgent need in the face of the Allied war of intervention. Thus that date, at least, for the military, became "Cryptographer Day."

Yet few cryptographers were on hand when diplomatic relations with the rest of the world began to open up, and the Bolsheviks were caught dangerously unprepared. Moreover, although the tsarist administration had had nothing to boast about with respect to military communications—indeed, much to regret given its woeful conduct of the war—its diplomatic codes and ciphers were regarded as "far ahead of anything anybody else had at that time." Its systems (complicated substitution and additive, with concealed indicators) might have appeared overelaborate, but they proved extremely effective.[1]

Making up for Lost Time

The Bolsheviks, of course, knew nothing about the revolution in cryptography in Britain and the United States that had occurred as a result of the First World War. Worse still, this was a province the all-powerful "Il'yich" thought he fully understood. But the limited use of ciphers in the Russian underground and Lenin's ignorance of the ease with which the police decrypted such communications left him with unjustified self-confidence. It was to cost the Bolsheviks dearly in both the short and long term.

The publication of a decrypted intercept (decrypt) in the *Times* of London during the crucial days of the Bolshevik march on Warsaw left no one in any doubt that Soviet codes and ciphers were an open book to the British.[2] At this stage the Russians were using "low-grade simple transposition systems"—the letters of the plain text in one column substituted for the letters of the code in another column (code but no cipher). These systems also used the Latin alphabet.[3]

Commissar Chicherin was a revolutionary, albeit in a frock coat, but he was also a knowledgeable former employee of the tsarist Foreign Ministry. He complained to Lenin that despatches were being deciphered by the adversary. This was not the result of betrayals, as Lenin and Kamenev automatically assumed. Instead, it had resulted from better decryption.

"From our employee [Andrei] Sabanin, son of an old cryptanalyst of the Ministry of Foreign Affairs [and formerly keeper of records at that ministry], we know that positively all foreign ciphers were broken by Russian cryptanalysts," Chicherin asserted. "In the latter days of the existence of Tsarism," he continued, "no foreign despatch was undeciphered, not because of treachery but due to the skills of Russian cryptanalysts. Bear in mind foreign governments have more complex ciphers than those used by ourselves. If we continually change the key, then the system itself will become known to tsarist civil servants and military currently in the White Guard camp abroad." The solution recommended was to send secret documents sealed in the diplomatic bag by courier.[4]

Lenin, however, had his own ideas. Tossing aside Chicherin's astute advice and failing to take into account the chronic shortage of staff, he suggested changing the key daily.[5] Given that Chicherin was simultaneously pleading with Commissar for Finance Nikolai Krestinsky that more cryptographers were "of the utmost importance," Lenin's response was, to say the least, unhelpful. The assumption continually made, as illustrated in Lenin's letter to Chicherin on September 24, 1920, was that the problem was one of efficiency, loyalty, and organisation, rather than of scarce resources. Lenin's proposals (the latest being to create special ciphers for each ambassador and also to introduce other measures, such as the use of book codes) were hopelessly impracticable for want of trained staff and lack of time. But Lenin was not to be contradicted. Following his philosophy, the interdepartmental committee under Commissar for Military and Naval Affairs Trotsky that "Il'yich" finally set up in January 1921 to sort out the problem of codes and ciphers handed over all control to the Cheka.[6]

No doubt at Lenin's prodding, the Russians tried new keys and a new cipher system.[7] Coded despatches were made more complex by inserting dinomal substitution underneath the transpositions—that is to say, encoded letters were ciphered into numbers, two for every letter of plain text, using a grid (a tsarist practice). Yet the eternal struggle between rival cryptographers is always a battle between the incompetence of each side. In this instance, a lazy cipher clerk could not be bothered to vary his usage to the extent that the system allowed. This lapse made it possible for the British to crack these systems without too much effort.[8]

John Tiltman was a young serviceman of unusual talents who had won a place at Oxford at the age of fourteen but was unable to take it up due to his father's premature demise. He had dabbled in Russian, but his personal experience of Russia, in this instance the icy wastes of Eastern Siberia during the Allied war of intervention, had been brief, as he was, during that conflict, still recovering from injuries sustained in World War I. With only the outlines of the language, Tiltman had joined the Government Code and Cypher School (GC&CS) at Watergate House in London as a translator in 1920, initially for a fortnight; he ended up staying on. He was taken up and trained by Ernst Feterlyain (or Fetterlein), a small, bespectacled cryptanalyst favored by Tsar Nicholas II. His brother was in the same line of work.

Tiltman recalled: "The [Soviet cipher] system was built so that each vowel could be substituted for by seven different dinomes [the insertion of two characters for every one in the plain text] that would reduce the chance that repetitions would reveal the frequency count cryptanalysts use to wedge their way into a cipher. In one particular message, however, a single word (the Russian *dogovor*, 'treaty') appeared multiple times. Each time the less-than-diligent clerk used the same vowel dinomes rather than the variants." Tiltman went on to work out the fact that the transposition keys came from lines of mid-seventeenth-century English poetry, based on an edition held by the British Museum (which refused him permission to copy even on security grounds).[9] When Tiltman left for Simla to work on Russian ciphers from the East, "Josh" Cooper was trained to replace him.

Bokii–"The Head of All Secrets"

Meanwhile, in Moscow, the Council of People's Commissars under Lenin set up the Spetsotdel (the Special Department, known as SPEKO) of the Cheka on May 5, 1921. It was to be headed by his friend and fanatic Gleb Bokii, a trained hydrologist, honoured veteran of the St. Petersburg revolutionary underground, and former secretary to the Petrograd revolutionary committee.

Bokii had been arrested and imprisoned repeatedly since his late teens. The cost was chiselled into his face and riddled his emaciated body. He had the gaunt looks of a former victim of tuberculosis. A tall man with a pronounced stoop, who invariably wore a raincoat, Bokii had Mongolian features braced by a pair of piercing eyes (sunken, cold blue) mounted on prominent cheekbones. He answered not to the head of the Cheka and its successors but directly to the Party leadership— which meant Lenin. There was no intervening or mediating level of analysis. (This practice of delivering raw data to the leadership continued after 1945.) Bokii had an initial advantage due to his having known Stalin during the struggle underground, but differences of opinion and the fact that Stalin had never been a leading figure in the Party, and therefore commanded little deference from Old Bolsheviks, soon began to sour relations after Lenin's death.[10] Stalin dearly wanted to dispose of Bokii, and would have done just that much earlier, had Bokii not made himself indispensable.

Uniquely privileged because of his direct access to the top, Bokii had "colossal influence" within the OGPU.[11] Chicherin nicknamed him "the head of all secrets," and described him as a man "difficult to deal with."[12] Like Bokii himself, the three sectors of SPEKO that dealt with codes and ciphers were peopled with eccentrics unusual within the Soviet apparat. The second section prepared codes and ciphers. The fourth and largest section (eight people in all) handled decryption. Structure, composition, tasks, and methods were all patterned largely on the tsarist special service.[13] The original core consisted of "elderly people, mostly men . . . mostly former Russian aristocrats, including numbers of Counts and Barons, who were employed because of their knowledge of foreign languages."[14] One former clerk recalls "old ladies with an aristocratic past"; "the majority were the most introverted and almost impossible to understand. There was a German with a beard practically down to his feet. There was a man who, according to almost all books on the First World War, was a double agent. There was Zybin, chairman of the party committee [*mestkom*], known as the man who deciphered Lenin's correspondence."[15] In fact, Ivan Zybin had been the tsarist police department's main specialist in deciphering revolutionary communications, an inspired genius at breaking book-based ciphers.[16]

Relying on this Pickwickian band had its problems. Despite Chicherin's eulogies, the tsarist service contained a serious defect in no way remedied by the Bolsheviks: it was unable to cover the entire range of foreign languages beyond European shores, Japanese being the notable exception. (Japan had been tsarist Russia's most embittered enemy after the latter's humiliating defeat in 1904.) Linguistic failings also confronted the Soviet diplomatic service and the human intelligence services. Moreover, the training of new recruits was scarcely thorough. At the outset, courses lasted merely two to six months.[17] The first graduating class yielded only fourteen, of which five engaged in decryption.[18] The second class, in 1922, yielded twenty-two cryptographers. Bokii headed the examination committee.[19] But talent proved hard to find.

SPEKO's offices for decryption were perched on the top two floors of a building belonging to the Commissariat of Foreign Affairs, at 21 Kuznetsky Most, on the corner of Lubyanka Street, a brief drive to the Kremlin. The lower floors were made up of apartments and the Commissariat Club. Employees could thus come and go, anonymously intermingling with residents.[20] The remainder, encryption, was located a short walk down the street, at the Lubyanka.

Bokii was seen by inquisitive subordinates as "a sinister and mysterious figure"; he kept his door shut at all times and used a peephole to inspect those knocking before admitting them. He would emerge from his bedroom at night to check with the duty officer on rotation as to whether anything required urgent attention. This caused some nervousness among younger female employees, as he was rumoured to engage in orgies involving occasional members of the department when on holiday in Batum, by the Black Sea.[21] Despite such salacious rumours, though, his obsession was with not sex but the supernatural. Indeed, whereas Yagoda's apartment was stacked with pornography, Bokii's was crammed with books on the occult, as the NKVD discovered when it came to arrest him. The cult of mystery certainly encouraged spicy gossip, but it was not always well informed.

Though of considerable importance, Bokii's department was starved of nourishment—indeed, stunted—during its infancy. Soviet Russia was after all grievously short of money, and while the Bolsheviks could still count on the prospects of revolution in Germany, building a sturdy state apparatus took lower priority. The impact made itself felt at the Foreign Commissariat, but most importantly on SPEKO.

By far the largest consumer of decrypts was the Foreign Commissariat. There, the sense of grievance and the feeling of frustration under Chicherin reached neurotic proportions. At the Commissariat, the ruling collegium in January 1923 reorganised the code and cipher section into a "code and secret section" of eleven people. Yet on May 8, 1923, British Foreign Secretary Lord Curzon published an ultimatum calling on Moscow to cease and desist from revolutionary agitation in the empire; decrypts from GC&CS underscored his accusations. This prompted further complaints from Chicherin, especially after cuts in the state budget produced a decrease rather than increases in numbers of staff. Somehow, the Kremlin could not get itself to take cryptography sufficiently seriously.

The euphoria of international diplomatic recognition early in 1924 was then followed by a serious and sustained deterioration in relations with Britain after the election of a conservative government that autumn. The die-hard conservatives had swept to power as the direct result of a scare created by the timely forgery of the "Zinoviev Letter." The letter purported to be instructions from Comintern to the British Communist Party calling for the subversion of the British armed forces. It was knowingly authenticated and deliberately leaked to the mass-circulation *Daily Mail* with the connivance of MI6.

The One-Time Pad

The British government again published decrypts on May 26, 1927, in this instance as the prelude to breaking off diplomatic relations. At last, the Kremlin woke up to its fundamental weakness in cryptography. Only adoption of the one-time pad (ciphers used only once and open only to the two parties communicating) made total secrecy possible. The shift to this kind of encryption was completed in November 1927, and had an immediate and dramatic effect. London's continuous stream of diplomatic intercepts suddenly dried up (though Tiltman, now in Simla, continued to break into communications in and out of Iran and Afghanistan). Russia's main adversary was now in the dark, with no idea how to confront and overcome such an unprecedented challenge. At a loss, London gave up prematurely, instead of seeking a solution to the one-time pad, which was unbreakable only in principle. Short of war, GC&CS lacked the necessary resources and failed to keep pace with technological innovation. Instead, it focused on an easier target, Comintern communications, and there it enjoyed some success, especially after Tiltman returned to London.

The one-time pad was a primitive but ruggedly effective solution, but it was bought at a price: the immediate security of communication was guaranteed at the expense of the incentive to innovate. Innovation would have been possible only through adopting the latest research in applying statistics to linguistics, and by exploiting the latest technologies. Soviet Russia was backward in these crucially important spheres, and was to remain so for quite some time.

Lack of innovation mattered less when London was the main adversary because the British were themselves laggards. Having found success too early and too easily, vested interests were largely averse to new ideas. But after 1929, Britain ceased to be the main enemy. As a result of the Kutyepov assassination, followed by Comintern's support for the revolution in colonial Indochina, France took its place. A minority Labour government had come to office in Britain, and it was obvious to the more sober-minded that the deep-seated confrontation with Moscow might finally be settled only by the one means the British could not afford: war. Yet for the new, revanchist Germany that took everyone by surprise from 1933, orthodox economics did not represent an obstacle. Hitler wasted no time in opening an international campaign against communism in general and, in a new twist, the Soviet Union in particular.

Germany had enormous strengths, not least in engineering. Berlin was quick to innovate if this could put it ahead of the game. Thus began the adaptation of the Enigma machine (originally devised to ensure commercial secrecy) for enciphering government communications. This fast created a more elaborate defence against decryption than the Russians had any hope of countering. Moscow was so far out of touch with the latest developments that, in response to the threat from Germany, it failed to procure manuals for the machine ciphers and did not even bother to buy the machines themselves.

Moreover, in direct contrast to neighbouring Poland, the Soviet Union failed to recruit and exploit plentiful mathematical talent from its best universities to attack codes and cyphers from a theoretical vantage point. Instead, cryptography was seen as a craft to which one was probably only born, a field entirely unconnected with advances in mathematics, the physical sciences, engineering, linguistics, or statistics.

The one-time pad was not a sensible long-term solution, either, as it took an excessive amount of time to encipher traffic by this means. Moreover, it was too unwieldy to use on a large scale because it depended crucially on no one duplicating pages, a provision that was breached when the volume of traffic grew incrementally (notably after the German invasion of 1941), and qualified staff proved hard to recruit and train at short notice. The use of the pad also sorely tested the temptation of a tired or simply lazy cipher clerk.

Purloining Codebooks

In turn, decryption became heavily reliant on an enticing short-cut that was hard to exploit over the long term: agents purloining codebooks and cribs of one kind or another from foreign ministries and embassies abroad. To this end, on May 5, 1921, the Cheka defined one of the Special Department's jobs as that of recruiting people who had access to "information on the organisation of cryptographic work by the Western special services."[22]

One of the most useful agents recruited was Francesco Constantini

("Duncan," "Langley") and his brother Secondo ("Dudley"), who had minor jobs at the British embassy in Rome. Recruited in 1924, the duo supplied a regular flow of classified Foreign Office documents to both the Russians and the Italians up to 1937. Crucial for SPEKO was the supply of changing codes and ciphers: the diplomatic code, Political B; the consular code, M-28; naval Reporting Officers Cyphers; the diplomatic code, K; the interdepartmental cypher; and the India Office cypher.[23]

Here, the dashing black-eyed Bystrolyotov, who started in the mid-1920s, proved a most successful forerunner of the "Romeo spies" of East Germany, in his seduction of vulnerable women in the inner offices of important officials. These predators were known in Russia as *vorony* ("ravens"); their female equivalents were *lastochki* ("swallows"). Born in the Crimea the illegitimate son of a local schoolteacher, Bystrolyotov drifted in and out of Russia before receiving cursory higher education in Constantinople (Istanbul after 1923). Following this, he registered for a law degree in Prague, at the Ukrainian University, where he became active in student union politics. This enabled him to visit the revolutionary heartland in 1925, where he encountered Artuzov, who played a role in recruiting him to the INO.

The problem with employing agents to purloin keys to foreign codes was that these were largely keys to diplomatic despatches. In the case of Germany, for instance, the Ausamt (its Foreign Ministry) was at more than one remove from Hitler's inner circle. Diplomatic correspondence was scarcely the best avenue to the dictator's true intentions. Stalin therefore became obsessed with penetrating the Führer's inner circle. Here, SPEKO was of no use—nor, in fact, were the Fourth and the INO.

SPEKO's counterpart at the Fourth (which pressed for its own independent operation) was established as a kind of substation in August 1930 on Bokii's floor; by January 1931 a joint decryption course had been established for both diplomatic and military specialists, and the course was further extended during the following year.[24] By 1934 the staff at SPEKO numbered one hundred.[25]

It was apparent, however, that the Fourth still lacked the decryption capabilities of the rival service, and despite the growing uncertainty of his own position, Berzin spoke out—to no avail. In a letter to Voroshilov on June 7, 1934, he emphasised the importance of improving work on codes and ciphers and the need to recruit more people of quality: these people would be not merely loyal but also highly educated, and fluent in more than one language; they would possess an independence of mind vital to research, a breadth of knowledge, extraordinary patience, and the ability to improvise. "Such employees," wrote Berzin, "take many years to bring on and only because of the accumulation of prior experience in specialist matters." Despite his warnings, decryption began only on the eve of war.

There were some successes—the most spectacular, in the decryption of Japanese ciphers, particularly military keys. The head of the British GC&CS commented later that "we knew . . . their work on Japanese cyphers was as good as ours."[26] In fact, it was better. In this sphere, the Russians kept pace with the Americans, and far outpaced the British. For good reason: until 1939, the East seemed the more probable theatre of war.

Voroshilov predictably failed to pursue Berzin's recommendations. Worse still, SPEKO—repeatedly renamed, as the ninth department, then the third, and finally the seventh—was decapitated during the Terror (July 1937), as were all branches of the service. Bokii was supplanted by an administrator, Isaak Shapiro. Shapiro himself was summarily replaced in March 1938, yielding to yet another administrator, Aleksandr Balamutov, who continued only until April 1939. Finally, a specialist, Aleksei Kopytsev, took over—but his brief interlude lasted only until July 1941, when Ivan Shevelyov, another administrator, succeeded.

The damage done required over a decade to repair. Training was inadequate—new recruits for the most part benefited only from a basic secondary education—the Soviet cryptographers were cut off entirely from their counterparts elsewhere, and they conducted no fundamental research. After 1945, when the Russians finally learned the sheer scale of the vast enterprise that GC&CS had established at Bletchley Park, midway between Oxford and Cambridge, and its focus on mechanising decryption, they were completely stunned.[27] An uneasy sense of backwardness reasserted itself with a vengeance.

The preventive war with Finland (November 1939 to April 1940) exposed the Soviet régime's deep-seated military failings. Embarked upon without due care, in the depths of winter, the conflict exposed the true cost of decapitating the officer corps and substituting raw operatives for trained professionals. The failure to handle codes and ciphers securely also proved a serious one. The Ninth and Seventh Armies, in particular, inadvertently gave Russia's enemies a back door into their systems, due to human error. On January 13, 1940, Beria reported to Stalin, Molotov, and Voroshilov:

> The management of secrecy by forces in parts of the ninth army is inadequate. All the keys to the code OKK-5 that we have in the form of eight copies were distributed all at once into the hands of the army's chief of staff and forces. One copy of the keys to the code in question was seized by the enemy from a dead commander, and the cipher was broken. For three days army units continued to use this cipher that the enemy was making use of. On January 4, by order of the army's former chief of staff divisional commander Sokolov, new keys had to be provided to units by aeroplane. However, Sokolov did not check whether his orders were carried out, as a result of which the keys lay undisturbed several more days with the army staff. The custody and use of cipher documents in units and the staff of the ninth army are utterly slipshod and irresponsible. The ciphers are not accounted for; they are handed out without being signed for. The chief of the cipher department of the ninth army—Captain Buinov—has inadequate knowledge; he shows no initiative; he has no managerial ability.[28]

Until this point, an inadvertent asymmetry, in the Russians' favour, had held: Soviet ciphers were secure from prying eyes, whereas foreign ciphers were accessible, but only aided by cribs or, in fact, entire codebooks, stolen from enemy hands. After the Soviet-Finnish War, however, Soviet codes and ciphers were more frequently broken. What is more, Moscow, in trying to break foreign codes, would require an entire technological revolution if it hoped to advance beyond deciphering purely by hand. Yet Stalin and his immediate successors never put sufficient resources into cryptanalysis, in terms either of manpower or of equipment. Inevitably, dependence upon agents to purloin foreign codes and ciphers grew rather than diminished in wartime. The fallible human factor reasserted itself as the immediate solution.

4. WHAT GERMAN THREAT?

The seismic impact of Stalin's personal priorities did not become apparent until the military disaster of June 22, 1941. Russia would never have suffered such horrendous casualties in the ensuing war—up to twenty-seven million dead—had Stalin been truly prepared for the worst. But, having banked so much on human intelligence while at the same time remaining morbidly mistrustful of those working under him, Stalin unwittingly undermined his own position—and a critical few, most notably Krivitsky and Orlov, who dreaded the ominous summons back to Moscow, lost no time in defecting to the West. How did Stalin really expect intelligent operatives to react?

An Artuzov favourite, Orlov had sufficient knowledge of the networks upon which Soviet security in Europe depended to undermine them entirely, had he chosen to do so. Instead he astutely made an offer to Yezhov through secret channels when he absconded: silence in exchange for his own and his family's protection. The concession was granted, but Stalin nonetheless doubted that Orlov could be trusted not to tell what he knew. Thus, the Lubyanka had good reason to mistrust what agents and friends had to say. That was certainly the case on the eve of war.

Although the Russians had some limited success in penetrating Nazi Germany, it was nothing compared to what had been achieved in

Britain. A great deal of attention has subsequently been given to the Rote Kapelle, the so-called Red Orchestra, a broad-brush German designation for the networks of Soviet spies operating against Berlin during the war. Martha Dodd, the daughter of the American ambassador, was an agent, as was her brother. The Russians could read Ausamt material through "Marta" in Berlin and through Rudolf von Scheliha, a diplomat at the German embassy in Warsaw. They had good access to the Finance Ministry through Arvid Harnack. They had low-level access to the Aviation Ministry through Harro Schultze-Boyson and to counterintelligence at the Gestapo via SS-Hauptsturmführer Willi Lehmann. But they never penetrated Hitler's circle, or even touched its outer rim.[1] Thus Soviet access to information was infinitely better in London than in Berlin, the corollary being that what they knew of Germany during hostilities largely came from Britain. That this was so had more to do with luck than purposeful planning.

Britain became the preeminent source for Soviet intelligence globally, and Anatoly Gorskii ("Henri," "Kap," "Vadim") played a crucial role. Born in 1907, in the Yenisei prefecture, he was educated in Kansk. Though devoid of charm, he was a clever man, and in 1928 he was recruited to SPEKO. In 1936, Gorskii was sent to London as assistant to the rezident and as code clerk for the legal rezidentura. His first boss was the legal rezident Adol'f Chapskii ("Klim"), who operated under cover as second secretary Anton Shuster at the embassy in London.[2] He was recalled in the summer of 1937, then arrested in his Moscow office, and shot on November 4. Grigorii Grafpen ("Sam," "Blank"), Chapskii's successor in April 1938, recalled that November, was arrested on December 29 and imprisoned for five years. Gorskii, who had none of Deutsch's spontaneous skill at handling young men, was thus stranded in London holding the bag by default, though technically he was still merely the assistant rezident. Under great stress he barked at his agents—all unpaid volunteers. Unsurprisingly, they found him much too demanding.[3]

At a critical time—from the Munich Agreement in September 1938 until March 1940—Gorskii alone was responsible for photography, cryptography, translation, typing, and communications. He also sustained contact with a total of fourteen agents, including Blunt, Burgess, Cairncross, and, on his return from Spain, Philby.[4] No wonder he could be grumpy.

Rebuilding the "Big House"

Before the war, Comintern headquarters occupied a smart turn-of-the-century building that stood at the corner of what is now Vozdvizhenka and Mokhovaya, opposite Tsar Alexander I's riding hall, to one side of the Kremlin. It was known as the Big House, a symbol of the radiant future, a cosmopolitan world under communism. But no longer, as Stalin's massacre of Bolsheviks had reduced Comintern to a shadow of its former self; so dumping it in the suburbs at Rostokino before abolishing it entirely in April 1943 was a logical move. The Lubyanka, on the other hand, having undergone two deadly purges, first under Yezhov and then under Beria, remained within easy reach of the Kremlin and was now hastily under reconstruction, transfused with fresh blood in a building subjected to ever-greater extension, vertical as well as horizontal. It now took over Comintern's sobriquet as the Big House. Nothing exemplified the changes in Russia since the revolution more than this.

The vacuum in the leadership of foreign intelligence was finally filled by a smart young pragmatist, Pavel Fitin, untainted by experience in the secret services. Born into a peasant family in tsarist Siberia on December 28, 1907, he grew up in Tobol'sk prefecture (its main city still a striking monument to prerevolutionary architecture) and became a full-time worker for Komsomol (Young Communists) after leaving school. At the astonishingly young age of twenty, Fitin was admitted into the Party proper, and after graduating from the engineering faculty of Russia's top agricultural university, he took charge of industrial literature at a publishing house. In 1934 he served briefly in the Red Army before returning to the publishing house as deputy chief editor. Then, in March 1938, he was selected to train at the central school for *enkavedisty*, where his education took place at an accelerated pace. In November, Fitin became a probationer at what had been the INO, swiftly rising to become deputy head at the age of only thirty-one; very soon, he was promoted to head of what had now become the fifth department.[5]

Almost all illegal rezidentury had been summarily shut down in 1938. Contacts with the most valuable sources were lost, some forever. The legal rezidentury remaining were at times reduced to just two operatives, often young and inexperienced. Most of those recalled to

Moscow were arrested; the rest were put on probation.[6] The losses were so great that in the course of six months in 1938, no information came into the Lubyanka from the field. Following Artuzov's arrest, Slutsky took over, only to have a heart attack in his office shortly thereafter. His two successors, Zelman Passov and Sergei Shpiegel'glas, were subsequently arrested, on October 23 and November 2, respectively. Beria's protégé, the diminutive Vladimir Dekanozov, took over at the beginning of 1939. It immediately became obvious that he was wholly unsuited to the task, and he was sent off to be ambassador in Berlin, a very demanding position for which he was even less suited. Yet to everyone's surprise, and no doubt to the consternation of some, his mania for dancing, even with Ribbentrop's amply proportioned wife, did demonstrate hidden talents of a kind as well as an avid interest in the opposite sex.[7]

Burgess now worked at MI6, in the newly formed Section D, which hid under cover as a statistical unit within the War Office. He had briefed Gorskii on two critical conversations. The first was with Horace Wilson, Prime Minister Neville Chamberlain's special advisor on foreign affairs. Gorskii was told that "the British chiefs of staff are firmly convinced that war with Germany can be won without difficulty and therefore the British government has no need to conclude a defence pact with the Soviet Union. In government circles the opinion expressed is that England never thought about concluding a serious pact with the USSR. The prime minister's advisors openly say that Great Britain can do without a Russian pact." The second conversation was with "Monty" (Montagu) Chidson, assistant to the head of Section D, Laurence Grand. On the eve of the negotiations with the Russians, Gorskii reported Burgess's account of what Chidson had said: "It is a fundamental aim of British policy to work with Germany whatever happens, and, in the end, against the USSR. But it is impossible to conduct this policy openly; one must manoeuvre every which way . . . Chidson told me unambiguously that our aim is not to resist German expansion to the east."[8]

As if this were not bad enough, while the British were still negotiating in Moscow, the indefatigable Burgess also conveyed to Gorskii the substance of a telegram from the British ambassador in Berlin, Sir Neville Henderson, dated August 21: "All measures have been taken for Herman Göring to arrive under secret cover in London on Wednesday 23rd. This will amount to an historic event and we are just waiting for confirmation of this from the German side."[9]

Doubtless finally convinced by such intelligence, and with no reason to trust Prime Minister Neville Chamberlain, on August 23 the Russians signed a pact with Germany that made possible Moscow's annexation of eastern Poland and its dominance (unspecified) over Latvia and Estonia. Stalin thus effectively solved the Soviet Union's own problem with Germany, at least for the short term, at the expense of everyone else. The road to war against Poland was now open, and with the Luftwaffe bombing Warsaw, the British reluctantly declared war on Germany on September 3.

Deprived of Deutsch, who was on his way to the United States to run the illegal rezidentura—on November 7, 1942, his ship, the *Donbass*, was torpedoed by a German submarine en route—Gorskii did his level best without the inestimable advantage of his old boss's charisma. His efforts were suddenly undermined when he was recalled to take charge of the British desk in February 1940, at a time when Moscow needed all the information it could get. The rezidentura in London was abruptly shut down as untrustworthy, and the Cambridge Five, among others, were left twisting in the wind.[10] They were forced to improvise. Philby, Burgess, and Blunt worked together as one and handed over their findings to Edith Tudor Hart, who passed them on to Bob Stewart, a trusted Communist who in turn arranged their transmission to Moscow.[11]

Meanwhile, ominous signs emerged that Britain and Germany were moving towards healing their rift. On July 9, Fitin submitted a disturbing secret report, No. 5/8175, which was already out of date on receipt: "The former King Edward together with his wife, Simpson, are currently in Madrid, from where they maintain contact with Hitler. Edward is conducting negotiations with Hitler on the question of forming a new English government and the conclusion of peace with Germany on the condition of a military alliance against the USSR."[12] Whether this was fact or rumour circulated by MI6 (very active in Spain and Portugal) to frighten the Russians into negotiations with the British is not known. Such tactics were later used in relation to the flight of Rudolf Hess to Britain in May 1941 (as explored later, on page 112), so the suggestion that this was a ruse is not entirely implausible.

Finally, common sense took hold in Moscow. Gorskii was sent back to Britain in August 1940. Of course, he did not arrive until November, having wasted months travelling to and fro. Moreover, on arrival, he once again found himself seriously short-staffed. His most promising assistant was the young Vadim Barkovskii. Born in Belgorod in 1913, Barkovskii lost his father in the First World War and was apprenticed to a furniture maker while still at school, making toys on the side. The aircraft designer Boris Sheremet'evo was also from Belgorod. He took on Barkovskii to help him build a glider in 1927. Finished with his schooling, Barkovskii worked as a mechanic, and after joining Komsomol in 1931, he entered the Moscow Institute of Machine-Building. He devoted his spare time to motorcycling, flying, parachuting, and giving gliding instruction. In the spring of 1939, this array of extreme sports led to his summons to the Central Committee at Staraya Ploshchad', the prelude to a further call to attend the Lubyanka, in May.[13]

Hitherto recruits to the INO—now the fifth department of the GUGB (NKVD)—were trained individually in "safe houses" (apartments) so that they did not know one another. They were chosen from the ranks of the NKVD. But this was obviously inefficient and needlessly complicated, particularly at a time when Stalin's Terror had inflicted so much loss of life (and defections) that training was required in number and at speed. Thus on October 3, 1938, the Specially Designated School (ShON) was set up to train young recruits for the NKVD.[14] "The course for intelligence operatives absolutely must be organised outside Moscow," Stalin insisted.[15] Five sites were chosen, two of which housed most recruits. Half were destined to become legals, the other half illegals. The main establishments were at Malakhova, along the Ryazan Chaussée, to the southeast of Moscow, where they trained illegals; and at Balashikh, twenty-five kilometres east of Moscow, along the Gor'kovskii Highway—nicknamed "the Twenty-Fifth" and "the woods"—where they trained the legals.[16]

The candidates were ultimately selected no longer from within the ranks of the NKVD or the Fourth but from the ranks of Komsomol by a committee chaired by Fitin. Initially only ten were trained for the Fifth at any given time, and only just over half ended up in the service.[17] Like Barkovskii, they had to be members of Komsomol and were required to have some form of higher education. At the Lubyanka, he and others were told they were now members of state security. On June 30 they were invited back, piled into covered lorries, and taken to ShON. Their destination was a two-storey wooden house in Balashikh.[18]

Conditions were spartan: five bedrooms, showers, and a rest and recreation room upstairs, two classrooms and a dining room downstairs.[19]

Barkovskii was allowed a week away to sit for the defence of his diploma. Thereafter, he disappeared from daily life. His friends naturally thought he had been arrested. At ShON, he received six hours of education a day, including tradecraft ("special disciplines"), economic geography, and political economy, but above all languages. Five took English, three took French, two took German; Oriental studies were conducted elsewhere. Everyone started from scratch.[20] Barkovskii spent six hours a day, evidently including work out of class, on English. He was taught through conversation. On completion, he replaced Gorskii on the British desk at the Lubyanka, where those working for foreign intelligence still amounted to no more than 120, including clerical staff.[21] That November, Fitin called him in. Barkovskii was assigned to London as an operative under diplomatic cover specialising in science and technology, NTR—those working in NTR were known as *ente-erovtsy*. Before leaving, he was briefed by Molotov on his diplomatic duties.

Knowing What the British Knew

Via Vladivostok, Tokyo, Honolulu, and New York, Barkovskii eventually reached the bustling port of Liverpool, under heavy German bombardment, in February 1941. Gorskii now had just two probationers, Barkovskii ("Dan," "Jerry") and Boris Kreshin ("Bob," "Max" to agents; né Kretenshil'd), to manage an ever-growing number of agents while also carrying a full diplomatic load. This meant a sixteen- to eighteen-hour day, at that time normal for Molotov and other commissars. For ordinary mortals it was too much. That summer Gorskii wrote to Fitin that "Although 'Bob' and 'Dan' are doing everything they can, they are not yet experienced intelligence agents. Each of us has ties with some twenty agents. We are all overburdened with meetings; moreover, this running about from safe house to safe house could have an extremely damaging impact on our work."[22] He saw two to three agents a day. Documents supplied by the network (including British diplomatic correspondence on a global scale, daily MI6 briefs, War Cabinet minutes and decisions) came into the Centre as high priority for Stalin, Molotov, and Beria.[23]

The need was so obvious that four more were despatched in November, which made Gorskii less cantankerous.

Moreover, disinformation circulated by the Germans reached Stalin through a double agent whom he naturally found more credible than the gloomy chorus wailing about impending invasion. He should have followed his own advice. "One must not be naïve in politics," Stalin cautioned, "but above all one must not be naïve in secret intelligence."[24] True enough, but it was always possible to be excessively suspicious. Before long, Stalin came to distrust even his best assets, including the Cambridge Five. Only the desperate need for continued secret intelligence from Allied sources in the face of the Nazi onslaught finally convinced the Russians that they had struck gold with their investment in British and American agents.

A key factor complicating Stalin's judgement was that the advice to the British War Cabinet, other than that based on interception of German communications given to Prime Minister Winston Churchill, indicated that, although Berlin might use force, it would do so in a limited way, to induce concessions. It has to be remembered that even the evidence from GC&CS was inconclusive. Also, Stalin had access only to what the Cabinet received; he knew nothing of the interception and decryption of Enigma communications. Blunt was running a former Trinity student, Leonard (Leo) Long, who was working in MI14. Long passed on to Blunt analyses of German military intentions.[25] This was the same kind of material that formed the basis of the assessments Stalin was already receiving as joint intelligence committee minutes and papers.

Philby reported the following to Gorskii:

According to reliable information received, Germany has rolled out 127 divisions up to the Soviet frontier. 58 Wehrmacht divisions have been deployed in former Poland alone. The German armed forces as a whole consist of 223 divisions which are fully up to strength.

Fitin commented:

Söhnchen evidently picked up this information from the British secret services. Up to now all the information received from him has as a rule been confirmed. Berlin, however, is in a state of war with England; German planes are daily bombing London and other cities of Great Britain. Is a German invasion of the Soviet Union possible in these conditions or have England's secret services deliberately chosen to deceive Moscow through Philby? This information must immediately be verified.[26]

Not least of Stalin's problems was that operatives with extensive experience had, in large part, been arrested without trial and then shot; this meant that his operatives were, on the whole, novices without direct experience of foreign countries. Some were not even competent in a foreign language. This was true especially at the most senior levels of the service, a fact that must have been deeply demoralising to their subordinates who were appropriately qualified.

The situation was perhaps at its worst in Nazi Germany. Neither Dekanozov, sent as envoy to Berlin, nor Amayak Kobulov, his deputy, serving as counsellor (and rezident), had any experience in secret intelligence, or even spoke German. Amayak ("Zakhar") was the younger brother of Beria's protégé, his arrogant deputy Bogdan Kobulov. Whereas Bogdan was ugly—small and fat with a vicious temperament to match—Amayak looked like a tall, well-built Charlie Chaplin, and was invariably the life and soul of any social occasion.[27] Yet as an interrogator who often beat his victims senseless, he was no different from his odious brother.[28]

Kobulov's ignorance soon led to gossip. Writing to Fitin, Beria delivered a severe rebuke: "I heard that the leadership of intelligence is dissatisfied with Zakhar's work and has simply washed its hands of him. Perhaps one should pay no attention to this chatter, but when it concerns responsible comrades with whom I personally maintain contact, such corridor conversations must not take place. I ask that you take measures to put an end henceforth to such tittle-tattle."[29] Failure to conform would have led to consequences best not risked.

Meanwhile, in Germany, Kobulov proved to be an utter failure. Even worse, he lent credibility to Stalin's treasured delusion that Germany would not attack. A rather different figure was cut by the young Aleksandr Korotkov, now promoted to deputy rezident under Kobulov in December 1940. He proved to be the rising talent, as evidenced by the fact that, in July 1940, he had already made a fleeting visit to Berlin to seek out agents with whom contact had been lost.[30]

Aleksandr Korotkov

Korotkov—an accomplished sportsman, tall, handsome, and athletic—was born on November 22, 1909, into a bourgeois family that was subsequently shorn of its wealth by the revolution. After an apprenticeship of only one year, he was hired as an electrician at the Lubyanka. Barely two months later, he came to the attention of the wife of Vilkoviskii, who no doubt found him rather agreeable; Vilkoviskii taught foreign languages to OGPU personnel.[31] On her recommendation, Korotkov was then recruited into the service by Veniamin Gerson, Yagoda's assistant. Two years later, he became a filing clerk in Artuzov's secretariat at the INO. His rise under Artuzov was meteoric. In 1930 he became assistant to the head of the second department, then rose in the ranks of the seventh, before finally taking charge of it. Meanwhile, he speedily assimilated French and German, the latter from a veteran of 1923; individual tutorials were the means by which this was done.

Korotkov's first assignments, under such code names as "Dlinnyi," "Korotin," and "Erdberg," included a brief sojourn during which he was under deep cover as a Czech, in Vienna in 1933, where he worked with Deutsch. Later that year, he moved to Paris, where he enrolled at the Sorbonne to study anthropology.[32] In Austria, he had worked on acquiring the distinctive local accent that obscured his native speech pattern. In Paris, under Orlov in the "Express" group, he ran a young man in the Deuxième Bureau and conducted missions to Switzerland and Germany, until his cover was jeopardised and he was forced to leave the country.

After a brief interval in Moscow, Korotkov returned to Berlin under official cover as representative of Soviet heavy industry at the trade delegation (April 1936 to December 1937). There, he gathered intelligence on the German production of synthetic rubber and oil, and on the latest weapons technology. Though Operation Krona steadily enveloped twenty informants, it remained undetected until the end of hostilities.[33] Korotkov was then tasked with assassinating the OGPU defector

Agabekov, but before the deed could be done, he was suddenly recalled to Moscow in January 1939 as a result of Orlov's defection. Back in Moscow, Korotkov faced the ever-present danger of Stalin's axe.

Korotkov was rendered idle for three months after abrupt dismissal from the service. He took the unusual step of appealing to Beria. "I do not see," Korotkov wrote, "that I have done anything which could give cause for depriving me of the honour of working in the organs. Finding oneself in this situation is infinitely distressing and offensive."[34] Uncharacteristically, Beria took a chance on him, and miraculously he avoided the fate of so many.

Korotkov did not resume operational activity for a year. In August 1940 he was sent on a brief trip to Berlin and restored contact with Schulze-Boysen ("Starshina") and Harnak ("Korsikanets"). A mere lieutenant, Korotkov was nevertheless raised to deputy rezident in Berlin, where he operated under diplomatic cover as "Stepanov," a lowly third secretary—only again to be withdrawn suddenly to Moscow.[35] Germany was a heavy burden. His agents were not the easiest to handle. They were not paid. They saw themselves as freedom fighters engaged in an ideological struggle, and so would not be disciplined—and their warnings to Kobulov and Dekanozov fell on deaf ears.

By early April 1941, tensions between Russia and Germany were rising rapidly. Korotkov—now back in Berlin—asked Kobulov to make a request of the leadership. Given the serious deterioration in the political situation, he said, "[W]e suggest that our every measure to set up an illegal rezidentura and guarantee its radio contact with the Centre should be speeded up. The 'Korsikanets-Starshina' group must be supplied with a cipher for a radio station and a sum of money of about 50–60,000 marks. This would secure their work in the event of their losing contact with us . . . We request that you immediately send a radio and ciphers for transmissions from the Berlin underground." Unfortunately, this request was ignored, and only on June 22 did the rezidentura receive instructions to supply them with money. By then, however, the embassy was entirely surrounded by the SS. Only through bribing Haupt-Stürmführer Heinemann, through the good offices of the young diplomat Valentin Berezhkov, was Korotkov able to catch the daily ride by car to Wilhelmstrasse on two successive days and managed to hand over first the money and then the radio transmitter/receiver.[36]

At intelligence headquarters in Berlin, the Gestapo chief Siegfried Müller had quickly taken the measure of Kobulov. Early in August 1940, Kobulov unknowingly recruited a double agent, the Lettish correspondent Orest Berlings, who was evidently not only short of money but also well connected in Nazi circles.[37] Recruitment required express permission from the Centre. Fitin was horrified at such credulousness and careless speed. Kobulov was warned, in no uncertain terms, that because Berlings had yet to be investigated, "we suggest you show reasonable caution in working with him and on no account put him into contact with any other operative of the rezidentura." The trouble was that Kobulov's despatches went over the heads of the department and landed directly in the hands of Stalin via Merkulov.[38]

Vsevolod Merkulov, a Beria protégé, was an aristocrat, born in 1895 in Zakatal, and educated first in the Georgian capital and then in Petrograd, where he attended university. His schooling was cut short when he was called to the colours, though he never actually fought; in fact, he was completely apolitical until discovering Marxist literature through his brother-in-law. He ended up in the Georgian Cheka because he grew bored teaching in a school for the blind. This was September 1921, after the Bolshevik takeover of Georgia. A year later, the ambitious Beria, now chairman of the Georgian Cheka, moved from Baku to Tiflis. He soon came across the modest and shy Merkulov.

Despite the burden of his high birth, Merkulov's career took off. To his role as first assistant, he brought unquestioning loyalty and a talent for articulating Beria's thoughts in print. He was most certainly not there to think for himself. In September 1938, Merkulov arrived in Moscow, where he was handed control of the GUGB and became first deputy commissar of internal affairs (NKVD). In exchange, Beria insisted that Merkulov participate in beating prisoners to extort confessions. For this gentle soul who never fought, even as a child, it was a craven surrender of his inner self. In February 1941, because of further reorganisation, Vsevolod Merkulov went on to head the newly formed NKGB.[39]

Kobulov's new agent, Berlings, was code-named "Litseist"—from *Lizeumsschüler*, or children educated privately. Berlings's job for the Nazis was to encourage Stalin to believe that troop concentrations on the Soviet border were designed to exert pressure on Moscow to negotiate concessions. The material Berlings passed on was prepared by

Ribbentrop and handed over only with Hitler's approval.[40] Molotov was deliberately flattered by a Nazi assessment of his disastrous visit in November 1940 as the beginning of "a new era."[41] This alone should have given rise to serious doubts. On May 19, 1941, Berlings reported that, in spite of Germany's deploying 160–200 divisions, "War between the Soviet Union and Germany is unlikely, although it would be very popular in Germany at a time when the present war with England does not meet with popular approval. Hitler cannot take such a risk as war with the USSR, fearing a breach in the unity of the national socialist party." Moreover, the Germans could not risk a loss of supplies from the Soviet Union for the six weeks that war would entail.[42] This logic sounded plausible to those—including the breezily overconfident Fitzroy Maclean at the Northern Department of the Foreign Office—who wished to believe it. The Russians also took these faulty but apparently authoritative judgements seriously.

The Importance of Rudolf Hess

The sudden and unanticipated flight of Rudolf Hess, Germany's third in line after Hitler and Göring, into Britain on May 10 appears to have confirmed Stalin in his unalterable conviction that any forceful reaction to a German breach of the Soviet border carried with it the risk of a united front from London to Berlin.

On the third floor at 19 Bol'shoi Znamensky Pereulok stood the office of the General Staff and of Lieutenant General Filipp Golikov, director of its intelligence directorate (once the Fourth). Director Golikov did not exactly cut an impressive figure. He was short, no more than five feet, two inches. He was stocky. He was completely bald. His face, like those of others in the Kremlin, was rather unpleasantly flushed. Golikov's power, however, was apparent in his eyes, not for their size but for the fact that they were a steely blue and exceptionally penetrating.[43] Yet he was actually no more than an intimidated novice in the secret world, easily browbeaten by those he answered to: Malenkov and Stalin. After all, every one of his immediate predecessors had been executed. Worse still, his understanding of the outside world was no better than that of the average soldier. "Could the Main Intelligence Directorate afford not to take into account the possibility that Germany and England might conclude peace during the course of the year preceding the attack by Hitlerite forces on the USSR?" Golikov asked rhetorically more than two decades later, older but not much the wiser.[44]

In an unprecedented speech to commanders of the armed forces on May 5, Stalin at last broke his silence and talked openly of mounting an offensive against Berlin.[45] Taking their cue from the speech, Chief of the General Staff Marshal Georgii Zhukov and Commissar for Military Affairs Marshal Semyon Timoshenko asked Deputy Head of the Operational Directorate of the General Staff Aleksandr Vasilevsky to prepare for the contingency of a first strike against the Germans. The plan was ready ten days later—which was, unfortunately for them, just five days after the Hess flight. On May 19, Timoshenko and Zhukov took the proposals to Stalin without signature as a precaution. As Zhukov recalls, Stalin erupted at the suggestion of preemption, insisting that he had spoken of an offensive merely to raise morale and to rebuff the damaging image of German invincibility.[46]

All too conscious that perfidious Albion was perpetually up to no good, Stalin became obsessed with uncovering the truth behind the Hess affair. One reason for his fixation was that, only a fortnight before the flight, a political appointee from the Independent Labour Party, Sir Stafford Cripps, Britain's ambassador in Moscow, had been flailing about desperately in search of a means of drawing Stalin into the war. Finally, in April 1941, Cripps suggested that the fear of a separate peace was the only card left to play. This telegram was intercepted, decrypted, and circulated to Stalin.[47]

But Philby, now back in London training intelligence operatives, had little to report on Hess. What he had to say was hurriedly circulated to rezidentury in other capitals so that they could fill in the details.[48] Not surprisingly, the news was that Hess had come to negotiate peace with Britain.[49] Yet the fact that everything was hidden from public view inevitably excited extravagant speculation as to whether he brought with him terms of peace and what exactly those terms might be. Philby's contact, Tom Dupree, deputy head of the press department of the Foreign Office, wryly remarked that "never in the field of human conflict has so much been hidden by so few from so many."

Summing up the intelligence available, Dekanozov cautiously described the Hess flight as "one of the most weighty events in the life of Germany in recent times." However, he also said the "circumstances and real meaning of this flight remain not entirely clear and are giving rise to contradictory and even mutually exclusive judgements from observers." All that could definitely be said was that there was "a crisis at the top" within Germany.[50]

The impact of ever more urgent warnings to Moscow from its agents in the field that the Germans were about to attack was negated by reports that the British did not believe in such an attack. On May 9, Merkulov had sent Stalin, Molotov, and Beria a despatch from London quoting from a War Office report for April 16–23, 1941: "German preparations for war with the USSR are continuing; however, up to now there is absolutely no evidence that the Germans are determined to attack the USSR in the summer of 1941."[51] Also, as late as May 23, 1941, the Joint Intelligence Committee's full prognosis on "Germany's intentions against the USSR" still assumed that Hitler was intent on feigning a fully fledged invasion in order to force negotiations on Stalin. Its report concluded, "With her usual thoroughness Germany is making all preparations for an attack so as to make the threat convincing."[52] Thus, the London rezidentura, in contrast to that in Berlin, never provided the date of invasion.[53] Of course, if an all-out assault were really Hitler's purpose, then a pretext would be needed to launch a minor skirmish, as in 1914.

Here, Soviet counterintelligence, now headed by the young Pyotr Fyodotov, played into Hitler's hands. Fyodotov had succeeded in planting a microphone in the office of the German military attaché. Stalin came to rely upon this intelligence as conclusive with respect to Nazi plans. But it seems that the Germans knew that the Russians could be eavesdropping. On May 31, Fyodotov relayed to Stalin a record of the attaché's conversation with the Slovakian envoy about war with the Soviet Union. What caught Stalin's eye was Ernst Köstring's statement: "Here what we need is to create some kind of provocation. We must arrange for some German or other to be murdered and by that means prompt war."[54] This was nonsense, of course, but Stalin had no way of judging whether it was true. His own obsession with the idea that war would begin by provocation, as at Sarajevo in 1914, held him back from mobilising against a likely attack.

Stalin had reason to be cautious in accepting at face value anything that London had to say. Cripps had, among other things, suggested making use of the Hess mission to heighten Soviet suspicions of Germany.

Orme ("Moley") Sargent, the most devious of foreign officials and deputy undersecretary, suggested that, given Stalin's panicky state of mind, this might result in territorial concessions from Moscow to Berlin that would scarcely be in British interests. Sargent favoured a "whisper" in the right ears courtesy of MI6. "The line of course to take is to give some assurance to the Soviet Government that they need not buy off Germany with a new and unfavourable agreement because there is clear evidence that Germany does not intend to embark on a war with the Soviet Union in present circumstances."[55] Indeed, a Joint Intelligence Committee report concluded that Stalin would make substantial concessions to Germany rather than risk open war.[56] In retrospect, much has been made of Churchill's warning, yet Enigma's secrets had by no means been broken at Bletchley: the warning was thinly based on the transfer of certain Luftwaffe squadrons to East Prussia. London evidently did not believe that a full-scale invasion was likely.

On June 17, Stalin brusquely dismissed Fitin's reports of imminent invasion as "disinformation."[57] Too late, covert information reaching the Soviet embassy in Berlin impressed even the usually indifferent Dekanozov, whose loyalty to Stalin could not be doubted. But even on the eve of invasion, as late as June 21, Beria, ever sensitive to Stalin's state of mind and ever conscious of the fate of his predecessors, overreacted, demanding Dekanozov's immediate recall and punishment for continually bombarding them with "disinformation" about an imminent German invasion—surely the nadir of Moscow's intelligence assessment.[58] Beria, utterly inexperienced but inebriated by overweening self-confidence, proved to be the most disastrous head of intelligence the Soviet Union ever had.

5. THE TEST OF WAR

It had been summer as usual along the shores of the balmy Black Sea and, with the unique exception of the courageous Colonel-General Yakov Cherevichenko, who commanded the Odessa military district and risked his life by mobilising his men in defiance of orders, war was wholly unanticipated. Life carried on as normal. Senior air force commanders were still being arrested. Leave had been granted to soldiers on a broad scale without a thought to the threat hanging over Russia. One observer recalls that "the resorts were full of army personnel, including from the western regions, and from the air force and navy as well."[1]

In Sochi alone, a grand total of 223 officers were taking a rest at the central military sanatorium. The Party's third most senior figure, Andrei Zhdanov, had only just arrived at the seaside for a break a little over a week earlier, and the people's commissar for the navy was sent there by the Politburo as late as June 21. None was actually ill; they were just taking a rest in the sun, oblivious to what was about to occur.[2]

The only straws in the wind indicating that some had serious concerns were reports reaching foreign diplomats of local Party meetings where the issue of war was now discussed and the fact that coverage given to military events in Soviet domestic broadcasts had increased.

Indeed, two children's programs on June 17 took up a military theme.[3] But such signs were faint, and acquired significance only in retrospect.

Just before dawn, at 4:00 a.m. on June 22, 1941, and with a low mist rising, the massed forces of Germany and its allies swept across eighteen hundred miles of the Soviet frontier and sliced through echelons of bewildered Russian troops, who emerged from their encampments bleary-eyed from sleep. As intended, Hitler had achieved full tactical surprise. Whole units were seized in place, aviation destroyed on the ground, and officers stationed close to the front line were so taken aback that they asked their commanders what to do. Belated instructions to mobilise had yet to reach the armed forces.

Demoralised Byelorussians, Russians, and Ukrainians fled their units. As the Germans arrived at the villages, dispossessed peasants followed tradition and greeted the Germans with bread and salt as liberators from socialist serfdom. The collective strength of Soviet secret intelligence was not the only organ of Soviet power put to the ultimate test.

The Kremlin machine was not even in gear when the collision occurred, and it still had no way of estimating the speed and direction of the Wehrmacht offensive because it was unable to decipher German strategic communications. As the 1930s progressed, decryption had become ever more difficult. Whereas a great number of cryptanalysts were needed, few were to be found. Also, lack of preparation had "a simply catastrophic" effect on the theory and practice of mechanising decryption.[4] Short-term needs had taken and held a vise-like grip. Long-standing dependence upon agents to purloin foreign codes and ciphers grew rather than diminished. At the same time, the means of penetrating the enemy camp had been immeasurably reduced because Europe was now a raging battlefield (in the east) or a fortified occupation zone (to the west).

The inability to break the ciphers of the German Enigma machine that transmitted crucial information on the order of battle, including the instructions of the High Command, would have proved crippling had it not been for human intelligence from London. Enigma was capable of producing more than one hundred fifty million permutations; it threatened to leave Russian cryptographers, armed only with pencil and paper, entirely overwhelmed.

The Costs of Backwardness

A momentary breakthrough miraculously occurred just in time for the massive Soviet counteroffensive at Stalingrad: the Russians captured an Enigma machine and several German cryptographers. Led by a brilliant cryptographer, Mikhail Sokolov, adopted by the OGPU as an orphan and educated entirely by it, the team succeeded in creating a mathematical model of Enigma, a feat for which they were decorated on November 29, 1942. But this vital advance proved agonisingly fleeting.[5] On January 17, 1943, the Germans, aware that they had abandoned twenty-six Enigma machines at Stalingrad, introduced changes that stumped the Russians.

Only with respect to Japan were the Russians consistently ahead. In the crisis year 1941, when Stalin waited anxiously in anticipation of a Japanese decision to take advantage of the German onslaught to attack Russia from the East, Boris Aronskii deciphered ambassadorial communications from a range of Germany's allies in Tokyo. A crucial despatch dated November 27 quoted the emperor as saying that although Japan would beat Russia, for the time being it would focus on the United States. Meanwhile, the leading specialists on Japanese ciphers, Sergei Tolstoi and Aronskii, cracked high-level communications within the Japanese government that confirmed these facts. For this, Aronskii and Tolstoi, the best among the earliest recruits to SPEKO in 1922, received the highest distinction, the Order of Lenin, on April 3, 1942.[6] Their decrypts allowed Stalin to transfer fresh forces in significant numbers from the Trans-Baikal and Siberian military districts to the Western Front when the need arose. Sorge was not only not needed; he was not trusted. If the Japanese had not arrested and executed him, the Russians would have done so themselves sooner or later.

In the spring of 1941, about fifty graduates in mathematics and physics were finally drafted in from Moscow University. It took a year for the new recruits to make an impact on the quantity of decrypts, and it was only in May 1942 that eight separate sections were set up by country. The most important among the new sections were those devoted to Germany, Japan, Britain, and the United States.[7]

Japan was very important as a potential adversary, but Germany was critical. Moscow was too far behind in electronics even to consider doing what London was doing on a massive scale at GC&CS in

Bletchley Park. The British could test Enigma's permutations at a rate of a thousand per minute. The Russians, on the other hand, had to rely for decrypts upon Cairncross, who had been at Bletchley Park since March 1942, but he did not have access to material on the Eastern Front until April 1943. Also, they were crucially dependent on the agent "Dolly" (one of few as yet unidentified, working for Soviet military intelligence) at the War Office, who gave the Russians access to Japanese diplomatic decrypts initially and, later, to German military decrypts on a vast scale throughout the latter half of the war.[8]

Technological backwardness meant that the Russians had no hope of winning the decryption race,[9] and not until the end of the decade were top mathematicians in the Soviet Union drawn into code and cipher cracking.[10] Instead, the Russians had to make do with human intelligence. After the Soviet counteroffensive that followed the disasters of 1941, Hitler issued secret directive No. 41 on April 5, 1942, for an all-out attack on the Caucasus, code-named "Blau" (Blue.) As in 1940, he launched a disinformation campaign, this time to confuse Stalin with the idea that instead of heading south, the Germans would immediately head east, to Moscow.

The Germans simultaneously moved to destroy Soviet intelligence operations in Central and Western Europe. Key spies within Germany, including Schultze-Boysen and Harnak, were arrested. About one hundred in all were rounded up, forty-six of whom were executed. Others, such as "Kent" (Anatoly Gurevich), who had operated abroad as a businessman until his arrest in 1942, were forced to conduct a radio game with Moscow to mislead the Russians about German capabilities and intentions. Gurevich managed to indicate to the Russians that he was acting under duress. Nonetheless, in every other respect, deception operations worked—despite the fact that some Soviet intelligence networks correctly reported the direction of the oncoming German offensive.

From London, on March 3, 1942, Major Aleksandr Sizov ("Edward") of what was now the GRU predicted that the objective was the Caucasus. Two days later, Bulgarian diplomatic communications purloined by the Soviet military rezident in Ankara indicated the same; as did Radó ("Dora") from Switzerland, on March 12. Dolly sent in the record of conversations between Ribbentrop and the Japanese ambassador to Germany, Hiroshi Oshima, that took place on February 18, 22, and 23, all to the same effect. On March 18, the GRU passed a special communication based on these sources to the General Staff. But Stalin was reluctant to give up offensive operations from Moscow, even as further corroboration came in—on this occasion from the main GRU rezident, Colonel Nikolai Nikitushev ("Akasto"), military attaché in Stockholm, based on the assessment of the Swedish General Staff. Finally, on June 28, German forces broke through into Voronezh, southeast of Moscow. It was Stalin's second major miscalculation, made because he ignored the best secret intelligence. Russia's prospects dimmed. It began to look like the beginning of the end.[11]

Deep-Seated Fears of a Separate Peace

Stalin's chronic mistrust of his sources had broken all hopes of a speedy victory; the events of 1942 demonstrated that it was potentially also a speedy route to catastrophic defeat. Bad faith pervaded not just intelligence gathering and assessment but also the diplomacy vigorously pursued by the same Molotov who had so trusted Hitler. As de facto allies of the Soviet Union, Britain and the United States were entirely innocent of the fact that Stalin was targeting them, or that he was driven by the deep-seated suspicion—indeed, imminent expectation—of their betrayal of Russia to Nazi Germany. Were they not all capitalists? Had not Neville Chamberlain envisaged Germany as the bulwark against encroaching Bolshevism in Europe? Why did they not immediately launch a second front in Europe? Stalin's abiding suspicions about the role of Hess indicated the compulsions that accelerated his frenzied imagination. It remained an obsession through to the end of hostilities, and beyond. Soviet use of the term *anti-Hitler* coalition rather than *anti-Nazi* coalition to describe the alliance underlined Kremlin suspicion that, were Hitler to be overthrown, the alliance would cease to exist. The Russians would then face the Germans alone.

The Allies were courted by German "opposition" to Hitler. The British held themselves in an attitude of studied reserve but, at the same time, refused to take any action that would entirely alienate potential oppositionists. As early as December 1942, Carl Langbehn, introduced as Himmler's personal advisor on legal affairs, met Professor Bruce Hopper in Stockholm. Hopper was a representative of the OSS, the U.S. secret intelligence service. At this meeting, Hopper was re-assured that "serious people" in Germany saw no point in war with the United States and Britain.[12] A further meeting, again unauthorised, this time with Allen Dulles, head of station in Switzerland, a genial but not a very smart man, took place in September 1943. Langbehn was subsequently arrested and executed along with the rest of the opposition just over a year later, after the attempt on Hitler's life.

The proposals included Hitler's demotion to a purely decorative role and Germany's confinement to ethnically "natural" frontiers. At the OSS in Washington, D.C., General William Donovan gave responsibility for sustaining contacts to Dulles. Between January and April 1943, another Himmler emissary, Prince Max Egon Hohenlohe-Langenburg, met Dulles in Geneva and Berne, on three occasions accompanied by an unidentified officer from Himmler's V Department (western Europe). Also present were the U.S. ambassador, Leland Harrison, and Lieutenant Colonel Duncan Lee, confidential assistant to General Donovan. Lee, a former Rhodes scholar at Oxford, where he was almost certainly recruited, was spying for Moscow under the code name "Koch."

From February 1943 to the end of the war, Dulles was in touch with Obergruppenführer Ernst Kaltenbrunner, who had just taken charge of the RSHA, the chief security office, through the deputy head of its southeast European department. Hohenlohe suggested "a cordon against Bolshevism and Panslavism" to be created by "expanding Poland to the East, maintaining the monarchy in Romania and a strong Hungary." Moscow, through Lee, was kept fully informed.

Further approaches were made, in this instance to the British, in May 1942, from von Papen, now Germany's ambassador in Ankara. Von Papen was an old hand at the spying game. He worked via intermediaries in Turkey, Sweden, and the Vatican. Yet they were firmly rebuffed from London. On June 19, Soviet intelligence reported from Istanbul that the German trade representative in Turkey had talked to Cardinal Angelo Roncalli (future Pope Saint John XXIII), the apostolic delegate, and subsequently visited Rome for further talks with Cardinal Giovanni Montini, future Pope Paul VI, and Luigi Maglione, secretary of state to the Vatican.

Meanwhile, in Berne, Dulles was contacted by a retired field marshal, Walther von Brauchitsch, who wanted a military dictatorship *tout court*. In this respect, he shared the views of Claus von

Stauffenberg—who tried to blow up Hitler on July 20, 1944—but unlike Stauffenberg, he never had the courage to act. As a quid pro quo for pulling Germany out of the war, Brauchitsch insisted that no part of the country should suffer Soviet occupation.[13]

No to Killing Hitler

All this might help explain Stalin's reluctance to assassinate Hitler, otherwise surprising given the policy of genocide implemented by the SS and the Wehrmacht on Soviet soil. Stalin's reticence stretched back to the early 1930s, when he held back from blocking Hitler's rise to power because of an even greater fear of a Franco-German axis pressed by von Papen and backed by populist military leaders such as the "social general" Kurt von Schleicher.[14] The bottom line was that Germany at war without Hitler would be more acceptable to the Allies; therefore it was not in the Soviet interest.

The fate of one of the conspirators illustrates well Stalin's abiding suspicions about the assassination attempt. When the plot failed, one of Stauffenberg's former aides, the young major Joachim Kuhn, who had manufactured the bombs, fled from his division on the Eastern Front and was captured by the Russians on July 27. He was incarcerated from August 12 until March 1, 1947, in Moscow's Butyrskii Prison under a false name. He revealed the location of the plans behind the bomb plot. The plot fit with Stalin's fixation that his allies had been engaged in an intrigue with the conspirators to oust Hitler and end the war only in the west. The Russians swooped in and snatched the plans on February 17, 1945, in Mauerwald, East Prussia. Kuhn was eventually sentenced as a war criminal, on October 17, 1951, by a special tribunal. The wording of the indictment clarifies why he was immured for so long in strict isolation: oddly but revealingly, it suggested that Kuhn's very participation in the bomb plot "demonstrated his guilt." It went on: "It has been established that the participants in the conspiracy [against Hitler] had in mind the following aim: Hitler's destruction; the conclusion of a separate peace with England, France, and the USA; [and] the continuation of the war against the Soviet Union together with these states."[15]

Stalin was not, of course, against assassination in principle; indeed, if anything, he was addicted to it. Proposals to assassinate Hitler had

been put to him at a time of desperation, when the population was fleeing Moscow in October 1941. These *mokrie dela* ("wet jobs") normally
fell to Sudoplatov. He cut an extraordinary figure: small but well-built,
with sparkling black eyes under heavy eyebrows. Self-possessed but
soft-spoken, with an easy smile, Sudoplatov combined deadly charm
with extreme toughness in equal measure.[16] He was born to a miller in
Melitopol', in the Ukraine, in 1907. His father died when he was ten.
When his brother joined the Red Army, he ran away from home with
the same idea in mind. After working in signals for the Reds, he soon
found himself in the Cheka at the tender age of fourteen, though his life
experience was already that of someone much older. When Balitsky
moved from the Ukraine to Moscow to head the special department
that policed the military, he took the young Pavel Sudoplatov with
him. Sudoplatov was put into the INO as chief inspector of personnel
at the unusually precocious age of twenty-six, where his talent was
spotted by Artuzov.

On October 23, 1933, Stalin received word in Gagra that the Organisation of Ukrainian Nationalists (OUN) had assassinated a Soviet diplomat at the consulate in Łwów. Artuzov's deputy Slutsky
suggested Sudoplatov become an illegal. He agreed and underwent
eight months' training. In July 1935, Sudoplatov crossed into Finland
as Pavel Grigdenko, the "nephew" of an agent already in place within
the OUN. From Helsinki he was sent by the OUN for training in Berlin,
at a Nazi Party school. It was here that he met Evgenii Konovalets, the
head of the OUN, who took to him immediately.[17] Then, on May 23, 1938,
Sudoplatov accomplished his mission: he assassinated Konovalets in
Rotterdam with an exploding cake.[18] Upon his return to Moscow, his
deputy, Eitingon, was given carte blanche to orchestrate the assassination of Trotsky. Operation Duck, Stalin's highest priority, proved
a startling success on August 20, 1940. Eitingon and the assassin's
mother fled from Mexico via Cuba, leaving the shameless Ramón Mercader to his fate.[19]

Action against Hitler, however, became feasible only in the autumn
of 1943, when the Russians obtained documentation on the layout of
"Wehrwolf," Hitler's field headquarters near Vinnitsa. Unfortunately,
Hitler ceased using it almost as soon as the Russians began laying
plans. It was decided instead to carry out the operation in Berlin, using
an officer under deep cover who had deserted the Red Army in January

1942, ostensibly with the aim of joining his uncle. His name was Igor' Miklashevskii.

The uncle had been a celebrated Soviet actor, Vsevolod Blumental'-Tamarin, who had himself been taken in by the Nazis and used for propaganda. Miklashevskii's task was to penetrate Hitler's circle with the aid of Olga Chekhova, an emigré Russian actress who had in the past carried out occasional duties of her own (unspecified), and Janusz Radziwiłł, a reluctant NKVD agent, having been imprisoned in the Lubyanka and turned. In the end, however, Stalin decided not to proceed, since Hitler's extinction would mean a government more acceptable to the Allies and therefore a separate peace at Russian expense.[20]

Evidence of Stalin's abiding concerns is abundant. When it was proposed that the title of the new highly centralised counterespionage organisation be Smernesh, which came from the current slogan "Death to German Spies," Stalin's immediate response echoed his general mistrust: "Do not other intelligence organisations work against our armies? Let us call it 'Death to Spies,' shortened to 'Smersh.' "[21] SMERSH came into being on April 19, 1943, as a department of the NKVD and two directorates for the armed forces (army and navy).[22]

That very month, Konstantin Kukin was to leave Moscow to take up the rezidentura in London. Born a *kuryanin* (native of Kursk) into a working-class family, Kukin volunteered for war in 1914 and in the course of the conflict received a commission. He fought with the partisans against the Germans in occupied Byelorussia before joining the Red Army during the civil war. Graduating from the Institute of Red Professors with a degree in the English language, he first served in London as a diplomat in 1931. Here, Kukin met an old comrade-in-arms, Evgenii Mitskevich, working for the OGPU. It was Mitskevich who convinced him to become an intelligence officer. His first deployment as such was in Kharbin, operating against the Japanese. From November 1937 he served briefly under cover as second secretary in Washington, D.C., before promotion to become deputy head of the first department (the USA and Canada) at the INO. Kukin was lucky enough to survive various denunciations and, in July 1942, accompanied Molotov on his visit to the United States for negotiations with President Franklin Roosevelt.[23]

Before Kukin left for London to take up the post, Merkulov gave him the following briefing:

Comrade Stalin has set intelligence an obligatory requirement to be up to date on the plans of our allies in the anti-Hitler coalition, including England. Therefore we are setting you four tasks: first, obtain reliable information about England's plans in the war against Germany; second, ascertain their standpoint on the postwar order in Europe and relations with the Soviet Union; third, gather information on the timing of the opening of the second front; fourth, ensure our scientists intelligence material on the creation of new weapons, especially on the problem of uranium.[24]

It was at this time that Stalin decided on "measures for the improvement of work abroad of the intelligence organs of the USSR." The point was to clarify a division of labour between the GRU and NKGB foreign intelligence. The GRU was to focus on Germany, Japan, Italy, Britain, and Turkey and to expand its activities by making greater use of delegations sent to these countries. Its illegal rezidentury had to expand under "natural cover": commercial enterprises such as cinemas, photographers, restaurants, and so on. The absence of a research and analysis directorate was finally to be remedied, but under joint leadership from the GRU and the NKGB.[25] Clearly Stalin's failure to heed incoming intelligence, which he held entirely within his own hands, now obliged him to spread responsibility more widely; though, ultimately, of course, there was nothing to stop his reverting to old habits, which, indeed, is exactly what he did by by the end of the war.

While working for Chancellor of the Duchy of Lancaster Lord Hankey, Cairncross ("Liszt") had managed to avoid army service by currying favour with a contact, Colonel Nicolls, to secure employment at Bletchley Park early in August 1942. He worked translating Luftwaffe decrypts. A breakthrough occurred when he sent word that Germany was determined to avenge its defeat at Stalingrad by launching a massive offensive called Operation Citadel in the region of Kursk and Oryol'.[26] In April 1943, Dolly reported Churchill's call for information on German plans for Kursk. Several days later, Dolly indicated that the British had "intercepted an order to the German air force eastern command . . . that those advanced units for Operation Citadel can begin preparing for the operation." Dolly continued: "On the basis of this material, British analysts at the Air Ministry have drawn the conclusion that the German Eighth Air Corps will be a part of this operation and suggest that the advanced units referred to above will be sent out from Germany. This operation may be the core of a future offensive against Kursk." This much was confirmed by further reports towards the end of April.[27]

On May 7, information from Cairncross prompted the NKGB to send the State Defence Committee (Stalin) a special communication (No. 136/M) outlining the details of Operation Citadel, along with German assessments of the readiness of Soviet forces in the direction of Kursk-Belgorod. Thereafter, Cairncross supplied the rough timing of the offensive; the technical characteristics of the new German "Tiger" and "Panzer" tanks and of the self-propelled weapon "Ferdinand," in which Hitler had placed so much hope for the summer campaign; and the numbers of German aircraft deployed from airfields in the Soviet Union. All his information was confirmed by field intelligence on the Bryansk front in May. On June 23 the GRU and the intelligence and sabotage directorate of the NKGB obtained even more precise data.

These reports convinced Stalin of the need to launch Operation Kutuzov, which began with a preemptive strike from the air that wiped out five hundred German aircraft and disabled hundreds more. The operation as a whole destroyed any hope of a German offensive and turned the balance of the war decisively to Soviet advantage.[28] The Nazis had no idea what had hit them.

The Cambridge Five Under a Cloud

Because of failing eyesight—only his right eye worked, and that, too, was now compromised by long hours of close reading in bad light—Cairncross left Bletchley Park on June 1 and, after a break, transferred to MI6 in London.[29] Thereafter, the Enigma material came to Moscow in bulk only through Dolly. The extraordinary contribution made by Cairncross to the Soviet victory at Kursk nonetheless failed to clear the air of foul suspicion hanging over the Cambridge Five. What is more, the appointment of Yelena Modrzhinskaya to head the British section at the NKGB's First Directorate in 1941 almost completely nullified all the advantages so painstakingly accrued with the recruitment of the Five.

Born on February 24, 1910, in Moscow to the son of Polish aristocrats in exile after the rebellion of 1863, Modrzhinskaya had a taste for languages. After graduating in international law from Moscow University, where she edited *Komsomol'skaya Pravda* and acted as a guide-interpreter for foreign visitors, Modrzhinskaya was sent to the Commissariat of Foreign Trade, where she took generic intelligence courses at its training school before Komsomol despatched her to work at the NKVD in, of all years, 1937. Here, over the bodies of others, she rose rapidly and was finally chosen, despite her pleas, to serve in German-occupied Warsaw, posing as the wife of the consul, Peter Gudimovich. In December 1940 she, as "Maria," and he, as "Ivan," endeavoured to resurrect a network shattered by the German invasion and the evacuation of the previous rezidentura. Their reports of the oncoming invasion were dismissed in Moscow.[30]

Modrzhinskaya was obviously more at home in Poland. Her ignorance of Britain, with the single exception of the language, was total. It did not help that she was by nature doctrinaire, domineering, and had a sharp tongue. But Modrzhinskaya was nonetheless backed by the rising star Sudoplatov, who had sided strongly with those who believed the Germans would not invade. His support guaranteed Beria's backing as well. Modrzhinskaya could not understand how, with the defections assumed to have been made by Orlov and Krivitsky in the late thirties, British "aristocrats" (*sic*) could still be working for the Soviet Union. Then, when long-awaited reports came in from London exposing the absence of operations against Soviet targets, incredulity took hold. That the British could be incompetent did not for a moment occur to them.

Blunt stated that MI5 was not watching the Soviet embassy in Britain, and Philby likewise reported that MI6 was not spying from its embassy in Moscow.[31] Modrzhinskaya, with her unwavering logic, came to the adamant conclusion that treachery was afoot. These must be double agents. Moreover, key members of the Cambridge Five—casually indifferent to elementary tradecraft, not least because Guy Liddell, who was then running anti-Soviet operations at MI5, had been completely taken in by the Five—were habitually staying at Victor Rothschild's apartment on Bentinck Street, despite express instruction from the rezident not to do so.[32]

The first result of Modrzhinskaya's morbid suspicions was a report to Fitin on November 17, 1942, that had been commissioned to sum up the achievements of the Five. But she contradicted herself by using information gathered from the Five already deemed accurate to demonstrate that they were in fact part of a double-cross system dispensing misleading intelligence. This was an act of gross stupidity that has to be understood in the context of the byzantine spy mania of 1937–1938.

Fitin was incensed at such blatant insubordination, but protected as she was by others with better access, Modrzhinskaya persisted.[33] In April 1943 she produced yet another report packed with irrelevant detail.[34] Her suspicions about the Five, in part shared by Boris Kreshin, who had replaced Gorskii, became obvious to the highly intelligent Burgess and formed the subject of open discussion between him and the rezident. In October, the Centre instructed the rezidentura to exercise greater care with its charges, and despite Cairncross's coup, which should have proved the loyalty of the group beyond question, a series of challenges was devised to test the Five's loyalty. By August 22, 1944, they had all passed with flying colours.[35]

Of course, Modrzhinskaya never changed her mind about the Five. When Burgess and Maclean finally defected in May 1951, she did her best to see that they were treated with the utmost suspicion, handled by counterintelligence, and safely bundled off to provincial Kuibyshev, in Siberia. Maclean did eventually secure a transfer to Moscow for both of them, in 1954, by means of a desperate appeal to Foreign Minister Molotov.[36]

Even though she was flushed out of the service after Stalin died, Modrzhinskaya's baleful influence remained, and her unceasing suspicions were reinforced by the bizarre leniency with which MI6 had indulged Philby until his defection in 1963. She spent her retirement perched in a sniper's nest at the headquarters of the Central Committee at Staraya Ploshchad', from which she could take pot shots at social scientists who strayed from the Party line, even inadvertently.[37]

Faltering Progress in the United States

Pro-Americanism—the *Amerikanomania* of the first Five-Year Plan—seriously diminished in Moscow after President Roosevelt's failure to agree to an alliance against Japan that the Russians had been fishing for since 1931.[38] The fighting on the border with Japanese troops in 1938 and 1939 showed that the Soviet Union would have to cope with Tokyo alone. Interest in the United States did not revive until the summer of 1940, when it became evident that Roosevelt was determined to prop up the British war effort against Germany, and as late as March 1941, it took second place to western Europe, where the war was progressing.

As part of the strategy to rebuild what had been the Fourth after only nine months on the job, Director Ivan Proskurov, a former bomber pilot in Spain, asked Lieutenant Lev Sergeev ("Morris") to go to the United States as rezident under cover as the military attaché's chauffeur. Hailing from Zakatal in Azerbaijan, Sergeev had fought in the Red Army at the age of fourteen and had only four years' experience in intelligence. Yet he had the best command of English in his department (the first), was good with people, and had demonstrated his capacity at analysing disparate information. His job, however, was not to build networks in the United States with a view to the future, but instead "to find and recruit people for shipment to Europe—Germany, Hungary, Romania and Italy and also to Britain." These recruits would be first-generation Americans, who would take some convincing to return to their erstwhile homes in current conditions. While Sergeev was settling in at the embassy—and it was a tricky task for someone of his ostensibly humble status to gain access to the cipher room—Colonel Golikov took over from Proskurov on July 11, 1940. By now Soviet interest in the United States for its own sake, particularly in the Far East, loomed large.[39] Despite the difficulties he encountered, Sergeev was to prove extremely successful in this alien American environment.

The same could not be said for the OGPU/NKVD rezidentury in the United States, which had been consistently dogged by bad luck. Yuri Markin ("Oskar"), the illegal rezident from 1932 to 1934, was murdered in circumstances unknown. He began as a young man of great promise, but as Elizabeth Poretsky relates, during his years in Germany working for the Fourth, "he almost immediately began drinking heavily and as he picked quarrels in bars he could by his carelessness have exposed the entire apparatus."[40] Later it came as no great surprise to those who knew him to learn that he ended up the victim of a casual, violent encounter in a New York City bar.

Boris Bazarov ("Kin," "Da Vinci," "Nord") was brought in to replace him. A former officer in the tsarist army who had retreated with General Denikin's men from southern Russia in 1920, Bazarov (né Shpak) was a quiet man ravaged by liver disease. Although unacceptable to the

Fourth because of his sustained service with the Whites, Bazarov typically had no trouble securing a post at the INO at its very inception. Unusually, he married a widow older than himself and adopted her child. Resigned to the ways of the world, when anything went wrong he would say, "These things will happen, you know."[41] A natural linguist and experienced illegal with a record of achievement in one of the toughest regions of Europe, the Balkans, Bazarov had been installed in Germany as one of several rezidents (the more liberal German governments operating the lightest-touch surveillance until Hitler came to power). From there, he ran operations in Britain and France. It was Bazarov, using Dmitrii Bystrolyotov, who recruited the Foreign Office cipher clerk Ernest Oldham, for which he had received praise from Artuzov back in 1931.

By now very much one of the "trusted"—he was one of the most experienced English-speaking illegals and had a talent for bringing on younger operatives—Bazarov was sent to New York in 1934. Backed up by the younger, indecisive Iskhak Akhmerov ("Yung") and the experienced Norman Borodin (son of Mikhail), he operated under cover as Gusev and worked in tandem with the first legal rezident in the United States, Pyotr Guttseit ("Nikolai"). Bazarov proved a great success. Moscow later admitted that he had "recruited some valuable agents with direct access to the State Department" and a "source with connexions to Roosevelt's circle." Even at the time it was known that Bazarov had reached the highest level of tradecraft. Yet, after being recalled to Moscow for a long-requested break, he was arrested in July 1937 and executed on February 21, 1939.[42]

Then came the turn of Akhmerov. In 1939, Beria wanted his rezidentura dissolved and everyone recalled. The fact that Akhmerov had asked permission to marry one of his agents—the pretty Helen Lowry ("Tanya"), a distant relative of U.S. Communist Party secretary Earl Browder—could not have helped. But, in September, Fitin fought to retain both him and his team, and somehow succeeded. Beria, however, took his revenge on Akhmerov when he returned in January 1940; Fitin eventually received his own retribution after the war. Akhmerov was reduced to the lowly rank of probationer in the American section, while his number two, Borodin, was tossed out of the service. Then, for two years, Akhmerov had to work under sustained scrutiny while his creative energies were lost to the illegal rezidentura. Only the German invasion brought his rehabilitation, and that of "Tanya." They settled in Baltimore, within immediate reach of Washington, D.C., where his agents were almost entirely based: in the White House, the State Department, the Treasury, the OSS, and the FBI. Akhmerov set up a textile company as cover and commuted into the capital two or three times a month.[43]

More trouble was to follow. Gaik Ovakimyan ("Gennadii") had arrived in 1934 and earned a PhD in chemistry in New York. In May 1941, as the most recent illegal rezident, posing under cover as an engineering consultant with the Soviet-owned trading company Amtorg, and the leading specialist in industrial intelligence (NTR), he was trapped by the FBI. Surprisingly, no dire consequences followed. On July 23, after the Germans invaded Russia, Roosevelt merely had him deported, displaying a soft touch in handling Soviet espionage that would prove even softer in the years that followed.[44] An honest man, on his return to Moscow, Ovakimyan incautiously expressed doubts about the guilt of those recalled, and Fitin had to intercede for his protection.[45]

Ovakimyan was replaced as head of the legal rezidentura by one of the most experienced rezidents at hand, but someone who was past his prime and ill-suited to American conditions: Zarubin. Having cooled his heels in Moscow on probation after Fitin saved him from execution, Zarubin had been sent out to occupied Poland, in October 1939, for counterintelligence work. His dispiriting mission was to recruit those captured Poles willing to turn coat and work for Moscow. Those he failed to bring on board were transported from the camps and shot by other hands at Katyn or, alternatively, transported to Siberia in April 1940. Now, having spent his entire career in Europe, Zarubin could leave the unsavory work behind him and pack for alien shores across the Atlantic.

On July 18, 1941, a Politburo resolution belatedly delegated to foreign intelligence the key task of ascertaining "the true plans and intentions of our allies especially the United States and England, on the questions of the conduct of the war, relations with the USSR, and the problems of postwar reconstruction."[46] On the night of October 12, 1941, when Zarubin was summoned to hear his duties, he was also informed that Stalin feared that the democracies would forge a separate peace with the Nazis.[47] On November 27, a directive from the Centre to rezidentury in the United States pointed out, "The USA presently plays the leading role in the world politics of capitalist countries. It is therefore very important for us to uncover in good time the political and diplomatic plans and activity of the USA whether in relation to the USSR or in relation to England, Japan, Germany and other countries."[48]

Golos of America

For a long time, the only notable exception to this uneven record of luckless NKVD rezidents was that of a mere agent who became, in the words of one operative, "a virtual station chief in the U.S."[49] The illegal Yakov Golos ("Zvuk") was one of the founders of the U.S. Communist Party. In time, he became a lynchpin for Soviet intelligence. A small man with simian features, close-cut frizzy hair, and a dome of a forehead, Golos always dressed the part of the successful businessman—which, in one sense, he was. On June 10, 1927, he set up for the Party a publicly traded company, World Tourists Inc., as a cover for the surreptitious movement of people and funds across borders; before long, he was obtaining foreign passports for the Russians as well. When the ambitious Browder succeeded to leadership of the Party with Stalinist backing in 1930, the work of the Soviet intelligence agencies and the Party became indistinguishable.

Golos's work for the INO under deep cover began in January 1933. He had been recruited by Abram Eingorn, who was also a pioneering figure in scientific and industrial intelligence (NTR), particularly in the United States.[50] Beginning in 1934, Golos headed the Party's powerful disciplinary body, the Central Control Commission. He also ran one of two secret Party organisations; the other, managed by Hungarian-born József Peter (Sándor Goldberger), had penetrated an array of federal institutions, partly due to help from Harold ("Hal") Ware. The Ware group—which included notable spies, including the diplomat Alger Hiss and his brother Donald—ultimately answered to the Fourth, now under Artuzov's direction. When Ware died in 1935, in an automobile accident in the mountains near Harrisburg, Pennsylvania, his group passed into Golos's hands. As a result, the two secret organisations, though they remained operationally distinct, were now combined under a single head.[51]

Golos was now juggling too many responsibilities, and the increased activity associated with helping volunteers fight in the Spanish

Civil War soon exposed him to FBI attention. In March 1940, he was arrested and sent to trial. The Party told him to plead guilty to a lesser charge, though, as a proud Communist, he saw a guilty plea as humiliating. Since the resulting sentence also deprived him of his American passport, the court inadvertently saved him from liquidation—the fate of his comrades—in Moscow. Even after the trial, Golos continued successfully recruiting. Indeed, he landed a key agent in the form of Harry Dexter White ("Richard"), Secretary of the Treasury Henry Morgenthau's right-hand man.[52]

The Zarubins arrived on American shores in January 1942. The outbreak of war meant that those at the rezidentura in New York were, like those in London, working sixteen- to eighteen-hour days.[53] The pace never diminished. The burden was unduly heavy because Zarubin ("Maksim") had to devote himself to rebuilding a network deserted by useful agents alienated, first, by Stalin's Terror, widely reported in the press at the time; then by the Nazi-Soviet Pact; and, for many the final straw, Trotsky's assassination. From 1939, these walking wounded were not only out of touch but also politically disorientated. At the State Department, Michael Straight, for example, was effectively lost to espionage. The idealist Larry Duggan, later head of the Latin American Division at State, was one of those disaffected. During the Moscow Show Trials, he used to say that he "could not understand how such things were possible," "something was rotten," and so forth. Duggan had to be manipulated back to the cause through a concerted appeal to his conscience.[54] Moreover, after Ovakimyan's arrest, an entirely new set of operatives had to be brought in from the Soviet Union. The intense pressure exerted from Moscow inevitably undermined Zarubin's natural sociability. As a man in a hurry, he possessed an underlying, patronising disdain for the American system of counterintelligence that made him unduly careless.

Despite Golos's continued successes, the Centre remained anxious to make up the depletion of the network since Stalin's bloodbath (1937–1939) and did not consider it sufficient for Zarubin just to take over Golos's assets. Writing to Zarubin on August 28, 1942, Fitin allowed "for the use of the illegal opportunities afforded by Communists (that is to say, opportunities made available by 'Golos'), in support of the rezidentura's work," but he also emphasised that "it would be a mistake to transform these opportunities into the core of [your] work."[55]

The strain ultimately proved too much. Golos had a preexisting heart condition, which deteriorated, no doubt aggravated by the stress of intensive FBI surveillance and the indignity of having his hard-earned agents abruptly snatched from him by the tactless Zarubin. On November 25, 1943, he finally succumbed to cardiac arrest. Stricken with grief and convinced that pressure from Moscow had hastened his demise, his lover, Elizabeth Bentley ("Umnitsa," which means "clever one"), soon betrayed the whole setup to the U.S. authorities.[56] This was an unforeseen disaster leading eventually to the unravelling of the entire network.

Zarubin held on to his position in New York until April 1943, when he was transferred to Washington, D.C., to become the legal rezident. Under cover at the embassy on Sixteenth Street as a workhorse second secretary, carrying a double workload, he nonetheless insisted on doing that which he enjoyed most: recruiting agents personally.[57] His actions were all too reminiscent of the Fourth under Berzin: rather more enthusiasm than due diligence. Devoid of any background in counterintelligence and rudely contemptuous of those he saw as pen pushers lacking in courage, he blurted out cover names—despite the fact that the FBI was at that very moment ratcheting up its surveillance—and was careless using codes and ciphers. These critical failings ultimately proved his undoing. He was clearly past his prime.[58]

The GRU rezident Sergeev was certainly in his prime, though Moscow did not always appreciate the fact. He recruited at the highest level, greatly aided by Russia's forced entry into the war and Roosevelt's decision to join in the European conflict after Japan bombed Pearl Harbor on December 7, 1941. With two assistants, by the end of the war he had penetrated seventy institutions, including the intelligence services and other government departments, committees, and subcommittees.[59]

Leonid Kvasnikov and the Bomb

Zarubin's arrival in New York was followed over a year later by that of a new deputy rezident for scientific and technical espionage, Leonid Kvasnikov ("Anton"). It was Stalin's unalterable conviction that once the war was over, his allies would inevitably become his future adversaries. "We are now with one faction against another; and in the future we will also be against this faction of capitalists," he said.[60] Their secrets had to become his secrets. An immense and high-risk espionage campaign was launched to uncover the formulae for the weapon of the future, the atomic bomb, first in Britain and then in the United States and Canada. As became apparent in decryption, a wide gap was opening in science that threatened to be compounded by weaknesses in technology. Russia was severely overstretched. As a consequence, military-industrial intelligence, hitherto something of a lucrative sideline of interest only to the Fourth, was finally coming into its own as equally valuable to political intelligence. It was here that Kvasnikov, known affectionately by members of his department as Uncle Kvas, was to make a signal contribution.[61]

Kvasnikov, like Zarubin, was a startling example of rapid social mobility. Born on June 2, 1905, into the family of a railway worker at a small station in Tula, he began his career as an unskilled labourer before training as an engine driver, a job that led almost immediately to further education as a chemical engineer and then later to graduate work in Moscow. As a mere research student in 1938, he was hired by a special investigative committee inspecting armaments plants for the Commissariat of the Defence Industry. In September he was drafted into ShON for training in foreign intelligence. After a very brief spell in the American section, at what had now become the fifth department of the GUGB, he found his calling, at the early age of thirty-four, as a senior operative in the section on scientific-technical intelligence.

Kvasnikov's first contact with the enemy came after the Soviet-German Treaty of Friendship of September 28, 1939. His intelligence missions to Germany and German-occupied Poland were masked by his role working for a committee under Soviet-German auspices tasked with managing the "refugee problem." Then, in February 1941, Kvasnikov was appointed head of the NTR section at the GUGB. Up to date on the latest developments in science, he must have been aware of recent speculation, widespread in the American press, concerning the feasibility of atomic weapons. Soviet intelligence was, in particular, alarmed to learn that Germany was working on a "super bomb" that would employ atomic energy. News of Albert Einstein's letter to Roosevelt on October 11, 1939, warning of German progress and Roosevelt's positive response, confirmed the need for countermeasures.

Kvasnikov took the initiative. On the eve of the German invasion, he despatched a circular to a series of rezidentury: London, New York,

Berlin, Stockholm, and Tokyo. The circular recommended penetration of the leading institutions in each foreign country researching nuclear physics. This was terra incognita to Soviet operatives. Nonetheless, information soon indicated that Kvasnikov's instincts had not led him astray. London was crucial. Here, the distinguished German-Jewish economist Jürgen Kuczynski ("Karo") played a significant role.

Leader of German Communists in Britain, Kuczynski was brother to Ursula ("Sonya"), an officer in Soviet military intelligence. Jürgen, who mixed in British socialist circles, had a code name and was therefore classed as an asset, but was never formally an officer in secret intelligence. Since 1936 he had been a regular visitor to the Soviet embassy in London. In August 1941 he told Ambassador Ivan Maisky of a conversation with the German Communist and physicist Klaus Fuchs in which Fuchs outlined his research in atomic physics at Birmingham University under Rudolf Peierls.[62]

Rumour had it that Maisky did not like Gorskii, the most obvious person to consult. So he passed the information instead to a military-intelligence officer, secretary to military attaché Ivan Sklyarov ("Briand"), Simyon Kremer ("Aleksandr," "Sergei," "Barch"). Kremer was a fellow Jew from Gomel and a veteran of the civil war who, as a cavalry officer, had joined the Fourth in September 1936. In January 1937 he was sent to London. On August 8, 1941, Kremer and Fuchs met.[63] Two days later, the attaché Sklyarov cabled the director, Ivan Il'ichyov, about Fuchs and briefly explained what the proposed weapon could do: "The contact gave a short briefing on the principles behind the use of uranium for these aims. Just 1% of the energy of a 10 kilogram uranium bomb would produce an explosion equivalent to 1000 tons of dynamite. I will send the text [of the briefing] at the earliest opportunity."[64]

Meanwhile, in September 1941, sensational news came in from London via Gorskii from Cairncross—who had wormed his way in as Lord Hankey's private secretary not only by his outstanding intelligence but also by befriending Hankey's son and then pretending to be a fellow vegetarian. The Uranium Committee, technically headed by the physicist Professor George Thomson of Imperial College, London, but chaired by Hankey, had recommended construction of an atomic bomb in cooperation with the Americans. On October 3, Gorskii reported that Cairncross had obtained a copy of Hankey's memorandum presented to the war minister. Gorskii handed it to Barkovskii, who had not seen anything of this kind before: "You know, this is scientific terminology of one kind or another. You are our engineer . . ." Sixty pages of text required translation. "Of course, I did not understand any of it," Barkovskii recalled. "Somehow I made sense of it with the help of a dictionary." Still, he had no understanding as to how important it was.[65] It was nonetheless despatched.[66]

In Moscow, Kvasnikov pressed ahead. The report was rapidly evaluated by colleagues in the Special Department of Operational Technology. On October 10, 1941, its head, Kravchenko, informed Beria of his conclusions: the report "is worthy of undoubted interest as evidence of substantial work conducted in England in the sphere of atomic energy for military ends."[67] Beria, however, was unmoved. Then, on November 24, the New York rezidentura telegraphed that American scientists were in London working on the construction of explosive material of massive destructive power.[68] London confirmed the presence of three American professors of physics, but could not explain why they were there.[69] The British and the Americans had in fact agreed to collaborate, as the Russians soon discovered. In March 1942, Kvasnikov reported to Stalin "On the intensive scientific research work for the creation of an atomic bomb carried out in England, the USA, Germany and France." The report, for Beria's signature, recommended that the Soviet Union follow suit with the aid of the NKVD's espionage.

Beria continued to hold out, however. He had to be outflanked. The key issue was what the main enemy, Germany, was doing. It was at this point that the GRU intervened. A German staff officer taken prisoner was found to have a pocketbook containing mysterious formulae. An officer who specialised in explosives, Ilya Starinov, guessed that the formulae had something to do with ordnance and sent it to Moscow. There, the State Defence Committee staff discovered that the hieroglyphs concerned a superbomb, perhaps atomic.[70] On September 28, 1942, atomic physicists were called in for a session of the committee chaired by Stalin. It was only after this that the critical decision was taken, on October 6, to gather further information through espionage, the Russians having been blocked a full seven months by Beria's ignorance and innate caution.

On December 22 an update on the research came in from London, but no equivalent was forthcoming for the United States, as a result of the tight cordon sanitaire enclosing the scientists in the desert at Los Alamos, New Mexico. Kvasnikov now managed to secure his own posting to the United States, where production was to be concentrated. The atomic espionage effort there was code-named "Enormoz." Kvasnikov was to head scientific and technical intelligence in New York. He left in mid-January 1943.

By now, Fuchs ("Otto," "Charles"), too, had come into his own. In May 1942 he handed over to Kremer of the GRU 155 pages of detail on the British atomic project. The quantity proved a burden, however. On May 25, Moscow instructed Sklyarev to despatch material by radio. Atomic espionage was now a going concern. However, it risked being jeopardised by MI5's sudden awareness of GRU networks penetrating War Office secrets. MI5 had, until then, been prepared, albeit reluctantly, to accept continued employment of Communists on war work, but Communists were systematically diverted to work on blue-sky projects such as atomic weapons in place of practical programs of immediate importance, and therefore highly sensitive, such as radar.

It was in May 1942 that the British authorities were once again alerted that the British Communist Party (CPGB) was involved in espionage. They were aware that such links had been officially discouraged since Berzin's day but breached subsequently. What they did not know was that for the GRU, the practice had never ceased. They may also have been aware of bad relations between the CPGB general secretary, Harry Pollitt, and the Party's national organiser, Douglas Springhall. Kremer reported that "Pollitt scolded Springhall for his links with me and for helping me with certain information."[71] Springhall was ordered "not to give us [Kremer] any people or material." In these circumstances the GRU asked Comintern to choose a couple of Party officials "for liaison with us and to select people to work on and transmit material."[72]

As a result of arresting Oliver Green, a secret Party member running a small network spying on British military secrets, MI5 learned of other Party activists engaged in military espionage. Springhall was among them. News of this important development came from Soviet agents in MI5, but the facts were only belatedly reported by Fitin to the Comintern chief Georgi Dimitrov in mid-April 1943.[73]

On June 16, Olive Sheehan, cadre leader for the Communist group in the Air Ministry, was arrested for espionage. She had asked her flatmate to pass on an envelope to a visitor, Springhall. The envelope was opened before Springhall saw it, and the contents were reported to MI5. Springhall was arrested the following day.[74] Pollitt had had enough. Springhall was promptly expelled from the Party.

Kremer, too, was in imminent danger of being exposed. Confusion and no small degree of friction arose with the rival service, the NKGB. This resulted from the fact that, not knowing what his counterparts at the GRU were up to, Gorskii had heard about Fuchs only from others, and sought to recruit him through Jürgen Kuczynski. It looked very much like a takeover. An almighty row broke out. In disgust, Kremer requested repatriation to fight on the front. In an evident attempt to calm tempers, the request was granted. Eventually such problems, which also arose in the United States, were solved by bringing all atomic espionage under one roof: that of the NKGB.

Meanwhile, Ursula ("Sonya"), despite having a babe in arms, assumed responsibility for Fuchs and met him regularly two to three times a month.[75] Kremer's replacement was the Ukrainian Nikolai Aptekar' ("Sergei," "Iris"). A tough-looking man—thick-set and balding, with a big nose and big ears—who clearly could take care of himself in a fight, Aptekar' worked officially as the chauffeur and secretary to the air attaché at the Soviet embassy.[76] He continued working through "Sonya" for access to Fuchs's documentation until the British team eventually left for the United States in August 1943.

Fuchs was to be met and indoctrinated by "Semyon Semyonov." Born Aba Taubman to a poor Jewish family in Odessa, Semyonov was brought up in an orphanage. After a cursory spell in secondary school, he was apprenticed to a local rope factory, where his natural talents, though wasted, were evidently soon spotted by others. Small and chubby, with a big nose, a large sensuous mouth, and round black eyes set below a receding hairline, he was also a veritable "ball of mercury"—endlessly curious, unthreatening, invariably convivial, and possessed of a wicked sense of humour.[77]

He was sufficiently gifted to become a scientist and was thus sent, accompanied by his immediate family, to take a postgraduate degree at MIT, from which he graduated in 1940.[78] Although he was forbidden from conducting operations while on cultural exchange in Boston, Semyonov proved impossible to rein in entirely. He became active in 1940 under the self-selected nom de guerre "Mark Twain"—after his favourite author. Against the odds, he succeeded in obtaining a sample of pure penicillin, as requested by Fitin in 1942, and innumerable specifications for aircraft and related armaments. The problem was that Semyonov's indefatigable charm eventually led to his undoing. In November 1943 the Centre advised the rezident Zarubin of the arrival of scientists from Britain working on the atomic bomb, among whom was Fuchs, who would turn out to be critical. He arrived the following month. When, finally, Fuchs's plane reached Los Angeles en route to Albuquerque, Semyonov had to call off the meeting, as his uninhibited behaviour and lack of tradecraft led to his being followed by the FBI and he was utterly unable to shake his tail. His place had to be taken by the recent arrivals Anatolii Yatskov ("Aleksei"), a talented scientific and technical intelligence probationer, and the dullard radio operator Aleksandr' Feklisov ("Kalistrat"). Contact was made through the New York rezidentura in February 1944. At the beginning of June, Fuchs handed over the details of the bomb's construction and told of the test forthcoming in July.[79]

The switch to handling Fuchs through the NKGB rather than the GRU (*gereushniki*) was initiated by Merkulov with the agreement of Il'ichyov, who effectively took charge of the GRU on August 28, 1942. Il'ichyov was a new broom. He had considerable talent and spoke nearly flawless English as well as French and German,[80] but his character left something to be desired. He had early on made an unpleasant name for himself denouncing others as traitors, doubtless on the principle that it was best to denounce them before they denounced you. Vitalii Nikol'skii, who joined the directorate at the same time as Il'ichyov, recalls, "He looked on all old employees of intelligence as potential 'enemies of the people,' and the agent network created by them as wholly hostile and therefore subject to liquidation."[81]

When Stalin considered the issue of efficiency in the management of secret intelligence, it became obvious that if both agencies, civilian and military, handled atomic matters, the result would be confusion. It was therefore decided that the GRU was, in principle, to concentrate its energies on the larger strategic issues connected with the war, and not on the bomb. In practice, however, controlling operatives in the field thousands of miles away was no easy matter. The illegal rezident of the NKGB in New York, Artur Adams ("Akhil"), in gathering intelligence on atomic secrets, broke the rules when, having unexpectedly encountered the GRU's legal rezident, Pavel Melkishev ("Molière"), in June 1944, he handed over atomic documents for despatch by diplomatic post, including 985 negatives. This clearly breached the long-standing rule that the two intelligence agencies had to keep a healthy distance from each other in the field to avoid the danger of compromising both if one were already under observation. A second such meeting, where he handed over 3,869 pages of material, was then monitored by the FBI. A trace was put on Adams, and before long he had to flee across the border.[82]

In retrospect, Russian atomic espionage was an outstanding success. It was also a close race against time. As late as November 1944, Fitin complained that "Despite the USA's participation in scientific work on the problem of 'Enormoz,' the large number of scientific organisations and employees, the bulk of whom are known to us through agent information, work cultivating them has been weak; thus the greater part of information we have on this country comes not from the rezidentura in the United States but from the rezidentura in England."[83]

The new NKGB rezident in London was a great success, but he felt unappreciated; his resources were never sufficient to the tasks required, and he was overburdened by pressure from the Foreign Commissariat to carry the full load of diplomatic work. At the end of 1943, Fitin told Kukin that eight more operatives were on their way. By then, however, the rezident had been struck down by ulcers and confined to bed. He begged Fitin to intercede with Deputy Commissar Andrei Vyshinsky to relieve him of the diplomatic burden (a lot of committee sitting, and Kukin could not even sit up). Instead the reply came that he should use his diplomatic role more effectively for intelligence purposes and provide detailed reports on all his operatives.

Barely containing his exasperation, Kukin dictated a letter from his bed. He pointed out that it was difficult in the face of the V-1 bombardment even to get out to see agents, and that hopes extravagantly held in Moscow of obtaining many more could be dashed: "In spite of the noticeable growth in the sympathies of ordinary people toward the Soviet Union in connexion with the success of our liberation mission in Europe, operational contacts in government and political circles in general have become much more difficult. The fact is that in the top echelons of English society [the favoured Soviet target] the attitude of suspicion towards the USSR is growing as a result of its great influence in

Europe."[84] In the past year, he reminded Fitin, "we have recruited twenty agents; contacts have been established with six of them. High dividends have come in from the 'Cambridge Five.' The rezidentura has regularly obtained for the Centre military, political, economic, and scientific information, especially on the uranium problem."[85]

Fitin ultimately backed his stricken rezident. He wrote that Kukin "managed not only to sustain the high level of operational work achieved but also to guarantee the delivery of important documentary material on all questions of interest to the Centre. From the London rezidentura we have continually received and are now receiving the most valuable political intelligence information, and also data on work carried out in Great Britain on the creation of the atomic bomb. The rezidentura led by Kukin has regularly informed our government about the postwar plans of England and the USA in relation to the order in Europe after the peace."

Written in February 1945, this assessment marked the highest point of intelligence operations in Britain. The Cambridge Five had yielded extraordinary results.

6. POSTWAR ADVANTAGE

By late 1944, Stalin had become convinced that the United States would supplant Britain as the leading capitalist power, just as Trotsky had predicted in the 1920s.[1] Acting on this correct but still controversial assumption, he sought to preempt the underpinning of American power and influence in Europe even before the end of the war.

He did this by oppressing the countries of Eastern Europe and—when this aroused growing resistance from the United States—threatening the security of Western Europe from within by driving the burgeoning Communist Parties of France and Italy to the verge of insurrection. Simultaneously, Moscow sustained a massive military capability in the Russian zone of Germany. The combination of these multiple threats collided with American expectations and ambitions and led to the Cold War between the Soviet Union and the democracies.[2]

The Balkans were a crucial sphere of influence for the Russians. Soviet-style régimes were installed in Bulgaria and Romania. SMERSH was summoned to remove all those on Stalin's blacklist for destinations unknown. Hungary lay in the firing line, literally, as the Russians encircled Budapest at the end of December 1944.

Prompted by the German occupation that began in mid-March of that year, the Americans had been active in Budapest anticipating the arrival of Soviet troops; their aim was to forestall a Hungarian surrender to the Russians. On July 9, 1944, the young and enthusiastically pro-American Raoul Wallenberg arrived to take up the post of second secretary at the Swedish diplomatic mission in Budapest. He had been specifically picked out by the U.S. authorities to avert the mass deportation and extinction of Jews by the Nazis. This he accomplished with tremendous skill. The problem for Stalin was that the line between the OSS and the organisation Wallenberg represented, the War Refugee Board, was blurred by the dual identity of the man in Stockholm who had selected him: Iver Olsen was employed by both in Sweden.[3]

For the Allies, the Communist occupation of Yugoslavia and the still-uncertain fate of Italy prompted the United States to keep one step ahead of the Red Army's entry into Austria, a high priority. Earlier, the OSS had run operations designed to secure the surrender of Hungary to Anglo-American forces, but they had failed.[4] Wallenberg appears to have filled more than one role, too, in the sense that he was also working *with* the OSS if not *for* it, an asset if not an agent. In October 1944, for example, Wallenberg made a covert trip back to Stockholm while secret negotiations concerning a separate peace were taking place with Hungary's Horthy régime.[5]

Without questioning his humanitarian commitment, the fact that Raoul was close to the minister at the Hungarian embassy in Stockholm and that two uncles, Jacob and Marcus, were variously identified with attempts to mediate between Britain (Marcus) and Germany (Jacob) meant that he was not as innocent as he appeared. The Wallenberg business empire was destined to gain no matter who won the war (except the Russians). It cannot have helped Wallenberg's case that, in an instruction issued to newspaper editors in Germany, the head of the SS, Heinrich Himmler, insisted that the Wallenbergs "have nothing at all to do with Jews"; they were "anti-Bolshevik" and they always behaved "very decently in economic negotiations with Germany."[6]

The NKGB had informers in Budapest. Among others, Count Golenishchev-Kutuzov-Tolstoi (sometimes Tolstoi-Kutuzov) had escaped the Bolshevik revolution with his life, but thereafter worked for the Cheka and its successors across Europe. In Budapest, he ran a Swedish Red Cross hospital for foreigners and managed a department for the Swedish embassy, looking after the interests of Soviet prisoners of war. He therefore knew Wallenberg well. On November 16 the Swedes commissioned him to establish and maintain contacts with the Red

Army. Before long, Kutuzov-Tolstoi had miraculously transformed himself into assistant to the head of the Soviet military commandatura while his wife, a Belgian contessa, became head of a commandatura department for liaison with foreign citizens and a language teacher to the chief of staff of the Allied commission, General Vladimir Sviridov.[7]

On January 14, 1945, Wallenberg and his driver were taken into custody as a result of his request to see the Soviet officer commanding. Since he was a relatively junior diplomat at the legation, the Russians would inevitably have assumed that Wallenberg was a senior intelligence operative under official cover, as a Russian would have been had he made such an unorthodox request. Orders came through to bring him in but, in the meantime, to forestall any contact between Wallenberg and the outside world. He was taken to see the divisional commander, to whom he delivered a long discourse on his work and the need to save the Jews in the ghetto. This was, after all, a man who had succeeded in saving tens of thousands from the extermination camps. But his humanitarianism fell on deaf ears. Stalin had already shown himself to be indifferent to the fate of the Jews.[8] He preferred to let the Jewish problem undermine Britain's unsustainable position in Palestine.[9] Helping Jews stay in Europe did not fit into the larger picture. Wallenberg was, unknowingly, in the way.

Three days after he was taken, orders came through from Deputy Commissar for Defence Marshal Nikolai Bulganin to arrest Wallenberg and hand him over to SMERSH. This took place on January 19. Subsequently, he was escorted from the command headquarters to Moscow, where he arrived on February 6. The first interrogation took place at the Lubyanka two days later, where Wallenberg was told, disconcertingly, that they knew him well. He was then confronted with an accusation of espionage. After interrogation, he was moved to another internal prison, at Lefortovo, for some months, before being returned to the Lubyanka in 1946.

The Soviet Foreign Ministry, as it was now named, was in receipt of multiple pressing enquiries from Sweden. It had asked SMERSH and the MGB (successor to the GUGB/NKGB) repeatedly whether they knew anything. The inexperienced Swedish ambassador, Staffan Söderblom, who as head of the political department was responsible for the pro-German line in Swedish diplomacy in 1940–1942, now seemed to see it as his job to appease the Russians. Perhaps this was an attempt to compensate. In any event, he failed to be forthright.[10] When he went to see Stalin on June 15, 1946, the general secretary implausibly pretended never to have heard the name Wallenberg and to know nothing about his disappearance.

In February 1947, Lieutenant General Fyodotov, the man who had bugged the German military attaché in 1941, oversaw foreign intelligence. He told the Foreign Ministry that Wallenberg was in the hands of the MGB. There the key post of deputy minister was held by Andrei Vyshinsky, formerly a notorious prosecutor of revolutionaries on behalf of the provisional government in 1917 and, later, an even more notorious prosecutor of former revolutionaries at Stalin's Show Trials of the 1930s. He wrote, "In so far as the Wallenberg case up to the present time continues to stand still, I must ask you to oblige Comrade Abakumov to present a report on the essence of the case and proposals for its liquidation." In the language of the day the term *liquidation* was superfluous unless Vyshinsky intended to imply that Wallenberg be executed. On May 18, Molotov wrote on the same memorandum: "Comrade Abakumov. I beg you to report back to me."[11]

But Vyshinsky's hint had had its intended effect. The Soviet embassy in Stockholm received a petition from a number of organisations on July 15. Wallenberg died not long thereafter, on July 17, 1947: the cause of death, heart failure, was most unlikely for a strong man in his mid-thirties without the administration of something sufficiently toxic to help him on his way.[12] Molotov was informed of this that same day by Viktor Abakumov in a personal letter drafted by the third main directorate.[13] These matters were kept in the strictest secrecy.

What Wallenberg may or may not have done in the last phase of the war was irrelevant. Stalin just wanted him out of the way as the Soviet occupation of Hungary proceeded apace, with SMERSH disposing of all potential opponents as the Red Army progressed. Having arrested Wallenberg on Stalin's instructions without knowing exactly what was to be done with him—waiting on orders that never came and not wanting to ask—Abakumov was not in a position to right the wrong that had been done. Treating a foreign diplomat just like any Soviet citizen or prisoner of war was potentially disastrous. Stalin's use of servile but inadequate men such as Abakumov in the intelligence services proved just as serious a matter after the war as it had been on the eve of war. Militarily, the Soviet Union was infinitely more powerful than it had been, but the price to be paid for casually disregarding international norms was going to be high.

Abakumov in Charge

Nowhere was the Cold War fought so sharply or extensively as at the level of secret intelligence. But the several branches in the Soviet Union (counterintelligence, foreign intelligence, military intelligence, and communications intelligence) had grown unevenly under the tremendous impact of a devastating war for survival.

Counterintelligence was enhanced immeasurably given Stalin's postwar priority of isolating the population from Western influence and contact. Foreign intelligence, with the crucial exception of atomic espionage, lived off the fat largely accumulated before the war. The GRU had, like counterintelligence, developed formidably under the exigencies of war, but it suffered from Stalin's inveterate suspicion of the military and its potential as a Napoleonic alternative to the police state—as the demotion of Marshal Georgii Zhukov proved in July 1946.

All these capabilities emerged as a result of an order of priorities unknown in the West. In other words, the Cold War began with asymmetrical capabilities between the two sides. The unanswered question was whether, overall, the asymmetries would prove more helpful to one side or the other.

Initially, the agents recruited abroad who had proven themselves loyal through the latter half of the war were now trusted to supply everything needed to outwit London and Washington. This, along with a sufficient measure of American naïveté in the White House and a seemingly inescapable class bias in British counterintelligence, inevitably encouraged Stalin to believe that it did not matter much who ran foreign operations, his agents would more or less be able to take care of themselves. There also lurked a hidden and damaging assumption emerging from the deep self-satisfaction of having won the war against the worst odds: it was all the easier to assume that the greater the degree of power, the less the need for vital intelligence. Thus the Kremlin's lethal combination of foreign intelligence assets and rigorous counterintelligence operations provided fertile ground for dangerous complacency over the longer term.

This is obvious from the reshuffling of key appointments: Stalin, as in 1938–1939, casually discarded experienced professionals for novices, on the assumption that he had time to spare. Abakumov, a good-looking man with ugly ambitions and a former head of SMERSH, had been appointed minister of state security on May 7, 1946. He was a very efficient operative, but had been promoted, on Peter's principle, to his level of incompetence. This appointment represented a serious setback for Beria, whose former protégé was now striking out on his own. It had damaging implications for foreign operations, just when they had settled down following the urgency of war, which had all too briefly forced common sense into decision making.

The minister, Merkulov, was rightly viewed as soft and too much Beria's lapdog, but he was at least intelligent, and he saw his role as guiding Beria without seeming to do so. He recalled that Abakumov was "a no less ambitious and imperious person than Beria, only more stupid than he was."[14] This was borne out by Abakumov's sudden, unexpected, and ultimately disastrous removal of Fitin as head of the First Directorate in December 1946. Thereafter, the friendless Fitin was progressively pushed down the ladder until, finally, in 1951, with Beria back at the top, the ladder, along with his pension in austerity Russia, was yanked out from under him.[15] The habit so evident in the late thirties of rewarding talent with ignominy, if not execution, looked to continue.

Merkulov's place was suddenly assumed by Pyotr Kubatkin, possibly at the recommendation of Andrei Zhdanov, Leningrad Party secretary and Stalin's new favourite. Kubatkin had also worked with Abakumov. He was a courageous man of principle and nobly tried to refuse the job, but was prevailed upon to accept.[16] His only hope in this new situation, given his lack of experience, was to draft those he had worked with in Leningrad. These included Alexei Krokhin, who had briefly been attached to the British Army on the Rhine, and Andrei Krasavin, later (1971) the head of radio-electronic intelligence. They remained in their posts when Kubatkin walked out only three months later. Lieutenant General Fyodotov from counterintelligence was regarded as a safe pair of hands. He took Kubatkin's place. Kubatkin eventually received retribution from Abakumov: he was executed on October 2, 1950, after a twenty-minute hearing.

Yet Stalin's indifference to talent led to no immediate adverse consequences. The reasons were simple. The White House took a less-than-professional attitude towards secret intelligence and counterespionage until the discovery of Soviet atomic espionage and hearings held by the House Un-American Activities Committee brought the issue dramatically to the public. As for Whitehall, if anything, it was more casual than the White House with respect to Soviet espionage. The resilient public image of the Russians defending Stalingrad to the last man made it hard to grasp the truth of Stalin's ambitions.

The worm was turning, however, and more rapidly than at first appeared. No sooner had the war in the Pacific ended with the dropping of the atomic bombs on Japan early in August 1945 than the first significant breach was made in the wall of Soviet secrecy. News of spying operations in the United States would soon expose Russia's atomic espionage. On September 15, Igor Gouzenko, the GRU cipher clerk at the Soviet embassy in Ottawa, defected.

Gouzenko had worked under a hopelessly ineffective military attaché named Nikolai Zabotin ("Grant"). Zabotin was supposedly assisted by three others—Colonel Pyotr Motinov, Major Aleksandr Rogov (later deputy director of the GRU), and Major Vsevolod Sokolov—all of whom failed him, though the disaster never prevented all three from eventually reaching the rank of major general. Gouzenko had slyly obtained a private apartment, in defiance of all the rules, because his small child cried most of the night; Zabotin's wife, living next door, could not bear the noise. Gouzenko also had the key to the embassy safe, and since the safe contained details of agents and their reporting, he was fully informed. Warned about Gouzenko, the head of the GRU, Fyodor Kuznetsov, ordered his recall. But the fact that Gouzenko had been the one to decipher this communication in August 1945 made this impossible.[17] It could not have been worse for the Russians: Gouzenko had a phenomenal memory for names.[18]

The shock of Gouzenko's defection was felt most strongly at 1125 Sixteenth Street, the Soviet embassy in the heart of Washington, D.C. Here the atmosphere was already polluted by the untimely arrival of a new and cantankerous ambassador, Nikolai Novikov, who replaced the more emollient Andrei Gromyko. It was evident that Gromyko and Novikov "simply hated one another." To say that Novikov was hard to get on with is an understatement. Indeed, he was actually feared. The reasons for this were not entirely a matter of bad character. The embassy was understaffed. It lacked two counsellors, two first secretaries, some second and third secretaries, and an attaché. There was no letup in the pressure of work. This painful squeeze was exacerbated by the fact that the embassy was split top to bottom between Novikov people and Gromyko people.

Gorskii's successor as rezident, Grigorii Dolbin, arrived in March 1946. He was also Novikov's first assistant and, not accidentally, gave the ambassador the code name "Wolf." Indeed, Novikov treated his personnel so badly that, on the former's arrival, Dolbin became seriously worried at the alarming prospect that Novikov's ill treatment of his subordinates might result in defections—a fear that had become ever more real since Gouzenko's disappearance in Ottawa. "The situation in the USA is now such that one cannot exclude the possibility that the most unstable members of the [Soviet] colony, having been maltreated from the top, being intimidated by threats, might take decisions that are most undesirable for us. The Americans well understand, I believe; they also know the character of our boss. Not for nothing do they use every fact of the failure to return to put pressure on our most unstable elements." The Canadian prime minister, for instance, had made much of the assertion that Gouzenko had experienced "free" elections and the fact that the Americans and Canadians had no defectors. On the contrary: "they make them [Soviet defectors] popular figures, making it easier for the unstable who have something in their past or are currently being bullied, to decide not to return to the Motherland." The "Canadian events followed by events in the USA" led to a frenzy of "spy mania," whipped up by the press, that terrified middle America. Meanwhile, the FBI had installed listening devices in the homes and cars of Soviet diplomats.[19]

Tension was mounting. The Americans kept digging up the road outside the embassy, apparently laying large quantities of cable. Dolbin suspected they were creating a massive eavesdropping system. In the prevailing atmosphere of suspicion, he found it impossible to make American acquaintances, and he needed more men. Early in August, Dolbin wrote, "I ask for only one thing: send me people. Without people the work does not improve. The quantity of information does not grow. The quality does not get better. All that increases are remarks to the effect that 'such a situation cannot be tolerated.'" The Centre responded to Dolbin's request with some frustration: "Very serious operational considerations are also the reason why the majority of the operatives of your office have been recalled home."[20]

As soon as the Gouzenko affair became public knowledge, in late 1945, Moscow began to pull in its horns. In Britain, however, it was still business as usual. The rezident, Nikolai Rodin ("Korovin"), proudly asserted that no country in the world had the kind of network Moscow had created in London; moreover, the web was woven from conviction, not payment for services rendered. The Russians continued to draw upon Burgess, who worked as secretary to the more junior minister at the Foreign Office, Hector McNeil, a clever but lazy man who allowed Burgess access to everything; Philby, who finally made headlong progress up the ladder at MI6; and Maclean, whose effortless elevation through the Foreign Office was never jeopardised by the fact that he often drank excessively to calm his nerves.

A new threat arose, however, this time directly jeopardising the Cambridge Five. The NKGB officer Colonel Konstantin Volkov, who had worked in the British department, tried in August 1945 to defect as vice-consul in Istanbul. He spoke of nine agents in London, one of whom was "head of a section of the British counter-espionage directorate." This could not have referred to Philby, who headed foreign counterintelligence at MI6. However, Volkov also claimed Moscow had two agents within the Foreign Office—Burgess and Maclean, most probably—and seven within British intelligence. (If Blunt is counted out, who were the others?)[21]

When the news came in to Philby, he told the rezidentura, which in turn notified Moscow. In Istanbul, Mikhail Baturin, the rezident, had to act quickly. Whether Volkov fell ill as a result of Baturin's intervention is not clear, but Volkov's sudden sickness warranted the speedy despatch of a doctor from Moscow. Accompanying him on the flight was Andrei Otroshchenko, head of the Near and Middle East department of the NKGB's First Main Directorate. The doctor persuaded Volkov that he needed to be evacuated back home. It was only once he entered the aircraft and it was too late that Volkov recognised Otroshchenko and the fact that he had been exposed.[22] The Cambridge Five were safe—for now.

Blunt had moved to care for the royal collection at Buckingham Palace, thereby advancing his career as a historian of art, which Moscow mistakenly supposed would give him access to King George VI and his secrets. Meanwhile, Cairncross transferred to the Treasury with Fitin's approval on June 25, 1945. Along with the other spies, he was put on ice for nearly two years after Gouzenko defected that September. Moscow resumed contact only in March 1947, by which time all hope of a postwar settlement had irretrievably broken down.

Cairncross's position improved when Cripps became chancellor of the exchequer, and by July 1948, code-named "Karel," he was once more passing on secrets, now relating to the financing of the armed forces.[23] His access to significant material vastly expanded with the outbreak of the war in Korea and the formation of a standing alliance, the North Atlantic Treaty Organization (NATO), with an operational command at Rocquencourt, just outside Paris, in July 1950. At the Treasury, Cairncross gained sudden access to vital details on the panic funding of new defence expenditure and the Allied plans that underlay them.[24] Meanwhile, Burgess and Maclean had enabled Stalin to outwit his erstwhile allies in negotiations at a succession of futile conferences of foreign ministers and at the Paris conference on the European Recovery Plan in 1947; as at Yalta, he had advance notice of the other side's position papers.[25]

In the United States, agents had also been kept on hold, and contact was not properly resumed until September 1947. Work then had to be taken up from scratch.[26] Moscow was not, however, entirely unresponsive to pleas for more resources from the overworked rezidentury. Washington received a complement of six in 1948, but there was more to do: a number of further betrayals then meant that almost half the U.S. network, sixty-two agents in total, had been exposed. The pressure from the Centre did not ease: "the rezidentury in the USA in 1948 has fundamentally not recruited one agent in U.S. institutions of basic political interest to us. Moreover, neither rezidentura has come up with future plans for further work with them."[27] Yet it made no difference to results. Finding experienced operatives who were also immune to American importuning was not easy. The fact that the rezident in New York, "Stepan," had to be recalled because he appeared about to defect, showed how serious was the crisis in American operations. On December 23, 1949, Gorskii, now back in the United States, reported that "up to mid-1949" the rezidentura had "effectively ceased work of any kind trying to find recruiters and new agents."[28]

The Main Enemy Must Nonetheless
Be Doing Something Right

The Americans were moving slowly but surely towards the creation of the Central Intelligence Agency (CIA). Keeping pace, on February 2, 1947, the MGB issued a decree "On the reinforcement of counter-intelligence work in the struggle with agents from the American and English intelligence services." At last, on February 26, 1947, the long-delayed provision for the creation of CIA went to Congress. Just four days later, Stalin had the Council of Ministers respond with a resolution creating the Committee of Information (KI) to run both the MGB First Directorate and the GRU. The KI was subordinate to Molotov, effectively run by his deputy, Vyshinsky. Within it, the Foreign Department of the MGB Fifth Directorate (codes and ciphers) was joined to the GRU equivalent but headed by its former chief at the MGB, Alexei Schyokoldin, inevitably irritating the General Staff. The whole enterprise was quartered in two former Comintern buildings at Rostokino with a number of branches at points across the city, including Gogolevskii Bul'var, parallel to Znamensky Pereulok, where military intelligence was still sited, in the Arbat.

The real work of taming this new bureaucratic mastodon fell to Fyodotov, who had been overseeing MGB foreign intelligence since September 7, 1946. A quiet man, who sported light metallic spectacles that gave him the look of the harmless professor, Fyodotov was reputed to be a "talented analyst and organiser" entirely suited to the purposes of centralising control, improving the selection of personnel, and allocating tasks to rezidentury around the globe. But he was insufficiently competent, a fact all too evident to his subordinates.[29]

The experiment with intelligence unification did not have a promising start, and it came at the worst possible time. In too many rezidentury, foreign operations were basically frozen in place. Furthermore, the foolhardy attempt to place both civilian foreign intelligence and military intelligence under one roof was beyond Fyodotov's abilities. Not only was the focus of the two agencies different but so, too, were their working practices.

Whereas the MGB tended to recruit agents one by one independently, the GRU created organic networks: an agent once recruited then set about recruiting friends from various backgrounds, rather in the manner of the Ware group in the United States. This was also how Burgess had wished to function within the NKVD. Yet it was a practice disapproved of by the rezident, who vetoed any direct approaches, and seen as an unsophisticated and a risky procedure limited to exceptional circumstances. Since Artuzov's time, recruitment had to be approved in advance by the Centre. The GRU, on the other hand, had no problems with local initiative. This was the way things had always been done. Moreover, the GRU's focus was explicitly on war fighting rather than on diplomatic priorities.

This bureaucratic rearrangement did not bode well for the future while Moscow was increasingly under siege. London and Washington, which had refused to recognise Soviet possession of Latvia, Estonia, and Lithuania, were both now backing resistance movements by Baltic nationalists. Although there had been raids into the Baltic states by armed groups after the end of hostilities in 1945, these were cut short by the Russians, with some success, until the autumn of 1946, when smaller-scale but more focused attacks were launched against the lives of Soviet officials. In November 1946, for instance, MI6 sent in a group of six, courtesy of the Estonian Committee in London, to set up a centre for Estonian nationalists. The Americans simultaneously despatched a group of agents for the purpose of espionage.[30] Raids across the Baltic Sea were organised by both with the help of neighbouring Sweden from 1947. Still, most were caught in traps as the Russians repeated their success with the Trust in the 1920s.

All restraint was abandoned by Washington and London as a consequence of the Soviet blockade of Berlin. On June 18, 1948, the Americans officially adopted covert operations as a means of dealing with the threat from the Soviet Union, and on December 14 the British moved in the same direction. The declared British aims included "making the Soviet Orbit so disaffected that in the event of war it would become a dangerous area requiring large armies of occupation" and inducing the captive countries to seek independence. Most important, the objectives now extended to encompass the "weakening" of Moscow "within the frontiers of the Soviet Union."[31]

By then plans were well advanced. Accordingly, on June 26, 1949, the London rezidentura sent the Centre news of British plans to drop agents into the Soviet bloc. A special communication to Stalin and Molotov on September 22 told them of Operation Valuable, the scheme to overthrow the Communist régime in Albania.[32] Thus it was crushed three months later without much difficulty.[33]

Closer to home, in the Ukraine, the involvement of the Western powers became more obvious over time due to the greater professionalisation of the operations and the fact that the insurgents increasingly wore the uniforms of border guards and other security personnel. In May 1951, however, no doubt due to a tip-off from Philby, the head of the OUN's security service, Miron Matvieiko, was caught, along with about thirty others, brought to Moscow, and turned. For the next decade, he played a radio game on behalf of the Russians to lure more unsuspecting victims and neutralise all further operations.[34]

Soviet counterintelligence thus benefited enormously from the secrets Philby provided. That said, Stalin also made mistakes, and the formation of the Committee of Information (KI) was definitely one of them. Finally, in January 1949, military intelligence was separated out as a reestablished GRU; it had become clear that the attempt to combine military and civilian foreign intelligence was not only impossible, but also counterproductive.[35] General Matvei Zakharov, deputy chief of the General Staff, took charge.

The First Directorate was thus all that remained of the KI. On September 19, 1949, the indecisive Fyodotov gave way to a more ruthless but no more inspired lieutenant general, Sergei Savchenko, former head of the MGB in the Ukraine. The son of a peasant, Savchenko had little education, let alone any experience in foreign operations. On November 2, 1951, the failure of the experiment now fully recognised, the directorate was reintegrated with the MGB.[36] Savchenko, tough and demanding in running operations, stayed in place.[37] In these conditions, foreign intelligence on the whole yielded results passively—that is, because of the investment made in foreign agents a decade before. The service was feasting off accumulated and depleting reserves. This could not last forever.

Cryptolinguistics

The situation with regard to decryption was even more problematic. It was American progress in decrypting wartime communications that finally broke Soviet ascendancy in human intelligence. The U.S. Army

Signals Intelligence Corps at Arlington Hall Station, Virginia, just across the Potomac from Washington, D.C., began studying the intercepts of Soviet-ciphered communications in February 1943. These intercepts had originally been encrypted with a numeric cipher superenciphered through the addition of a numeric key stream taken from a one-time pad. The British had introduced mechanical comparators as a means of breaking Enigma. A comparator was a device used to count the coincidences of words or letters. In October, the army lieutenant Richard Halleck ran ten thousand ciphered Soviet trade mission messages through an IBM electronic comparator to identify any repetitions. These American comparators now began the slow process of methodically checking Soviet-ciphered communications at an ever-greater speed to detect repetitions that could then be isolated and worked upon. Halleck soon found seven cases of a duplicate key. This discovery inspired further searches through intercepts that, at the time, the Americans had no idea were communications between Moscow and its rezidentury.[38]

The theory behind the use of comparators is easily explained. It was the gifted son of Russian emigrés in the United States, William Friedman, who discovered the index of coincidence: the likelihood of a given letter in any text finding itself in exactly the same position in another text, even a ciphered text.[39] This approach was then trumped by research into the application of statistics to linguistics pioneered by George Zipf in 1935[40] and more rigorously articulated in mathematical form by Benoît Mandelbrot after the war, funded by the U.S. armed services.[41]

Zipf found degrees of probability of a word appearing in a text; more than that, a fixed ratio of repetition between the commonest word and the next most common word, and so forth. As he wrote, words are not deliberately chosen for their frequency, but they "have a frequency distribution of great orderliness which for a large portion of the curve seems to be constant for language in general."[42] In the United States, cryptolinguistics was coming into being as a field in its own right. The implications for cryptography as a whole were not to be ignored, particularly when machinery could be used to break open the text at speeds far beyond what pencil and paper could achieve.

What Moscow was slow to realise was what the British had hitherto never believed likely: careless use of the one-time pad and the use of duplicated pages from pads made decryption possible. By 1945, fifty

Americans were working on Soviet intercepts,[43] but as NSA historians note, "in 1945 and 1946 even the President was unsure of the relationship between the United States and the Soviets and argued against reading their messages."[44] Truman was under heavy pressure to launch a serious intelligence effort.

Cipher Warfare

A breakthrough occurred with the defection of Gouzenko, who made a significant contribution to explaining how the codebooks were compiled and how the additives worked.[45] Thus the telegrams used by Moscow were vulnerable. At the beginning of the following year, 1946, Meredith Gardner, an outstanding cryptanalyst good at languages and capable of lateral thinking, joined this ambitious enterprise. The official account explains that Gardner identified "the 'spell' and 'end spell' indicators" and was thereby "able to recover the portion of the codebook used for spelling English names and phrases in a message. He continued to build on his success, recovering more and more code groups." Gardner broke the first message in February 1946. The following year, close collaboration with the FBI yielded cribs that could further develop the process.[46]

The British were critical to the general problem of breaking Soviet ciphers. The Americans did not have the skills to make independent attacks on non-Morse, enciphered, radio teletype traffic, whereas the British had already had some success against Soviet cipher machines because they could intercept and process non-Morse transmissions.[47] They were doing so with the aid of new generations of computers that went beyond Colossus, the machine designed by Tommy Flowers that had cracked the Fuhrer's non-Morse ciphered teleprinter, the Geheimschreiber, Lorenz Schlüsselzusatz 42. This breakthrough was made possible by means of a crib in the form of a very lengthy signal repeated with abbreviations by a lazy German operator. That signal enabled Bill Tutte to work out the logical framework of the machine. As a result of a great deal of ingenuity, Colossus became operational in January 1944. It was followed by Mark 2 in June. Mark 2 was hard-wired and switch-programmed, not a memory-stored computer, but it was incredibly fast, reading five thousand characters a second.[48]

That lead held by Britain was "critical" in convincing U.S. agencies to extend World War II cooperation, now formalised into the BRUSA, the Anglo-American intelligence-sharing agreement of March 5, 1946.[49] Ciphered teletype was important because not everything could be distributed through one-time pads. They were too labour-intensive to produce in the tens of thousands, and it was almost impossible, with mass production by hand, to ensure no repetitions of words or letters. Arlington Hall had long been working on the Soviet-ciphered teleprinter machine they called Longfellow. The Japanese had created a machine (the Tan) to break into it.[50]

Knowledge of the Japanese system undoubtedly raised the game. The Soviet machine targeted first by the British appears to have been the M-101, otherwise known as Izumrud ("Emerald"). It was used for top-level military communications. Izumrud first came into action in 1943.[51] Its basic design was by Nikolai Sharygin, but it was the entire team, also composed of Ivan Volosk, Pavel Sudakov, and Valentin Rytov, who won the State Prize. More than ninety such machines were produced for the armed forces. The Russians had also ransacked German facilities at the end of the war to update their cipher machine technology, the very technology the British and Americans had already mastered. From Berlin alone, three railway carriages of equipment were transported out to the Soviet Union in May 1945.[52]

Through combined effort, London and Washington were soon breaking into several different classes of enciphering systems. Indeed, progress was such that by the end of 1946, signs emerged that some of the most crucial Soviet civil and military systems were vulnerable. The game had been made all the easier by new developments in technology. The mistakes made by the Russians in construction (weaknesses in the design of the cipher equipment) also made their enciphering teleprinter machines vulnerable to penetration. The Americans began to dream of duplicating the Russian equipment. The Russians, they were relieved to discover, "had yet to perfect their cryptosecurity procedures."[53]

New American comparators (such as Warlock) were already operating at speed by weighing each letter according to language frequency.[54] The next step was to replicate the chi-square distribution test mechanically, to compare the frequency with which a letter appeared in one text to the frequency with which it appeared in another, and testing to ensure that this was not just a matter of chance. This had to be done through thousands of multiplications and additions—and at speed.[55]

Meanwhile, cryptolinguistics were developing with increasing so-phistication under Benoît Mandelbrot. Though apparently produced at random with respect to the probability of repetition, words emerge in the text in a discernible pattern that bears no relationship to gram-mar or meaning. This means that even were a text enciphered, the probability of a word appearing remained just as it did in plain text. Mandelbrot, who linked these insights to information theory, summed it up when he said that word frequency is in inverse proportion to ranking.

Critically, hopes of breaking the one-time pad used by Soviet diplo-mats and intelligence operatives also rose.[56] Were this to happen, the postwar advantage in secret intelligence that underpinned Stalin's for-eign policy of bluff would be thrown into jeopardy. More than that, the agency networks upon which all Soviet intelligence hinged—composed most notably of the Cambridge Five (now effectively down to three)—would be exposed. Moscow had unthinkingly allowed the West a criti-cal advantage through falling behind in cryptography.

By 1948 the Americans were also intercepting more than a million plain-text messages and subjecting undeciphered messages to traffic analysis—tracing the source of intercepted military communications was a critical advantage for determining the Soviet order of battle. Knowing who had sent a message could be as important as, if not more important than, reading the contents of the message. Fusing the find-ings of traffic analysis with the process of decryption, a technique de-veloped by GC&CS at Bletchley Park in World War II, made all the difference. That was why the very practice of fusion was kept secret for so many years after the war.[57]

In view of growing Anglo-American capabilities, the decision was taken in Moscow to hand over all the communications systems of the legal rezidentury to the illegals, including contacts with agents.[58] The race was on. One indicator was the fact that in 1947 the leading math-ematician Ivan Verchenko, who had published with the world-famous specialist on probability Andrei Kolmogorov, was invited to work for the MGB on the most important and most complicated part of research in the analysis and synthesis of machine cipher systems. He spent most of his time on the highest priority, given Stalin's long absences from Moscow spent at distant datchas in Sochi, of encrypting telephone conversations between members of the leadership.[59]

William Weisband

A crucial agent had been recruited over a decade before, in 1934, for whom little use had arisen. He was William Weisband, of Russian extraction. In July 1944, as part of his urgent search for agents in the United States, the rezident instructed Feklisov to resume contact with Weisband (code-named "Rupert"). This proved a difficult challenge because Weisband, in army signals, was on the road in various theatres of war. After a series of mishaps, the two finally met, outside a cinema in New York City in February 1945. Weisband broke the alarming news that the Americans had cracked the Japanese diplomatic cipher— which meant they could follow the course of Soviet negotiations with Tokyo at a time when the Japanese were bidding to keep the Russians out of the war in the Pacific. Weisband also told Feklisov that the Americans had somehow also managed to read a one-time pad communication between the Centre and the consulate in New York. Although this particular piece of news initially induced something akin to panic, the cryptographers in Moscow, having identified the precise telegram, heaved a sigh of relief that the Americans' deciphering it was merely the result of an error in encryption.[60]

On the eve of the Berlin Blockade in February 1948, Moscow again renewed contact with Weisband, who was now working full time for the Russian section at Arlington Hall Station, translating intercepted Soviet communications. On this occasion he startled the Centre with the appalling news that the Americans were "decrypting Soviet ciphers, and intercepting and analysing unciphered radio communications."[61] The Americans could no longer be underestimated.

Washington had also ambitiously decided to invest in the creation of two special-purpose electronic comparators and anticipated massive funding for an "Electronic Super Bombe."[62] The Bombes had been the machines created to break Enigma. This was news to Moscow, because Cairncross had left Bletchley Park at the end of 1943, well before the Post Office engineers under Tommy Flowers succeeded in re-creating the Lorenz cipher machine without seeing the original. The Kremlin had thus unknowingly continued using vulnerable ciphered teleprinters well after the war without being alerted to the capacity of Colossus and its successors to break open their transmissions. As time went on, however, the Russians came to the sobering realisation that London and

Washington were well ahead. The danger that Moscow's entire network, atomic and civilian, would be exposed was all too real. Switching cipher systems was a lengthy, tortuous, and risky process, however. It took the best part of six months, given the scale of the internal and external Soviet communications systems, and was implemented in the strictest secrecy. Finally, all Moscow's communications with the outside world were suddenly severed. For Washington, this was Black Friday: October 29, 1948. When signals resumed on Monday, nothing could be deciphered.

Computer Catch-Up

At the Institute for Advanced Study the publication in 1946 by the Hungarian-born mathematician John von Neumann of a seminal article on the construction of the computer and the appearance of the first American civilian computer, ENIAC, that same year served to warn the Russians that the United States was moving into more innovative computation. This was despite the fact that it was a symbolic rather than a genuine threat, since the machine was digital with an outside program driven slowly, step by step, with only a single memory. Most viewed this as inappropriate for codebreaking compared to parallel processing, which meant speedier results.[63] For the Russians, with so much to reconstruct after a devastating war and next to no experience in this complex field of electronic computation, the development of a computer for cryptographic purposes was not seen as urgent. Acquiring the atomic bomb and a means of delivery were more pressing priorities. It was here that electronic computation was seen to be valuable.

The years 1948 and 1949 proved a turning point. The atomic bomb was within reach, and Stalin's interest in missiles as the best means of delivery meant that computer technology would be needed. Sergei Lebedev led the way from Kiev, where he headed the Institute of Electrotechnology and had been working towards the construction of a computer when the outbreak of war interrupted his early efforts. In Moscow, the Institute of Precision Mechanics and Computer Technology had been established on July 16, 1948, to build a computer. Towards the end of that year, Lebedev was put in charge of a secret laboratory under the auspices of the Moscow Institute, which he also formally headed (though Nikolai Bruevich actually ran it). The newly commissioned laboratory was constructed just outside Kiev, on the grounds of an old monastery, St. Panteleimon the Healer, in Feofaniya. Lebedev's task was to build a small computer.

Two years and the combined effort of seventeen men (twelve scientists and five technicians) were needed to complete the job. The machine was not finally tested until November 6, 1950, and it went into regular use on December 25, 1951.[64] For over a year, it remained the only working computer in the country.[65] On December 17, 1948, at around the same time that the Kiev laboratory came into being, Stalin issued an order that created the Special Construction Bureau 245 (SKB-245) under Mikhail Lesechko, a leading aviation engineer.[66] The job of building a computer was then handed over to Yuri Bazilevskii in January 1950. He produced the Strela in 1953, which could manage two thousand operations a second (as many as the American UNIVAC machine in 1951). Seven Strely were introduced that year, and not phased out until 1956.[67]

With respect to cryptography, Stalin finally lost patience and snatched the code and cipher business from the control of the intelligence agencies, including the MGB's Sixth Directorate, in 1949. On October 19, he handed them to two new organisations, GUSS (the Main Directorate of the Special Service) and the Advanced School of Cryptography (VShK), though it would not go by this name formally until August of the following year. The Vyshka, as the school was known, provided two years' training for graduates in engineering or the physical sciences. Then, at the beginning of 1950, Scientific Research Institute No. 1 came into being. The mathematician Verchenko was appointed deputy head of research.[68] It appears that this initiative had no bearing, however, on the Eighth Directorate of the General Staff, where Pyotr Belyusov continued successfully to run the bureau for construction of cipher machinery until 1961.

In the teaching of cryptography, hasty improvisation was the order of the day. No up-to-date textbooks existed. Instead, students were taught by instructors illustrating their work through wartime decryption, "working ciphers" (*boevye shifry*) mimeographed for class work. Moreover, most of the teaching was remedial, designed to raise the level of existing cryptanalysts, most of whom at the time had no more than rudimentary secondary education. Because of the pressure of work, this had to be done through evening classes. The shortage of trained talent was so great that the top of the class immediately became instructors upon graduating. (This included the "Three Musketeers," Boris Antonov, Yuri Davydov, and Leonid Kuz'min.) At least the Russians were finally on the road to professionalisation. The very best and most experienced ran the show. The outstanding cryptanalyst Aleksandr Sokolov, who had broken into the Japanese systems, was the first dean of the cryptological faculty. He was deputised by his fellow star Boris Aronskii.[69]

At GUSS, the First Directorate dealt exclusively with cryptanalysis. The first department covered the United States; the second, Britain; the third, Europe; and the fourth, the rest. As the Russian archives tell us, a new scientific research institute encompassed the theoretical bases of decryption, mainly the use of machines for that purpose in the United States and Britain, above all "the problem of creating and using fast analytical calculating machines and the problem of new methods of intercepting communications."[70]

Deflated by an Intellectual Vacuum

Research was all to the good, but as the one-time chief cryptographer General Nikolai Andreev has pointed out, one cannot develop sophisticated cipher-cracking institutions in an intellectual vacuum. This was not like building the bomb, which was a process completely isolated under Beria's supervision. For cryptography, not only was a high level of science and technology required, but so were contiguous fields of knowledge in the humanities. The cipher war, Andreev reminds us, is "an unending struggle," "a war of minds" that requires conditions conducive to "study, research, creativity."[71] Under high Stalinism, however, the long-standing isolation of the cryptographic effort from mainstream academic life was a crucial defect, and even though it was reconnected to the world beyond, academic life was under barbaric assault.

This had never before been considered an issue. In the Soviet Union of the 1930s, cryptography had been regarded as a purely practical enterprise unrelated to the advances in the sciences, a skill to which people were born rather than educated. It was in grudging and partial recognition of this error that Stalin simultaneously set up a "closed" department of mechanics and mathematics, "Mekhmata," at Moscow

University, to train the mathematicians required for cryptography. Although, remarkably, given the state of terror in which most lived, the most prestigious in the field courageously refused to contribute their talents because of cryptography's long-standing association with the secret police. Moreover, the prestige still lay with pure mathematics, whereas, at this early stage, what were needed above all were more applied mathematicians.[72]

The underlying problem was intractable given the nature of the régime. High Stalinism was wreaking enormous damage on the very disciplines that would make this organisational revolution fully effective. Mainstream academic life was itself increasingly paralysed discipline by discipline as little Stalins clawed their way up the heap through ritual denunciation of their rivals in every field both publicly and by means of libellous anonymous letters—*anonimki* (a term so widespread as to deserve a place in the dictionary)—to the security organs.

The Cost of Politicising Science

During the late 1940s in Russia, both linguistics and statistics were under blistering attack from high Stalinists due to the virulent campaign against scientific biology by an ambitious fraudster, Trofim Lysenko. The entire field of genetics was underpinned by statistics, since inherited characteristics could be calculated only on the basis of probability.

This crucial contribution to genetics was made by Andrei Kolmogorov (1903–1987), a name known worldwide and the Soviet Union's greatest theorist of probability: in 1940 he had confirmed Mendel's laws of heredity.[73] Thus, when, in August 1948, with Stalin's explicit support, Lysenko launched his assault on Mendel's genetics as a bourgeois distortion, his main opponent, Vasilii Nemchinov, reasserted the statistical validity of Mendelian genetics only to be forced out of his post as director of the K. A. Timiryazev All-Union Agricultural Academy. What the critics did not know was that Stalin had actually edited and rewritten Lysenko's speech, including its conclusion.[74] Statistics as a discipline thus stood directly in Stalin's line of fire, which meant this was not the time to revolutionise cryptanalysis according to Western principles and practices. These were desperate times. Kolmogorov took the obvious course and shamelessly disowned his previous findings.

The lamentable fact was that Soviet cryptographers at the time were unaware of the innovations in statistical application, and no serious attention was paid to their fundamental importance in breaking codes and ciphers. The persecution of those who believed in the use of statistics for general purposes held matters back even further. For a considerable time thereafter, training suffered a severe shortage of those capable of teaching the application of probability theory to cryptography.[75]

Resistance to innovation on the Western model was never far away. It is striking that, when Semyonov served in Paris after the war, he collided with the rezident there, Nikolai Lysenkov, a former teacher, a miserable-looking man, but a formidable operative. Two issues turned Lysenkov against Semyonov: first, what were regarded as his subordinate's loose morals; and, second, his interest in cybernetics, the science of automated control systems. In the late 1940s, Lysenkov, although an educated man, reacted badly when Semyonov handed him documents on the latest developments in cybernetics. He simply refused to mail them to Moscow. Then, when Semyonov, who had not been home since 1946, applied for and was granted leave, Lysenkov was dismissive: "you will be able to study your, what do you call it, cy-ber-net-ics." Sure enough, a denunciation stalked Semyonov all the way home, and in the midst of the anti-Semitic wave, his promising career, as with many others, ground to an abrupt halt. Like Fitin, he was brusquely dismissed without income or pension.[76] Ten years earlier, he would not have been so lucky; he would almost certainly have been shot.

7. BREAKDOWN

Soviet reliance on human intelligence inevitably increased as decryption became ever more problematic. Thus, the collapse of long-standing human intelligence networks spelled disaster. That this occurred at the height of East-West tension was due entirely to Stalin's policy of calculated risk, which went badly wrong on June 25, 1950, when a Soviet planned invasion of South Korea precipitated U.S. military intervention.[1]

Stalin had been exerting pressure on Western Europe since the Cold War began. The governments of Eastern Europe, dominated by minority Communist parties, stifled all opposition. After the introduction of the Marshall Plan for European economic recovery, accepted by Western Europe in June 1947, the Russians lost not a moment in mobilising foreign Communist parties to undermine its implementation. Under sustained pressure from Moscow, in February 1948 the Communists seized power in Czechoslovakia. Stalin then cut off all communications by road and rail from the Western zones of Germany through to Berlin from March 1948. It was a war of nerves made possible only through Stalin's direct knowledge of British and American decision making supplied by the Cambridge Five.

Included among Stalin's calculations was that the West did not believe the Russians would consider resorting to war until at least 1955, given the time needed to recover from devastation at the hands of the Germans and the effort subsequently required to match the United States in atomic capability. Yet the assumption that because Moscow could not contemplate the prospect of world war it would do everything to avoid local war for fear it could escalate to a global scale proved entirely false.

War in Korea

Since early 1949, Stalin had repeatedly turned down pleas from Kim Il-Sung of North Korea to launch a surprise attack that would unify the country at the expense of the South. The lobbying began before the crisis over the Western presence in Berlin, as well as before Mao Tsetung's final victory in China that October. The failure in Berlin foiled Stalin's plans for Europe. The rise of Communist China shifted the balance of power in Asia potentially to Soviet advantage. Thus Stalin thought the time ripe to follow through by seizing South Korea. The attack was thus a calculated risk predicated on immediate success achieved by virtue of surprise and in the absence of U.S. forces, now on the other side of the Sea of Japan.[2]

The trouble was that, although taken entirely by surprise, the U.S. president startled everyone by acting decisively to defend South Korea by means of a counteroffensive launched from the sea by General Douglas MacArthur. This was done with authorisation from the UN Security Council in the absence of Yakov Malik, the Soviet permanent representative, and therefore with freedom to act without the threat of Soviet veto. Malik's absence was a formal retaliation against Washington's refusal to recognise Communist China's right to take up the Chinese seat on the council. Stalin had unwisely taken this course of action against the advice of his diplomats.[3]

Two days after the North Korean attack, Stalin explained his reasoning to Klement Gottwald, his counterpart in Czechoslovakia. Stalin defended Malik's absence from the UN Security Council, saying it underscored "the stupidity and idiocy of the U.S.A.'s policy of recognising the Kuomintang 'scarecrow' as China's representative in the Security Council." Rationalising Truman's resort to the Security Council, Stalin suggested that the absence of the Soviet Union had "untied the hands of the American government and made it possible for it, making use of the majority on the Security Council, to commit new stupidities so that public opinion could make out the true face of the American government." By intervening in Korea, he continued, the United States would lose military prestige and moral authority. More important:

> Besides, it is clear that the United States of America is now distracted from Europe by the Far East. Does this add up to a plus for us in respect to the global balance of power? Undoubtedly it does. Let us assume that the American government will get further entangled in the Far East and will draw China into the fight for the liberation of Korea and for its own independence and what will come out of this? First, America, like any other state, cannot cope with China, which has more armed forces at its disposal. Therefore, America will fall apart in such a fight. Second, in falling apart as a result of this business, America will be unable in the near future to conduct a third world war. Therefore a third world war will be delayed for an indefinite period, that will guarantee the time needed for the reinforcement of Socialism in Europe. That is leaving aside the fact that America's fight with China must revolutionise all of the Far East. Does all that add up to a plus for us from the standpoint of balance of global power? Absolutely.[4]

The beginning of the Korean War was undoubtedly the high point of Stalin's postwar strategy. Thereafter, the entire edifice began rapidly to crumble away, including the advantage in human intelligence, which had sustained Soviet foreign policy and underpinned what was essentially a policy of calculated bluff.

The Cambridge Five in Jeopardy

The new illegal rezident in New York, Valerii Makayev ("Harry"), arrived in the United States in 1948. He was not entirely reliable, having lived off his wits as an orphan running wild amid famine and chaos after the civil war, which meant that he was not entirely trustworthy with money. Moreover, his training was minimal. He had one hundred twenty hours of Polish to sustain his cover, just eighty hours of English, thirty hours of technical tuition, and only ten hours of conversation with Akhmerov (to brief him on the American context) before embarking on his new role.[5] This was important because he took responsibility for Philby, who was attached to the British embassy in Washington as head of station to liaise for MI6 with CIA and the FBI in 1949. Burgess, as first secretary, surreptitiously acted as courier to Makayev, when a breakthrough occurred that would soon unmask Maclean.[6]

Maclean was under extreme pressure and had been taking to the bottle more heavily than ever. As minister at the embassy in Cairo from 1948, he began to unravel, drinking excessively and carousing openly with promiscuous young men he picked up while cruising through town. His antics were observed with disapproval by the military attaché, among others, and reported to London.[7] Of course, nothing happened. It was from Cairo that Maclean first signalled to the Centre his urgent desire to be exfiltrated to Moscow.[8] But his request went unnoticed, and even when it was repeated in 1950, nothing was done about it. By then his anti-American sentiments proved hard to contain and inevitably infused the minutes he wrote when Cold War issues arose after his transfer back to London as head of the American Department.

In the United States, anticommunist sentiment had reached fever pitch with the outbreak of war in Korea. In Europe, the Americans insisted on turning the North Atlantic pact into a permanent organisation ready for war: NATO. McCarthyism took off. Maclean was certainly close to breaking, and any sustained close interrogation by MI5, such as Fuchs received, would have destroyed the entire network. In April 1951, the British and the American services finally determined that Maclean was "Homer."[9] The Soviet failure to prioritise cryptography now jeopardised its lead in human intelligence.

Up to this point Philby had never met the rezident Makayev, who had arrived in New York the year before. Contact was maintained through "Paul," whose real name is unknown. When Philby learned of this breakthrough, he asked "Paul" urgently to set up a meeting with Makayev. Here he conveyed the disturbing news that Maclean's cover had been blown. Moscow was immediately informed, and the rezident in London made arrangements to spirit Maclean out of Britain.[10]

In a scene worthy of a French farce, Maclean fled across the Channel, from Southampton for St. Malo, on the SS *Falaise*, a packet boat (no passports required), with Guy Burgess on May 25, 1951, a Friday. MI5 had bugged Maclean's house. However, the escape proved no great challenge. The reaction of Liddell at MI5 was, characteristically, innocent bafflement. "It seemed to me unlikely that a man of BURGESS's intelligence could imagine that he had any future in Russia." Liddell took advice from Anthony (Blunt), who was being "persecuted by the press" (Liddell's words), and Victor and Tess (Rothschild), who offered nothing but empty words.[11] As late as August 20, Liddell still refused to believe that Burgess and Maclean could have been Soviet spies.[12]

Philby was obviously too close to Burgess, who had stayed at his home while in Washington. Moreover, Philby's anti-American prejudices were not always fully concealed by the superficial charm showered on his acquaintances in Washington. Called home, Philby was questioned by MI5. He lied about the date that his marriage to Lizy came to an end. (He claimed 1936, and MI5 later discovered it was actually 1940.) Even then Liddell remained reluctant to "prejudge"—in fact "to judge"—Philby's case.[13] It was, he firmly believed, quite possibly a matter of "pure coincidences."[14] The same indulgent and myopic view was taken by chums such as George Young, Tim Milne, and Nicholas Elliott.[15] "My dear boy," Elliott once observed. "One of us."[16] Belief in Philby's innocence was also the firm conviction of the man who headed MI6 from 1953 to 1956, Sir John Sinclair,[17] a belief shared by his predecessor, Sir Stewart Menzies.[18]

Indeed, Liddell was also "convinced" that Blunt had never been a Communist, even though no less a figure than the experienced Russia watcher Owen O'Malley, formerly of the Foreign Office, reported evidence that Blunt most definitely had been a Communist at Cambridge.[19] Somehow, resistance to hearing the unpleasant truth seemed to strengthen rather than weaken as more direct evidence flowed in.

Meanwhile, Burgess and Maclean reached Prague via Switzerland; from there they were whisked off to Moscow. In the Soviet capital, they were extensively debriefed over the course of five months. Thereafter, both were effectively ostracised—relegated to occasional editorial work for the publishers of foreign literature, though Maclean set about learning Russian with characteristic vigour and then teaching English to eager Russians. On October 24 they were granted Soviet citizenship by the Politburo, each handed a generous salary and a three- to four-bedroom apartment on condition that they live not in Moscow but distant Kuibyshev, in Siberia, watched by the MGB.[20] For those accustomed to the great metropolis of London, this was punishment rather than reward for outstanding service. They had come not to the socialist paradise of which they had dreamed but instead to a glorified prison, which may have appealed to Maclean's more ascetic qualities but did nothing for the self-indulgent Burgess, who longed for the comforts of home.

MI5 clung desperately to its touching belief that insiders would never betray their own, as American suspicions inevitably rose. Eventually, London was, albeit with the deepest reluctance, forced to take action, at the very least to preserve appearances, and Philby was removed from the inner sanctum of MI6. Yet he continued to be protected by influential figures (most notably Elliott) who later had good cause to repent, though affection for Philby appears never to have dimmed. Perhaps he had been framed by the Americans and MI5 was trying to get even with them? This was of little consolation to the Russians, however, for the sound reason that Stalin's investment, painstakingly accumulated since the 1930s, was rapidly dissolving overnight—and there was nothing comparable to replace it.

The Collapse of U.S. Networks

The loss of high-level sources in London was soon paralleled in Washington, D.C. On January 21, 1950, the former diplomat and GRU agent Alger Hiss, quondam director of the Office of Special Political Affairs, at State, was convicted of perjury rather than treason, only because the authorities were reluctant to reveal to the Russians all of their sources. On February 2, Fuchs faced imprisonment in Britain; he was the most important of the atomic spies to go down. He identified Harry Gold, who on May 22 confessed to the FBI. Gold led the FBI to David Greenglass, who on June 15 named Julius Rosenberg. Two days later Julius and Ethel were arrested and subsequently executed.

The sequence of events had a chilling effect on Kremlin hopes. It indicated that the rest of the American atomic network was in immediate danger.

It seemed only a matter of time before the Cohens (code-named "the Volunteers") were also swept up into the FBI's nets. Moscow decided to withdraw its most vulnerable assets, particularly those who could yet play the role of illegals elsewhere in the English-speaking world. Given the critical role of Morris ("Luis") Cohen and his wife, Leontina ("Leslie"), in procuring atomic secrets, the Centre telegraphed the rezident in New York: "In connexion with the situation that has arisen into which Luis and Leslie may be drawn, every measure must be taken to preserve them as sources of information. Convince Luis and Leslie that this turn of events threatens arrest; it is therefore proposed that they leave the borders of the USA."

Breaking the rules of tradecraft because there was no time to lose, Yuri Sokolov ("Claude"), an operative at the New York rezidentura, visited the Cohens' apartment. There he wrote on a notepad, "We will conduct the conversation on paper. I must ask you to burn the notes in front of me. It is possible that your apartment is bugged. Exercise the utmost caution in communicating." The Cohens were baffled and looked at Sokolov with suspicion. He continued writing: "At the end of the month you have to leave the USA." Leontina, always the more forceful, burst out, "Bullshit! We are not going to do that." "Why not?" Sokolov whispered. They were reluctant to leave because Morris had ageing parents who could not be left to cope alone. At the end of further exchanges on paper, Sokolov, no doubt utterly exasperated, insisted that this was an order.

The Cohens left for Mexico, where they stayed for nearly two months while suitable American passports could be found in the names of Pedro and Maria Sanchez. To allow them passage through Europe, passports were produced in the names of Benjamin and Emily Briggs. In October, the Cohens left for the Netherlands, Switzerland, Austria, West Germany, and, finally, Czechoslovakia. In the Soviet Union and Poland, they both underwent retraining before embarking for Britain with new identities.[21]

The Cold War promised to continue indefinitely. On March 1, 1951, a directive from the KI instructed that every operative "must get it firmly into his head that the struggle against the main enemy [the

United States] is no short-term undertaking but will constitute the fundamental substance of our work as a whole for a long time."[22] The MGB now moved to create rezidentury in reserve for the moment when legal rezidentury could no longer operate.[23] The stark fact facing Stalin was that these devastating losses in human intelligence could not be compensated for by communications intelligence. He had lived long enough for the serious consequences of earlier neglect to haunt him, in cryptography no less than the disaster in agriculture. GUSS had barely taken off. The construction of computers that could create and tackle ciphers at speed and in depth was merely a distant dream.

On October 6, 1951, just before Maclean and Burgess left for Kuibyshev, and with Philby in the doghouse, Yevgenii Pitovranov, deputy minister for state security, responsible inter alia for GUSS, signed a directive circulated to all rezidentury impressing upon them the importance of targeting those who had access to British or American codebooks.[24] The instruction went by diplomatic bag, not because any complacency existed on this score, but because the Russians could not be sure that their ciphers had not already been compromised by the other side. In June 1952, operatives throughout the West were told to construct illegal organisations to "function without interruption under any conditions."[25]

Thus, before he died, Stalin had to come to terms with the failings in foreign intelligence. He set up a meeting with the deputy ministers of state security, Sergo Gogilidze, Sergei Ogol'tsov, and Yevgenii Pitovranov, on November 20, 1952, to discuss the reorganisation of the GRU. In an atmosphere he poisoned by ghoulish recrimination and foul-mouthed threats, Stalin accused the MGB of committing the most basic mistakes in covert operations abroad. The MGB had refused to conduct terrorism against the enemy because of terrorism's supposed inconsistency with Marxism-Leninism. The fact was, Stalin ranted, the MGB had thereby adopted a position of bourgeois liberalism and pacifism.[26] Unknown to the rest of the leadership, in February 1953 Stalin summoned Korotkov, then heading illegal operations, to orchestrate the troublesome Yugoslavian leader Tito's assassination.[27] It was one of his last instructions.

Late in the evening on March 2, Dr. Aleksandr Myasnikov answered the door to a member of the Special Department (MVD) of the Kremlin hospital: "I have come to take you to the boss, who is ill."

Stalin had suffered a brain haemorrhage earlier that evening.[28] His death on March 4, 1953, was greeted by Beria with enormous relief—and he was not alone. In the weeks of mourning that ensued, Beria could not resist a broad smile of satisfaction, even in public. Stalin's demise, however, also presented its difficulties. The Cold War was at its peak. Having acquired Eastern Germany in war, the Russians were determined not to let go, even though the occupation of the rest of the country was too costly to contemplate while the main enemy, the United States, guarded the gates to the West. Beria, the one man most insistent on the need to end the Cold War by yielding Soviet hegemony over East Germany, was shot at the end of 1953. For the rest of the leadership—with the exception of Georgii Malenkov, who now stood alone—there was no real inclination to fold the tents and return home. On the contrary: it was deemed essential to hold and if possible extend the bridgehead at the very centre of Europe through means other than the force of arms. Once again, intelligence was in high demand.

However, cuts in government expenditure after Stalin's death, the urgent need to train the military as well as civilians in cryptography, and the liquidation of GUSS as an independent institution—it had been absorbed into the new all-purpose MVD (successor to the MGB)—all dealt a severe blow to communications intelligence, as two leading lights with the greatest experience, Boris Aronskii and David Truskanov, were summoned to operations, where they were most urgently needed.[29] On April 24, 1953, GUSS was carved up into three discrete institutions: the special service of the security organs as the Eighth Directorate (the *vos 'myorka*) of the MVD, the special service of the army General Staff, and the special service of the navy General Staff.[30]

Vadim Kirpichenko, who entered the service in Stalin's last years, recalled his own dismay at the "state of neglect" of Soviet intelligence.[31] Indeed, at a meeting of the leadership on February 8, 1954, no less a figure than Chairman of the Council of Ministers Georgii Malenkov complained that foreign intelligence as a whole was at a "low level." Indeed, he went so far as to use the word *breakdown* to describe its parlous condition.[32]

Whenever the Soviet régime faced a problem of some magnitude, the instinctive response was to engage in frantic bureaucratic reorganisation. It was from this crisis of confidence that on March 13 the Committee of State Security (KGB) emerged, separated out from the

Ministry of Internal Affairs, as a self-conscious continuation of the Cheka. Its employees were thereafter known as *kagebisty* or *komitet-chiki*. The Eighth Directorate of the MVD became the Eighth Main Directorate of the KGB. On June 30, 1954, the Presidium followed through with a resolution "On measures for the strengthening of intelligence work by the organs of state security of the USSR abroad." In particular, this meant constructing networks of illegals in Britain and the United States.[33]

8. THE GERMAN THEATRE

From the end of 1944, Stalin had highlighted the United States as the next main enemy.[1] Germany, where the Russians held the advantage, remained the chief theatre of potential conflict where this rivalry was played out. "Our main enemy is America," Stalin said only a few months before he died. "But the main emphasis should be directed not at America itself. The starting point, where we need to have our own people, is Western Germany."[2]

Much hinged upon selecting leaders of the best calibre, in particular to head the First Main Directorate of what became the KGB, and the GRU. The former, however, predictably went to a bureaucrat with limited experience of foreign operations: Aleksandr Sakharovskii.

The son of a paper hanger, Sakharovskii was born on September 3, 1909. He had limited secondary education, augmented by experience building up the Romanian security services, but no knowledge of foreign languages. Sakharovskii became deputy head of the First Main Directorate on March 18, 1954. On June 23, 1955, he was appointed acting head of the directorate until full promotion on May 12, 1956, recommended by his sick and inept predecessor, Aleksandr Panyushkin.[3] Good-looking and demanding without being petty, Sakharovskii was cautious, made friends only very slowly, and was staunchly independent. His contacts abroad were limited to his counterparts in the

Warsaw Pact. His fundamental problem was a lack of any systematic education or serious experience abroad. This in part explains his reluctance to innovate, a feature worsened by his health, which deteriorated as the requirements for foreign intelligence expanded exponentially. He breathed a sigh of relief nonetheless when, on December 8, 1958, Ivan Serov was transferred out of the KGB to head the GRU. Yet, as the years rolled by and the remit of the First Main Directorate grew with expansion of the formerly colonial Third World, Sakharovskii's poor health, notably continual headaches, prevented him from keeping pace.[4]

Korotkov, now raised to the rank of general, was passed over despite the fact that he was vastly more qualified and had been entrusted with illegal operations since May 22, 1946. It could not have helped matters that, as an experienced and hardworking professional, he was notoriously direct. Now he was also too closely identified with Beria. The fact that he had survived even the ill-fated Yagoda and the hated Yezhov did not help.[5]

Striking continuities persisted, even following the spring cleaning after Stalin's death. On September 3, 1953, for example, proposals put forward by First Deputy Minister of the MVD Sergei Kruglov and by Panyushkin, "to recognise the value of engaging in acts of terrorism"—a term later euphemistically changed to *aktivka*, or "active measures"—were turned into a decree providing for the organisation of a twelfth (special) department within the MVD's foreign directorate.[6] These were plans carried over from Beria by the head of the MVD's First Directorate, Pyotr Fyodotov, and his deputy, Oleg Gribanov.[7] Yet the men of the greatest experience most capable of leading the campaign, Pavel Sudoplatov and Naum Eitingon, remained incarcerated under special interrogation for having been closely associated with Beria.

The twelfth was not an entirely new outfit; it was based on Bureau No. 1 of the MGB, headed by Sudoplatov from 1945.[8] Immediately after the war, composed as it was mainly of those who conducted sabotage behind enemy lines within the Soviet Union, the Bureau was scarcely used. Sudoplatov tried to keep training going within the new dictatorships of Eastern Europe, but it was the GRU that took the lion's share of special operations, having operatives who had been actively engaged across the whole of occupied Europe during the war. What Sudoplatov did succeed in doing, once the Cold War got under way, was to infiltrate the flood of refugees fleeing from the East, particularly into the

Allied occupation zone in western Austria. For this purpose a special group was sent over in 1950 to recruit minor bureaucrats with access to official documents (especially passports) that could authenticate the "legends" of incoming operatives.[9] Thereafter, Austria, even with Allied and Soviet withdrawal on its neutralisation by treaty in 1955, remained a focus for such activities.

The task of the twelfth included raids against military-political objectives and communications on American and British soil. The proposals also provided for "terrorist acts against the most active and die-hard enemies of the Soviet Union and individuals in capitalist countries, especially foreign intelligence agents, leaders of anti-Soviet emigrant organisations and traitors to the Motherland."[10]

Inevitably, improvisation became the order of the day. First, on Nikita Khrushchev's personal orders in February 1954, an attempt was made on the life of Georgii Okolovich, head of the emigré NTS (Narodno-Trudovoi Soyuz), located in Germany under CIA auspices.[11] It failed because the assassin, Nikolai Khokhlov, defected and, within three years, published his memoirs. In April the head of NTS in West Germany, Aleksandr Trushnovich, was murdered by accident during an attempted kidnapping. By June a few lessons had been learned. The head of NTS in Austria, Valerii Tremmel', was successfully kidnapped. Then, in October 1957, the KGB assassin Bogdan Stashin'skii killed Lev Rebet, a leading Ukrainian nationalist. On October 15, 1959, he sprayed Stefan Bandera, head of the OUN, with cyanide, only to defect and tell all just two years later.

It is sobering to recall that in spite of the damaging publicity that resulted from these notorious episodes, on November 1, 1962, Semichastny approved plans for further operations. The decision was justified by the fact that, from 1954 to 1961, of 329 instances of treachery, only 23 traitors had been lured back to Russia for the highest penalty. The task fell to the thirteenth department of the First Main Directorate and the fourteenth department (later K Directorate), in cooperation with the eighth department of the Second Main Directorate (counter-intelligence).[12]

In one key respect, change was very apparent—though it was not always to the benefit of the intelligence services. As already evident with respect to the First Main Directorate, those regarded as too closely associated with Beria were purged—more than 50 percent in all.

Leading figures such as Beria himself, Abakumov, and Merkulov had already been shot on the usual trumped-up charges of spying for the enemy. Sudoplatov, imprisoned, remained defiantly unrepentant.

The figure who won the intense power struggle following Stalin's death was Khrushchev, semiliterate (he could read but not write), a natural bully, but innately clever. He had worked closely in the Ukraine with his new, ruthless but loyal chief at the KGB, Ivan Serov. A relative of Khrushchev's, small but strong, resilient, inordinately proud, and ferociously ambitious, Serov had been born into a poor peasant family in Vologda. He became chairman of a district soviet at the early age of eighteen and rose through the army, where he is said to have assisted in the deportation of recalcitrant peasants to Siberia. By 1935 he had become chief of staff of an artillery regiment, later attending the Frunze military academy, where he was picked out for the NKVD, and in 1940 he became Ukrainian commissar for internal affairs. Assigned to the Baltic states, that year he oversaw yet more mass deportations.[13] Later, in March 1945, it was Serov who orchestrated the notorious disappearance of the emigré Polish representatives when they ill-advisedly parachuted into Soviet-occupied Poland on the assumption that Stalin meant what he had said at Yalta about negotiating a government of all talents.[14]

Mikhail Mil'shtein at the GRU, who, being Jewish, suffered a foreshortened career, was "astonished at the narrow-mindedness, the hidebound nature of [Serov's] views." Ivan Serov was, Mil'shtein recalls, a small man in every meaning of the word.[15] He never could sit still. He was also vain, particularly about his muscularity, and vociferously xenophobic. He was prone to heavy sarcasm, while his wife was a notorious battle-axe, and he could not tolerate anyone smoking in his presence, so entertaining fellow Russians must have been difficult. Not surprisingly, Serov luxuriated in the company of pretty women, though they were not allowed to become operatives. He very much regretted that his son, Vladimir, a young officer in the air force, did "not value our regime in the way that I do."[16]

Yet, unlike his predecessors, Serov held no senior rank in the Party. His entire authority rested upon especially close relations with his patron Khrushchev. The rest of the leadership was, to say the least, uncomfortable with Khrushchev's choice. Serov was, of course, cut from the same cloth as Beria. Mikhail Suslov, an ideologue, disapproved of him because he spoke to Party organisations "from on high," while another member of the leadership, Mikhail Pervukhin, considered him "ill-mannered" (*grubyi*)[17]—criticisms that were soon borne out. Operationally, he left much to be desired. Not only did he take a backwards step in bluntly refusing to employ women other than for clerical duties, but he was also scandalised at the thought of homosexuals as agents. He nearly vetoed recruitment of the naval clerk John Vassall, who had been caught in a male honey trap set in Moscow, but who proved an invaluable spy at the Admiralty in London until his exposure.

By far the greatest damage to the services, however, was done by Khrushchev's sensational denunciation of Stalin at the Twentieth Party Congress on February 25, 1956. Since by far the greatest number of foreign agents worked not for money but out of blind belief in the Communist cause, which was by then inseparable from the glorious memory of Stalin, Khrushchev's speech, delivered to a closed session, shattered the faith of many when it was later read to Party cells. Not even news of the notorious Nazi-Soviet pact had caused such disarray in the ranks of the international Communist movement. Worse still for the now-embattled régime, hatred, pride, and personal integrity drove significant numbers into the hands of the adversary's intelligence services.[18]

Pitovranov

The KGB mission in Eastern Germany, now the German Democratic Republic (GDR), was "by rights considered the strongest external point of Soviet foreign intelligence," a former operative recalls.[19] The mission stood proud within the spacious Soviet compound at Karlshorst, in the distant suburbs of Berlin, bounded by Bodenmaiser Weg, Zwieseler Strasse, Dewetallee, and Aberstrasse. Built like a barracks with tall antennae on the roof, the compound was easily identifiable. The key figure in place was Lieutenant General Yevgenii ("Zhenya") Pitovranov, the MVD/KGB plenipotentiary in the GDR from May 17, 1953.[20] The address was Field Post Office No. 62706. From here the MGB/KGB operated as a law unto itself, its fleet of cars spewing forth at midnight to pick up whomsoever they chose: the sombre world of John le Carré's classic *The Spy Who Came in from the Cold.*[21]

Pitovranov began his career in counterintelligence. In 1946 he became deputy head of the MGB's Second Main Directorate. There, a "safe group" of seven, under the direction of Tokhchianov, head of the European department, broke into the vaults of foreign embassies after conducting a meticulous study of the movements of the employees and copying full sets of keys (via the embassy cleaners) for the task. They had installed microphones at leisure under plinths and in the ceilings of all the embassies during the long evacuation to Kuibyshev between October 15, 1941, and the summer of 1942. The Americans had their suspicions, however, and in the winter of 1946–1947, they were about to call in the FBI.

Abakumov hurriedly summoned a meeting. All the microphones had to be removed as soon as possible. A solution was speedily found: the American mission was deliberately contaminated so that diarrhoea spread throughout, keeping officials away from their desks for half the week, while the Russians hastily extracted all their equipment.[22]

Abakumov's arrest in July 1951, however, jolted Pitovranov's career off course. He was imprisoned and subjected to repeated beatings for over a year (between October 28, 1951, and November 1, 1952). He used that time to appeal to Stalin, arguing for reform of the entire service. As a result, he was eventually released and summoned to see the "Big Boss" on November 20, 1952, after being reinstated by Stalin himself. Impressed with his extraordinary resilience and persistence, Stalin then turned to Pitovranov for ideas about reforming the structure of the service as a whole.

An impressive personality with Tatar traces in his bloodline, Pitovranov was certainly not without ability. A tall, sharp-featured man, he had an acute and decisive mind. He spoke quietly but firmly. He was praised by one of his subordinates (out of his hearing) as "a fighter" who "stands up for his people." This, it has to be said, was a most unusual attribute in the Soviet Union of the time.[23] At a critical moment after the Berlin uprising, Pitovranov was appointed deputy supreme commissar responsible for security in occupied Germany, where he now ran what was effectively a "super rezidentura" overseeing several hundred officers at Karlshorst.

Markus Wolf

Known as "the fisherman," for invariably exaggerating the size of his catch, Pitovranov undoubtedly inflated his own achievement in penetrating the West German security services. His ego also made him easy prey to sycophancy from Markus Wolf. The son of German Communist emigrés in the Soviet Union, Wolf was a bear of a man. Highly intelligent, he skillfully manoeuvred his way to the top of secret intelligence in the GDR. Wolf spoke Russian with perfect fluency, marred only by the occasional guttural pronunciation of the r—a characteristic of Germans, Russian Jews, and, indeed, Lenin. Despite Wolf's Russian persona, he was derided as "the crafty Jew" by the anti-Semitic commander in chief of the Soviet Group of Forces in Germany, Marshal Andrei Grechko (later defence minister). It did Wolf no harm, however. He had the right kind of patronage.

In August 1951, Wolf was summoned to Berlin from Moscow, where he was serving as counsellor at the GDR's embassy, and redeployed to the Institute for Economic Research, headed by Anton Ackermann. This innocently named institute was actually the emergent secret intelligence service, the HVA (Hauptwerwaltung Aufklärung), which Wolf took over in December 1952.[24] "Wolf is himself a Russian," insisted Colonel Hans Knaust of the HVA. "He knows how the Russians think like no other. He thinks and feels like a Muscovite. In any event he is Moscow's rezident in Western Europe."[25] Russian cuisine, Russian holidays, Russian friends, Russian literature and cinema—all were an inalienable part of Wolf's hybrid life.

New Recruits

Pitovranov's notorious lack of modesty was not entirely unjustified given the incompetence of others at the top. The defector Pyotr Deriabin said Pitovranov was considered by Moscow "to be extremely capable." Unusually, he explained, the "responsibility for an operation, which otherwise would be handled by Moscow directly, is often given to him to manage at his own discretion. On previous occasions when less capable persons, such as [Colonel German] Chaikovski, were at the head in Germany, most of these operations were handled directly from Moscow for fear that the Russians in Germany would fumble the job."[26]

Despite what Stalin and Malenkov said, foreign intelligence had not been idle. In 1949 it had recruited agent "Paul," Heinz Felfe, a former junior officer in the SS and former agent for MI6 (1947–1949). He was a rare find, eventually heading the counterintelligence section of the German secret service, the BND, successor to the unit run by General Gehlen, formerly a senior officer in the SS. Philby, for one, did not think much of it. He "knew about the Gehlen unit from the summer of 1943 onwards. It was the anti-Soviet section of the poor Abwehr, and the British were reading the majority of its signals. It seemed to be no better than the other sections of the Abwehr (on which I had been continuously engaged since 1941), which means that it was very bad indeed. No exaggeration, no joke. So I was undismayed when CIA took it over."[27]

Otto John, the first head of West German counterintelligence, was Pitovranov's own catch. Having spoken out against the employment of ex-Nazis, John, along with his friend Dr. Wolfgang Wohlgemuth, was lured over to East Berlin on the evening of July 20, 1954, to discuss matters informally with the Russians.

What tempted John was that German reunification was still very much in the air. Once he had crossed to the East, however, he was detained against his will and divulged information on the Gehlen organisation.[28] Not only did the Russians benefit from the great many secrets disclosed, but they also scored a massive propaganda coup by claiming that John had defected. By the end of December 1955, however, they had lost all interest in this asset, and John was allowed to return home in disgrace. No doubt the chaos and disorientation wrought in Bonn was deemed to be worth all the trouble. By then, the spy Felfe was pulling his weight as the emerging expert in Soviet operations, having joined the Gehlen organisation in November 1951. More were to follow, as the Russians found a productive use for the files of SS and Gestapo personnel that they had captured at the end of the war. The Free Democratic Party in West Germany provided particularly rich pickings for blackmail in this respect.

Agent "Grail Spice"

The top-heavy Soviet presence in Germany brought mixed blessings to Soviet intelligence, however. The massive Soviet Group of Forces in the Eastern zone presented NATO with prime targets for penetration, despite strict measures designed to keep personnel away from the local population. The most impressive catch was the GRU major, later lieutenant colonel, Pyotr Popov. Popov owed his position to Serov's patronage, which had allowed him to advance despite lack of talent, a pronounced inferiority complex, mental rigidity, and a bombastic manner, combined with poor knowledge of German.

At the time, CIA was running "Redcap" operations under Henry Hecksher, which were designed to lure Soviet servicemen into working for the West by inducing them to defect in situ. A key figure here went under the cover name of "Gary Grossman"—though in fact he was a Russian emigré named George Kisevalter (pronounced "Keesevalter" in Russian). Born in St. Petersburg, Kisevalter was stranded in the United States with his grandfather, former deputy finance minister to the tsar, buying arms from the Americans, when the Bolshevik revolution broke out. He joined intelligence in the U.S. Army in 1944 and found his métier attached to the U.S. military mission in north Russia.[29] A gifted scalp hunter, in pursuing Popov, Kisevalter had been tipped off by the gardener (agent "Hans") working at the Soviet mission. Popov, a graduate of the Military-Diplomatic Academy, was due to replace someone identified by the Americans as a *gereushnik* (GRU officer) at the Central Group of Forces in Vienna.

Kisevalter had apprenticed with Gehlen after the war and worked as a CIA officer since 1951, assisting the heads of operational bases in Vienna and Berlin. Married, with two children, Popov fell in love with Gretchen Ritzler, a Walter Schellenberg contact in the guise of an Austrian Communist (Kochanek). And it was only a matter of time before he was recruited by Kisevalter. With the Popov operation under way, a special department (SR-9) was established under Kisevalter to handle Soviet moles. On January 25, 1953, the Gehlen organisation followed suit with a strategy for the deep penetration of the Soviet Union, using Soviet servicemen whom they had recruited.

In Berlin, Popov ("Grail Spice") handed over increasing amounts of valuable military information to Kisevalter. But the relationship with his Austrian "Communist" lover was not forgotten. Popov asked permission to write to her, but was told to do so only in order to end the relationship. He did not. Instead, a series of love letters followed that were eventually brought to the attention of his commanding officer, who took immediate action. In November 1958, Popov was sent home to Kalinin, where he served in the air defence forces. Before he left, Kisevalter arranged a meeting with the officer who would be handling him in Moscow.[30]

Moscow itself was a graveyard for CIA operations. The State Department saw the presence of the agency as a menace to its primary mission—this is well reflected in the writings of George Kennan, whose scepticism about secret intelligence deepened with advancing years—so initially such officers had only military cover, which made them all the easier to spot. The veteran Paul Redmond recalls the agency sending in two heads of station in 1948–1950: "The first had eight days of training, the second one had 21 hours. One of them was almost blind, he wore glasses which fogged up, or iced up, depending on the weather." The situation remained dire throughout the fifties.[31]

CIA officer and junior American diplomat Russell Langelle ("Daniel"), turned up in Moscow at the end of 1957 ostensibly as the embassy's chief security officer. The KGB was baffled when it observed that Langelle was greeted at the Byelorusskii railway terminal by, among others, First Secretary (consular) Idar Rimstead, identified as a CIA officer in Moscow since the beginning of the month. Why should a first secretary be going out of his way to welcome a subordinate? Further investigation suggested that Langelle and Rimstead knew each other well.

As a result, Langelle was closely watched. The walks he subsequently took with his colleague George Winters, who arrived in June 1958, intensified suspicion. It became apparent that Winters was a CIA officer. Moreover, Langelle's behaviour in itself was not well calculated to avert unnecessary suspicion. In his apartment, he turned up the radio whenever speaking to his wife, for the evident purpose of overwhelming the microphones installed by the KGB, a rather unusual procedure for purely domestic chitchat. On one occasion, he took off in the car, with his wife, ran a red light, and showed every indication of trying to lose a tail. On exiting the car at a Metro station, he raced onto the very last carriage of a train and ran off at the very last minute before departure. In the street, he was seen passing close to an army officer. Something was exchanged between them. They separated. The officer then returned to Hotel Ostankino, near the main botanic gardens (well out of the city centre), where it turned out the officer was staying.

Popov was arrested by operatives from the Second Main Directorate under Colonel Ivan Yermolaev on February 18, 1959. This was Operation Boomerang. Popov—"Iuda" (Judas)—was then turned and sent to convey disinformation to CIA. On a trip to the Lenin Hills on May 28 with his entire family, Langelle was filmed hiding something. The container was found to have within it instructions and cash.[32] A succession of meetings and exchanges of money and (false) intelligence with Popov ensued, under discreet KGB control, until October 16, when, finally, Langelle was seized and, on proving unresponsive to the suggestion that he accept (in his words) "information that would help with my promotion as part of a gentleman's agreement," he was promptly declared persona non grata.[33] Popov was tried and executed in January 1960. CIA had still much to learn about operating in Moscow.

The life expectancy of any Russian run as an American agent was extremely brief, whereas, at least until 1961, the British were largely invisible. It took the directorate a long time before it identified a small, plump, ever-so-polite second secretary, a woman, no less, as MI6's undaunted resident running a network in the Baltic states with caring as well as purposeful diligence. This was Daphne Park, though the Russians had her name down as "Daphna," exactly as it would have sounded on concealed microphones.[34]

The Berlin Tunnel

The British and the Americans had, however, two major successes that could be chalked up to both technological superiority and entrepreneurial ingenuity. Vienna, like Berlin, had been divided between the British and Americans on the one side and the Russians on the other. Peter Lunn, the son of a travel company entrepreneur and a great skier, was, in the words of his fellow MI6 officer and Soviet spy George Blake, a "very experienced and very skilful intelligence officer" yet "a man you wouldn't notice in a crowd." A sharp-minded, imaginative second secretary at the British mission and head of station in Vienna, Lunn had built tunnels beneath Soviet communication systems that enabled the

British to intercept communications and thereby re-create the Soviet order of battle in the Balkans between 1949 and 1951. This enabled them to barter genuine intercepts with the Americans.

Blake, while starving as a prisoner of war in North Korea in the spring of 1951, was fed bread and chocolate by an astute MGB officer, Nikolai Loenko, who groomed him as a future agent.[35] Blake, a cosmopolitan Dutch Jew, had been a favourite of a die-hard anticommunist emigré, Professor Elizabeth Hill in Cambridge. She taught him and, unwisely, as it turned out, imbued him with her romanticised image of the Mother Russia she had fled as a result of the revolution. Happily for his Soviet controllers, Blake returned to London to become deputy head of Section Y, processing the Vienna intercepts.

The Balkans was not the crucial theatre of battle, so the information obtained was not of the greatest value, unlike that offered by Berlin, Lunn's new posting at the very core of the Soviet Group of Forces, in 1953.[36] Blake tells the story of Lunn's initiative:

> Naturally, having so successfully operated telephone taps in Vienna, his first thought was how we can find a place where we can tap either the East German telephone line, the official lines or the Soviet lines? Through his sources in the Berlin telephone office, he discovered these three cables which went along at a distance of about twelve hundred feet from the American sector boundary. So it was clear. He knew that these cables, of which there were twelve hundred communications [lines], were used by the Soviet forces in East Germany, by the Soviet Administration and Embassy in East Berlin. So it was a very—would be a very promising target. But of course, the British couldn't just start digging a tunnel from the American sector. They had to bring the Americans in, which had a . . . further advantage because the Americans had lots of money . . .[37]

Blake was secretary and note taker at the subsequent Allied meeting (December 15–18, 1953). Within hours a copy of the minutes reached his controller, the rezident Sergei Kondrashyov. He was young, energetic, determined to do well, and beamed with pride at having once been privileged with the task of interpreting for Stalin in German. Yet, though his linguistic abilities were astonishing, Kondrashyov was utterly devoid of any imaginative capacity. That October, he had arrived in London under cover as first secretary at the Soviet embassy for the very purpose of running Blake.[38]

The two of them used to meet "after office hours in one of the London suburbs. We . . . came from different directions, and we walked for about half an hour through the crowded street. And we discussed operation[al] material." They then exchanged film. Top-secret documents were always photographed and then despatched by courier undeveloped, so they could be exposed to light in the event of seizure. On this occasion, because of the significance of the material, they limited themselves to a brief exchange.[39] For the West, the Berlin Tunnel provided the best strategic early-warning system imaginable.

Thereafter, in East Berlin and Moscow, knowledge of the tunnel was highly restricted for fear that Blake's cover would be blown. The KGB had to hurry to implement any major operation in Germany, before the operation got under way. In March 1955, Blake began work with MI6 in Berlin. It did not take long for him to transfer information from existing files on current agents in the Russian zone to Moscow.[40] In anticipation of what was to follow, General Serov moved quickly. In April, the Second Main Directorate launched Operation Spring, which, in one decisive blow, wiped out all known American, British, and West German networks in the East. By May, more than 500 agents had been detained, of whom 221 were from U.S. agencies, 105 were British, and 45 from the Gehlen organisation. In total, four U.S., five British, and three German bases were closed down.[41]

Tunnel construction was finally completed on March 28, 1955, but interception began only in May. Even after the lines were tapped, the logistics for translating and analysing the intercepts presented an extraordinary challenge. Interception lasted until a showcase "discovery" by the East Germans arranged by the Russians a year later, on April 21, 1956. Blake was tipped off shortly before the event.

By then, however, the loss of secret information from the Soviet side was colossal—the tunnel had tapped twenty-five telephone lines serving the GRU alone. A total of 368,000 conversations were recorded and processed at Clarence Terrace, Regent's Park, in London. A similar operation took place in Washington, D.C. The backlog was so great that it took until the end of September 1958 to transcribe it all. The intercepts were of prime importance for NATO's understanding of Warsaw Pact intentions and capabilities,[42] and yielded a treasure trove of personal information on those serving in the Soviet Group of Forces in Germany during that fateful year. They also cast a much-needed spotlight on the order of battle in Central Europe and the entire structure of both military and intelligence systems operating out of Berlin.

The few Russians who knew of the tunnel were no doubt tempted to feed disinformation via their communications systems in Berlin, to wreck Allied objectives. Instead, ever conscious of the damage being inflicted but mindful of the need not to jeopardise their most promising agent in place, the Soviet military authorities were allowed only to issue regular warnings to officers that they restrict the length and content of their telephone calls. Sometimes officers even received verbatim printouts of their calls as a stern reminder to remain vigilant— not that it had much noticeable effect.[43]

The Betrayal of William Fisher

Berlin held centre stage in the Cold War for many years, but the United States was always the ultimate objective. Early on, after the war, as Washington was closing in on existing Soviet intelligence assets, the Russians awoke to the urgency of introducing new talent into the United States. The Soviet services uniquely made extensive use of illegals, but even these were few and far between.[44] It took at least seven years to train an illegal from scratch so that he or she would pass unnoticed. Moreover, life under deep cover was very demanding. The illegal had "to act no differently from the inhabitants of the country where he lives," Yuri Drozdov, former head of illegals, reminds us. "In illegal intelligence there is no privacy, almost everything will be painful and uncomfortable if one does not submit oneself to the demands of the service. Above all one must be completely open and account for everything one does, including one's personal life."[45] In the meantime, suitable candidates had to be found who could pass muster at short notice. One operative chosen for this difficult task was William Fisher.

Fisher was born in Newcastle, England, on July 11, 1903, of Russified German parentage. His father, Genrikh, and his mother, Lyubov, had both fallen out with the tsarist authorities and found exile in Britain. There, William received his education, and went up to London University at the unusually early age of sixteen, but his family returned to Russia during the revolution, so he did not complete his degree. Despite extra coaching on arrival, his spoken Russian was faltering. Fisher spent the rest of his life sounding unmistakeably like a Geordie (that is, hailing from Newcastle), a foreigner to Russian kith and kin.[46] After military service and on the recommendation of the Young Communist League, in 1927 he was asked to join the OGPU. He was told that his knowledge of foreign languages would be useful.[47] Yet Fisher had his doubts, as he revealed to Trilisser in an interview: only as the result of his father's insistence did he agree to sign up.[48]

Fisher joined the eighth section, focusing on scientific and technical intelligence. His immediate superior was Aleksandr Orlov, for whom he had worked in Britain. During his brief spell in the Red Army, Fisher trained as a radio operator, and this became his métier in the intelligence service. Before long, however, he was moved over to the first section, illegal intelligence, which was being rolled out on a much wider scale by Artuzov. He applied for and received his British passport in 1931. Thereafter, he served first in Oslo, where he became known for his meticulous attention to detail and his Prussian rigidity (for which he was very nearly dismissed).[49] After Oslo, he moved to London, where he handled radio communications for Orlov, now launching the Cambridge Five.

Orlov's subsequent defection therefore jeopardised Fisher's very existence. At the end of 1938, Fisher was abruptly dismissed from the service as suspect. He was reinstated almost exactly three years later, only after the Germans invaded.[50] Fisher was then welcomed into the famed Fourth Directorate, run by Sudoplatov, sending men who could pass as enemy officers for intelligence gathering and sabotage behind the lines. Very much his father's son, Fisher had such good German that it is claimed he could and did pass for a regular Wehrmacht officer. His appetite for action had been whetted.

After hostilities, Fisher volunteered for further work, this time in France. Yet, at the end of 1947, Korotkov, charged with illegals, decided to send him on a more urgent assignment, to the United States. According to Fuchs, now returned from the States to continue work in Britain, America was close to developing a hydrogen bomb. After six months' intensive preparation, Fisher was despatched to Canada via Hamburg on the *Scythia*. It arrived in Quebec on November 14, 1948. Fisher had the passport of a Latvian American, Andrew Kayotis, who had died visiting relatives in his homeland.[51] En route to New York, he saw little of the rest of the United States but later took trips inland for further acquaintance. Under the nom de guerre "Arach," Fisher reported that he was ready to work. Every illegal had a "legend," a false identity. His legend was as Emil Goldfus, a bohemian American artist and photographer of German-Jewish extraction. Within a month he was in touch with the Cohens. They—Leontina, in particular—had been the most ingenious and fearless conduit for atomic secrets from Los Alamos. Resumption of operations earned Fisher the Order of the Red Banner within a couple of months. He had also established a new illegal network in California to track arms shipments to Chiang Kai-shek in China.

In 1952, Fisher acquired a new nom de guerre, "Mark," and was given a courier who proved to be his downfall. The cover name of this supposedly American-born Finn, Reino Hayhanen, was Eugene Maki, his code name "Vik." Hayhanen arrived in New York on October 20, 1950, barely able to make himself understood in English, a situation that showed no sign of improvement over time, particularly given his habit of drowning his sorrows by bar hopping through Brooklyn. By the end of 1953, Hayhanen had come to the attention of the FBI. He left the country briefly the following April.

On his return to the United States, he met Fisher for the first time in the summer of 1954. The contrast between the two men could not have been greater: the Karelian was an idle, inept, unmotivated alcoholic; his boss, a dedicated and pedantic workaholic. While Fisher was away in Moscow for nine months for rest and retraining, Hayhanen not only married a foreigner without permission but embezzled five thousand dollars that should have gone to agents.

In exasperation, Fisher complained vociferously upon returning to New York in 1956, as a result of which Hayhanen was finally recalled, supposedly because he was being promoted to lieutenant colonel, which even he thought unlikely. After sailing for France, he took the money given to him in Paris by the KGB and, on May 6, staggered drunk and incoherent into the U.S. embassy requesting asylum.[52] The Centre warned Fisher of the likely danger resulting from Hayhanen's defection. He promptly left New York for Florida, under the name Martin Collins, and broke off contact with his agents. But, impatient after eighteen days of forced inactivity at Daytona Beach, he returned and was soon caught, after twice returning to his apartment.[53]

Although his knowledge was not detailed, Hayhanen was able to tip off the FBI that Fisher usually wore an unusual dark snap-brim fedora with a white band. The FBI tracked him down and arrested him at the Hotel Latham on East Twenty-eighth Street in Manhattan early on June 21, without even a warrant to search the room.[54] Fisher refused to talk but conceded that he was not Goldfus, instead giving the name of his friend and fellow KGB operative Colonel Rudolf Abel, knowing that when word reached Moscow, his superiors, knowing the real Abel to be safe, would quickly understand that it was he, William Fisher, who had been taken.[55] As far as the American media were concerned, however, this was none other than Rudolf Abel.

The entire episode cast Serov's leadership of the KGB in a bad light. Its best illegal operating in the United States had been compromised by someone who should never have been permitted to enter the service. It was not the last of such clumsy amateurism under a Party secretary who had once haughtily declared with a straight face that the USSR did not engage in espionage.

Ivan Serov

In appointing Serov head of the KGB, Khrushchev no doubt hoped that their former close association meant he had found someone who would be entirely responsive to his demands. That this was not so became apparent when Serov identified himself entirely with his service (the sin of "departmental patriotism"). He stubbornly refused to implement cuts in personnel, oblivious of the consequences, and openly expressed resentment at Party intrusion. In the summer of 1957, Khrushchev greeted him maliciously in front of other members of the leadership: "The KGB is our eyes and ears. But if it doesn't avert its eyes . . . then we will pluck them out and rip off the ears and do as Taras Bulba said: I gave birth to you, and I will slaughter you."[56] Serov was lucky: his punishment was only a new assignment as head of the GRU.

In his place on Christmas Day 1958 appeared Aleksandr Shelepin, an efficiency advocate, a party apparatchik eager to amalgamate departments and cut away surplus labour, and a man with no loyalty to those he managed.[57] The latecomers to secret intelligence who were running various branches of the KGB now saw an opportunity to assert themselves at the expense of the old guard.

Serov's KGB was mediaeval in structure. Both Serov and Shelepin were always determined to bombard and demolish every castle in sight. This was especially important since there were many pretenders to the throne—including Korotkov, who, before Stalin's death, rose all too briefly to become deputy head of the First Main Directorate (foreign intelligence). He was reappointed head of illegals on July 16, 1954, with Serov's backing.

On March 23, 1957, Korotkov gave up illegals and moved back to Berlin, still the cornerstone of Soviet operations in Europe. Karlshorst, home to the Berlin office, was the largest fiefdom of them all. Here Korotkov's close relations with the Party leader Walter Ulbricht and Markus Wolf, head of the HVA (East German foreign intelligence), made for a more harmonious workplace, especially compared to the endless bickering he had endured under Sakharovskii at the Lubyanka. Yet Korotkov's career came to an abrupt end when he collapsed and died of a heart attack while playing tennis with the fitness fanatic Serov in Moscow on June 27, 1961. (Tennis had now become an essential means of advancement among the elite.) By then, his work had been done. It was all too obvious that their HVA counterparts knew more about West Germany than the KGB did.[58] Wolf was more than capable of striking out on his own without close supervision from his friends at Karlshorst. He was a man Moscow could rely upon.

Shelepin was not to last long, however, as he was deeply involved in the continuing struggle for power and appeared to be heading for the very top of the Party. Three years later, he gave way to Vladimir Semichastny, another Komsomol leader, this time from the Ukraine. Semichastny was no great asset to the KGB.[59] He is described bluntly by one who knew him in the 1940s as "lively, wilful, voluble and completely empty."[60]

The Portland Spies

Throughout the Cold War the Russians were impelled to devote a great deal of intelligence activity merely to acquiring military technology from their adversaries. This was the entire purpose of what became known as the Portland spy ring. The spies involved two sets of Soviet illegals: the aforementioned Cohens ("Helen and Peter Kroger"), who lived in suburbia and ran communications, and Konon Molody ("Gordon Lonsdale"), who was the illegal rezident.

The ring came into being initially with Harry Houghton ("Miron"), who worked as secretary to the naval attaché at the British embassy in Warsaw. He volunteered his secrets to the Poles by letter in January 1952. In return, he demanded "Sufficient local currency to meet his local requirements . . . A sum, to be agreed upon, placed to his credit in England . . . The lease of a nicely furnished flat in a nice neighbourhood, and well heated in winter."[61] Since the Poles were not allowed to conduct such operations on their own account, his file was turned over to the Russians without his knowledge. It was arranged that he meet Feklisov, who, as deputy rezident for scientific and technical intelligence, had handled Fuchs.[62]

In receipt of the first batch of material, the Lubyanka was, as usual, chiefly interested in the codebooks Houghton had managed to obtain for them. When Houghton (now "Shah") returned to Britain in February 1952, he met his handler, Lieutenant Colonel Nikita Deryabkin, in the Dulwich Picture Gallery. He was posted by Whitehall to the Royal Navy's Underwater Weapons Research Establishment at Portland, Dorset. This somewhat recondite organisation housed the technical specifications of the latest NATO submarines, including their atomic capability. Although the Russians were never confident that Houghton was truthful about his access to material, they had no complaints about its quality, including a subject index of secret documents, a veritable shopping list that enabled them to cherry-pick and order exactly what they required. From January 1955, Houghton was being handled by Aleksandr Baranov ("Bron"). They met monthly.[63] The only hiccup was the defection of the assistant trade attaché at the Polish embassy on August 19, 1957. It was thought best that Houghton be told that in fact he worked for Moscow so that he need not worry about exposure by the Polish defector. After permission from Moscow, this was done on October 26, 1957.

Houghton had recruited a girlfriend, Ethel Gee ("Asya"), who worked at Portland in the drawing office; her job, unsupervised, included disposal of classified documents, which she now simply took home. Gee had taken some convincing (at least according to Houghton), and was initially told she was working for the Americans, though in the end that mattered little to her as long as she was paid well. The success of the London legal rezidentura and the heavy workload—"a string of quite valuable agents"—that inevitably resulted led Sakharovskii to recommend that more work be transferred to the illegal rezidentura under Konon Molody.[64]

Molody ("Ben") easily passed as an American, which aroused Houghton's suspicions given his strongly anti-American prejudices. But "Ben" was an exceptional figure. He had been born in Moscow on January 17, 1922, the second child to a teacher of physics at Moscow University and a surgeon (his mother). His father died when he was just seven. Two years later, his mother's older sister, Anastasia, visited for a few days from California and offered to take Konon home with her. It proved difficult to obtain a visa for a Soviet citizen, but through family contacts they succeeded in gaining Yagoda's help (no doubt at Artuzov's instigation) to create a legend for the boy, who travelled to California via Estonia.

Molody eventually returned to Moscow in 1938, against his aunt's wishes. He fought in the war and then studied Chinese at the Institute for Foreign Trade, from which he emerged with top marks in July 1951. Molody stayed on to teach at the institute until the KGB came for him; once in the service, he worked for Vitalii Pavlov, head of the Anglo-American department of the illegal service and one of the brightest of the new generation. A hard-nosed professional, Pavlov was impressed with Molody, even after twelve years of experience during which up to a hundred aspirant illegals had come before him. Pavlov determined that Molody was the model candidate and that the timing was perfect.[65] On June 30, 1954, the Soviet leadership resolved to intensify intelligence work abroad, particularly in Britain and the United States.[66] As part of that effort, Molody was trained to adopt the role of a Canadian businessman. This was relatively easy, as Pavlov had already served there as rezident. In 1954 Molody was sent to Vancouver to build his legend.[67]

From there he moved to London, as the illegal rezident, in March 1955. He enrolled to study Chinese at the School of Oriental and African Studies (used by MI6 and CIA) and set up business under deep cover, as "Gordon Lonsdale," leasing jukeboxes and vending machines; ultimately, he owned four different companies. We have no idea what other agents he ran until he took over Houghton on July 11, 1959, when they were introduced by Vasilii Dozhdalyov, Houghton's latest handler and later head of illegals at the KGB.[68]

In retrospect, Dozhdalyov recalled the reasons: with restrictions on legals travelling beyond twenty-five miles of London, only an illegal could safely handle Houghton. It was also the case that the legals had their hands full, though none of the many agents they ran has since come to light; one can only guess who they were. When Feklisov was assigned to Britain in the late 1940s, he took up recruitment of two entirely new categories: those who admired Red Army achievements in World War II and those who disliked those Americans who were both notoriously "oversexed" as well as "over here."[69] Specifically referring to the young, Feklisov recalled, "Among the new agents, young people predominated who did not have the possibility of obtaining important secret information but who with time and our help could settle down in a job with governmental institutions in need and military establishments and become valued sources."[70]

Molody's modus operandi was to take the Portland documents to the Cohens, who ran operations from a little bungalow at 45 Cranley Drive, Ruislip, in the depths of the London suburbs, where they lived under deep cover as the New Zealanders Helen Kroger and her husband, Peter, the sort of kindly, middle-aged neighbours one might wish to have; certainly able to fix any minor electrical problems in the house. There, documents photographed could be formed into microdots and inserted into antique books that were mailed from the Krogers' shop, opposite St. Clement Danes Church on the Strand. They also operated an extraordinarily powerful transmitter that could send two hundred fifty words a minute.

The fact that Houghton had been recruited in Poland ultimately proved Lonsdale's undoing. In 1958, CIA recruited Colonel Michael Goleniewski ("Sniper"), who was in charge of the British section in the Polish secret service. Yet he was not just a senior figure in the Polish service; he also spied for the Russians, delivering to them details of everything he found in Warsaw. This was evidently a habit difficult to shake. In mid-1960, he tipped off the Americans about Lonsdale and the Krogers. Thereafter, MI5 watched the suspects in order to encompass the entire network. Yet its hand was forced when Goleniewski defected on January 5, 1961. The Portland spy ring was rounded up just two days later, to the utter amazement of the sedate residents of Cranley Drive and to the consternation of Lonsdale's business associates in London.[71] Worse still for Moscow, on December 15, 1961, the KGB officer Anatoly Golytsin defected to the Americans in Helsinki, bringing with him news of the British naval clerk John Vassall's treachery. Blake's cover was also blown.

Oleg Pen'kovskii: Agent "Young"

The GRU's main duty was to provide early warning against thermonuclear war from the United States, which possessed overwhelming strategic superiority in bomber power and, soon, intercontinental ballistic missiles.[72] June 22, 1941, was a searing memory, but the Soviet Union had no strategic nuclear-detection system comparable to the American BMEWS (Ballistic Missile Early Warning System) until the middle of the 1960s. Lacking the strategic reach of the United States, the Soviet Union under Khrushchev got by through bluff. That bluff would be called, however, if the West were to penetrate the higher reaches of the Soviet military establishment. It finally succeeded through the person of Colonel Oleg Pen'kovskii of the GRU. To their astonishment, the Americans discovered that Moscow had proved incapable of engineering intercontinental missile superiority, despite having led the world in launching the first artificial orbital satellite, *Sputnik*. It took twenty analysts in the United States and ten in Britain to work through all the material Pen'kovskii handed over, so great was the damage done to Soviet interests.

Pen'kovskii was handled by MI6 and CIA. His contact was Anne Chisholm, wife of the rezident, Ruari. Normally, MI6 was invisible in Moscow. The Chisholms, however, were a team known to the Russians from their service in Berlin, courtesy of Blake. Anne was followed, and after a second careless encounter, KGB counterintelligence started watching Pen'kovskii. Having found out who he was, on January 29, 1962, Lieutenant General Oleg Gribanov, head of KGB counterintelligence, arranged close surveillance.

At the GRU, Serov did not learn of all this until April 1962, the very month that the Soviet leadership decided to place medium- and intermediate-range ballistic missiles in Cuba. The head of the Third

Directorate of the KGB (military counterintelligence), Anatolii Gus'kov briefed Serov at the Main Military Council. Serov then called Lieutenant General Smolikov, head of the GRU's personnel directorate, and told him to have Pen'kovskii dismissed. In May, Pen'kovskii was summoned and told he would be ejected from the GRU and redeployed to teach foreign languages. When he learned of this indiscretion, Gribanov, normally deferential to his former boss, barely suppressed his fury. He immediately impressed upon Serov the importance of reversing the decision in order that counterintelligence could proceed unhindered.[73]

The operation was called "Open Caesar!" Its initiator, Gribanov, who had served as deputy to Fyodotov in the early 1950s, was a small man of unsual hypnotic power known as "the little Bonaparte."[74] His deputy, Colonel Leonid Pasholikov, handled the detail. Lieutenants Alexei Kiselev and Nikolai Ionov were moved into the apartment above Pen'kovskii's, deceiving the family there into moving out with a free holiday to a GRU sanatorium on the Black Sea. From the balcony of the flat above, they dropped a miniature periscope to the level of Pen'kovskii's apartment below to film evidence that he was photographing secret documents. Rather than act immediately and search the apartment, Gribanov covered his exposed position by taking the matter to Semichastny at the top of the KGB; this had to be done because Pen'kovskii's two patrons, Serov and Marshal Sergei Varentsov, had direct access both to Khrushchev and to Defence Minister Marshal Rodion Malinovsky.

Approval was cautiously granted "For the possible exposure of facts relating to unsanctioned work with secret materials by Colonel Pen'kovskii in his place of habitation [sic]." To ensure the absence of the Pen'kovskii family, the KGB scattered toxins on the table and chairs of the apartment to induce excema, which was duly diagnosed by the GRU doctor. This led to the hospitalisation of the entire family while a thorough search was to take place. But they failed to take into account the ever-present Russian mother-in-law, Klavdiya Vlas'evna, who then thoughtfully took it upon herself to move in. An initial search had to be hurried while she was at the market. To find all that was needed, however, they had to create an incident at a market stall, resulting in her interrogation by the police for purported theft, which implausibly stretched out for a total of five gruelling hours, surely a record even for the militia.

The burglars found what they were looking for: three Minox

cameras, dictaphones, cipher tables, instructions on communications, and money. Fearing he might flee, and with Khrushchev's permission, they arrested Pen'kovskii (by then handled by the Americans) on October 22, 1962, the height of the Cuban Missile Crisis. Since all the evidence was in, and he was a weak man in an impossible situation, it was not hard to find Pen'kovskii guilty of having passed to CIA and MI5 more than five thousand photographs of secret information. After standing trial, he was shot on May 18, 1963.[75]

Serov, too, was punished for being duped so easily. He was dismissed on February 2, 1963, and successively demoted and stripped of Party membership. Humiliated, he survived in disgrace until he finally passed away on July 1, 1990. The tracking down and arrest of Pen'kovskii came under the supervision of Gribanov and stood to his credit. However, scandal soon enveloped Gribanov himself. He fell from office, just as had Serov, because of indiscreet relations with a subordinate turned traitor.

"Murat": The GRU Within NATO

The GRU suffered a severe reputational blow because of Pen'kovskii's treachery, but at least the fault for employing, trusting, and promoting him could be placed at the feet of Serov, whom Khrushchev had imposed on the directorate. Moreover, the GRU had successes to its credit, notably the agent "Murat."

In 1961 there appeared a new naval attaché in Paris by the name of Viktor Lyubimov, a bold and outstanding operative who impressed his superiors by taking the initiative. Even castigation for "arrogance" and "tactlessness" at his previous post in Washington, D.C., had done him no harm. Paris was the headquarters of NATO and therefore a prime target. General Charles de Gaulle had swept to power in 1958 on the back of French indignation at the various insults to national pride inflicted by a combination of violent colonial rebellion and American high-handedness. Here was a post to test Lyubimov's mettle.

He did not disappoint. Lyubimov soon recruited Colonel Charles d'Anfreville de Jurquet de la Salle ("Murat"), a count, a veteran of the war, and at first glance a most unlikely candidate. But he, too, was affronted at having to work as a subordinate to Americans in the NATO high command who had been too young to experience the reality of war. From de la Salle, Moscow secured NATO's plans for war, including the entire list of targets and the payload destined for the destruction of Warsaw Pact forces.[76]

Crisis over Missiles in Cuba: Operation Anadyr

Lagging behind in the strategic nuclear arms race as the Americans extended their advantage with every passing year, Khrushchev sought a short cut. This was how the Cuban Missile Crisis erupted in October 1962. The Russians always called this the Caribbean crisis—that is to say, it had little to do with Cuba itself.

At this point, Georgii Bol'shakov found a place in history. Trained for military intelligence in 1943, Bol'shakov was soon fluent in English. In 1951 he was despatched to the United States under cover as the TASS correspondent in Washington, D.C. There he established working relationships with American journalists before returning to Moscow. Bol'shakov was posted back to the capital in the inglorious aftermath of the Bay of Pigs, and renewed his contacts with the journalist Frank Holman at the National Press Club. There, on April 29, 1961, he received the surprising suggestion that he meet the president's brother, Attorney General Robert ("Bobby") Kennedy.

The Bay of Pigs (Baya de Cochinos) was the beach in Cuba where U.S.-backed forces landed in the expectation of overthrowing the Communist government led by Fidel Castro; the United States was especially troubled by Cuba's export of revolution across the Caribbean. Advanced word of the attack and details of the plans reached Moscow through various sources, including a GRU illegal working out of New York: this was Masha ("Maria") Dobrova, code name "Maisy."

Something of a polyglot, Dobrova had fought in the Spanish Civil War and worked at the Soviet consulate in Colombia after World War II. Charming as well as pretty, she was fluent in both English and French. Dobrova began serving in the GRU on September 5, 1951. To establish her legend, she was sent on a circuitous itinerary through Western Europe over a two-year period, which entailed her receiving cosmetic training and further language instruction while travelling on an American passport. Finally, in the summer of 1954, she settled in the United States. She was kept on ice for up to three years while she established a legitimate new identity, qualified at the Banford Academy of Beauty Culture, and opened up her own business ("Glen's Visiting") in a small house in the Bronx on the Grand Concourse. She met the illegal rezident once every three months. After a full briefing in Moscow, she began running and recruiting agents. Her work as a cosmetician was designed to bring her into close contact with the wives of influential Americans who, relaxing in congenial female company, would gossip about their spouses, to Soviet advantage.[77] Her information invariably checked out when arrayed against other valued indicators.

Dobrova's first case officer, Colonel Sergei Lebedev, a sympathetic figure, emphasised to her the importance of patience; she would be kept in reserve in case of war.[78] Arguably, Dobrova should have been in Washington, but Serov, then director of the GRU, did not believe in having women as operatives. So, instead of her revelations about the Bay of Pigs leading to a more prominent role, Dobrova languished; at a time of mounting crisis between the United States and the Soviet Union over the fate of Berlin, she had little to do.

The GRU was naturally made up of believers in rank, and although Bol'shakov was not the most junior at the embassy, he ranked about fortieth in the Soviet diplomatic list for Washington. Moscow was therefore puzzled, if not suspicious and indignant, at the suggestion that so lowly a figure could become the back channel with, of all people, the U.S. attorney general.

Maj. Gen. Sokolov, head of the American directorate at the GRU, cannot have been alone in his suspicions as to why such an extraordinary offer should come to someone so obscure. It was almost a calculated affront; indeed, a provocation. The response was predictably negative. Nonetheless, a meeting did eventually take place—Bol'shakov was finally unable to prevent it—on the evening of May 9 at the Department of Justice. Kennedy was extraordinarily frank, expressing worry lest Khrushchev underestimate the president after the Bay of Pigs fiasco. He insisted that his brother be taken seriously. At the same time, however, he argued that the president wished to take a nontraditional approach to relations with Moscow, hence the opening of this unofficial line between the Kremlin and the White House. From May 1961 to November 1962, some fifty meetings took place between

Bol'shakov and the attorney general, of which there appears to be no American record.

The problem was that the president's brother made clear from the outset that the White House regarded Cuba as "a dead problem" that should not stand in the way of relations between the two superpowers; that, contrary to appearances, the president wanted much closer relations with Moscow.[79] Inevitably, Khrushchev being Khrushchev, he took such gauche ineptitude as a sign of weakness. The president and his brother remained boys "in short trousers," as Ambassador Mikhail Menshikov quipped. Thus, the back channel reinforced the belief prevalent in the Kremlin that risks could be taken in relations with Washington without dire consequences.

The Russians were outgunned. To resolve the long-standing dispute over the possession of West Berlin, they needed more firepower. Lacking an intercontinental capability, Khrushchev decided to install medium- and intermediate-range nuclear-tipped ballistic missiles in Cuba. Deploying the missiles was viewed as a quick fix for the gross imbalance of strategic nuclear power that stood to American advantage; at the time, U.S. superiority in intercontinental bombers and intercontinental ballistic missiles (including those at sea) was no secret, supplemented as it was by carrier-based dual-capable aircraft and medium-range missiles in Western Europe and Turkey. The Russians lacked intercontinental ballistic missiles, their long-range air force was of dubious effectiveness, and their diesel-powered submarines could deliver only a nuclear torpedo.

Khrushchev cajoled the rest of the leadership into accepting the idea of this "offensive policy" on May 24, 1962.[80] But Operation Anadyr had to be implemented in the strictest secrecy, during a communications blackout, until the missiles were up and ready for firing, in order to forestall any American attempt to prevent their installation. Radio silence was complete. Not a word of instruction or information went along electronic wires that could be intercepted by the NSA or GCHQ, which had succeeded the GC&CS, in Cheltenham. Everything went by hand.[81] Anticipating a crisis, Serov instructed all illegals in the United States with the right to communicate directly with Moscow that, in the event of extreme need, they could contact the Soviet diplomatic mission on Sixty-seventh Street in New York City.[82]

It was, of course, to the Bol'shakov back channel that the White

House turned when intelligence confirmed that offensive Soviet missiles were being shipped into Cuba for deployment. But, at a meeting on October 5, before the president was finally convinced by image intelligence that such missiles had indeed arrived, Bol'shakov, in perfect ignorance, and under instruction, denied to Robert Kennedy that anything other than "defensive" weapons were being put in. When Gromyko arrived in Washington to see the president, knowing perfectly well that Moscow was deceiving the Americans, he refused even to listen to a briefing from the KGB rezidents and the two new and very senior military attachés, Lieutenant General Vladimir Dubovik and Rear Adm. Leonid Bekrenyov, before concluding that everything was just fine according to both official and "unofficial channels."[83]

Everything was not fine—and as the crisis broke out, it was the attorney general who activated his contact with Bol'shakov through Holman in order to find a solution that took the missiles out of Cuba but allowed the Russians to save face. On October 25, Holman suggested to Bol'shakov that American missile bases in Turkey be exchanged for those in Cuba. It was this proposal that formed the core of the agreement reached by Ambassador Anatoly Dobrynin and Bobby Kennedy between October 26 and 28.[84]

Throughout the month of October, the two GRU rezidentury in the United States sent a total of 268 reports to Moscow. All information that came in went to a group of analysts under the chairmanship of the KGB chief Semichastny, including representatives from the First Main Directorate, the Foreign Ministry, the Ministry of Defence, and the GRU. While back-channel efforts to resolve the crisis were being made in Washington, the Russians were closely monitoring the communications systems of the U.S. Strategic Air Command. At 10:00 a.m. on October 24, Eastern Standard Time, the GRU intercepted an order from the Joint Chiefs of Staff to ready for a nuclear attack. The rezidentura reported, "For twenty-four hours from October 23, 85 planes belonging to strategic aviation were flying above the USA. Of these 22 were B-52 bombers. 57 B-47s left the United States for Europe." The GRU picked up the order "Maintain course even in the event of one engine going out of commission."

The tension grew. Kennedy issued his ultimatum for removal of Soviet missiles at 2:00 p.m. on October 26. At 12:00 p.m. the following day, the Soviet rezident noted, "The next 24 hours will be decisive."

Secretary of Defense Robert McNamara had called up reserves, and although Soviet attachés could not reach Florida because of travel restrictions, their allies from Poland and Czechoslovakia were able to report back on contingents of U.S. forces ready to invade Cuba. Meanwhile, the rezident reported a comment from a member of the British embassy, who was at the Pentagon every day for several hours, to the effect that "invasion will take place in 5–7 days."[85]

The Eighth Main Directorate of the KGB, under Lieutenant General Serafim Lyalin, had also made progress breaking American ciphers. Nikolai Andreev, among the cryptanalysts, recalls that "the most important thing in those days was that the country's leadership knew precisely at what stage in the development of the crisis the Americans were prepared to use nuclear weapons. Knowing where this threshold lay enabled it to control the situation, hold the initiative in decision making, [and to decide] whether to advance or to stop."[86] An array of those from the directorate were subsequently given medals; the most outstanding secretly awarded the coveted Lenin Prize.[87] This was the kind of prestige the special service had always sought but had invariably found beyond reach. Unfortunately for Moscow, Khrushchev then boasted of this victory, the Americans promptly took countermeasures, and the special service was back to square one.[88]

The Downfall of Gribanov

The entrapment and exposure of Pen'kovskii showed counterintelligence at its most effective. The operation also followed a series of offensives against Western officials from within Moscow that took full advantage of a strategy pursued with some success in the late 1920s: the honey trap. The first example postwar was the recruitment in 1955 of the junior naval clerk at the British embassy in Moscow, a homosexual named John Vassall. The second was sprung to entrap a visiting Tory MP and former intelligence officer, Commander Anthony Courtney, in May 1961. Courtney refused to cooperate, however, and indeed bravely publicised the whole affair. The third was laid against a notably perceptive French ambassador, Louis Joxe. Then came the Canadian ambassador John Watkins, who in 1964 died under interrogation; and Joxe's successor, Maurice Dejean, a friend of de Gaulle's who had relied upon Gribanov (operating under another name) to extricate him from the awkward consequences of a romantic entanglement until he was removed from his post in 1963. The setup was the customary one of the victim caught in flagrante delicto by the supposed husband who threatened to make everything known. The aim here was to turn Dejean into an "agent of influence" rather than a spy, a face-saving distinction.[89]

Yet Gribanov was also personally vulnerable, no less so than Serov. This became evident with the baffling defection to the United States of Yuri Nosenko. A man driven by a taste for the sensual side of life, Nosenko joined the MGB, where his fluency in foreign languages made him stand out, and served under Gribanov, initially in the first department (anti-American operations) and then as deputy head of the seventh department.

As a result of his father's former post as minister of the shipbuilding industry, Nosenko established a network of contacts across subsections of the Second Main Directorate, a ready source of information. From 1957, by virtue of backing from Dmitrii Ustinov, later minister of defence, he was permitted trips to Britain, Cuba, and Switzerland, a most unusual privilege for someone at his level.

This enabled him to give the Americans secret intelligence of interest in June 1962, when he made his first approach in Geneva, having been sent with the Soviet delegation to the disarmament talks as the watchman, or *kirpich*, which literally means "brick," a term taken from the No Entry/No Exit sign on roads. Nosenko had stolen money from the rezidentura to fund an evening out. He needed cash, rapidly, and approached an American diplomat. The CIA scalp hunter Kisevalter was called in, and in return for information, Nosenko received more than enough for his immediate purpose: nine hundred Swiss francs.[90]

Nosenko's access to secrets was greatly enhanced by the fact that he was close to Gribanov himself and attended his drunken parties. Indeed, immediately before Nosenko's departure for Geneva as the counterintelligence officer responsible for the Soviet delegation to the International Committee on Disarmament, he and Gribanov caroused together all night in the same apartment.

After a fortnight in Geneva, Nosenko asked the Americans for political asylum. In March 1964, Moscow began recalling rezidents from across the globe whom Nosenko may have known. The damage was

considerable. Moreover, Nosenko was privy to Gribanov's most inti-
mate secrets, including the fact that he lived with a female operative
by the name of Churaeva, who worked for the First Main Directorate.
Gribanov should have known of Nosenko's planned defection, but if he
did, he certainly took no action to forestall it and, according to Viktor
Martynov, who was leading the investigation, subsequently attempted
to cover everything up.

The fact that Gribanov was a protégé of the ideologue Mikhail
Suslov, éminence grise of the Soviet régime, made matters all the more
difficult. Finally, not only was Gribanov sacked, he was also removed
from the Party Central Committee for "political duplicity," a most
unusual occurrence within the organs.[91] Gribanov was then excluded
from the Party entirely, in August 1965, and took to writing spy fiction
as a sideline under a pseudonym; his first best seller, *The Secret Agent's
Blunder*, was turned into a very popular film in 1968.[92] Serov should
perhaps have spent less time in the gym.

The Profumo Affair

The hostile presence of both the KGB and the GRU in London was
larger than in any city other than New York and Washington, and for
good reason. The British were still second only to the main enemy, or
"the probable enemy," as the GRU used to say. "Both rezidentury—KGB
and GRU—were absolutely independent from one another and were in
no way subordinated to the embassy even though they worked under its
roof. However, not all employees of either rezidentura worked only in the
Soviet embassy. Many of them were senior officials at the USSR's trade
delegation in London, on the premises of various Soviet periodicals
and information agencies, in the offices of such agencies as Aeroflot,
Intourist etc. But wherever these employees were formally categorised,
their work was supervised by the rezident, in turn receiving instructions
from the centre."[93]

The Profumo affair blew up in the summer of 1963. This was the
worst possible moment for Prime Minister Harold Macmillan. Only
six months earlier, having been alerted to the danger of exposure by
Blunt (visiting ostensibly in search of a flower actually easily found in
Britain rather than Lebanon), Philby had absconded from Beirut. But

the Profumo problem actually began in 1961, and it highlighted a problem that had persisted since MI5's Liddell sought endless, utterly implausible excuses for members of the Cambridge Five. Harold Wilson, leader of the Labour Party opposition, rightly summed up this "lapse" as a consequence of the security services being run with "nonchalant amateurism in a world of ruthless professionalism."[94]

John ("Jack") Profumo was, on the face of it, merely a junior minister, but his formal status was misleading. He had access to high-level military secrets, due to his role in facilitating the acquisition of Polaris (a submarine-launched ballistic missile system) from the United States and, latterly, his membership on the Cabinet Defence Committee.

It is unclear when exactly Stephen Ward, the charming, sexually charged society osteopath, first met the GRU officer and assistant naval attaché Evgenii Ivanov. Ivanov was a bulky man with a broken nose and a louche manner that some women found irresistible. Ward might in fact have come to the attention of the GRU before Ivanov's arrival in London on March 27, 1960; we simply do not know. He was fiercely anti-American and pro-Soviet—and it was scarcely a well kept secret. His prejudices will have made Ward the object of attention from Soviet intelligence given that his clientèle included high society. Ward was a conspicuous and regular guest at Soviet embassy receptions. He also supplied women as well as osteopathy to those in high society needing various forms of therapy. It might not have been entirely accidental that Ivanov was posted to London on the back of his own reputation on assignment in Norway as a serial womaniser. Christine Keeler, the boldly sensuous young woman who ended up sleeping initially with Ivanov and then with "Jack," claims Ward and Ivanov knew each other even before Sir Colin Coote, manager of the *Daily Telegraph* (himself previously associated with MI6), supposedly introduced one to the other.

On June 8, 1961, Ward, as he explained in detail to Ivanov, was called to an interview with the MI5 officer Keith Wagstaffe ("Woods"), an avuncular and self-satisfied figure in a bowler hat who was all too easily palmed off with comforting reassurance. "I do not think that he [Ward] is of security interest," Wagstaffe complacently concluded. This was, after all, preeminently the age of deference in postwar Britain. Barely a month later, on July 8–9, entirely unknown to anyone from MI5, Ward's young plaything Keeler was swimming naked in the pool at Lord ("Billy") Astor's house at Cliveden in front of the secretary of state for war. Not that nudity was required to launch the priapic Profumo into action.

By the time Wagstaffe and Ward met a second time, on May 28, 1962, the affair between Keeler and Profumo was already fully under way. Rather than hearing of this crucial news, Wagstaffe instead sat through a tediously pro-Soviet diatribe from Ward, and came away recalling only his "queer opinions about Russia's aims in international affairs." Of course, MI5 had no idea that Ward's protégé, Keeler, had slept with both the secretary of state for war and Ivanov.[95]

When the scandal finally made headlines on June 12, 1963, Prime Minister Harold Macmillan noted hastily, with prematurely smug satisfaction, that "there appeared to be no truth in Mr. Ward's assertion that he had given the Secret Service information about the relationship between Mr. Profumo and Miss Keeler."[96] Finally, on November 2, MI5 acknowledged to the Foreign Office that Ward indeed had "a number of titled and influential friends and patients, including several members of the Cabinet," but the agency still held firmly to the belief that Ward was "not a man who would be actively disloyal." The furthest it would go, belatedly to protect its all-too-vulnerable backside, was to say that he was not to be trusted.[97]

It was very late in the day indeed, on June 13, 1963, that a baffled prime minister and an equally disconcerted Cabinet at last learned of Keeler's statement on January 30 (the day after Ivanov left for Moscow), "to the effect that only a few weeks previously she had been asked by Mr. Ward to try to obtain secret information from Mr. Profumo." But it had taken nearly six months for the prime minister to be informed of the fact. It emerged only as a result of an investigation by Lord Chancellor Reginald Manningham-Buller, the 1st Baron Dilhorne. At a stroke, he revealed that this was not just a matter of impropriety but crucially also of espionage. Not suprisingly, Macmillan admonished his slumbering security service for not realising the risk and failing to be prompt in warning the government.[98]

Red faces all round at MI5, no doubt, when a double agent in Moscow sent word on June 14 that "the Russians had in fact received a lot of useful information from Profumo from Christine Keeler, with whom Ivanov had even been able to lay on eaves-dropping operations at the appropriate times."[99] Not only had Keeler handed over to Ivanov

Profumo's love letters, but Ward had thoughtfully and discreetly photographed Keeler and "Jack" making love at 17 Wimpole Mews.[100] Ward "practically worked for me and concealed nothing," Ivanov recalled.[101]

Not everything depended upon Ward, the eager accomplice. Ivanov had twice used a Minox camera at Profumo's home, Nash House, on Chester Terrace, when Valerie Hobson, the minister's wife, left him alone in the study. He subsequently despatched details of the top-secret X-15 experimental high-altitude, hypersonic aircraft. He also revealed, for example, "Long Trust," contingency plans for the rotation of individual battle groups after the Berlin Wall went up in August 1961.

Had a conflict between NATO and the Warsaw Pact broken out at that moment, Soviet knowledge of these plans would have enabled them to inflict severe damage on Western conventional forces that held the line in Berlin. Ivanov also revealed MC-70: top-secret plans for the dual deployment of tactical nuclear weapons in Europe.[102] These were matters of considerable importance for NATO during a period of heightened international tension, especially given the ever-present danger of miscalculation on the part of the unpredictable Nikita Khrushchev leading to war.

In Moscow, Captain Ievlev, head of the British department at the GRU, had the responsibility of putting together the entire operation. When Ivanov returned to Moscow at the end of 1961, he was carefully debriefed for that purpose. The idea was to use an illegal to confront Profumo with the evidence of his indiscretions, including photocopies of the documents obtained, in order to press him into service.[103] Had the scandal not exploded into public view so quickly, and had Profumo reached the point of being blackmailed, the security implications would have been even more serious.

Through membership of the Cabinet Defence Committee, Profumo had direct knowledge of the extent of disarray within NATO; the details of negotiations with Secretary of Defense Robert McNamara that aimed to create a multilateral force controversially designed to give West Germany access to nuclear weapons (a contingency that Moscow greatly feared); plans to hand over naval facilities in Scotland to the Americans in return for Polaris-firing submarines to replace the bomber force; and the severe weaknesses in British preparations for chemical and biological warfare, use of which was anticipated in the event of a war limited to the European theatre.[104]

Not surprisingly, General Joseph Carroll, former FBI agent and head of the Defense Intelligence Agency, told the Bureau that "Defense Secretary McNamara is extremely interested in the Keeler case and has asked to be kept promptly informed on all developments."[105] That was an understatement.

Ivashutin Takes Charge of the GRU

The scandal enveloping Macmillan's government complicated relations with the Kennedy administration to Moscow's advantage. It had, however, also exposed the GRU to further unwanted publicity after the arrest and execution of the traitor Pen'kovskii. Its new director, appointed on March 18, 1963, was Colonel-General Pyotr Ivashutin (né Ivashutich). There were thousands of generals in the military, yet Khrushchev appointed a man from the KGB whom he could trust. The GRU, which answered directly only to the General Staff, clearly needed house cleaning and updating.

In terms of overseas posts, the GRU saw itself as more in the business of "pure intelligence" than its counterpart and as more effective, certainly in science and technology. It was also better connected to national liberation movements in the Third World, including terrorist organisations, which gave it a reach that the KGB never possessed and seriously envied. Its Military-Diplomatic Academy, until 1948 the Soviet Army Academy, was nicknamed Konservatoriya ("the Conservatoire"). Its new location could be found at 50 Narodnogo Opolcheniya, near Oktyabr'skoe Pole Metro station, which had been built as recently as 1972. Here stood the first faculty, for intelligence training. Various other faculties were scattered across the city.

The GRU was highly selective. It took in junior officers, though no lower than the rank of captain, no younger than thirty and no older than thirty-five years of age. Only one in ten was accepted. Two hundred graduated at the end of each year.[106] Conditions for entry were never made explicit, but apart from the age qualification, they included exemplary military service, membership of the Party, military education to degree level, physical fitness, and an additional, idiosyncratic requirement: candidates had to be married with children. Wives were also indoctrinated.[107] The head of the Academy was a deputy director of the GRU.

The syllabus was not much different from that of the KGB, including the teaching of *spets podgotovka* ("tradecraft") along with area studies, foreign languages, and so on. At the KGB, the training was arguably less thorough: those who already had foreign languages received only one year's instruction. Those who were in science or technology had to start learning languages from scratch, which took three years. Other than proficiency in foreign languages, knowledge of human psychology was the most valued asset. In addition, knowledge of other countries and a "healthy cynicism" were of course also prized.[108]

Ivashutin was obsessively professional, having overseen counterintelligence since 1954. The only drawback, given the history of KGB-GRU rivalry, was that he had been transferred between rival institutions and, being in counterintelligence, he had been a watchman for the KGB. In other respects, however, he was not a typical *kagebist*. Ivashutin was ready to make the GRU his own, having all but exhausted himself filling the vacuum at the top of the KGB as first deputy chairman; he also stood in as chairman for a week after Shelepin's resignation, though given the highly political nature of the job, he was never likely to be given the chair permanently. At the Lubyanka, Shelepin had focused his energies on transforming his position into a springboard to supreme power. Semichastny, Shelepin's protégé, who replaced him on November 13, 1961, turned out to be no great improvement.[109] Thereafter, Ivashutin had as little to do with his former home as he could. Indeed, he did nothing to facilitate close cooperation, even to the detriment of the common cause.

Born in 1909 to a Ukrainian father and a Byelorussian mother, Ivashutin started out as a metalworker. At the age of twenty-four, he trained as a bomber pilot and instructor in the air force. Then, in January 1939, before he could complete senior officer's training at the Zhukovskii Air Force Academy, he was directed into the murky world of counterintelligence at the NKVD. For the latter half of the war he served in SMERSH. Here, he rose rapidly from the rank of captain to lieutenant general under Abakumov. In the second half of the decade, Ivashutin was fully engaged in suppressing nationalist rebels in the Ukraine, backed by the British and American secret services.[110]

Ivashutin headed the GRU for a quarter of a century. A private man and a fervent patriot who believed secrets should remain secret, he kept his head down and never gave interviews except to brief those fictionalising the work of the GRU, including the life and career of Sorge (deemed necessary after the GRU's proud image was sullied by Pen'kovskii's betrayal). This was an issue not merely of personal preference. Whereas his counterpart at the Lubyanka had the privilege of direct access to the Party's general secretary, the director of the GRU had to operate indirectly through the chief of the General Staff and the defence minister, who could not even be certain of a seat on the Politburo until 1973.

Ivashutin lived well within his means: in retirement he had the same modest datcha and car acquired in the 1950s. He could not tolerate flattery, never drank alcohol, and was more than a little moralistic, though he could take a joke; he was a convinced anti-Semite, had a love of technology, a formidable memory for detail, and strange to relate, he was a great lover of poetry who knew many contemporary poets and would recite their work at length.[111] Rear Adm. Anatoly Rimskii recalls, "His intuition was astonishing. He saw the whole picture. Thus certain operations promising, it would seem, guaranteed success would suddenly be cancelled by him and, as it turned out later, he always turned out to be right."[112] Not an insecure personality in need of yes-men, to the amazement of his colleagues the only person he brought in to the GRU from the Lubyanka was his assistant, Igor Popov.[113]

By the early 1960s the massive investment that followed Stalin's death finally began yielding returns. Although cryptography was still feeling the strain (more of this later), advances in human intelligence put the Americans and their allies on their mettle. Moreover, the latter were still reeling from the aftermath of Black Friday 1948. To the extent that winning the Cold War depended upon gaining the edge in intelligence, Moscow showed every evidence of striding ahead. It was also confident of being able to match the spy satellite capabilities of the Americans before the decade was out.

Under Khrushchev, the moments of relief from constant confrontation proved fleeting. The pressure exerted on the West in Europe and the Third World was persistent and probing. The détente that the European democracies, in particular, had dreamed of under Khrushchev faded all too rapidly with the Berlin crisis between 1958 and 1961, capped by the Cuban Missile Crisis of October 1962. However much both sides in the Cold War wished to avoid open conflict, the search for marginal advantage proved unending. There would therefore be no relief from the ongoing Cold War, in spite of treaties on the banning of atomic tests and a treaty on the nonproliferation of nuclear weapons. These measures were simply palliatives, not significant enough to halt further intensification of the war between intelligence services. Here the crucial weakness now emerging within the Soviet Union was something the services could do little or nothing about: disillusionment with the entire socialist system.

9. LOSS OF FAITH

The paradox of Soviet espionage was that Stalin rated human intelligence above cryptography and valued recruitment of the ideologically like-minded above those with mercenary motives. This high-minded preference was that of a revolutionary. As a strategy, however, it could succeed only if communism as a cause remained a credible focus of belief for those disillusioned with democracy under capitalism. That faith, however, was severely strained by Khrushchev's denunciation of Stalin in 1956, and it could not survive the Warsaw Pact invasion of Czechoslovakia twelve years later.

The shock of the invasion and occupation of Prague made it extremely unlikely that recruitment in the West could continue to be based on ideology, certainly among the better educated, such as university students. The dramatic loss of innocence could not be reversed. Worse still, disillusionment began to set in; a condition that became chronic when, after the fears and hopes unleashed by Khrushchev, the Soviet Union in Leonid Brezhnev's later years succumbed to a stultifying inertia and widespread corruption at every level of society. However disciplined, the intelligence services could not entirely escape the consequences, most seriously the loss of faith. Instead, those disillusioned by the West were increasingly enlisted under a "false flag." Within West Germany, in some notable instances (such as secretaries in the BND and the office of the president) this could even mean neo-Nazi movements created entirely for that purpose.

Andropov Takes Charge

The setback for the First Main Directorate in the loss of the priceless asset that Stalin so much relied upon was matched in counterintelligence by the crumbling of faith in the revolution at home. Although protests at the invasion of Hungary caused problems only among Soviet students, the destruction of the Prague Spring, the opening of Czechoslovakia to social-democratic reform in 1968, prompted discontent even within the Party apparat. This played to NATO's advantage. Russians were increasingly losing their commitment to communism, a commitment that had never been shared by the captive populations of Eastern Europe. Younger Russians, in particular, increasingly understood that they had been lied to about the reality of living conditions in the West, especially as tourists began flocking into Moscow and Leningrad from the early 1970s, a logistical nightmare requiring special measures at the Lubyanka.

Discontented Russians thus fell easy prey to NATO intelligence. Indeed, of the Soviet citizens working as spies exposed by the Second Main Directorate between 1972 and 1982, one half had offered their services to the enemy, above all the United States.[1] This was the era of the bitterest and most brilliant satire of Soviet society, published in 1976 by a former professor of logic at Moscow University, Alexander Zinoviev, *Yawning Heights*, all the more damaging because it took so much of the Soviet system, *sotsizm*, as a given. Prostitution was rife, and even waiters serving foreign tourists in hotels within sight of the Kremlin openly offered to change money on the black market (an offence that would normally have led to a labour camp sentence). The irony was that this revolutionary sclerosis at home had become so well entrenched that it reached its peak just at the point that the KGB acquired as chief Yuri Andropov ("Yuva"), ideologically the most committed and intelligent Leninist that Russia had seen for decades.

It was said that Andropov had no liking for the KGB before he was handed the poisoned chalice of chairmanship on May 18, 1967. But if he were ever to realize his ambition to follow in Lenin's footsteps, he would have to prove himself. By the time Andropov took charge, his outlook had been hardened by the trauma experienced as Soviet ambassador to Hungary in October 1956, from which he drew the "sad lesson" that "truth" could not be defended merely by "word and pen" but also "if needs be, with the hatchet." Andropov was nonetheless a purposeful innovator, setting up closed research institutes not only in areas of former interest (the economics of socialist countries, which he once supervised from his perch in the Central Committee) but also across the board, in computer science, electronics, communications, and cryptography.[2]

At home, Andropov moved further toward a more efficient and sophisticated repression of dissent, which involved both widespread mentoring and a system of probation for minor malefactors. This policy, though more "liberal" than that which led to massacres ineptly perpetrated in panic under Khrushchev, should not be confused with leniency. Andropov also introduced the truly horrifying abuse of psychiatric confinement on a broad scale, inflicting debilitating drugs on those such as Vladimir Bukovsky who were insane enough to believe that the Soviet system had failed.

Andropov tried, with marginal success, to cut away at excessively corrupt practices and the baronial patronage that encouraged them, but it was an uphill battle, and corruption ultimately proved a hurdle impossible to clear. He was more successful abroad, at ramping up military-industrial espionage to enhance Soviet technology and in tireless efforts to subvert the "main enemy."

In May 1968, Andropov briefed Brezhnev on "the reinforcement above all of foreign political intelligence," particularly in the field of human intelligence. Of the 218 foreigners recruited in 1967, 64 were in a position to operate against the United States. Meanwhile, counterintelligence forestalled the entrapment of twenty-two KGB and GRU operatives and agents and eight more from Allied countries. Nonetheless, Andropov was dissatisfied that the KGB had "still not established the agents needed within the governmental, military and intelligence organs and ideological centres of the enemy" to give up-to-date guidance on its intentions and plans. The same could also be said for counterintelligence on Soviet soil.[3]

Brezhnev, who had ousted Khrushchev in October 1964, did not entirely trust Andropov. So the latter was surrounded by Brezhnev protégés, and the consequences of their corruptive influence became a major headache. A comfortable office in a prestigious institution was just the thing for hangers-on. Even Semichastny had tried to root them out: Right before he was ousted from office as head of the KGB, he tried to lay his hands on Sakharovskii's fiefdom. He appointed the former rezident in Israel, Ivan Dedulya, as a roving inspector with oversight on operations, answering directly to the chairman. By the time Dedulya got to work, however, Andropov was in charge.

Over the course of the next eight years, Andropov clashed increasingly with Brezhnev appointees such as the counterintelligence chief Georgii Tsinyov and, the least agreeable of all, Viktor Alidin, in trying to clean house of widespread incompetence and corruption. As Dedulya has pointed out, in 1954 there were no generals in the KGB. Within a few years the group could count three: Sakharovskii, Korotkov, and Aleksei Krokhin (first deputy to Sakharovskii). By 1985, there were more than fifty.[4]

At the time the Soviet Union collapsed, the First Main Directorate amounted to twelve thousand people.[5] "There was paper in unbelievable quantities, as every document spawned several more," recalled one veteran of those times. "The only difference from other Soviet organisations consisted in the fact that paper got lost in only the rarest of cases, and deadlines were quite strictly adhered to. Intelligence in any country is part of the bureaucratic apparatus. And insofar as we were concerned, especially during the latter days of Brezhnev, bureaucracy was at its most decadent, intelligence followed suit."

The perils of stagnation, from recruitment on up, were apparent throughout the KGB. Playing it safe (*perestrakhovka*) was the watchword. As a consequence, "They selected not those who could make the best contribution, but above all those who would wreak the least damage." Signs of initiative in a candidate evoked mistrust: "Why is he like that? Wouldn't he be likely to flee abroad?" In the first round, they eliminated clever intellectuals: "They were considered (true, not unnaturally) as being psychologically unstable." Those who were ambitious were also cut out. If they were undervalued, they would no doubt resort to intrigues. Overall, the preference was for "solid mediocrities." These were more likely to be appreciative of the many benefits the service afforded them. Moreover, the practice of handing out "gifts" purchased abroad on foreign postings to superiors (or their wives) became the norm rather than exception; it was standard practice at the Foreign Ministry under Gromyko. And in terms of sheer numbers, the KGB was growing exponentially.[6]

In these conditions, maintaining strict security proved impossible. On January 18, 1983, for example, an order was issued tightening up procedures and condemning private sharing of operational details, the movement of personnel from one distinct set of functions in the office to another, the unsystematic allocation of tasks to operatives, and the sharing of secrets in conversation.[7]

Furthermore, the world of intelligence had changed a great deal from the early days, when the head of the service would personally brief those joining a rezidentura; this procedure had long become utterly impracticable. One former officer witheringly caricatured KGB practice in assigning men to the field; they were posted, he said, "like parcels to the places where they were needed."[8] In return for such manifest indifference to individual talents, no one was removed from the First Main Directorate except through retirement, and even these were kept on as consultants. This was a world that easily accommodated a time server like Vladimir Kryuchkov.[9]

Typically in intelligence, successes remained hidden, whereas failures had an awkwardly uncontrollable tendency to become publicly known. Almost immediately after the First Main Directorate was handed over to Andropov's right-hand man, the timid Kryuchkov, a crisis exploded in London. A mediocre apparatchik of no known ability, and possessed of no experience whatsoever, Kryuchkov, who had served under Andropov since 1956, was someone Andropov trusted and groomed for advancement. He had been put in charge of European operations, the archives, the new analytical service, and collaboration with Warsaw Pact allies, until eventually he took over the reins of the First Main Directorate (foreign intelligence) from an increasingly infirm Sakharovskii.[10] The KGB had once again to suffer the indignity of being managed by novices, albeit some more enlightened than usual.

The London Purge

The KGB department responsible for paramilitary preparation for war behind enemy lines, V department (terrorism and subversion), could hardly have been more sensitive. On September 3, 1971, the operative Major Oleg Lyalin defected. Lyalin was under cover as a senior engineer for the massive Soviet trade mission in Highgate, London. His job was to hire agents capable of carrying out assassination and sabotage in the event of war and searching out likely targets—in his case, ports and naval communications. The fact that this role had been given to someone so fond of the bottle indicates that it cannot have been high on the list of KGB priorities. Indeed, V department had been crippled by Sakharovskii when he was under pressure to reduce costs: obliged to absorb the illegal intelligence directorate, he retaliated by simultaneously cutting operatives.[11]

With détente in prospect, cost cutting seemed to make good sense to those in charge of the economy. Between 1969 and 1975, a postwar settlement in Europe was finally being orchestrated, though one that bricked in the territorial status quo and, at least in Brezhnev's eyes, also cemented Soviet hegemony over Central and Eastern Europe.[12] At the same time, however, Andropov in particular showed no sign of abandoning the ideological struggle. On the contrary, the more inert and decrepit the revolution became at home, the more actively was the cause of communism pushed abroad, and the reaction this caused in the West ultimately put détente in reverse. Instead of cutting its team, the KGB had significantly increased the number of spies in London, which MI6 and MI5 were extremely anxious to reduce.

These spies and associated Soviet citizens in foreign capitals were obliged to live within an official ghetto, the Soviet "colony" in London. KGB operative Oleg Lyalin was unsuited to his role because, although knowledgeable about shipping and very effective at running what amounted to a subordinate rezidentura in London made up of Armenian Cypriots, who even had their own radio communications, he and his wife did not feel at home. Lyalin's only real experience had been observing shipping on the Lithuanian coast; his wife, Tamara, never settled in. The selection of Lyalin for the mission was another example of the then-current trend of offering jobs to those from the periphery. Little thought had been given, however, as to how such people would cope not only with a great metropolis (compared to which Moscow resembled little more than an overgrown village), with all its advantages as well as disadvantages, but also how to fend off what was now a proactive counterintelligence service. MI5 by now ensured that it had at its disposal all the personal gossip that the large Soviet official community generated.

When Tamara, lonely and frustrated, finally abandoned her friendless existence and went back home, Lyalin promptly began living with a local girl while simultaneously carrying on an affair with the wife of a colleague. To say the least, this was more than a little risky. It was not long before Special Branch and MI5 caught on to what was happening. Lyalin began cooperating with them voluntarily from April 1971, and was debriefed at a safe house, 24 Collingham Gardens, near the Earls Court Underground station. But the idea of long-term collaboration was seriously jeopardised by a drunk-driving incident that could not be covered up and that, had it been reported to the embassy, would have resulted in immediate disgrace and hasty repatriation.[13]

Lyalin therefore asked for and received political asylum, prompting London to seize this once-in-a-lifetime opportunity to eject a sufficient number of Soviet intelligence officers to make counterintelligence manageable. On September 24, ninety officers were unceremoniously removed from Britain and a further fifteen denied the right of return.[14] This amounted to 20 percent of the five hundred fifty Soviet officials in London. Ironically, the preference for stationing "peripherals" in Britain was only reinforced by these measures, since undetectability became the crucial criterion. Clearly, Moscow never bothered to plumb the underlying reasons for the Lyalin affair.[15] This had the long-term effect of seriously undercutting the Soviet intelligence effort in Britain— though one prize agent, Geoffrey Prime ("Rowlands"), a Russian linguist and pederast, was still securely on the books. Prime, then in the Royal Air Force, had been recruited in January 1968 on his own initiative. He was enrolled in Berlin, then under the jurisidiction of the Third Main Directorate, which handled counterintelligence for the Soviet Group of Forces in Germany. For this reason, Prime was run outside Britain and thus fortuitously insulated from the leakages of information from the KGB rezidentura in London.[16] By the mid-1970s, he was working as a transcriber and translator at GCHQ.[17]

"Aktivka"

The Lyalin defection and the surrounding scandal was Kryuchkov's uncomfortable introduction to a world he had yet to assimilate. The unexpected inflammation of relations with Britain might explain why, in the summer of 1972, Andropov finally acceded to a repeated request from the general secretary of the Irish Communist Party, Michael O'Riordan, for military assistance in Northern Ireland, where, since 1969, an armed struggle had been renewed against an intolerant Protestant ascendancy.[18] Andropov presented the Politburo with a plan for secret arms shipments to the Soviet Union's Irish "friends." This was Operation Vsplesk ("splash"). O'Riordan ended up obtaining plastic explosives from the Russians that had originated with the British Army on the Rhine (BAOR).[19]

More such operations were to follow, though largely in the Third World. After Israel humiliated the front-line Arab states in the Six-Day War (June 1967), the Soviet leadership came under surprise attack at the subsequent Central Committee plenum for lack of belligerence. The chief of the First Main Directorate, Sakharovskii, who had "advised" the Romanian security services between November 13, 1949, and November 19, 1952, flew into Bucharest shortly thereafter to inform his counterparts that Moscow was determined to bolster its Arab friends by helping them in terrorist operations against Israeli targets.[20]

For this purpose, the Russians turned to one of their agents, Dr. Wadi Haddad, deputy head and chief of foreign operations of the Popular Front for the Liberation of Palestine (PFLP), himself a victim of Israeli terrorism. Haddad ("Natsionalist") was assisted with "special actions" (otherwise known as terrorism) throughout the Middle East, even a bizarre operation to kidnap the head of the CIA station in Beirut, which fell through.[21]

The better-known Palestine Liberation Organization, headed by Yasser Arafat from 1969, was less attractive to the Russians, as it had been opportunist in its search for allies. Under Arafat's predecessor, Shukeiri, the PLO's ties with China irritated Moscow; China was now an adversary and a fierce rival for influence in the Third World.[22] Undeterred, on September 7, 1973, the Soviet leadership authorised secret contacts with Arafat's people through the rezidentura in Lebanon.[23] Training for PLO operatives was organised within the Soviet Union.[24]

The blurring between "active measures" and terrorism was unavoidable, and with Moscow behind the idea of sustaining and developing terrorism in the Middle East, it was only a brief step to doing so in Europe, where the regular Communist parties had become so constitutionalist that they all but accepted a status quo that was intolerable to the Russians over the long term. Here the Brigate Rosse (Red Brigades) had emerged in Italy and the Rote Armee Fraktion (Red Army Faction) in West Germany on the back of the failed student unrest of the late 1960s. The idea of providing arms, including bomb-making equipment, and training to the Italian and German terrorists using the PFLP as a cutout no doubt seemed obvious. But training facilities were also incautiously afforded in Czechoslovakia and East Germany.

The Russians thus worked through the Czech (StB) and East German (BStU, or Stasi) intelligence services. Researching the Brigate Rosse in the Stasi archive, Antonio Selvatici found that imprinted on the photographs of the BR's leading members were the words "Album of Friends in International Terrorism." When he asked the archivist what this meant, he was told "it is a catalogue of terrorists compiled by the KGB in the form of a book." The associated database was shared by Russia with trusted allied intelligence in Bulgaria, Poland, Czechoslovakia, Outer Mongolia, Cuba, East Germany, and Vietnam.[25] This was not a form of stamp collecting but something much more sinister.

It was not only the KGB that formed these ties. Indeed, the GRU simultaneously operated throughout the Middle East in greater numbers and with more of an open mind than did the rival KGB. Since one of its primary tasks was to acquire weapons technology of Western manufacture, the GRU would cooperate with anyone in the market with access to a supply. The GRU also had on offer a greater range of training in weapons and explosives, which meant that it had extensive informal contacts with extremist elements—this was the job of the GRU's Third Directorate—that the KGB, with its focus on governments, never cultivated. The KGB was uncomfortable with this. The rivalry between the two was in fact so fierce that operatives of the one were not even entirely safe from the protégés of the other.[26]

Dmitrii Polyakov: "Top Hat," "Bourbon,"
"Spectre," "Diplomat"

Following the execution of Pen'kovskii, the drain of high-level secret
intelligence unaccountably continued. This was because its source,
Dmitrii Polyakov, had none of Popov's or Pen'kovskii's weakness of
character; on the contrary, Polyakov had a distinguished war record
and unusual self-discipline, which meant that he passed by counterintelligence unnoticed. This allowed him to escape detection over a long
period. Within the GRU, he was as ruthless as the best of them. Most
important, he kept the head of personnel, Lieutenant General Izotov,
fully supplied with expensive gifts, including an entire silver service
paid for out of GRU funds.[27]

The Americans did not recruit Polyakov. It was Polyakov who recruited the Americans. Everyone's image of the fit Soviet army officer
(an unpretentious man), he combined a pleasing smile with acute intelligence and unbending firmness of character. His former subordinate,
Leonid Gul'yov, found him "severe" and was even "afraid" of him.[28]
While he was stationed at the United Nations in New York, between
1951 and 1956, one of the major's sons, a three-year-old, fell gravely ill;
soon he was in dire need of specialist treatment for a heart condition.
An initial operation failed, and Polyakov sought money for a second, at
the Sloane Hospital, which was very expensive. But the Soviet UN
Mission said it did not have the money. Tragically, the child died for
want of the best treatment. Apparently, this was significant in turning Polyakov against the Soviet régime. Yet he made that fateful decision only on returning, this time as a lieutenant colonel, to head the
secretariat of Soviet military representatives at the UN in 1961; by this
time, he was deputy rezident, and his disillusionment with Khrushchev
was total.

The denunciation of Stalin, followed by the ejection of the prestigious Marshal Zhukov from his post as minister of defence just over
a year later, as well as severe cuts in conventional forces, proved the
last straw for some in the military. Moreover, Polyakov believed that
the Soviet Union was in real danger of precipitating World War III, a
fear shared by many under the mercurial and ignorant Khrushchev
and later borne out by his deployment of missiles in Cuba in 1962. At
the UN, Polyakov approached General Edward O'Neill, the senior U.S.

Army representative on the military staff committee and asked to be put in touch with the U.S. intelligence authorities.

On November 16, 1961, at a reception courtesy of O'Neill, Polyakov met John Mabey of the FBI's New York office. The office had been running Operation Courtship to win over members of the Soviet missions, but no one anticipated Polyakov would take the initiative. At first Polyakov, naturally cautious, hesitated, but Mabey persisted through two further meetings, and in January work began. The first step was for Polyakov to provide proof: specimen ciphers and the rezidentura's personnel list. He quickly obliged and became the FBI's agent (code name "Tophat," also referred to using the designation "3549S") through to the autumn of 1962, when he returned home.

One notable exposure during this time was that of the illegal Dobrova ("Maisy"), who suffered a tragic fate as a result. While Khrushchev was despatching missiles to Cuba, it was Polyakov who, as deputy rezident, ran illegals such as Dobrova. When he left for Moscow, on October 10, 1962, with the missile crisis in full sway, the FBI photographed Dobrova depositing something at a dead drop. Polyakov's replacement, Colonel Maslov, collected it. Dobrova sensed that she was being observed after noticing a Plymouth conspicuously parked along her street rather too frequently. She reported her sighting to Moscow. The return telegram was brief: "Cease active work. Hold firm and stay quiet. If the situation requires and you judge it necessary, leave town without being noticed and head for Canada." She did so, via Chicago. On May 14, 1963, the FBI agent Ronald Brighton knocked on her hotel room door. Rather than risk capture, Dobrova plunged from the window to certain death.[29]

Polyakov revealed the identity of four further agents, including Sgt. Jack Dunlap, chauffeur and courier to successive heads of the NSA, Generals Robert Coverdale and Thomas Watlington. Knowing he had been discovered, Dunlap succeeded in committing suicide on July 22, 1963, on his third attempt. Later, Polyakov informed on Sgt. Herbert Boeckenhaupt, USAF communications technician, who was arrested in 1966; Lieutenant Colonel William Henry Wahlen, head of the cipher section at the Joint Chiefs of Staff from December 1959 to March 1961, and later at the Pentagon as a civilian with continued access to military plans and net estimates, who was also arrested in 1966;

and Nelson Drummond, a naval yeoman first class, blackmailed into revealing top-secret NATO and technical naval data.

In November 1965, Polyakov arrived in Rangoon as military attaché and rezident. Because Polyakov's English had deteriorated and much of the vocabulary needed was technical, concerning weapons systems and plans, Mabey was out of his depth, as he had no Russian. After several wasted months, Polyakov became "Bourbon," a CIA asset. His handler, a second secretary at the U.S. embassy, was an abrasive Russian-speaker, Jim Flint. Influenced by the paranoid chief of counterintelligence, James Angleton, who had become unhinged by Philby's betrayal, Flint treated Polyakov as a potential mole, plying him with endless questions that could be double-checked from the files back home. To enable them to meet in the open, Polyakov developed a cover story that claimed Flint was a recruitment prospect.[30] In August 1969, Polyakov returned to work in Moscow, where he soon took up the reins as head of the China department.

His next foreign assignment was in New Delhi, where he served from 1974 to August 1976. Here, he was handled very differently, by a highly competent Russianist, Paul Dillon, who, perhaps because he was a fellow Catholic, had miraculously evaded the inquisition led by Angleton. On his return, Polyakov ran the second faculty of the Military-Diplomatic Academy. He was a fox in the henhouse. The damage he inflicted was in some instances lethal. Lists of the graduating classes for over three years were not the least of what he supplied from the inside.

Polyakov's contribution to the Americans in the course of two decades spanned the gamut of what Washington needed to know. First, having been the desk officer responsible for illegals sent to the United States, he disclosed a total of a hundred fifty agents working for the Russians plus nineteen Soviet operatives under cover as illegals from 1956 to 1959. Second, he exposed fifteen hundred GRU and KGB officers. Third, he revealed details on weapons systems and their capabilities (unspecified). Fourth, he handed over secret intelligence relating to parallel institutions: the KGB and the Foreign Ministry. What is more, the fact that he headed the China department of the GRU when President Nixon opened up relations with Mao's régime in the early 1970s gave Washington an enormous advantage. The Americans could calibrate their moves precisely according to the Russian reading of the situation.

What came into Langley was both so extensive and so specialized that a separate branch at CIA had to be set up to handle the information—called the "GRU Branch" as cover, so that no one outside could realise the significance of this unique source. It was a disaster for Soviet intelligence. In 1976, conscious that Polyakov demanded only the most secure communications, CIA created a device that enabled short-range communication by hand releasing a 2.6-second burst of encrypted material. This made it possible for Polyakov to have a direct line to CIA by taking public transport down Tchaikovsky Street past the embassy.[31]

Polyakov had attained the rank of major general when, in June 1980, after four years in India, he was suddenly recalled and retired from the service. The circle of suspicion had narrowed from one hundred to just five. By then, leaks had begun from within Washington, including comments by the investigative journalist Edward Epstein to the effect that two Russians serving at the UN in the early 1960s had been spying for the United States. This may have been a leak by the disaffected former deputy director of the FBI (counterintelligence) William Sullivan. Epstein even named one as "Tophat," the FBI's code name for Polyakov. He said that CIA assumed they were double agents, but of course the Russians would have known that at least one—whoever "Tophat" was—could not have been a double. Polyakov was already under suspicion; this, however, could have been the final missing piece in the jigsaw.[32] Not surprisingly after this slipup, U.S. officials, particularly at CIA, became extraordinarily agitated and tight-lipped when questioned concerning their knowledge of the latest Soviet nuclear weapons systems. Now we know why.

Meanwhile, in Moscow, all five suspects were gently eased out of active service. Polyakov was given a fake medical diagnosis by KGB counterintelligence. Finally, an American traitor heading counterintelligence at CIA, Aldrich Ames, sealed the Russian's fate. Before President Ronald Reagan could plead for his life, Polyakov was executed on March 15, 1988. As head of section in the KGB investigative directorate, Aleksandr Dukhanin noted that Polyakov "stood firm" until the very end.[33] They could not but admire his unrelenting defiance despite what he had done.

The bottom line for the Soviet Union was that loyalty was increasingly a rare commodity. For Soviet counterintelligence, the potential defector could be tempted into treachery because the socialist system had let its people down so completely. For foreign intelligence, the problem was one of recruitment. When Andropov took power at the KGB, he immediately wanted to know why the Soviet Union had no one operating in the United States who could be as significant as Kim Philby had been in Britain.[34] The obvious answer was that no one of that quality in the West had any reason to believe in the Soviet Union as the future. Andropov would have to look to a completely different constituency.

Boris Solomatin

Andropov's hope for a new Philby was not fulfilled in his lifetime. But in October 1967, Chief Warrant Officer John Walker dropped in at the Soviet embassy on Sixteenth Street in Washington, D.C., offering to become a Soviet agent. Walker was a watch officer at the U.S. submarine fleet message center (NAVCAMS). He faced bankruptcy after failing in a personal business venture he was engaged in out of hours. "We were all wary of walk-ins; for every one true intelligence asset there were a hundred crazies or FBI plants who came in off the street," recalls Oleg Kalugin, then head of foreign counterintelligence at the embassy.[35]

Walker was thus met and cautiously received at the embassy by Aleksandr Sokolov, an operative from K Directorate. Sokolov and his colleagues were then astounded to be presented with "keys to ciphers of the National Security Agency."[36] On the second visit, the KGB resident himself recruited Walker after two hours of discussion, against all the rules. "I immediately decided to take a major risk." "I like risks, at least risks that seem to me reasonable. I am sure that without risk there can be no real productive intelligence," the resident recalled. In contrast, most intelligence officers could not be bothered to take such risks, and preferred to play it safe.[37]

The resident was Boris Solomatin. Born in Odessa on October 31, 1924, to a soldier father who was frequently transferred from post to post, Solomatin also joined the ranks. Just before the end of the war, he transferred from artillery to the intelligence department of his regiment as assistant to its head. In 1946 he enrolled at the Moscow state institute of international relations (MGIMO) and joined foreign intelligence for formal training in 1951. In 1954 the KGB sent him to India on a four-year tour, and after returning to Moscow, he went to New Delhi in 1960, this time as rezident. This was followed by a short spell in the American department and then what would turn out to be a fascinating and rewarding three-year assignment as rezident to Washington, beginning in 1965.

Perpetually "wreathed in a cloud of smoke," the small, stocky, well-dressed Solomatin, with fluent English and a sharp sense of irony, cut an unusually sophisticated figure for a Soviet intelligence operative.[38] Over the next seventeen years, the Walker network would turn out to be the most important source of strategic intelligence since Dolly. "It was impossible for you to bluff when we were reading your cables. This helped us determine when you were willing to fight and when you were simply puffing your cheeks," Solomatin told his American interviewer. "Walker was not an ordinary man," he added. "He always wanted to be the one at the center of attention," however, "and he was ambitious without limits, was shameless, and even cynical. As it happens with such people, he was let down by his own extreme self-assurances [sic] . . . The character traits that made him such a successful spy for us were also the main sources that led to his capture. And this is always the truth when it comes to such men. They become careless because they believe they are wiser than their peers, more talented, even invulnerable."[39]

Not surprisingly, Andropov once hailed Solomatin as "a classic secret service man." When Andropov decided to have the U.S. deputy resident in Beirut kidnapped (with Brezhnev's permission) in May 1970, to extort information from him, Solomatin was one of two tasked with planning the operation.[40] Even though the operation was unsuccessful, it did no harm to Solomatin's career. The following year, he was appointed rezident in New York.

Not only a classic secret service man, Solomatin was also an opinionated one, and that would normally have been enough to cut short his career—but under Andropov, he thrived because their political views coincided, as did their sense of timing. Both thought détente with the United States had played itself out. Andropov was far more interested in lessening tensions with Bonn than Washington, for the simple reason that the Germans might be lured out of the American grip (something Henry Kissinger seriously feared). Kalugin recalls, "Several times, Solomatin—who held tough, anti-American views—attacked Foreign Minister Andrei Gromyko for taking too soft a line with the United States."[41]

At the very moment Brezhnev's hold on the leadership began to waver as a result of ill health, the enemies of détente in and around the Kremlin took their opportunity to assert revolutionary internationalism against the United States in line with Castro's Cuba. Solomatin was now main rezident in New York (where he served from 1971 to 1975 as one of forty-four operatives). He saw things the same way:

> In these years, especially toward the end of 1974 to the beginning of 1975, it became clear that détente in relations with the USA for a whole raft of reasons gave rise to real conflict. At the beginning of 1975, I sent the Centre a telegram in which I suggested that we had to prepare ourselves for a new, less pleasant stage in Soviet-American relations, to try to expose the reasons for what had happened, and I put forward proposals as to what should be done in the situation that had come about. Chairman of the KGB Y. V. Andropov agreed with my conclusions and, on the basis of the telegram, sent a memorandum personally to L. I. Brezhnev. However, the memorandum was returned with the statement "Who has given permission for the general line of the Party in foreign policy to be revised?" Shortly thereafter I was recalled to Moscow.[42]

Yuri Drozdov

The despatch caused outrage. As a result, Solomatin was rapidly supplanted by Yuri Drozdov. Born on September 19, 1925, Drozdov was the son of a former officer in the tsarist army who switched sides in the civil war. Drozdov served during the last year of World War II and, in 1956, after German language training, he moved from the army to the KGB. From August 1957, he worked out of Karlshorst, in a subunit of illegals commanded by Colonel V. Kiryukhin, who in turn came under Korotkov. Drozdov assumed the guise of an illegal ("Kleinert"), brought his German up to scratch in the safety of Leipzig, where he passed for a Silesian, then made frequent forays into West Berlin to pick up the local patois, habits, and customs.

The Americanists were naturally and openly resentful. The choice was met with undisguised mistrust: after all, Drozdov was a trained Germanist; he had served in China, where he used his legal cover, as counsellor at the Soviet embassy, to reestablish a rezidentura during the most difficult years of the Cultural Revolution (1964–1968), only to be reprimanded in Moscow for delivering bad news; and the final straw in their eyes: he hailed from illegal intelligence. "What need is there of someone like that?" the Americanists scoffed.

Drozdov had indeed for the last six years been running illegals from the S Directorate, latterly with Vadim Kirpichenko as his new deputy. But he did serve two rounds in the United States. He had also penetrated West German intelligence through an elaborate scheme involving the creation of a dummy organisation of German Nazis in Latin America. The purpose was to recruit a fervent Hitler supporter within the heart of the BND. Drozdov took on the identity of the former SS officer Baron von Hoenstein, and after some time and effort, the ruse exceeded expectations: Drozdov was able to attract agent D-104 ("Rosie"), who was working in one of the most sensitive sections of the BND, that dealing with liaison with Allied intelligence agencies. The operation lasted five years.[43]

While visiting New York at the end of 1974, Drozdov was briefed by Solomatin. From an intelligence viewpoint, conditions in the United States had seriously deteriorated. Drozdov was told to take a fresh look and judge whether the KGB should move to a more active form of intelligence gathering without worrying about détente. That, and his experience under deep cover in the face of vigilant counterintelligence, doubtless made him a better choice than those who came to the problem loaded with departmental preconceptions and accustomed to a lighter touch from Washington. Kryuchkov, as head of the First Main Directorate, personally favoured taking the offensive, which was precisely what Drozdov could deliver.

Drozdov took up his post in August 1975. He spent four years in a tense operational environment. The situation he found in New York needed shaking up. He responded by taking direct responsibility for everything: political intelligence, counterintelligence, support for illegals, contacts with agents, and technological espionage.[44] The Russians realised that they had been taken in by the apparently "primitive forms and methods" used by the FBI, that these were designed to deceive. It was discovered that the Americans were using radio frequencies other than anticipated and equipment unknown to the KGB. The Americans were even using small sporting planes for surveillance of Soviet dead drops; operatives were under observation without knowing it.[45] In 1976 a special group from K Directorate flew in to analyse the means by which the rezidentura could deflect FBI surveillance.[46] Eight "experienced operatives" were sent in: Krasovskii, Khrenov, Galenovich, Zhuravlyov, Volotskov, Aver'yanov, Androsov, and Kreptgorskii.[47]

Drozdov knew that there had to be a traitor in the midst of the Soviet colony in Riverdale, in the northwest of the Bronx, where some fifteen hundred people were housed in a massive complex that some jokingly referred to as the "Big White House." Deputy Secretary-General of the UN Arkady Shevchenko turned out to be their man. Shevchenko had access to directives from the Centre and knowledge of certain operations.[48] His peculiar behaviour drew Drozdov's attention to him long before Shevchenko formally defected. The Centre was, however, unwilling to listen—not least because Shevchenko was close to Gromyko—and Drozdov was told to halt surveillance (which he did not do). His warnings to Oleg Troyanovsky, Soviet ambassador to the UN, merely elicited hostile remarks about "1937." Yet, when Shevchenko did defect, in March 1978, Gromyko wanted to know why Drozdov had not come to see him in person. The attempt to find fault with Drozdov failed. In this case, Andropov's firm support clearly mattered.[49]

In 1980, Solomatin, who had returned to active duty as rezident and minister-counsellor at the Soviet embassy in Rome, recruited Glenn Souther, a photographer currently serving with the U.S. Sixth Fleet in the Mediterranean, and recently with naval command at Norfolk, Virginia. Souther, Solomatin discovered, had access to image intelligence secrets far above his rank. He was, unusually, spying out of conviction rather than for money, and lasted only until 1985. Solomatin also ran three senior "men of gold" in Rome and one in northern Italy, including a spy with high-level access to the Vatican.[50]

10. THE COMPUTER GAP

By the time Solomatin was recalled from Washington for insubordination, the gap between the Soviet Union and the United States in computing power had expanded to an unprecedented degree.

Soviet Russia was known more for its advances in the fundamental, rather than the applied, sciences. The hazards that arose after the war for those in the applied sciences meant that many sought safe haven in fields that would not be subjected to Stalinist criticism from ambitious careerists. Such cultures are not easily changed: they become far too ingrained; they pass from generation to generation intact, regardless of society's travails and traumas.

Stalin, having subjected the applied sciences, including cybernetics, to a witch hunt, was finally alerted to the costs of continued Soviet backwardness. As a result, he imposed drastic change on the intelligence agencies: codes and ciphers in particular. But these seeds of modernisation had difficulty growing in infertile Russian soil. They went untended, and it was thought, why make such an effort to produce your own harvest when you can buy the crop elsewhere? Soviet technology thus had every prospect of going the same way as Soviet agriculture, into ever-greater dependence on foreign imports, cheaper to acquire than to produce.

The focus on human intelligence was an issue not just of

preference—many at CIA, particularly of World War II vintage, felt the same way—but also emerged and predominated by default. Even after the fall of the Soviet Union, the senior KGB defector Sergei Tretyakov insisted that for the Russians, intelligence was "mainly a matter of human intelligence," that the rest was purely "auxiliary."[1] Technology was always the Soviet Union's Achilles' heel. Getting a satellite into outer space at any price, as Moscow did on November 3, 1957, was a single-focused objective that could be accomplished ahead of the United States. Engineering intercontinental ballistic missiles on a massive scale was another question entirely. Similarly, Soviet computer production lagged seriously behind that in the West, and no sooner had the Russians, against the best advice, decided to make their machinery compatible with the superior IBM-360 system in the 1960s, than the Americans embargoed sales.

Hence the critical importance of military-industrial intelligence programs while disinformation (the bomber gap and the missile gap that so worried the American public) filled the breach. Under Ivashutin, when artificial satellites took on an additional role in espionage from outer space, the GRU was able to monitor wireless traffic in and out of all U.S. bases even on American soil. It was Ivashutin who paid full attention to the *polyarniki* (the Polar lobby) at the GRU: those who specialised in gathering intelligence on U.S. strategic aviation flying in across the North Pole.

The new head of the Sixth Directorate (electronic intelligence), Georgii Stroilov, quartered at "K-500," on Volokolamskoe Chaussée, initiated the creation of a forward intelligence base in Cuba. He worked through Defence Minister Rodion Malinovsky and his Cuban equivalent, Raúl Castro, Fidel's trusted brother, so the operation took some time to set up. The new communications intelligence facility received the cover name "Trostnik" and was established in November 1963, at Lourdes, not far from Havana. Personnel wore plain clothes and were formally subordinate to General Ivan Shkadov, consultant to the Cuban Defence Ministry, but in practice they answered to their commander, the former head of radio intelligence in Germany, Valentin Kudryashov; he was succeeded by Lieutenant Colonel Vladimir Rogovoi, later head of the GRU's newly created Directorate of Missile and Space Weapons Intelligence. It was a popular posting—the Russians invariably enjoyed Cuba. (The reverse was never true because of racial prejudice in the Soviet Union against blacks and mestizos.) They were, however, perpetually short of personnel to meet all the tasks confronting them.[2] The GRU was thus not allowed to monopolise this precious and prestigious asset. On April 25, 1975, the Council of Ministers ratified a decision to augment the GRU station with the installation of radio interception controlled by the Sixteenth Directorate of the KGB. Construction began in June, and six months later "Termit P" and then "Termit S" went into operation. At its peak, three thousand Soviet specialists worked at Lourdes. These listening posts, in combination with smaller stations at Soviet diplomatic premises in New York (Proba 1), Washington (Pochin-1 and Pochin-2), and Los Angeles (Proba-2), gave the Russians unusual reach, enabling them to intercept and then decrypt official conversations snatched from the ether just as the GRU intercepted and decrypted the traffic in and out of all U.S. air, naval, and military bases.[3]

The GRU, under Ivashutin, led the way. Andropov therefore knew where to look for talent. On July 2, 1968, he appointed Major General Nikolai Emokhonov, who had headed the special research institute in radio-technology at the Ministry of Defence, head of the Eighth Main Directorate of the KGB, the *vos'myorka* (which dealt with interception, decryption, and encryption). In recognition of the importance of this field, on July 8, 1971, Emokhonov was made a deputy chairman of the KGB.

Under Ivashutin, however, the GRU was nonetheless able to sustain a monopoly on intelligence from outer space. On May 22, 1959, the Americans sent up the first spy satellite (Discoverer); by August 1960, they had successfully mapped all possible targets in the USSR from orbit. The Soviet leadership decided on their own program, Zenit, in 1961, directed by the head of the Centre for Intelligence in Outer Space, Major General Pyotr Trofimovich Kostin. Kostin was not only talented but a consummate operator who also treated his men properly, which doubtless encouraged them to outperform. Progress was delayed, however, because the political priority was that of launching a man into space. The first launch of Zenit-2 thus did not take place until December 11, 1961, and failed to get into orbit. Of course, all this was in the service of image intelligence. The second launch, on April 26, 1962, partly succeeded, but the third, on July 18, 1962, carrying two high-resolution cameras and two low-resolution cameras, came as a much-needed boost to morale just as Soviet missiles were bound for Cuba. Within two years, more progress had been made, and by 1967 the entire United States had been photographed sufficiently to detail missile silos, ships, even railway carriages and trucks, among other targets.[4]

The Americans unquestionably held the lead. They had the technology to send photographic images remotely, whereas the Russians had to rely on cannisters ejected to earth in order to recover the film. Moreover, the cost of the highest-quality photographic equipment required was prohibitive, and serious problems remained throughout the rest of the decade.[5] But nothing presented more of a threat than the advance in U.S. cryptography signalled by the Cray 1A and IBM 3033 computers just over a decade later.

Human intelligence somehow always seemed a speedier and easier, though at times erratic, way into the other side's secrets. The U.S. model in creating an independent National Security Agency (1952) was ignored. "Copying" what the Russians imagined CIA to be with the Committee on Information had turned out to be disastrous. So Moscow went its own way. On Stalin's death, codes and ciphers were reincorporated into and therefore subordinated to the intelligence community proper, and this meant that human intelligence predominated. Lack of autonomy for cryptography inevitably had an impact on the allocation of resources. Partly as a result, the Russians fell even further behind.

Help from Human Intelligence

The KGB general Vitalii Pavlov recalled that the continuing priority in foreign intelligence encompassed two tasks: "obtaining foreign ciphers and the interception of foreign communications by which means secret messages are sent; plus obtaining cryptographic information to assist the decryption services." The only difference between this and the policy during the interwar period was that "whereas in the prewar years the emphasis was more upon obtaining ciphers," the war itself highlighted the importance of "gathering of cryptographic and cryptological information as much for protecting our own lines of communication as for decrypting foreign ciphered messages."[6] As long as the Russians were unable to safeguard their own secret communications through cryptographic means, human intelligence operations would become ever more vital.

Under Khrushchev in the late 1950s, a directive (reaffirmed under Brezhnev in 1975) called for "great attention" to the recruitment of U.S. agents with "access to encrypted and other secret correspondence, such as code clerks, secretaries and typists."[7] This signalled a major advance. In 1957 two young men, the statistician Bernon Mitchell and the mathematician William Martin, joined the NSA, and after two years they decided to expose the immorality of their government. They secretly visited revolutionary Cuba for a few days, and it was no doubt there that they contacted Soviet intelligence about fleeing to Moscow. On June 22, 1960, they placed a declaration explaining their motives for moving to the Soviet Union in safe-deposit box 174 at the State Bank of Laurel, Maryland. They then announced that they were off to see family on the West Coast. Instead, on July 25, both of them flew to Mexico and on to Cuba; from there, they took a Soviet transport to Odessa, then to the Soviet capital.

On September 6, 1960, Mitchell and Martin appeared at a press conference in Moscow to reveal the extent to which the U.S. government was reading the mail of other countries (especially that of its allies) and their own naïve belief that somehow the Soviet Union was morally superior. They had been particularly shocked to learn that their own government had bribed the cipher clerk of an allied embassy in Washington in order to read its traffic. They went on to reveal all they knew of the structure and functions of the NSA, the very size of which (ten thousand employees) must have come as bad news to the Kremlin when they first learned about it.[8] Rumour has it that when an aerial photograph revealed the dimensions of the parking lot, the sheer scale of the American effort dawned on Moscow. The good news for the Kremlin, however, was that its "main government ciphers" remained unbroken.[9]

It is often claimed that the two American defectors could have offered little that the Russians did not already know. But Mitchell and Martin did grant them direct insight into the priorities and working practices of the NSA, which may in turn have influenced a shift in Russia's own intelligence priorities and working practices. This awareness soon made itself apparent. In 1960 the Advanced School of Cryptography was turned into the fourth (technical) faculty of the KGB Dzerzhinsky Advanced School. In 1961 the budget cut in early 1953 was finally reversed, and cryptography was given more serious priority, particularly with respect to upgrading mathematical capability. Engineering and mathematics became full degree-level courses. To accomplish all this, the star mathematician Ivan Verchenko was brought back into the system in 1961. In May of the following year, a full-time five-year course was instituted in place of evening classes. Two months later, Verchenko was appointed head of the special division of higher mathematics. He held the position for a decade and transformed radically the level of training received.[10]

Human intelligence continued to bring in the goods, though never consistently. One unpromising American agent, Sgt. Robert Lee Johnson, suddenly struck gold in 1961. Stationed in West Berlin in 1953, Johnson crossed into the East in search of political asylum along with his Austrian wife, Heidi. He said he had been badly treated by his commander and wanted to avenge himself at his expense.[11] There, despite his rough appearance, Soviet intelligence persuaded him to return and work under cover after a few weeks' training for them both (she as courier) while they were purportedly on vacation in Bavaria. Back in the United States, guarding a missile base in Texas after renewing his military service, Johnson provided Moscow with photographs and even fuel samples. He was then transferred to Rouen, France, to work for the U.S. European Command. During the summer of 1960, Heidi, who was mentally unstable, had to be hospitalised in Paris. Johnson requested a transfer to be with her and managed to obtain a post in the U.S. courier centre on the outskirts of Orly Airport, the hub for all secret communications on paper between the Pentagon and every U.S. command throughout Europe, including NATO headquarters.

It is at this delicate point that an operative specialising in the English-speaking world arrived at the Paris embassy, to the surprise of the rezident, Colonel Lazarev. Vitalii Urzhumov ("Viktor") had been despatched to handle Johnson's new mission, Operation Karfagen, which required access to the massive safe room locked behind two huge steel doors within a concrete bunker at Orly. After copying the key while the duty officer was distracted, Johnson was gifted with an extraordinary stroke of luck: he heard the code read out loud over the phone in his presence. The first opportunity to access the safe on night duty came over the weekend of December 15–16, 1962. Johnson had only one hour to remove the documents, take them to the third floor of the embassy, a fashionable mansion at 79 rue de Grenelle, where they were photographed, and then put them back. There was a second attempt the following weekend. This continued through to the autumn of 1963, when Johnson was transferred to Sennes, despite Heidi screaming from her hospital bed that her husband was a Soviet spy. It was only when he moved back to the Pentagon, in May 1964, that Johnson was fingered by the defector Nosenko, arrested, and sentenced to twenty-five years' imprisonment. What Johnson gave the Eighth Main Directorate was an array of vital military codes and ciphers, including all the mobilisation plans for war in Europe in the event of a Soviet invasion.[12]

One other recruit to the Soviet cause with direct knowledge of NSA secrets was Victor Hamilton, an American of Palestinian origin who, along with his American-born wife, Lilly, applied for diplomatic asylum at the Soviet embassy in Prague. Lilly was just a language teacher; Hamilton, however, had worked at the NSA from July 1957 to June 1959, as an analyst and translator in Arabic. His section covered the Middle East and North Africa plus Greece and Turkey. Hamilton was sacked as a result of trying to make contact by letter with relatives in Syria. Unable to find appropriate employment, the couple moved to Iraq, where he could work as an interpreter. Hamilton brought little to the Soviet table in terms of recent NSA material and methods. Instead, the word from on high, which came down on June 25, 1962, was that the defection would be used for propaganda, though a press conference for these purposes was not called until over a year later, after a sensational article titled "I Chose Freedom" was published in *Izvestiya*, evidently with no irony intended.[13]

In January 1963, Warrant Officer Joseph Helmich of the Army Signals Corps, a crypto-custodian at the U.S. embassy in Paris, offered the Russians the secrets of the KL-7 cryptosystem, and a sophisticated teletype ciphering machine that was a descendant of the Enigma machine. The secrets included technical details of rotors and settings that would enable Moscow to reverse-engineer the mechanism, in return for a considerable sum of money. The passing of information continued through to July 1964. The Russians put it to good use intercepting and decrypting U.S. military communications during the Vietnam War.

They were further helped on January 23, 1968, by the capture of the USS *Pueblo*, off the North Korean coastline, a spy ship that had on board a whole generation of code machines, nineteen different types in total, including the KL-7 systems.[14] John Walker's spy ring kept the Russians updated on changes in the equipment that ensured Moscow's continued monitoring of such intelligence through the 1970s.

From Bits to Bytes

The demand for more effective cryptography grew as the Soviet Union's superpower role expanded in the 1960s, but it soon hit a wall in both human and physical resources. Priorities lay elsewhere. When the Soviet Union first began producing computers, its primary application had been for artillery: missiles that could eventually deliver nuclear warheads or antimissiles that could intercept and shoot down incoming missiles at precise coordinates. Cryptographic needs were secondary, and in general, computation was associated more with the needs of defence than those of intelligence. Whereas digital computers were needed for cryptography, those best suited to ballistics were analog.

It was no accident, therefore, that the first Soviet textbook on computers was published in 1956 by an artillery man, Anatoly Kitov, who had made a name for himself with his dissertation on "The Tasks for Programming the External Ballistics of Long-Distance Missiles." For him, however, computer-aided control systems were merely a crucial by-product of a more general mission. It was Kitov who broke through the Stalinist objections to cybernetics as a "fake bourgeois science," though it took him three full years (1952–1955). By then, he was already director of the Defence Ministry Computer Centre (and therefore a general), with carte blanche for recruitment, and a military representative at a key new body, SKB-245, at the Ministry of Machine Tool Building, which was tasked with pioneering defence-related technologies.[15] Thus, although Kitov had no direct interest in the world of codes and ciphers, he legitimised information theory for cryptographic exploration.

Kitov's infatuation with computer electronics as *the* solution to society's problems drove him headlong into a clash with the authorities through his ludicrous proposal for a unique programmed directing system for national defence and the economy—as if the planned economy were not already creaking at the seams. Under Khrushchev, the

GRU had, however, successfully commissioned his organisation to meet its needs, including the enciphering of open information. But the spirit of voluntarism so characteristic of the Khrushchevian era also steered Kitov down such dead-end streets as translation by machine, which followed the scientistic fallacy of confusing literal fact with semantic truth.[16]

The challenges facing cryptography proved altogether more complicated than Kitov's engineering solutions would allow. The bottom line was that computers needed to be faster; but greater speed comes at the price of reducing security in the transmission of ciphered communications. This is a trade-off that has never entirely been resolved.

The ideal was to create a culture in which the computer specialist was also a cryptanalyst. The only notable cryptanalyst innovating computer technology from the outset was Vladimir Polin (1908–1975). He took charge of the Construction Bureau of Industrial Automation (KBPA), which belonged to the Ministry of the Radio Industry, creating specialist computer technology. It soon became known as "Polin's Enterprise."[17] Here, Polin and his team could work closely with the Soviet Union's first computer engineers, Lebedev and Bashir Rameev. In the end it was Lebedev who came out ahead of his rivals Isaak Bruk and Rameev at the SKB-245 in producing the best computers. Yet even Lebedev's best in 1958, the M-20, which was as fast as the American IBM NORC, had a severe deficiency: it boasted less than half the NORC's operating memory.[18] The Russians still had to turn to the West to attain the level of mathematical modelling needed.[19]

Behind the updating of Soviet code and cipher technology stood several cryptographers. One was Vladimir Kozlov, a new kind of scholar-manager, the first cryptographer to reach the rank of general, also elected a corresponding member of the Academy of Sciences in 1966.[20] Two others were products of Stalin's attempts to revive and develop cryptography just before his demise: Nikolai Andreev and Aleksei Bosik, both pioneers in the application of electronics and physics to cryptography.

Andreev, like Bokii a geologist, graduated from GUSS in 1953 and went into what became the Eighth Main Directorate, which covered all aspects of cryptography. One of the new problems that arose in the use of machinery for enciphered communication was that the machines themselves gave off electronic radiation and inadvertent acoustic signals. These emissions could be recorded and interpreted to reveal plain text. When outlines of the problem first emerged in the early 1950s the Americans called it TEMPEST, or Transient Electromagnetic Pulse Emanation Standard. Before the decade was out, further acoustic leakage was discovered. The Russians grouped it all under the acronym PEMNI, or Collateral Electromagnetic Emanation and Acoustic Emission. The phenomenon did not become public knowledge until much later, when it was revealed by the Swedish cryptographer and Russian specialist Bengt Beckman in 1983. Enciphering equipment was in this respect no different from telephones, computers, fax machines, or electronic typewriters. "At that time," Andreev noted, "no one could imagine that the detection and recording of electromagnetic emanations have the capability of giving away secret information more than any traitor."[21]

Though a mild-mannered man, Andreev was also an extremely determined one. In 1959 a group working under him confronted the dilemma of finding weaknesses in the coding machine within the U.S. embassy in Moscow. They eventually succeeded and built equipment able to read part of its secret communications by monitoring acoustic emissions. For this critical breakthrough, Andreev was awarded the prestigious Lenin Prize. It took over a decade for CIA to find a way to circumvent these practices. A disaffected former CIA employee revealed the adjustments made by the late 1960s: "The machines and other equipment are cushioned and covered to mute the sounds emanating from them. The rooms themselves are encased in lead and rest on huge springs that further reduce the internal noises. Resembling large camping trailers, the code rooms now are normally located deep in the concrete basements of embassy buildings."[22]

Andreev was involved in the decryption of dozens of foreign ciphers. In this he was something of an enthusiast. "With time," he recalled, "any cryptographer ceases to be interested in the meaning of decrypted communications. The most interesting and complicated is understanding the logic of the cipher. This is because each cipher is a unique construct. It is always new; it never poses itself in the same way. Hand the cipher to some mathematician or physicist. He will say the problem is not soluble, and he will be right. A contemporary cipher can be unravelled only through the use of a complex of disciplines: mathematics, physics, radio electronics, and computer technology. Otherwise nothing can be done." In short, the academic context mattered.

Andreev realised that separating out decryption from the making of codes and ciphers would allow the Soviet Union to upgrade the security of its own codes and ciphers. To get the country into this position required greater resources and the mobilisation of both academic and industrial manpower. Andreev stated the case simply: "Good cryptography yields nothing if it has no firm foundation in the form of a strong production base that allows one to reproduce equipment, to create it according to the highest technological specification and in a sufficiently large quantity. It is the level of the technology in particular that enables us to cover the broadest range with the same amount of expenditure."

Andreev's reasoning was accepted. "It was therefore decided that each should do his own thing."[23] Accepting Andreev's arguments, Kozlov drove forward an institutional divorce. On June 21, 1973, in recognition of the expansion in the scope of Soviet cryptography and of the urgent need to catch up with the West, which meant a separate and substantial budget, KGB order No. 0056 split interception from the Eighth into its own domain, the Sixteenth Directorate. Decryption was moved along with it. General Andreev was put in at the top. Whole branches of industry and entire institutions were rolled out to meet the new directorate's exclusive needs.

Bosik, the other, no-less-dynamic half of the pair, was a small, slight man with a high-pitched voice and jet black hair (hence his nickname, "Gipsy"). He was "a compelling, charismatic figure" with an "uncommonly sharp" mind and a "voracious" appetite for work. "His ingenuity and resourcefulness were legendary," an immediate subordinate recalls.[24] Bosik was also unselfish, honest, a lover of life, and, a real compliment for a Russian, "a truly cultivated intellectual."[25] Thus, once Andreev set the wheels in motion and, in August 1975, moved back to head the Eighth, he took Colonel Bosik as his first deputy. The Sixteenth was taken over by Igor' Vasil'evich Maslov.

In 1974 the young Mikhail Maslennikov entered the fourth faculty on Bol'shoi Kisel'nyi Pereulok, not far from the Lubyanka, to train in cryptography. He was initially overwhelmed by the high standards expected in mathematics (largely algebra) and probability theory (where logic, statistics, and knowledge of linguistic pecularities held sway). "Between the algebra people and the probability people, sharp exchanges had always taken place on the subject of whose truth was more genuine and who brought more to cryptography."[26] Then there was linguistics, a sphere also viewed with suspicion under Stalin, and finally accepted only in 1957.[27]

Yet, just as Andreev had anticipated, a new era was dawning: that of powerful high-speed computers with integrated circuit chips and the arrival of public-key cryptography in 1977. This tipped the balance between pure and applied sciences in cryptography. All of a sudden, pure mathematicians working with prime numbers, whom the Cambridge mathematician G. H. Hardy once consigned as useless "for any warlike purpose," were in demand.[28] For once, the Russians could exploit their strength in pure mathematics. The prospect of mechanically applying high-speed solutions by means of algorithms suddenly loomed. At the Eighth and the Sixteenth Main Directorates, however, they were still working in bits rather than bytes—the latter with eight times the former's capacity for data transfer and storage, so the Russians were well behind the game and ill fitted to catch up.

Having sold out by adopting IBM in the 1960s, against Lebedev's strict advice, Moscow inadvertently made the fatal mistake of rendering itself vulnerable to pressure from the United States. The Russians were warned that this could happen. The Stasi (the East German Ministry of State Security) had in fact recommended that the Russians instead buy British (ICL) computing technology, which they believed was just as advanced as IBM, but that came without the attendant danger of embargo.[29]

Although under President Nixon the Americans proved more easygoing about enforcing the strategic trade embargo against the Soviet Union, passage in the U.S. Congress of the Jackson-Vanik Amendment on January 3, 1975, stripping Russia of its most favoured nation status in trade, was nevertheless cause for concern. It meant that the warnings from East Berlin should have been taken seriously. Additional dependence on American technology therefore placed a new burden on human intelligence at both the KGB and the GRU. Increased dependence then made the Russians vulnerable from another angle. If the West exposed the burgeoning Soviet network gathering vital industrial intelligence, then the Russians would have nowhere to turn; and if the

West simultaneously ratcheted up the technological competition in the arms race, the Soviet Union would lose.

By the beginning of the 1970s the KBPA scientific research institute, later known as Kvant, had engineered the Soviet Union's most powerful computer yet, known as the Bulat ("Sword"); its integrated systems were produced by the Mikron factory in Zelenograd. The Bulat may well have been an adaptation of the M-10 computer built by Mikhail Kartsev, who had astonishingly won the State Prize for his doctoral dissertation: Bulat Okudzhava, the celebrated and iconoclastic balladeer, was his favourite singer. The Bulat was sited in the first department of the twenty-one-floor building on Prospekt Vernadskogo. The GRU's decryption service could be found along Komsomol'skii Prospekt, but its computer centre, on the other hand, stood forty kilometres away, outside Moscow, in the settlement of Sokolovskii.

Despite the existence of this powerful computer, most of the analytical work at the KGB's Eighth continued to be done by hand. "We did not even dare dream, like the Americans, of putting each interception through computer analysis," a former employee recalls. "I remember long rows of cupboards packed with dusty files with intercepted but undeciphered material. In essence we worked with cupboards."[30]

In stark contrast, the NSA bought the second Cray-1A, produced in 1977. (The national weather service took the first and GCHQ bought the third.) It cost more than eight million dollars, weighed five and a half tons, and took more than thirty men to get into the computer room. Crucially, its design was simple compared to its predecessors, it could run for several days before failing, and it outpaced all rivals. Then, in 1980, another striking advance: the IBM 3033 attached processor complex enabled the operator to deal with up to sixteen million characters under a single system control program with a fifty-seven-billionth-of-a-second cycle time.

Thus, once détente was truly dead and buried, the Russians were significantly outgunned. The best computer the Russians produced at that time was still Kartsev's M-10, designed for early warning of a missile attack. But because its microelectronics were not up to scratch (a standard Soviet problem), it could not run as fast as the Cray. The maximum number of processor cycles for the M-10 was 5.3; for the Cray, it was 27.6.[31]

Maslennikov recalls arriving at Subdirectorate S, the fifth department, which specialised in cryptographic theory. It was headed by Vadim Stepanov, who lectured on the theory of probability and mathematical statistics, and was quartered at Kuntsevo, Fili, a suburb in northwestern Moscow that housed senior KGB officers and the datchas of many Soviet leaders, including, at one time, Stalin. The main building of the Eighth, at the intersection of two streets, Mologvardeiskaya and Yel'ninskaya, was a glass house (*steklyashka*) designed like an open book. It stood in a deserted urban landscape for security reasons. Once, an American diplomat inadvertently parked there, on what appeared to be an abandoned plot, and doubtless assumed that his diplomatic license plate would protect him from prying hands; he was startled to find on his return that his car had disappeared (unheard of in Moscow in those days).

Maslennikov's arrival coincided with the dismantling of an outmoded computer, Vesna, in the courtyard of a building. He recalled those moments when "one of the last of the purely Soviet computer models received a uniquely Soviet death." A Hewlett-Packard was installed. "I went to the machine" became the byword for those looking for some free creative mathematical activity, especially after dinner. "But all the same," Maslennikov noted, "basic work in the theoretical department was with pencil and paper."[32]

The contrast between the situation in Fort Meade and Moscow is striking. The technological advantage achieved by the Americans yielded rapid and substantial results, especially at the NSA, where Anna Caracristi's A Group took full advantage of errors made by Soviet cipher operators to break into an array of hitherto impenetrable systems. By 1979 the Americans were able to use the knowledge gained from reading the traffic to trick the Russians into invading Afghanistan by the end of that year.[33]

Fortunately for Moscow, Geoffrey Prime, who had resigned from his job at GCHQ on September 28, 1977, where he regularly photographed classified material, suddenly had second thoughts about his decision. Now short of money, in 1980 he turned the secrets he had harvested three years earlier over to the KGB. It was this treasure trove that exposed the extent to which Washington and London were reading Moscow's most secret traffic, engineering the USSR's disastrous invasion of

Afghanistan.[34] The Americans "were more interested in the entry of our forces than we were," General Valentin Varennikov has noted. "We set ourselves the task of stabilising the situation; they prepared a trap."[35]

Prime handed over fifteen reels of film to the KGB in May.[36] Washington's hard-earned advantage was lost in an instant. The Russians had momentarily evened up the odds, once again due to human intelligence. Though the fact that they received the material three years later made all the difference to the survival of the régime: by that time, the calamitous invasion of Afghanistan had already brought to a head the long-ignored social, economic, and political problems confronting the Kremlin.

Viktor Sheymov

Prime was a disaster for the Americans and British, but a piece of luck brought them a new prize from an increasingly war-weary society that had crucially lost the confidence of its youth. This prize came in the form of Viktor Sheymov. Sheymov was one of the best, and, reared within the postwar elite, he had had every conceivable advantage. Born in 1946 to a colonel, an engineer who built the first missile-testing sites, Sheymov went on to train in the construction of space vehicles. A young man of great promise, he married a classmate and, no doubt to advance his career, joined the Party. A year after graduating he was hand-picked to join the Eighth Directorate. By 1979 he had risen to head a department that was responsible for cipher links with legal rezidentury abroad. In Warsaw on business, on October 31 of that same year, he slipped out of the embassy unseen and made contact with CIA. Unable to persuade him to remain an agent in place, the agency guaranteed his family's evacuation from Moscow (which would doubtless pose a tremendous challenge) in return for information.

The timing could not have been better. Counterintelligence was focused on the mass influx of visitors expected for the Summer Olympics. No special measures were in place for those leaving. CIA officer David Rolph oversaw the operation. Dressed as an airline pilot, and with his wife, Ol'ga, and daughter, Lenochka, secreted in a container that was then placed on board a plane by the U.S. embassy, Sheymov

("Ckutopia," later "Ckquartz") abruptly disappeared. He had absconded with comprehensive knowledge of KGB secret communications: it was, in short, a disaster. Nothing had been taken from his apartment, so it would have been easy to assume that the family had been kidnapped or perhaps had died without a trace in a car accident.[37] His parents could not be forewarned, for obvious reasons. The most Sheymov could do was warn his mother that unless she knew with certainty of his demise, she should not believe any such speculation.

The investigation into Sheymov's disappearance was led by Anatoly Zhuchkov. Zhuchkov headed the Second Main Directorate's investigation department, which handled especially important cases. Another such case fortuitously appeared not long after the Sheymovs disappeared, when the body of Major Vladimir Afanas'ev, deputy head of the main secretariat at the Lubyanka, was discovered on December 27, 1980, not far from the road to Bykovo Airport. It was determined that he had been murdered on his way home to a KGB datcha at Pekhorka after birthday celebrations in town. Eight militia men were under investigation for the crime. The militia was accustomed to beating up drunks for entertainment, a practice not uncommon at that time. Four of them were tried in secret and shot. Minister of the Interior Nikolai Shchelokov, a Brezhnev crony, who had succeeded in hushing everything up, was dismissed when Andropov became general secretary on November 12, 1982. He was thrown out of the Party and eventually shot himself on December 13, 1984.[38]

As far as the KGB was concerned, Sheymov and his family had simply disappeared without a trace. Codes and ciphers were thus still secure. Everyone breathed a welcome sigh of relief. The KGB could not have been more mistaken—but of course no one of any seniority wanted to rock the boat with anything akin to panic. Reality did not finally dawn until the summer of 1985, when Aldrich Ames reported from CIA that the Americans had, since June 10, 1980, been tapping the cables leading in and out of Yasenevo, with incalculable consequences for KGB operations abroad.[39]

II. PRIDE BEFORE THE FALL

The 1970s had seemed something of a golden age to the Soviet régime and especially to Soviet intelligence. For the rulers of the Soviet Union, however, it turned out to be nothing other than reflected twilight. The turning point came with the Soviet invasion of Afghanistan, which accelerated the Soviet Union's unstoppable drift into steep decline.

From 1921 through to 1947, Afghanistan remained a buffer state between British India and the Soviet Union. When at birth the new India split in two, Afghanistan found itself neighbouring Pakistan, which instead of following India in a pro-Soviet direction, took another path, toward U.S. patronage. Thereafter, Afghanistan's nonalignment depended on American and Russian self-restraint, which, as it turned out, was effective only if neither side was presented with an opportunity too good to be rejected.

A coup d'état in the Afghan capital, Kabul, on April 27, 1978, brought to office but not to power a group of Communists led by two KGB agents, Nur Mohammad Taraki and Babrak Karmal. The attempt to gain control over the state as a whole, in particular the massive countryside, resistant to radical change, inevitably required ever greater quantities of Soviet military aid. The Soviet invasion followed after a year of frustration at the failure of the Afghan leadership to make haste slowly and win over a people disgruntled and wedded to the traditions of the distant past.

The Afghan leadership failed to pace its reforms as opposition mounted. Instead of staging a tactical retreat, the more fanatical came to believe that ever-greater repression was needed. On September 16, 1979, the vengeful and ambitious Hafizullah Amin seized power from the more pro-Soviet Taraki. Thereafter, Moscow took fright. Reading Soviet ciphers to the highest level, the Americans knew full well that the Russians were very reluctant to force their way in and impose their will for fear of creating their own "Vietnam."[1] Chairman of the Council of Ministers Alexei Kosygin had been particularly vehement in his warnings of what might come to pass were intervention to take place.

The full invasion that followed involved nearly one hundred thousand men and was a fatal error by the Soviet leadership. It was championed by a small cabal, the Afghan committee of the Politburo, headed by Andropov, Ustinov, and Gromyko, dogmatists all, under the notional chairmanship of their much-decorated leader, Brezhnev, who was crippled by cerebral atrophy. Brezhnev's personal assistant, Aleksandrov-Agentov, was not even informed of the decision that had been reached. All the specialists were ignored. "On Afghanistan we gave no recommendations whatever," the GRU director Ivashutin recalled; "and we were modest in the information we gave." When Chief of the General Staff Nikolai Ogarkov got together heads of all nine departments, plus the head of the main political directorate, every one of them opposed going in.[2] With the exception of the Politburo member Kosygin, who was confined to bed, the remainder of the leadership were bulldozed by Andropov, Ustinov, and Gromyko into taking the crucial decision, regardless of the consequences correctly predicted by the professionals. The Americans purposefully lured them in, making it look as though Amin, a Columbia University graduate, were about to switch sides and turn to the United States for support. By this means the Americans snatched from Moscow the ultimate prize of incorporating what had been a nonaligned country on its southern flank into the Soviet bloc. The first deputy head of the First Main Directorate, General Vadim Kirpichenko, chaired the planning process for "Baikal-79," the invasion itself. The prelude was Operation Shtorm-333, scheduled for 9:30 p.m. on December 27, 1979.

The attack on Amin's palace was led by KGB *spetsnaz* ("special forces") and backed up by GRU *spetsnaz*. The GRU forces were originally set up in the heat of the Korean War through a special directive (Org/2/395832) on October 24, 1950. Forty-six units were created across the military districts of the Red Army. Each unit contained one hundred twenty men. On May 2, 1979, Ivashutin instructed Colonel Vasily Kolesnik to form the 154th separate detachment of *spetznaz* (ooSpN), made up exclusively of Uzbeks, Turkmen, and Tadzhiks. This became a battalion commanded by Major Khabib Khalbaev.

The other, main element came from the Lubyanka. Andropov had instructed the creation of KGB *spetsnaz* on March 19, 1969, with what was euphemistically called "Advanced Courses for Officers" (KUOS). Initially twenty-eight officers were chosen for special training under Grigory Boyarinov, at Balashikh. The aim was to establish an operational reserve for special tasks. The idea had been in the air for some time, and KUOS was the culmination of several false starts and prolonged debate, as some veterans insisted that officers from the First Main Directorate be excluded, that the *spetsnaz* be purely military in formation. They had their way.[3]

KUOS was situated within S Directorate (illegals). Andropov approved the formation of A (Alfa) Group on July 29, 1974, within the Seventh Directorate, responsible for surveillance of suspect spies.[4] Thus Alfa was for domestic purposes, and the *alfovtsy* were recruited from operatives with no fewer than three years' experience in the field and trained like the British SAS for immediate action, with or without weapons.[5] The training was one year in length, carried out at the famous (in closed circles) Leningrad 401st special school of the KGB.[6] Nonetheless, Afghanistan required an assemblage of skills that included those peculiar to Alfa.

Drozdov, now head of a Directorate, and Vasily Kolesnik, representing the GRU, along with delegates from the *spetsnaz* of both organisations, put together the planned assault on the presidential palace in Kabul. They were sent in early as "advisors" to the Afghans. The only hiccup came when the Afghan hosts expressed puzzlement at the presence of Drozdov, perennially bald and somewhat wizened, who seemed too old to hold such a lowly position.

In order to dull the vigilance of the commanders whose forces they would have to overcome, Drozdov and Kolesnik tried to persuade them to come to a birthday party earlier that same day, but failing to lure the most important and fearing that they had aroused suspicion, they brought forward the assault to 7:30 p.m. The attack directly involved only sixty men (KGB)—those from KUOS were called "Zenit"; those from Alfa, "Grom"—backed by the Muslim battalion under Major Khalbaev, providing cover and bringing out the wounded. The operation lasted only forty-three minutes, but the fighting was savage; there was a veritable sea of blood when combat ended. It left eighteen dead, including eight *spetsnaz*, and a further thirty-seven men who perished in an aircraft crash; plus fifty-seven wounded, of whom thirty-seven were *spetsnaz*. Boyarinov was one of those who died in the fighting. In return, they killed one hundred eighty and captured twenty-five hundred. As far away as the Soviet embassy, on the other side of the city, one could hear the roar of gunfire and see the flames.[7] "They have taken the bait!" crowed the U.S. national security advisor, Zbigniew Brzezinski, clenching his fist in the air.[8] Once committed, Ivashutin poured into Afghanistan all that the GRU could spare to win the war.

The Extraordinary Achievements of Yuri Totrov

Whereas it could rightly be said that the Americans held the lead in technology, the Russians managed to make up much of the distance in other ways. Stymied by backwardness in invention, Soviet engineers in the military-industrial complex proved their genius through mastering the art of improvisation. They applied the law of comparative advantage: making full use of what lay at hand rather than mimicking the other side, treating fundamental asymmetries not as reason for regret but as opportunities to exploit. The substitution of brain matter for high technology was, therefore, a matter of necessity. But because Soviet bureaucracy was weighed down by routine that stifled initiative at every turn, the West could be forgiven for assuming that only the expected could happen. What eventually shook CIA (and doubtless MI6) to the core was the discovery of what KGB foreign counterintelligence could achieve through inspired leadership followed through by systematic research and analysis, conducted mostly by one man. His name was Yuri Totrov. Totrov owed his career to a leading figure, a pioneer in foreign counterintelligence: Grigorii Grigorenko.

Grigorenko had forged foreign counterintelligence into a distinctive and high-profile entity within the First Main Directorate—and it acquired a fearsome reputation. Grigorenko was an odd entrant into the secret service: a thinker, deceptively mild in manner, but with an indomitable will. He was not only clever. He also had a formidable memory for detail. He had trained as a teacher of physics and mathematics in the Ukraine before he was conscripted into the NKVD in 1940. Subsequently wounded on the Southwestern Front, he went on to graduate from the NKVD higher school. At SMERSH, beginning in 1943, he was responsible for 181 radio games misdirecting the Germans. His most notable achievement was in giving them to believe that the road was clear for a full frontal attack at the fateful Battle of Kursk, in July 1943. After the war, he operated in military counterintelligence at the Third Main Directorate until 1949. He was then transferred to the First Main Directorate specialising in counterintelligence. In Hungary during the turmoil of 1956, as first deputy representative of the KGB, he saw his judgement as to the perilous scale of the rebellion against Communist power meet with open disapproval from Serov. He also received a grievous head wound from artillery fire during the uprising.

Thereafter, Grigorenko ran a department of the Second Main Directorate, suppressing the activities of emigré organisations within Russia sponsored by the Americans. In 1959 he was moved over to become deputy head of the "active measures" service, heading the counterintelligence (fourteenth) department of the First Main Directorate. It was here that he came up with the idea of elevating and professionalising the department: turning it into a complete service, within the First Main Directorate, that would devote itself exclusively and systematically to foreign counterintelligence, with an emphasis on analysis as well as active penetration of enemy intelligence.

In February 1963, the second service of the First Main Directorate finally came into being, incorporating the ninth and fourteenth departments of the First Main Directorate, subdivisions of the Second Main Directorate and the Third Directorate of the KGB. It added up to 104 operatives in Moscow, and by the end of the year 1,037 abroad. The plan for 1965 provided for the creation of counterintelligence rezidentury under deep cover in the United States, France, Britain, Italy, and Austria. The Americans felt its impact straightaway. The idea was to try to turn U.S. intelligence officers in third countries and, in individual cases, compromise those who refused to cooperate. The fact that few such officers were competent in Russian made targeting them particularly valuable, as it would reduce the ability of CIA capabilities against Moscow. In addition, plans were laid to send over two or three agents to penetrate the U.S. intelligence services within the United States. These would not have the option of ever returning home.[9]

Grigorenko had impressed everyone with his cool judgement under fire in 1956. Thus it prompted no surprise when Semichastry placed Grigorenko as head of this new service. He also served simultaneously as deputy chairman of the KGB until 1983.[10] A veritable "golden age" of counterintelligence dawned: U.S. agents began to be mopped up with relentless thoroughness.

One of Grigorenko's particular skills was in nurturing young talent. Yuri Totrov, for example, came in as a complete novice. Born in Moscow in 1933, Totrov was a slim, small man of Turkic roots and appearance. He passed through the customary training at MGIMO and intelligence school, and emerged as an Orientalist destined to become a *kagebist* (KGB operative). His first foreign posting allowed him field experience first in Bangkok (1958–1960) and then in Tokyo (1967–1971 and 1975–1980). But he was no ordinary operative.

Totrov was as unusual as Grigorenko—perhaps more so. He was highly intelligent, deeply analytical, doggedly persistent, averse to letting others do his thinking for him, and a highly intuitive social psychologist. Counterintelligence was certainly not the most glamorous or prestigious section of the First Main Directorate, but he made it his own. One of his crucial tasks was to identify the main adversary's operatives under diplomatic cover. Two main deficiencies were immediately apparent in the way the KGB looked at the problem. First, the culture favoured secret over open sources for no reason other than the former were held in higher esteem. *Kagebisty* tended to be dismissive of CIA's practice of spending so much time and effort reading newspapers. Second, the Russians assumed Western behaviour would necessarily be the same as their own, which reflected a degree of provincialism inevitably strengthened daily by their living tightly compartmentalised lives within the Soviet colony abroad under the ever-watchful eyes of their own counterintelligence operatives.

Totrov's work on the problem of identifying U.S. intelligence officers began at foreign counterintelligence, after his return from Thailand in 1961–1962. Little did he know that the project would absorb twenty of his thirty-two years in the field. Totrov started with the obvious, searching through official manuals such as the diplomatic list. The fact that a rezident abroad could send in the names of supposed American intelligence officers who turned out to be mere marines and request that they be added to the *kartoteka* ("card index") struck Totrov as incompetent and reinforced his commitment to precision. The mistake made by the rezident was to misread the State Department's listings of diplomatic personnel and to assume that a name followed by *SY* for "Security" necessarily meant intelligence, as it would have been in the Soviet Union. The reasoning was straightforward but demonstrated the fallacy of mirror-imaging the enemy.[11] The colossal waste of resources expended as a result of misclassifying potential counterparts for fear of letting one pass unnoticed was obvious.

In 1964, David Wise and Thomas Ross published *The Invisible Government*, which confirmed Totrov's initial findings. It also complicated matters. As a consequence, the standard listing ceased. After withdrawing the original foreign service list, however, the State Department's new reference works—the *Foreign Service List* and the *Biographic Register* ("the stud book")—maintained propriety by listing an *R* for "Reserve" after the names of some, including CIA officers. The *R* meant that they were not regular foreign service officers and therefore could be, though were not necessarily, officers in CIA.

At the agency, Ray Cline, in charge of operations, tried in vain to end this practice but was unable to do anything into the late 1960s.[12] Of course, the fallout would not have touched officers under deep cover, who were unknown even to the local station chief. Yet even in these cases, the agency was not safe. Totrov went on to comb through other official open sources and cross-check the results with intelligence from operations, using the archives of the fifteenth sector of the directorate to see how other intelligence agencies spotted CIA people and how Western governments worked out who was who.

Packed off to Japan for a long stay (1967–1971) at the height of the Vietnam War, Totrov was obliged to pass the baton. In his absence, Grigorenko was promoted in November 1969 to head the Second Main Directorate. His first deputy, Vitalii Boyarov, replaced him in January 1970; so there was no break in Totrov's project, which continued after

Boyarov moved to deputise to Grigorenko three years later. The rising star Oleg Kalugin was then in charge when, in 1974, Totrov returned home. The second service had also been elevated to the role of K Directorate. Within it, Totrov's seventh department was innocuously retitled the "Information and Reference Store," no doubt to discourage inquisitive questions.[13] In practice, of course, its chief function remained analysis.

Thereafter, Totrov could legitimately focus on perfecting his method of ferreting out CIA personnel from their foxholes. Inspired by a reliable source supplying data on CIA diplomats, he ploughed on. Philip Agee, a CIA officer who had resigned in 1969, offered himself to the Russians but was turned down. No doubt they feared a trap. The less-inhibited Cubans, however, accepted. The results were turned into a book by the KGB's A Service (disinformation). It was published as *Inside the Company: CIA Diary*, by Penguin in London (1975).[14]

But Totrov, of course, went much further. One crucial breakthrough was in realising that the agency's bureaucracy, not unlike Totrov's own, was a creature enslaved by habit. To a bureaucrat, change was always disruptive and to be avoided. So when an officer was assigned to a particular mission, the tendency was to place him at the same rank as his predecessor. More than that, from bureaucratic inertia, intelligence officers were then allocated the same apartments, even the same car, as previous incumbents.

Totrov's first challenge was to build the model. This was followed by a slow process of testing and fine-tuning until he felt confident enough to present his conclusions. The old hands, including his superiors, took some convincing, however, as they steadfastly believed they always knew best and that intuition guided by direct experience in the field was a far better guide than systematic research. "Unfortunately," Totrov recalled, "even one of my chiefs, not wishing to make a special effort to get into the essence of the system, for a long time could not believe that with its help one could with surgical precision establish which people belonged to CIA." The system worked even on those under deep cover.

The model contained twenty-six indicators that in combination enabled the identification of an officer from CIA under cover as a genuine foreign service officer (FSO). They are worth listing here, as they show the relentless precision and intricacy of Totrov's fine needlework:

1. The "R" shown after the name of a foreign service office (FSO) was a necessary but not sufficient condition;
2. The payscale at entry level for an agency officer was substantially higher than normal;
3. After 3–4 years abroad the regular FSO could return home. This rule did not apply to officers from the agency;
4. Mention of military service;
5. Genuine FSOs were recruited between the ages of 21 and 31. This did not apply to agency personnel;
6. Only genuine FSOs were required to attend the Institute of Foreign Service for three months prior to entry;
7. Naturalised Americans could not become regular FSOs for at least nine years;
8. When agency officers returned from overseas, they normally no longer appeared on the State Department list;
9. If they did appear, they were classified as research and planning, research and intelligence, consular or chancelry (security affairs);
10. Unlike FSOs, agency officers could change their place of work for no apparent reason;
11. Missing data in the published biography;
12. Agency officers could be relocated within the host country; they had no right to leave for home in between postings; and whereas genuine FSOs had to pay their passage, CIA officers had theirs paid for;
13. Agency personnel were frequently alumni of Harvard, Yale, or Columbia;
14. These officers usually had more than one working foreign language;
15. In the guise of FSOs they were usually "political" or "consular" (often vice-consul);
16. On arriving at a new post, a visit to a known CIA officer's home was a strong indicator;
17. Positions vacated by agency officers were usually filled by the same;
18. Embassy reorganisations left agency personnel untouched— positions, offices and telephones;

19. Agency officers were restricted to security zones out of bounds to local employees;
20. Host country intelligence agencies usually had a fair idea who was who;
21. If an American offered to introduce a Soviet diplomat to a friend, then that friend was usually CIA;
22. Agency officers would appear in the streets during the working day to use public telephone boxes;
23. Host country observation posts would be positioned outside agency premises;
24. CIA officers would arrange meetings for the evening, usually around 7:30 or 8:00 pm, in out of town locations;
25. FSOs had to observe strict rules as to the hours of attendance at dinner, whereas agency officers could come and go as they pleased; and, lastly,
26. If visitors to the FSO's home were concealed from the domestic staff, then CIA was hosting.[15]

Once identified by these means, U.S. intelligence officers were subjected to sustained unwanted attention that nipped operations in the bud and, in some instances, endangered their personal safety, mostly as a result of staged car accidents. The accumulative cost to the Americans was serious, and the true causes of the problem remained a complete mystery for two decades. CIA knew something was going wrong but had not worked out what lay behind it. The more paranoid and unimaginative in its Soviet department, still in the shadow of the counterintelligence chief James Angleton, such as "Pete" Bagley, naturally but wrongly assumed that the explanation had to be treachery. Thus Totrov's system had a double advantage for Soviet foreign counterintelligence: identification of the main enemy's operatives and the disorientation and demoralisation of the main enemy's intelligence and counterintelligence services. In 1980 alone, the first department (for the United States) of K Directorate unmasked 168 CIA officers and 77 agents.[16]

Totrov emerged into the light of day only after the end of the Cold War. At Langley, they joked bitterly that he was "the shadow head of personnel at CIA." In their desperation to find out precisely how he had uncovered their officers with such unerring precision, on September 5, 1991, with the Soviet Union collapsing, the agency authorised a senior officer to recruit Totrov in Osaka with the offer of a million-dollar book deal. The officer was disconcerted to receive a typically defiant retort. Totrov insisted that he was not to be turned, that his dossier at Langley was stamped "Not to Be Pitched."[17] Presumably he knew as much from Aldrich Ames, the turncoat head of CIA counterintelligence. Totrov nonetheless spent a fortnight at the family home in Virginia discussing general methods with the same CIA officer. Close audiovisual surveillance from cameras hidden in a table lamp ensured that a full record resulted.

Totrov's great success notwithstanding, the outcome for Grigorenko personally illustrated what was wrong with the Soviet system generally: ability at the top of the ladder counted for less than networking and casuistry. Vladimir Kryuchkov, whom Grigorenko despised as a mere party hack, manoeuvred unerringly to forestall Grigorenko's succession to the chair of the KGB in the early 1980s.[18] The main enemy could thus in the end count on the Soviet Union's own corruptibility.

The Pope in the Line of Fire

It was not easy for Totrov to convince his superiors that he was right, in part because, when pressed, the KGB and the Soviet leadership found it extremely hard to let go of old habits that had proven a welcome comfort in times of trouble. The physical liquidation of adversaries, one of its worst practices, was one such habit. Under Andropov, operations from which Moscow needed to distance itself, including logistical support for terrorism, were, where possible, delegated to allies. Each ally had its own expertise to contribute. Bulgaria—specifically the "Seventh Service" of the D"zhavna Sigurnost' (the DS)—specialised in "severe measures" (OM), including assassination. When the proposal to establish the Seventh Service first emerged in the summer of 1963, Minister of the Interior General Diko Dikov wrote to Semichastny at the KGB for assistance in bringing the project to fruition.

Bulgaria's Seventh Service began with only four operatives, but by the time its chief, Colonel Petko Kovachev, requested more help from the Soviet comrades in 1967, it had expanded to thirty-nine—and

Kovachev was not sitting on his hands. On September 7, 1978, Georgi Markov, a Bulgarian emigré, was assassinated. He worked for the World Service of the BBC (paid for from Foreign and Commonwealth Office funds) and moonlighted for Western intelligence agencies. The telltale documents were willfully destroyed by the former head of the DS, but circumstantial evidence from the archives available indicates that the culprit was an agent working for the Bulgarians. The murder was evidently a birthday present for Todor Zhivkov, leader of the Bulgarian Communist Party, who found Markov a thorn in his flesh.[19] This was the eleventh assassination the Bulgarian service had accomplished undetected. Such silent successes could well have gone to its head.

Cardinal Karol Wojtyła was elected Pope John Paul II on October 16, 1978, just as an avalanche of misjudgements by Soviet leaders was about to crash down upon their heads. Within a month of the papal election, Vyacheslav Dashichev's international relations section at the Institute for the Economics of the World Socialist System (a closed institute created by Andropov in 1967 and never part of the Soviet Academy of Sciences) produced a measured but disturbing assessment of the threat posed to Soviet interests.

Moscow's anxieties increased at meetings with the Poles in anticipation of the Pope's visit to Poland. On July 15, 1980, a total of eighty-nine pages was produced by Dashichev for the leadership. It pointed to the manner in which the Vatican had increasingly become a catalyst for unwelcome developments not just in Poland but also in Lithuania (Catholic), Latvia, the Western Ukraine (Uniate), and Byelorussia.[20]

The Russians sought to weaken the international underpinning of Solidarity, the opposition workers' movement that threatened Communist rule in neighbouring Poland. In October 1984, for instance, the turbulent priest Jerzy Popiełuszko was murdered by Polish state security. Clearly, a person or persons unknown had declared open season against prominent enemies of the existing order. The Soviet leadership was fearful of mass disobedience in Poland, having abandoned plans far advanced for invasion and occupation in the summer of 1980 because of the incalculable damage this would have done to East-West relations, already crippled by Afghanistan. The dire prospect stubbornly remained, however, of a revolution succeeding that would turn Moscow's main ally into, at the very least, an indifferent or, indeed, hostile neighbour, leaving the Soviet position in East Germany untenable.

It is not hard to imagine Russian leaders, in such calamitous circumstances, repeating the words of Henry II of England: "Who will rid me of this turbulent priest?"—in that instance his erstwhile friend, Archbishop of Canterbury Thomas à Beckett—and for this to have been acted upon by an eager ally, through an untraceable cutout. After visiting the Soviet embassy in October to overhaul cipher security, Viktor Sheymov reported that he was present at a conversation between the illegal rezident and the head of the legal KGB mission in Poland. The Centre wanted all information on the Pope urgently, in particular anything that could get them "physically" closer to him, a KGB euphemism for assassination.[21] But how was this to be done?

On May 13, 1981, an attempt was made on the life of the Pope by a Turk, Mehmet Ali Ağca. The Pope recognised that Ağca was "a professional assassin. This means that he was not his own initiator, it was someone else's idea, someone else had commissioned him to carry it out."[22] Ağca identified his Bulgarian handlers in some detail. Yet, whereas the Bulgarian authorities had a direct interest in silencing Markov, they had no interest at all in extinguishing the Pope. The Russians, on the other hand, had every interest in doing so, provided no one could find out who was actually responsible. Inevitably, suspicion for the attempt on the Pope soon fell directly upon Moscow, but the Kremlin remained resolutely impervious to world opinion; instead, it issued disinformation to create a smokescreen to hide its worst excesses.

Bulgaria had had a special relationship with Russia since its liberation from Ottoman rule courtesy of Tsar Alexander II in 1878. Eclipsed by monarchical allegiance during the First World War, when Bulgaria fought on the side of the Central Powers, and by the October Revolution that made the two states ideological enemies, the relationship was rekindled under Soviet occupation and forced adoption of socialist rule after the Second World War.

"The closest and most multidimensional contacts were maintained with GDR intelligence," former head of the KGB First Main Directorate Vadim Kirpichenko recalls. "Beyond that I would place Bulgaria as having the most intensive degree of interaction; then the Czechoslovaks."[23] The quondam head of K Directorate, Oleg Kalugin, has emphatically denied that the KGB attempted to assassinate the Pope, but only on the basis of guesswork. Kalugin nonetheless acknowledges that "As close as we were to Marcus [sic] Wolf and East German intelligence, we had an even tighter relationship with the secret service of Bulgaria. That Eastern European country . . . was so firmly bound to the USSR that people in both countries referred to Bulgaria as the sixteenth Soviet republic. The Bulgarian Interior Ministry was little more than a branch of the KGB. Our station chief in Sofia for many years, General Ivan Savchenko, virtually ran Bulgaria's secret services; no general in Bulgarian intelligence or in the Interior Ministry dared do anything of consequence without first picking up the telephone and checking with Savchenko."[24] Major General Vadim Udilov, formerly deputy head of the Second Main Directorate, recalls that relations with the Bulgarians were "beyond reproach."[25] Indeed, as early as the mid-1970s, Andropov "instructed his men to create a network among those around the leader of the Bulgarian Communist Party, Todor Zhivkov." As a result, it is asserted, Andropov sometimes saw documents destined for Zhivkov before Zhivkov himself had seen them.[26]

If one can establish a Bulgarian connexion, one might reasonably assume Soviet complicity. The link between Ağca and the Bulgarian secret service came through Balkan Air's representative in Rome, Sergei Antonov, who was identified in a photograph by Ağca on November 8, 1982.[27] Antonov's cover name, according to Ağca, was "Bayramic." Ağca went on to demonstrate an extraordinarily detailed knowledge of Antonov's apartment when Antonov, arrested on November 25, 1982, denied knowing him. Antonov's identity as an operative of the Bulgarian service was also confirmed by former colonel Günther Bohnsack of the Stasi.[28] Ağca claimed Antonov was in St. Peter's Square with him when he shot the Pope. It was impossible to prove this from the photographs available at the time of the original investigation, but later image technology is said to show that Antonov was standing behind him.[29]

Thereafter, as the enquiries continued, the investigating magistrate, Ilario Martella, began receiving threats against himself and his family. The threats came from Germany and contained private information about his niece, for example, who was unknown to anyone beyond the household. Moreover, his son-in-law, working for an aerospace company in Britain, was threatened with dismissal on the grounds that he had placed the firm in jeopardy—until, that is, the leader of the Socialist

Party, Bettino Craxi, intervened.[30] Later Bohnsack reported that the HVA in Berlin was asked to circulate disinformation on behalf of the Bulgarians. Among other active measures, they "sent messages signed by Turkish terrorists."[31] When the *Bild Zeitung* sent a reporter and a historian to interview Antonov at his apartment in Sofia, they were greeted by his wife and two men, one of whom introduced himself as Marin Petkov, president of the Association of Ex–Intelligence Officials. Bohnsack later identified Petkov as having headed active measures in the Bulgarian secret service.[32]

On May 28, 1983, two Bulgarians, "Jordan" Ormankov and "Stefan" Petkov, arrived in Italy, claiming to be magistrates. They gained access to Ağca in October 1983. The meetings apparently gave Petkov the opportunity to threaten that if Ağca did not disrupt the forthcoming trial, the Russians would take revenge.[33] Thereafter, Ağca wrecked any attempt to sort out the true facts of the case and to prosecute anyone other than himself by feigning madness, declaring himself to be Jesus Christ.

At the outset of the investigation, Ağca was identified as a member of a right-wing Turkish terrorist organisation, the Grey Wolves. He had in fact been trained in Palestine with the terrorist PFLP, headed by a KGB agent through a process that was overseen by the GRU.[34] Given Moscow's close relations with the PFLP and the Bulgarians, its role in this murky affair would have been hard to cover up but for the fact that the U.S. government was eager, as it had been when confronted with likely Cuban complicity in the Kennedy assassination, not to fan the flames and create a political conflagration it could not control, or expose an agent in place that could alone have informed them of what had occurred. Moscow had, anyway, failed to remove the Pope, and the Polish problem was about to get much worse; ultimately, it would bring down the entire bloc.

Never had the two great rivals, the KGB and GRU, seemed so powerful. Yet not since the height of Stalin's Terror was the ground beneath their feet so unstable—and their inability to cooperate closely was a part of the problem only too visible to their allies in the Warsaw Pact, who fretted at the consequences. On October 19, 1965, both Ivashutin as GRU director and Sakharovskii as head of the KGB's First Main Directorate instructed their respective rezidentury to collaborate at moments of crisis, coups d'état or military operations within the host state.

They were told to share information, and in particular, the KGB had to ensure that all military intelligence went to the GRU. In such circumstances they were also to make joint recommendations to Moscow.[35]

In practice, however, little changed. Meeting with Sakharovskii on November 11, 1969, at a time when Moscow was contemplating détente with the Willy Brandt coalition in the West, East Germany's minister of state security, Erich Mielke, bluntly pointed out that, for the organs of state security, the central question remained: when is the enemy going to strike? His concern was not nuclear weapons as such. It was the issue of being taken by surprise—*das Überraschungsmoment*, or strategic early warning, as the Americans would have put it. What Moscow needed, he said, was a centre for the analysis and utilisation of all information bearing on "the joint struggle against the common enemy," adding, for good measure: "In this connexion it seems what is required is to improve working cooperation between the KGB and the organs of military intelligence (General Ivashutin). It would appear that working cooperation between the Ministry of State Security and Comrade Ivashutin is better than working cooperation between the KGB and Comrade Ivashutin."[36]

Insults came in many forms: clearly the East German worm was turning. The Russians were being put in their place. Once Erich Honecker replaced Walter Ulbricht at the top, Moscow's communications with East Berlin had to be delivered not in Russian as usual, but in German.

The Strange Case of Vetrov

A key failure, the betrayal of the KGB's entire military-industrial intelligence network by Vladimir Vetrov (agent "Farewell") to the French in 1981–1982, seriously undermined a branch of the service critical to meeting the American challenge presented by the Strategic Defense Initiative, the American project for space-based defence with the potential for a preemptive first strike against missiles in their launch phase.

Born in 1932 to Muscovite industrial workers, Vladimir Vetrov came to the attention of the KGB in 1959 while working as an engineer at a computer factory. On July 9 he sent in a letter of application that succceeded in gaining him admission to the KGB. A handsome young man with every advantage, three years later he graduated from the 101 training school. For his first assignment abroad, he was posted to Paris under cover as an illegal; he travelled as a senior engineer for V.O. Mashpriborintorg, trading in instrumentation devices. In Paris he recruited agents and demonstrated a high degree of competence, for which he was duly singled out for praise. His second mission proved a disaster, however. Now a lieutenant colonel, but unable to hold his drink, he received unwanted attention from the RCMP security service in Canada, as a result of which he was swiftly repatriated, removed from operations, and put to work in analysis for the Aviation Industry Ministry at T Directorate (technical and industrial espionage).

Vetrov was well regarded as a creative man of initiative. He rose to become assistant head of department at T Directorate. It was not enough, however; the years abroad had made him hungry for more. Now in his mid-forties, with all prospects of promotion gone (and with them, his patriotism), Vetrov, an unstable personality given to swings of exhilaration and depression, was evidently both in search of excitement and embittered by what the KGB had to offer him. Finally, in February 1981, at an exhibition for hydrometeorology in Moscow, he encountered a representative from Schlumberger (the international oil and gas exploration company), Alexandre de Paul. Vetrov asked if de Paul would, on his return to Paris, be seeing someone he had known during his Paris posting: Jacques Prévost, commercial director of Thomson-CSF, a leading French electronics and defence manufacturer. Vetrov gave Prévost a message to deliver, offering to spy on his own directorate, which had been set up in 1967 and was extremely active in France; personnel at the Soviet embassy had climbed from 200 to 750 within a decade.

This offer resulted in Vetrov's recruitment to the DST, Direction de la surveillance du territoire (French counterintelligence), under Raymond Nart. The DST was the main link between Thomson and the French services, as the foreign intelligence service, DGSE (Direction générale de la sécurité extérieure), was regarded as leaky. Delivery of data began in February 1981 via the Thomson engineer Xavier Amiel ("Volodia"), who was in Moscow negotiating the modernisation of Soviet television.

Thereafter, Madeleine Ferrant, the wife of the French military attaché, Major Patrick Ferrant, took over, since she was less likely than he to be tailed. Each Friday, Vetrov and Madeleine met at 11:00 a.m. near the Cheremushkinskii exit of the Vavilov market. The following day, at the same time, the documents were returned to Vetrov in the square outside the museum Borodin Panorama, just off one of Moscow's main roads, Kutuzovskii Prospekt. But after a strange incident—Vetrov had slipped a new-model pistol in with the documents—Ferrant's wife took fright and refused to continue. Her husband then stepped in and met Vetrov for the first time on May 28, 1981.[37]

Vetrov handed over a detailed image of the structure of technological intelligence, including three thousand pages that exposed the names of 422 operatives working abroad, 222 of whom were acting under diplomatic cover, and 57 of the agents who had been recruited in the West and were now working for either the KGB or the GRU.[38] Vetrov was eventually unmasked after he was imprisoned for killing his mistress. He was subsequently executed for treason on September 24, 1983.

GRU Research and Analysis

The Reagan administration calculated that it could destabilise the economic foundations of the Soviet Union by depriving it of the technologies essential to war while simultaneously ratcheting up the arms race (hence the SDI). Much, therefore, came to hinge upon Moscow's ability to give an objective assessment of the threat truly posed by the United States: its capacity to mobilise for war.

The Soviet response was exacerbated by the GRU's failure to make an accurate assessment of NATO's mobilisational capabilities. Gauging the capacity of "the probable enemy," a GRU term as against the KGB's "main enemy," to wage war was critical to Soviet defence planning, including the configuration of armaments required and, most important of all, the correct allocation of ever-scarcer economic resources. The failure to draw up accurate assessments would have far-reaching consequences for not only Soviet war fighting but also expenditure. The Russians were in danger of spending money they did not have, and to no useful purpose. It therefore mattered that intelligence coming in was properly assessed before it reached the leadership that ultimately made the decisions. For different reasons, the two rival services, the KGB and GRU, failed to do what was vitally necessary in terms of evaluation. The fault was by no means entirely theirs. Handing over evaluation to the experts was not something the Party wished to do any more than Stalin was prepared to do.

The KGB was conscious of its unique status. It encompassed domestic as well as foreign intelligence, which the GRU did not. Yet the KGB liked to think of itself as the supreme guardian of national security against the main enemy. It alone of the two intelligence organisations had direct access to the very top. According to an officer of the Eighth Main Directorate, "intercept information was so highly valued that it was transmitted directly to the Politburo, bypassing all regular KGB information channels."[39] But in the wrong hands, the raw material of intelligence could easily be misinterpreted. Moreover, if it got into the hands of the adversary, sensitive sources could be compromised. In short, this was a risky procedure. Although Brezhnev could be trusted, Khrushchev, who could not resist an opportunity to boast, used to blurt out when chatting to foreign ambassadors that he and his men were reading intercepted information.

It helped to some degree that, under Andropov's leadership, an analytical unit—Service No. 1 (information)—was created in 1973, under Nikolai Leonov, though it focused mainly on military affairs. There, a team of twenty-five eventually grew to five hundred, servicing requests from above. Information was transformed into "pooled" communications sent through to the "Instantsiya"—the Politburo and the secretariat of the Central Committee, plus the General Staff, the Ministry of Defence, other parts of the KGB, and, last but not least, allied governments. The analysts did not just sit around in their offices exchanging ideas. They met with subdivisions and specialist groups within the KGB and also so-called "friends" within the Academy of Sciences. They held brainstorming sessions ("situational analysis") on the most pressing issues.[40] Yet not until September 15, 1989, was a comprehensive Service of Operational Analysis and Information (SOAI) finally set up within the KGB, under Valerii Lebedev.[41] Well after Stalin, the Party leadership continued to hold tight to the unique privilege of being the ultimate arbiter of intelligence analysis because of the implications of its findings for the decisions to be taken.

The destruction of the Fourth's research and analytical section in 1935 meant that although the Soviet régime could be adequately equipped to assess the adversary's order of battle, it had no understanding of its economic underpinnings. However, under Stalin, no attempt was made to compensate for this serious loss. Also, whereas the size of the GRU increased tenfold through the Cold War, the Ministry of Defence, the General Staff, and the GRU did not have much interest in economic issues related to military matters. Under Khrushchev in 1960 a closed "department of technical and economic research" was set up at the Institute of World Economy and International Relations (IMEMO) within the Academy of Sciences, headed by the undercover KGB officer Nikolai Inozemtsev. Made up of an astounding number, four hundred out of seven hundred, of IMEMO researchers, it was designed to focus on military-economic issues. Other institutes at the academy, covering various areas of the globe, contained closed, and much smaller, sections that focused on similar work, but these remained on the margins, with no institutional pull within the military hierarchy.

Finally, at the end of 1971, on the advice of the General Staff, the Politburo passed Resolution 229: to concentrate assessments of foreign military-economic capabilities in the hands of the GRU. The Military-Economic Directorate (the Tenth) that came into being was headed by a former colonel, now a general, with no knowledge of either economics or foreign languages. This made all the difference to its operations, since members of the group were classed as regular soldiers and were therefore individually subject to military discipline and thus vulnerable to pressure from within the General Staff to produce the results desired. The very fact of centralisation was an attempt by the military to rein in autonomous sources of knowledge and to keep everything in the hands of the generals. The Strategic Arms Limitation Talks (SALT), the first round of which concluded in May 1972, were to continue through to a second round, ultimately threatening to lay bare to prying political eyes the crucial process of Soviet arms acquisition. It was therefore imperative that civilians be firmly shut out of the reasoning behind that process and the evidence adduced in support of it.[42]

The Tenth Directorate thus lasted only until 1978. The economists, predictably perhaps, proved difficult to keep in line. The reports, produced with great effort, were bound and distributed to Brezhnev and other members of the Politburo. Their real value was limited by the fact that priceless material from human intelligence was cut out of the process of assessment because its product was too unpredictable and could contradict the GRU's consensus in support of maximising military expenditure. For if the enemy were not ten feet tall, why should the USSR stand so high? In 1976, the GRU paved the way for liquidating the directorate by setting up a research institute for the study of the military potential of foreign countries. When the economic directorate was dissolved, the research institute was incorporated into the more general information directorate (the Third.)

Incorporation produced a clash between alien cultures that was eventually resolved at the expense of the outsiders, the economists. Whereas the information people worked to serve operational needs at speed, taking personal responsibility on a daily basis, the Tenth worked as a collective on long-term work, hammering out a consensus from conflicting individual appraisals in depth over extended periods of time. The economists responded by drifting off into academic work. The team effectively dissolved. By 1988 only one man remained who specialised in both the economics of military power and mobilisational capabilities. This was a very determined analyst and skilled operative in the field, Vasilii Shlykov, the courageous deputy head of the institute created in 1976. The problem was deep-seated, Shlykov recalled: "During thirty years of service in the GRU, particularly in the last years, all too often I saw that the most valuable documents acquired by human intelligence, including those relating to mobilisation preparations, obtained at great expense and no little risk to agents and intelligence operatives, were cast aside without hesitation if they contradicted the views of an ignorant minister of defence or chief of the General Staff."[43]

Worse still, perhaps, was the ideological challenge. The accumulated impact of what American insiders called the "Marshall Plan of the Mind"—the mass distribution of forbidden books within the Soviet bloc, Radio Free Europe, Radio Liberty, Deutsche Welle, the Voice of America, the BBC World Service; and "Basket Three" (freedom of communications and human rights), agreed to under the Helsinki Final Act of the Conference on Security and Co-operation in Europe in 1975—finally proved too much for the Soviet system to bear. Not only had the appeal to foreign idealists fallen away, but the appeal of the Western way of life had penetrated the Soviet bloc not least due to the flood of foreign tourists. Under Andropov, the KGB had to create an entire directorate, the Fifth, focusing entirely upon insulating the Soviet Union from ideological subversion.[44]

Human Intelligence Triumphant

The Russians had the edge in human intelligence, however, and this they now tried to exploit to the full. It is estimated that 40 to 60 percent of all diplomats at Soviet embassies were in fact intelligence officers under diplomatic cover.[45] The late KGB general Leonid Shebarshin once boasted that Soviet intelligence was "the best in the world." The extraordinary advances made by the Russians in penetrating U.S. intelligence and counterintelligence after years of effort were realized just as Gorbachev was en route to power in Moscow.

The contrast with latter-day American priorities is instructive. "The Soviets were obsessed with human intelligence," recalls Kalugin, "and not only in terms of collection of intelligence, but as a means to promote the cause . . . all the great collection of information provided by Soviet intelligence was subordinated to a single cause: to weaken, deceive, confuse, injure, damage, and destroy the other side." It was also the case that "Soviet intelligence thrived on a great cause for which we were willing to fight and die. This cause gradually faded away and evaporated, because the system proved to be incapable of delivering the pledge [of a better life] they had made for so many years."[46]

As Solomatin demonstrated, the KGB understood the main enemy sufficiently after the U.S. humiliations of the 1970s (the Vietnam War and the Iranian hostage crisis, to give just two examples) to focus on bribery rather than winning over hearts and minds.[47] Only the Cubans still managed a successful appeal to idealists, and only while Fidel was alive and well. That was how they recruited Kendall Myers, a Washington snob from a patrician family whose PhD dissertation was in part a justification of Neville Chamberlain's misguided policy of appeasing Nazi Germany, a point of view to which he remained stubbornly attached, in spite of the evidence. Myers thus had already demonstrated a capacity to disregard reality when it interfered with his prejudices. He worked as an analyst at INR, where the most sensitive secret intelligence was synthesised for the White House. He actively disliked the Soviet Union but was romantically committed (as was his second wife, Gwendolyn) to the Cuban revolutionary dream. Disillusionment with U.S. foreign policy following the catastrophic war in Vietnam and revelations concerning CIA covert action in the Third World undoubtedly provided fertile ground for recuitment along anti-American lines, even among U.S. officials.

Yet intelligence is only as good as those who analyse it and those who have access to it for policy making and execution. Much therefore hinges upon the integrity of the intelligence process. As we have seen, the Soviet General Staff choked off accurate assessments based on intelligence gathered where it conflicted with its own objectives. In turn, the KGB, with its close proximity to the Politburo, lost its core integrity in foreign operations with Andropov's elevation to the post of general secretary of the Party. The man responsible, Kryuchkov, ever anxious to secure his own future, and heartily disliked by Andropov's anointed successor as general secretary, Konstantin Chernenko, was more concerned with guarding his own back rather than owning up to failure where it occurred. This is easily illustrated.

After Ronald Reagan assumed the U.S. presidency in 1981, Stanislav Androsov, a creature of Kryuchkov, was appointed KGB rezident in Washington, D.C. He decided to pin up next to his office a massive map of the district. Every operative, on leaving the premises, had to indicate with a pin on the map his precise location, so that Androsov could tell at a glance where everyone was. Colonel Viktor Cherkashin, head of foreign counterintelligence at the rezidentura, was never consulted on this, and on returning from leave in March 1984 expressed his horror. All it needed was an American agent in their midst, and the FBI could watch for all operatives meeting their contacts to roll up whatever activities were in progress. When Cherkashin tested his hunch by creating a fictitious new operative, only to find the FBI on the ground awaiting him, Androsov refused to acknowledge the implications of this discovery—that there was, indeed, an FBI agent in their midst—since reporting it would jeopardise his own continuation in post and Kryuchkov's standing, too. Even when Cherkashin identified Valerii Martynov as the culprit, nothing was done until eventually Martynov was named by others.[48]

U.S. human intelligence operations in the Soviet Union, always a point of vulnerability, collapsed under the successful Soviet counterintelligence drive accelerated by Andropov—at least that is what Major General Rem Krasil'nikov, head of the first (American) department of the KGB's Second Main Directorate (1979–1992), claims. In fact, the American effort collapsed under the weight of the greed at the heart of its own intelligence establishment. Robert Hanssen at the FBI was responsible for counterintelligence against Soviet operations. From 1979 to 2001, Hanssen gave Moscow the names of those Russians he knew to have been recruited by the American services within the United States. "Perhaps for some in Russia, the 1960s and the beginning of the 1980s were the years of social stagnation," the former KGB rezident Solomatin recalled with smug satisfaction. "But as the John Walker affair shows, this was not true for the Soviet intelligence service."[49]

After William Casey took over CIA under Reagan, the Americans combined a diplomatic offensive against the Soviet Union with a frontal assault on its entire intelligence network. A number of agents were recruited: Gennadii Varenik ("Fitness"), Valerii Martynov ("Gentile"), Sergei Motorin ("Gauze"), Vladimir Piguzov ("Jogger"), Gennady Smetanin ("Million"), Boris Yuzhin ("Twine"), Vyacheslav Baranov ("Tony"), and Sergei Bokhan ("Blizzard").[50] CIA veteran Paul Redmond has estimated that "we had well into the double digits of good penetrations of the Soviet government, most of them being run out of Moscow."[51]

The British already had an unusually well-informed asset, Oleg Gordievsky, in place as deputy rezident in London. Among other issues, he reported a state of alarm in Moscow at the prospective deployment of ground-launched cruise missiles and Pershing II missiles in Western Europe in 1983. This was how he explained Operation Ryan, measures for strategic early warning that included widespread monitoring for signs that the West was readying for a preemptive strike. This met with a certain scepticism from Fritz Ermarth, the national intelligence officer for the USSR and Eastern Europe, not least because another double agent, Boris Yuzhin ("Twine"), a KGB operative on the West Coast, considered it to be "another make work project."[52]

All the American agents were betrayed by Aldrich Ames ("Kolokol"), who headed counterintelligence against the Russians at CIA from 1985 to 1993. On April 16, 1985, Ames began trading top-secret information of the most sensitive (life-threatening) kind to the KGB for fifty thousand dollars. Just over one month later, an agreement was reached with the head of counterintelligence at the Soviet embassy, Cherkashin, subject to clearance in Moscow. Cherkashin left for the Soviet Union five days later with classified documents in hand exposing a range of U.S. agents. He returned at the end of the month.[53]

The loss to the Americans was catastrophic. The reaction of the U.S.

bureaucracy was predictable. "The message was clear," the CIA counterintelligence officers Sandra Grimes and Jeanne Vertefeuille recall. "Running well-thought-out operations against the KGB target was no longer a career-enhancing activity. Stations reacted accordingly."[54] Everyone ducked for cover. The contrast with the immediate past is striking.

Ames also betrayed Polyakov; like Polyakov, he had approached the adversary—in his case, Cherkashin—rather than the reverse. In Moscow, the KGB head, Kryuchkov, knew enough to keep the truth of Ames's voluntary recruitment to himself. By this means, those uncovered spying for the West were seen as discoveries made by hardworking counterintelligence men, rather than as unsolicited gifts offered by embittered and greedy American counterintelligence officers.[55]

The KGB were astute in other respects. The web of deception woven around Ames to hoodwink mole hunters within CIA counterintelligence proved state of the art. Yet the true test for secret intelligence in Moscow came with the collapse of the Soviet Union. Its allies, both ideological (those who believed in communism) and military (the conscripted allies within the Warsaw Pact in Central and Eastern Europe), had been lost. What was worse, Russia's new leadership was now tempted to cut away at what had been the foundations of the old system, including intelligence, not least because of severe budgetary constraints. Unsurprisingly, morale hit rock bottom.

CONCLUSION: Out from the Shadows

When the Bolsheviks set up the Cheka and the Fourth, their model for foreign operations was MI6—but it bore little relation to reality. Shadowboxing a massive, imaginary opponent, they created for themselves agencies that were far larger than was absolutely necessary. The strengths of Soviet intelligence even survived the miasma of corruption under Brezhnev, though neither the GRU nor the KGB emerged untarnished.

In turn, although steadfastly alert to the threat posed by Moscow to the stability of the realm and the empire, the British made the fatal error of severely and consistently underestimating their main adversary. The Government Code and Cypher School's own initial successes in codebreaking were taken for granted and carelessly exploited by ministers ignorant of the serious consequences of publication, and human intelligence operations against the Kremlin (whether in the 1920s, 1930s, 1940s, or 1950s) were hopelessly compromised from the start. Nonetheless, the Bolsheviks had to compensate for their deficiencies in cryptography through creative human intelligence, and it was undoubtedly the case that in the first phase of Soviet power, from 1917 through to 1927, Bolshevik intelligence was on the back foot.

It is striking that the great achievements of the prewar period emerged out of counterintelligence (notably Artuzov and the Trust) and that only once the leaders of counterintelligence took over foreign intelligence did the Soviet Union finally strike gold with the Cambridge Five. The greatest talents among the illegals were spotted and brought on by Artuzov. Without Artuzov, there would not have been Deutsch or Orlov, and without them, no Cambridge Five.

The subsequent decade from 1934 to 1944 proved one of outstanding, though not unalloyed, success. Its limitations were most apparent in the failure to penetrate the Nazi inner circle. The achievements, such as they were, met with little appreciation by Stalin because he was not, as we would normally understand the term, a completely rational statesman. He mistrusted research and analysis, preferring to hold on tight to the interpretation of raw intelligence. He neglected cryptography. Moreover, the deeply flawed features of his own personality combined with his near-absolute power seriously interfered with the processes of gathering and analysing intelligence.

In the circumstances, Stalin was extraordinarily lucky that those who volunteered unpaid for the privilege of serving him from abroad had no idea at all what the Soviet Union was really like until it was too late (when they defected and had to endure life there in premature if mind-numbing retirement). Stalin was also served loyally and to the limit by Soviet revolutionaries and patriots who had no idea as to the true nature of the régime for which they had risked their lives.

It was deeply ironical that, although the Cambridge Five were viewed with suspicion, it was their joint effort, massively bolstered by agent Dolly, that enabled Stalin to turn the tide of war in July 1943. Finally, the Fabian investment in penetrating the ruling caste in Britain paid off, not least due to the hidebound class consciousness of those senior officials who protected the Five. Indeed, the biographies of the Five should be subtitled "one of us." Consciousness of their value by Stalin became all too clear after the defection by Burgess and Maclean in the early 1950s. For although that hard-earned capital paid such lucrative dividends in the earliest phase of the Cold War, Stalin failed to invest for the future. Undoubtedly, the possession of overwhelming military power at the heart of Europe and his underestimation of Truman contributed to such perilous complacency.

Thus, Stalin's successors found their account drawn down to the point where Soviet intelligence was yielding dwindling returns. The business of rebuilding networks of illegals had to be done in haste.

Although cryptography remained the victim of relative neglect, it is remarkable how much progress was made in human intelligence, despite the revelations in 1956 about the truth of the Soviet Union's bloody past, which undercut the traditional bases for recruitment abroad. From then on, the intelligence services had to prove that they could operate as a profession entirely from their own resources, without foreign Communist help. Where they did not enlist agents under false flags, the practice of recruiting spies for Russia began to resemble American practices, which the Russians had always disparaged as blatantly commercial ("Maidens, like moths, are ever caught by glare, / And Mammon wins his way where seraphs might despair").

It is striking that successful agents such as Ames signed up purely for money. Only the U.S. naval intelligence petty officer Glenn Souther, spying from 1980 to 1985, believed in the radiant Soviet future. According to his handler, Solomatin, Souther was, indeed, an outstanding exception given that "Most spies are men who sell their souls for cash."[1] Head of the GRU until July 9, 1987, and a noted hawk, Ivashutin continued to the very end steadfast in the belief that "the human factor was and remains at the forefront of intelligence."[2] It is just that the "human factor" was no longer naïve belief but plain greed.

Counterintelligence in the 1950s produced noted achievements under Gribanov. It had been the success story of the 1920s, with the adoption of tsarist best practice. The loss of faith abroad may have been a serious setback, but it did not yet halt the influx of Russians, patriotic or not, eager to find a life of adventure and in search of a standard of living out of reach of the Soviet citizen through service in secret intelligence. This, however, meant that the First Main Directorate, in particular, became a major attraction for the offspring of the spoiled elite. Inevitably, the corrupt practices of an addled bureaucracy under Brezhnev in the era of stagnation (*zastoi*) spread through the intelligence services, despite the innovator Andropov's best efforts.

Native talent there was, nonetheless, as evidenced by highly skilled operatives such as Solomatin, Drozdov, and Totrov. This was especially important because human intelligence all too frequently had to make up the deficit in communications intelligence. The latter was held back by the technological backwardness of the Soviet Union. Thus, to those in communications intelligence, the demise of a system unable to compete could not have come as a surprise, whereas those in human intelligence were only now reaping the harvest sown in recent years and were inevitably both more shocked and all the more embittered by the collapse of the régime.

Holding the diehards at bay, Gorbachev defied every expectation at home and abroad by permitting the Berlin Wall to be breached in November 1989. He had finally allowed the imbalance of military power in Europe, which had stood provocatively and overwhelmingly to Soviet advantage since 1945, to be broken unopposed. Behind all this lay a basic truth: Moscow had effectively already given up the ideological struggle. The Russia reborn in 1992 had to confront the unexpected need to substitute at short notice raw patriotism for a long-outmoded belief in a global ideal, all in the face of falling living standards and full consciousness—not least via MTV, now beamed freely into city apartments—of what the West could offer in return for betrayal.

The negative impact on intelligence assets and their recruitment was severe, given how heavily Moscow depended upon human resources once attracted by and tied to the Soviet model. Only with the emergence of their own man, former Lieutenant Colonel Vladimir Putin, as president in 2000 could the "organs" hope to regain lost ground. He rose to power as a result of the chaotic conditions prevailing in Yeltsin's Russia, the state in retreat, criminality rife, and widespread corruption associated with the liberation of the state's assets to the market. Putin's message in 1999 was twofold: reestablishment of order and restoration of the Soviet Union, not as a Communist entity but as an imperial stronghold. Inevitably, practices rapidly reverted to those of an era we had all thought dead and buried.

How much was all this an essentially Russian phenomenon rather than the temporary aberration produced by the Communist order? The saying goes that when the tide goes out, you can see who is swimming naked. Once the Soviet régime collapsed, we could begin to separate out what was essentially Russian (that which remained) and that which was peculiarly Communist (which is largely in the process of falling away despite the nostalgia it evokes). Ugly practices, such as assassination, reemerged within a decade after Soviet rule had ended for good. The role of the GRU special forces in the takeover of the Crimea in the spring of 2014 and in the undeclared war to take over the Eastern Ukraine is an ugly reminder of times past, the *aktivka* against Poland in the 1920s.

Such phenomena cannot be viewed as accidental. Their occurrence suggests that rather than being a complete displacement of and substitution for traditional ways and means, the Soviet model was in some fundamental way their continuation, albeit in revised form. Is one to forget that assassination was an instrument much favoured by the Narodniki, the forerunners of the left Socialist Revolutionaries and the Bolsheviks? Were they so different from the Rote Armee Fraktion and the Brigate Rosse, who found favour in Moscow? As distance grew from the time of the old autocracy, it became easier to imagine that the horrors that emerged under Stalin were unprecedented rather than a reversion to earlier times, the ruthless systematisation and application of older practices under new guises.

After the final collapse of Soviet power, a golden opportunity arose to break completely with the past. To reduce the disproportionate reach of the security services within Russian politics, President Boris Yeltsin splintered the KGB into three: the FSB (domestic intelligence), the SVR (foreign service), and the FAPSI (communications intelligence). Necessary cuts in government expenditures in order to substitute a welfare state for the warfare state and a market for the Five-Year Plan reduced the relentless growth of the fighting services. These changes in priorities failed, however, to make a lasting impact on attitudes. Although redundancies followed, and the private sector soon absorbed many of the more entrepreneurial and technologically sophisticated, by the mid-1990s cutbacks were being reversed.

Moreover, although the goal of communism disappeared, methods tried and tested from the more distant past reasserted themselves with the wars against Islamic-led separatism to the south and the postimperial resentment at U.S. supremacy. It is no coincidence that Putin's emergence and speedy ascendance, culminating in his electoral victory in March 2000, coincide with both. By 2003, the *siloviki* ("men of power"), who were figures from the security services, held all the reins. They had come from out of the shadows for everyone to see, a caste that owed its very existence and identity to the history of the Cheka. It is striking, however, that the dominant element has been counterintelligence, represented in the FSB, rather than foreign intelligence represented in the SVR. Counterintelligence was, after all, where Putin served. The FSB, some claim, has become a law unto itself.

One symptom of this reversion to the past was the reappearance of the expression *Eto ne telefonnyi razgovor* ("This is not a telephone conversation"), meaning "We can speak openly." Those in the business of intercepting communications and who were destined to become unemployed in the early 1990s soon found themselves back at work. And instead of interception being run as a monopoly by the twelfth department of the KGB, any number of agencies have been conducting their own operations. The official number of intercepts, for example, doubled between 2007 and 2011. But it is doubtful whether this tells the whole story.[3] Another symptom, of a more sinister nature, was the shattering news of the ex-FSB officer Alexander Litvinenko's assassination.

Instead of the Soviet Union's collapse leading directly to the dismantling of the security organs, a decade later they had taken over the Russian Federation. It did not take long after Putin's electoral triumph for the Jewish oligarchs (who had acquired much of the Soviet Union's capital portfolio and were now seeking leverage for political purposes) to be driven out of Russia. The sole dogged figure of resistance, the ruthless Mikhail Khodorkovsky, was brutally given to understand that he was digging himself ever deeper into a hole of his own making by continuing to oppose the inevitable.[4] Simultaneously, every vital post in the public and private sectors of the economy was appropriated by either a former *gebist*, a close relative of the same, or an asset of the security organs.

The Russian sociologist Ol'ga Kryshtanovskaya, director of the study of the elite at the Institute of Sociology (Russian Academy of Sciences), in her earlier guise as critic, pointed to the formation of a new elite and the incorporation of the state by the security services.[5] Nikolai Patrushev, who succeeded Putin as director of the FSB, described them as Russia's "new nobility."[6] Former general of the KGB Alexei Kondaurov boasted, "There is nobody today who can say no to the FSB." He added: "Communist ideology has gone, but the methods and psychology of its secret police have remained."[7]

For a while it looked as though the GRU was heading for dismemberment under Putin as a force that no longer served a useful purpose. Yet the operations launched against the Crimea, with "little green men," and against the rest of the Eastern Ukraine propelled the GRU back into life. Until 2014, its role as policeman of the "near abroad" (former Soviet republics) looked redundant. All of a sudden the GRU has found a new role in what might be described as "implausibly deniable" *aktivka*, operations not unlike those conducted against Poland by the Fourth in the 1920s: sufficient to keep the wound bleeding but insufficient, thus far, to warrant massive retaliation.[8]

These forms of covert operations were heralded by the new chief of the General Staff, Valery Gerasimov, in January 2013. The business-speak within the army today is "outsourcing," which has been coined as a new Russian word. Now it has acquired a new meaning altogether. Moscow "outsources" its war fighting. Considered "an intellectual," in the words of the editor of *Natsional'naya oborona*, Gerasimov assured those assembled at the Academy of Military Sciences that force continued to play an important role in resolving disputes between countries and that "hot points" existed close to Russian frontiers. Referring to the spring revolutions in various states, he went on to point out that even a country in good condition could fall victim to foreign intervention and descend into chaos. A broad range of nonmilitary measures could be used in support of popular protest, plus the use of "covert military means."[9]

We began with the emergence of the Cheka out of the dust of Russia's ancien régime. We end with Russia incorporated by the diehards of the Cheka. Even the GRU has rediscovered a role hitherto lost in the mists of the past. The history of the Soviet intelligence services thus becomes not just an end in itself but also a vantage point into the story of the present, a state within a state retreating into the past with the destruction of pluralism and the recentralisation of power then exerting itself to determine the future through a process of stealthy expansion into the former territories of the Soviet Union.

APPENDIX I
Soviet Foreign Intelligence Organisations

Cheka/KGB

December 20, 1920	INO Cheka, then GPU and OGPU
June 10, 1934	INO GUGB NKVD
December 25, 1936	7 otdel GUGB NKVD
June 9, 1938	5 otdel 1 upravlenie NKGB
September 29, 1938	5 otdel GUGB NKVD
February 26, 1941	1 upravlenie NKBG
July 31, 1941	1 upravlenie NKVD
April 14, 1943	1 upravlenie NKGB
May 4, 1946	1 glavnoe upravlenie MGB
May 30, 1947	Komitet Informatsii (Sovmin)
1949	(Minindel)
November 2, 1951	1 glavnoe upravlenie MGB
March 14, 1953	1 glavnoe upravlenie MVD
March 18, 1954	1 glavnoe upravlenie KGB (Sovmin)

Registrupr/GRU

November 5, 1918	Registrupr (*Registratsionnoe upravlenie*)
April 4, 1921	Razvedupr (*Razvedyvatel'noe upravlenie*)
September 1926	Fourth Directorate/Razvedupr
February 16, 1942	GRU

Cryptography and Decryption

July 10, 1934	Spetsotdel GUGB NKVD
December 25, 1936	9 otdel GUGB NKVD
June 9, 1938	Spetsotdel NKVD
September 29, 1938	7 otdel GUGB NKVD
February 26, 1941	5 otdel NKGB and 6 otdelenie NKVD
July 31, 1941	5 spetsotdel NKVD
November 3, 1942	5 upravlenie NKVD
April 14, 1943	5 upravlenie NKGB and 2 spetsotdel NKVD

May 4, 1946	6 upravlenie MGB
November 19, 1949	GUSS (CC)
March 14, 1953	8 upravlenie MVD
March 18, 1954	8 glavnoe upravlenie KGB
June 21, 1973	8 glavnoe upravlenie and 16 glavnoe upravlenie

APPENDIX 2
Operatives Who Betrayed the Régime, Including Defectors

1922   Smirnov—the Fourth
       Yashin-Sumarokov (Pavlunovskii)—GPU
1925   Nesterovich (Yaroslavskii)—the Fourth
       Dzevaltovskii—the Fourth
1927   Opperput-Straunits—OGPU
       Miller—OGPU
1928   Petrov—OGPU
       Birger (Maksimov)—OGPU
1929   Blyumkin—OGPU
1930   Agabekov—OGPU
       Svitts—Fourth
       Sobolev—Fourth
1933   Trossin—Fourth
1937   Poretskii—NKVD
       Krivitsky—NKVD
       Barmine—NKVD
1938   Orlov—NKVD
       Lyushkov—NKVD
       Uspenskii—NKVD
1940   Gel'fand—NKVD
1942   Akhmedov—NKVD
       Bart—GRU
1944   Mironov—NKGB
1945   Volkov—NKGB
       Gouzenko—GRU
1946   Granovskii—MGB
       Skripkin—GRU
1947   Baklanov—MGB
1949   Shelaputin—GRU
1950   Dzhirkvelov—MGB
1953   Popov—GRU

1954   Petrov and Petrova—KGB
       Rastvorov—KGB
       Deryabin—KGB
       Khokhlov—KGB
       "Gart"—KGB
       Heyhanen—KGB
1958   Cheishvili—KGB
       Fedorov—GRU
1961   Loginov—KGB
       Stashinskii—KGB
       Golitsyn—KGB
       Pen'kovskii—GRU
1962   Nosenko—KGB
       Kulak—KGB
       Polyakov—GRU
1963   Chernov—GRU
1968   Runge—KGB
1970   Orekhov—KGB
1971   Lyalin—KGB
       Sakharov—KGB
       Petrov—GRU
1972   Oganesyan—KGB
       Sorokin—GRU
1974   Gordievsky—KGB
       Grigoryan—KGB
       Poleshchuk—KGB
       Filatov—GRU
       Smetanin—GRU
1976   Semenov—KGB
       Piguzov—KGB
       Bokhan—GRU
       Yuzhin—KGB
1977   Zemenek—KGB
       Ogorodnik—KGB
1978   Rezun—GRU
1979   Levchenko—KGB
       Sheimov—KGB
1980   Vetrov—KGB
1982   Kuzichkin—KGB
       Bogatyi—KGB
       Martynov—KGB
1983   Motorin—KGB

1984   Vorontsov—KGB
       Vasil'ev—GRU
1985   Yurchenko—KGB
       Makarov—KGB
1987   Varenik—KGB

NOTES

Preface

1. The late Sir Harry Hinsley, the late Ernest May, and Christopher Andrew: see J. Haslam and K. Urbach, eds., *Secret Intelligence in the European States System, 1918–1989* (Stanford, CA: Stanford University Press, 2013), pp. 1–2. And from outside academia, David Kahn and Nigel West.
2. Christopher Andrew and Vasili Mitrokhin, *The Sword and the Shield: The Mitrokhin Archive and the Secret History of the KGB* (New York: Allen Lane, 1999); and Andrew and Mitrokhin, *The Mitrokhin Archive: The KGB and the World*, part 2 (New York: Allen Lane, 2006).
3. Inventory list, The Papers of Vasiliy Mitrokhin, janus.lib.cam.ac.uk; and House of Commons, Intelligence and Security Committee, Cm 4764: "The Mitrokhin Inquiry Report," June 2000, p. 54.
4. RTS with the FSB, "Pen'kovskii—agent trekh razvedok," February 6, 2012: available at www.youtube.com/watch?v=173CLBrsP20.
5. Photocopy of the first page of the text and copy of the rest released by Yuri Titov (FSB), July 1, 2014, available in Russian at www.lustration.ru.
6. R. Benson, *The Venona Story* (Meade, MD: NSA, 2000).
7. The threat was made by Nikolai Andreev, then head of FAPSI, the Russian code and cipher establishment, for oral transmission to the NSA via David Kahn, who had finally secured an interview with him. "Interview with the former head of the Eighth Main Directorate of the KGB, N. Andreev," vif2ne.ru.

Introduction

1. Lecture notes reprinted in T. Gladkov and N. Zaitsev, *I ya emu ne mogu ne verit'* (Moscow: Politizdat, 1983), p. 222. Of course Artuzov's knowledge of the history of MI6 was somewhat defective.
2. V. Solov'ev and V. Trifonov, "Svezho predatel'stvo," *Kommersant*, November 11, 2010.
3. BBC Press Office, *Newsnight* broadcast February 7, 2007, BBC 2. Gusak, who came to loathe Litvinenko for being arrogant and utterly self-centered, had previously accused him of treachery when the latter published a book with accusations levelled against the FSB: "Govorit Aleksandr' Gusak," *Zavtra*, September 10, 2001.
4. *Daily Mail*, January 28, 2012; *Sunday Times*, March 17, 2013.
5. Conversation with Yevgenii Savast'yanov, March 9, 2012. Savost'yanov headed the Moscow KGB from September 1991 to December 1994. General Trofimov took over until his own dismissal in February 1997.
6. "Tekst prigovora Gusaku i Litvinenko," November 26, 1999, www.compromat.ru.
7. Roger Boyse, *The Times*, www.inopressa.ru, November 24, 2010; also "Byvshii shef Litvinenko: plany ubit' Berezovskogo deistvitel'no obsuzhdalis'," February 9, 2007, www.news.ru.com.
8. J. Haslam, *Soviet Foreign Policy 1930-33: The Impact of the Depression* (London: Macmillan/New York, St. Martin's Press, 1983), p. 23.
9. V. Antonov, "Yakov Serebryanskii—trizhdy uznik Lubyanki," *Voenno-promyshlennyi kur'er*, November 1, 2006. Antonov was an administrator at the SVR archives, the successor to the KGB in foreign intelligence. The best account from French sources remains M. Grey, *Le Général Meurt à Minuit: L'enlèvement des généraux Koutiepov (1930) et Miller (1937)* (Paris: Plon, 1981).
10. B. Gudz', "Ya videl, kak Dzerzhinskii tseloval dame ruku," *Trud*, December 20, 2002.
11. S. Dmitrievskii, *Sovetskie portrety* (Berlin: Strela, 1932), pp. 218-20. Dmitrievskii was an early defector.
12. Ibid., p. 225.
13. L. Trotsky, "Jakob Blumkin Shot by the Stalinists," January 4, 1930, *Writings of Leon Trotsky* (1930, New York, 1975).
14. "Razvedka—svyatoe, ideal'noe dlya nas delo," enclosed in "Zapiska Yu. Andropova L Brezhnevu," April 15, 1973, *Istochnik* 5, no. 53 (2001): 132.
15. Recorded by Vyacheslav Molotov: V. Nikonov, *Molotov: Molodost'* (Moscow: Vagrius, 2005), pp. 704-5.
16. Stalin to Lenin, July 24, 1920, *Bol'shevistskoe rukovodstvo. Perepiska, 1912-1927*, ed. A. Kvashonkin et al. (Moscow: Rosspen, 1996), doc. 91.
17. Stalin's reply to Thalheim, September 13, 1923, quoted in P. Makarenko, "'Nemetskii Oktyabr' 1923 g. i sovetskaya vneshnyaya politika," *Voprosy istorii* 3 (March, 2012): 43.
18. Speech at a reception, uncorrected stenogram, May 4, 1935, V. Nevezhin, ed., *Stalin o voine: Zastol'nye rechi 1933-1945gg.* (Moscow: Eksmo, 2007), doc. 8.

19. Quoted in A. Ciliga, *The Russian Enigma* (republished London: Routledge, 1979), p. 85. This was quite possibly Litvinov, in one of his more cynical moments.

20. Nikonov, *Molotov: Molodost'*.

21. Speech delivered sometime in the second half of 1937 or the first two months of 1938, "Pravil'naya politika pravitel'stva reshaet uspekh armii," *Istochnik* 3, no. 57 (Olma Press, 2002): 75.

22. R. Krasil'nikov, *Novye krestonostsy: TsRU i perestroika* (Moscow, 2003), p. 225.

23. Memorandum for his successor: "Zdes' lezhit Chicherin, zhertva sokrashchenii i chistok," *Kommersant vlast'* 4, no. 858 (February 1, 2010).

I. Starting from Scratch

1. There is only one, hard-to-obtain biography: V. I. Viktorov, *Podpol'shchik, voin, chekist* (Moscow: Politiicheskaya Literatura, 1963). For recollections of the period, B. Gudz', "Ya videl."

2. Recollections of Boris Gudz' in T. Gladkov, *Nagrada za vernost'* (Moscow: Tsentrpoligraf, 2000), pp. 150–52.

3. *Ocherki istorii Rossiiskoi vneshnei razvedki*, vol. 2 (Moscow: Mezhdunarodyne Otnosheniya, 1996), p. 62.

4. Artuzov's report, November 30, 1924, quoted at length in V. Abramov, *Kontrrazvedka: Shchit i mech protiv Abvera i TsRU* (Moscow: Eksmo, 2006), p. 12.

5. From a memorandum by Artuzov, April 15, 1924, reprinted in A. Zdanovich, *Organy gosudarstvennoi bezopasnosti i Krasnaya Armiya. Deyatel'nost' organov VChK-OGPU po obespecheniyu bezopasnosti RKKA (1921–1934)* (Moscow: Kuchkovo Pole, 2008), doc. 16, pp. 575–80.

6. Ibid.

7. Artuzov's report, in Abramov, *Kontrrazvedka*, p. 19.

8. By riding in the German delegation's cars, which were allowed to speed through the city, the Soviet delegation avoided their adversaries. Similarly at public venues, the delegates slipped out of sight and gave out false information as to their likely movements: *Ocherki istorii Rossiiskoi vneshnei razvedki*, vol. 2 (Moscow: Mezhdunarodyne Otnosheniya, 1996), pp. 54–55.

9. O. Matveev and V. Merzlyakov, "Azbuka Kontrrazvedka," *Nezavisimoe voennoe obozrenie*, March 3, 2000.

10. On Dzhunkovskii, see N. Sysoev, "Zhandarm, konsul'tirovavshii chekistov," November 2002, www. bratishka.ru. For tsarist operations, see A. Vasil'ev, "Okhrana. Russkaya sekretnaya politsiya," in *"Okhranka": Vospominaniya rukovoditelei okhrannykh otdelenii*, ed. Z. Peregudova: vol. 2 (Moscow: Novoe literaturnoe obozrenie, 2004), pp. 346–81; also S. Galvazin, *Okhrannye struktury Rossiiskoi Imperii. Formirovanie apparata, analiz operativnoi praktiki* (Moscow: Kollektsiya Sovershenno Sekietno, 2001).

11. Quoted at length in *Ocherki istorii Rossiiskoi vneshnei razvedki*, vol. 2, p. 112.

12. Memorandum by Artuzov, April 18, 1927, Zdanovich, *Organy gosudarstvennoi*, doc. 33, pp. 630–33.
13. For description of an associate in 1922–1923, see *The Trust*, Security and Intelligence Foundation Reprint Series, July 1989, p. 19.
14. *Ocherki istorii Rossiiskoi vneshnei razvedki*, vol. 2, pp. 116–19.
15. S. Voitsekhovskii, *Trest* (Ontario: Zaria, 1974), p. 10.
16. See Wrangel's letter of March 12, 1925, in ibid., pp. 141–42.
17. Gladkov and Zaitsev, *I ya emu ne mogu ne verit'*, pp. 70–73; and A. Gasparyan, *Operatsiya "Trest," Sovetskaya razvedka protiv russkoi emigratsii 1921–1937* (Moscow: Politizdat, 1983), pp. 134–79.
18. MI6 was taken in. See K. Jeffery, *MI6: The History of the Secret Intelligence Service 1909–1949* (London: Bloomsbury, 2011), pp. 271–73.
19. Vladimir Antonov, "Razgrom belogvardeiskogo gnezda," *Nezavisimoe voennoe obozrenie*, October 19, 2012.
20. The Mitrokhin Archive, Churchill College, Cambridge, MITN 1/7.
21. Davtyan was in the INO and the Commissariat of Foreign Affairs simultaneously until eventually edged out of both: V. Antonov, "Iskusstvo vybirat' druzei i vragov," *Nezavisimoe voennoe obozrenie*, October 31, 2013.
22. Gladkov, *Nagrada na vernost'—Kazn'*, p. 325.
23. I. Damaskin, *Stalin i razvedka* (Moscow: Veche, 2004), p. 43.
24. "Poslednyaya sluzhebnaya zapiska G. V. Chicherina," Foreign Ministry archives, AVPRF, f.08, op. 11, n. 47, d. 63, ll. 81–83. Also www.idd.mid.ru and *Kommersant vlast'*, 4, February 1, 2010.
25. A. Kolpakidi and D. Prokhorov, *Imperiya GRU* (Moscow: Olma Press, 2000), pp. 142–44.
26. The defector Krivitsky, who initially served in the Fourth and later moved over to the NKVD, testifies to the bad relations between the two organisations: "Iz vospominaniya sovetskogo kommunista," *Sotsialisticheskii vestnik* 8, no. 412 (April 29, 1938): 3.
27. Pre-Bolshevik terms and titles were restored to the military at Tukhachevsky's insistence on September 22, 1935.
28. May 25, 1920, quoted in V. Kochik, "Sovetskaya voennaya razvedka: struktura i kadry," *Svobodnaya mysl'* 6, no. 1475 (June 1998): 96.
29. G. Nowik, "Znaczenie i zakres deszyfracji depesz bolszewickich w latach 1919–1920," *Gazeta Wyborcza*, August 7, 2005.
30. *Ocherki istorii Rossiiskoi vneshnei razvedki*, vol. 2, p. 10.
31. Stalin to Minister Ignat'ev, August 1952, Ignat'ev memorandum to Beria, March 27, 1953, reprinted in N. Petrov, *Palachi: Oni vypolnyali zakazy Stalina* (Moscow: Novaya Gazeta, 2011), pp. 299–300.
32. M. Alekseev, *Sovetskaya voennaya razvedka v kitae i khronika "kitaiskoi smuty" (1922–1929)* (Moscow: Kuchkovo Pole, 2010), pp. 230–31.
33. V. Kochik, "Sovetskaya voennaya razvedka: struktura i kadry," *Svobodnaya mysl'* 7, no. 1476 (July 1998): 102; M. K. Zaleskaya, *Oni rukovodili GRU* (Moscow: Veche, 2010), pp. 94–108.

34. O. Gorchakov, *Yan Berzin—komandarm GRU* (Moscow: Neva, 2004).

35. L. Trepper, *Le Grand Jeu* (Paris: A. Michel, 1975), p. 78.

36. Testimony of V. Sukhorukov, in Zalesskaya, *Oni rukovodili GRU*, pp. 109–10.

37. Recollections of Mil'shtein in M. Mil'shtein, *Skvoz' gody voin i nishchety* (Moscow: Itar-TASS, 2000).

38. Alekseev, *Sovetskaya voennaya razvedka*, pp. 231–32.

39. W. Krivitsky, *In Stalin's Secret Service* (New York: Enigma Books, 2000), p. 123.

40. Damaskin, *Stalin i razvedka*, pp. 62–63.

41. Elizabeth Poretsky, *Our Own People* (London: Oxford University Press, 1969), p. 104.

42. J. and J. MacKinnon, *Agnes Smedley: The Life and Times of an American Radical* (Berkeley: University of California Press, 1998), p. 147. This is useful but in other respects far too credulous of claims about the innocence of the Rudniks.

43. N. and M. Ulanovskii, *Istoriya odnoi sem'i* (New York: Chalidze, 1982), pp. 78–79.

44. A reprimand from the head of the standing committee of the Comintern secretariat, Vasil'ev, December 6, 1928: M. Alekseev, *"Vash Ramzai." Rikhard Zorge i sovetskaya voennaya razvedka v Kitae 1930–1933 gg.* (Moscow: Kuchkovo Pole, 2010), p. 115.

45. Ibid., p. 134.

46. F. Firsov, *Sekretnye kody istorii Kominterna 1919–1943* (Moscow: Airo-XXI, 2007), part 1, chap. 4; also Damaskin, *Stalin i razvedka*, pp. 65–66.

47. E. Zhirnov, "Pri nashem sodeistvii rabotayut bandy za kordonom," *Kommersant Vlast'*, 33, no. 586 (August 23, 2004); E. Gorbunov, "Aktivnaya razvedka, perekhodyashchaya v banditizm," *Nezavisimoe voennoe obozrenie*, September 9, 2005.

48. Report from the directorate of the GPU border guards, January 5, 1925: E. D. Solov'ev, *Pogranichnye voiska SSSR 1918–1928: Sbornik documentov i materialov*, ed. P. Zyryanov et al. (Moscow: Nauka, 1973), doc. 363.

49. A. Plekhanov, *Dzerzhinskii. Pervyi chekist Rossii* (Moscow: Olma Media Group, 2007), pp. 388–91.

50. *Lubyanka (January 1922–December 1936), Dokumenty*, p. 795.

51. Politburo resolution, June 23, 1927, in ibid., doc. 156.

52. Politburo resolution, February 25, 1925, in *Lubyanka, Dokumenty*, doc. 105.

53. "Poslednyaya sluzhebnaya zapiska G. V. Chicherina."

54. Debriefing London, sent to Vivian, MI6, March 13, 1940, KV/2/804, National Archives, London.

55. *Nezavisimoe voennoe obozrenie*, February 28, 2003.

56. Styrne's report of December 9, 1924, in M. Alekseev, *Sovetskaya voennaya razvedka*, p. 586.

57. "Kratkaya spravka," quoted in Abramov, *Kontrrazvedka*, p. 7.

58. This much is apparent on reading a letter from the leading Old Bolshevik Leonid Krasin to his daughters, then in Stockholm, that month. Krasin Papers, International Institute of Social History, Amsterdam, 1–4. I inspected these papers when they were still held by the family, in the late 1970s, before they were bought by the Institute. Also see the testimony of A. Borman, *Moskva—1918: Iz*

zapisok sekretnogo agenta v Kremle (Leningrad: Russkoe proshloe, 1991), vol. 1, pp. 126 and 133.

59. Artuzov's report of November 30, 1924, in Abramov, *Kontrrazvedka*, pp. 17–18.
60. Artuzov's report of April 18, 1927, in Zdanovich, *Organy gosudarstvennoi*, doc. 33.
61. M. Alekseev, *Sovetskaya voennaya razvedka*, p. 586.
62. *Ocherki istorii Rossiiskoi vneshnei razvedki*, p. 122.
63. Abramov, *Kontrrazvedka*, p. 27.
64. This was a forgery purchased by the head of station for MI6 in Riga for five hundred pounds produced by a man named Pokrowski, purporting to be a letter from the president of Comintern pressing for subversion of the British armed forces. See G. Adibekov et al., eds., *Politburo TsK RKP (b)—VKP(b) i Evropa: resheniya 'Osoboi papki' 1923–1939* (Moscow: Rosspen, 2001), p. 53n1.
65. C. Andrew, *The Defence of the Realm: The Authorized History of MI5* (London: Allen Lane, 2009), pp. 139–59; also O. Tsarev, *KGB v Anglii* (Moscow: Tsentrpoligraf, 1999), chap. 2.
66. I. Simbirtsev, *Spetssluzhby pervykh let SSSR 1923–1939* (Moscow: Tsentrpoligraf, 2008), pp. 90–91.
67. Alekseev, *Sovetskaya voennaya razvedka*, pp. 235–36.
68. Ibid., p. 240.
69. Damaskin, *Semnadtsat' imyon Kitti Kharris* (Moscow: Geia Iterum, 1999), p. 85.
70. V. Khaustov et al., eds., *Lubyanka, Stalin i VChK-GPU-OGPU-NKVD 1922–1936* (Moscow: Mezhdunarodnyi fond Demokratiya, 2003), doc. 152.
71. S. Ostrjakow, *Militär—Tschekisten* (Berlin: Militär Verlag, 1984), p. 109.
72. Abramov, *Kontrrazvedka*, p. 28.
73. Quoted at length in *Ocherki istorii Rossiiskoi vneshnei razvedki*, pp. 127–28.
74. G. Agabekov, *Sekretnyi terror: Zapiski razvedchika* (Moscow: Sovremennik, 1996), p. 10.
75. Dmitrievskii, *Sovetskie portrety*, pp. 222–23.
76. Documentary, November 22, 2012, itemising the inventory from the NKVD files: warfiles.ru/show-2472-tayny-veka-padenie-marshala-lubyanki.html.
77. M. Alekseev, *Leksika russkoi razvedki* (Moscow: Mezhdunarodnye Otnosheniya, 1996), pp. 100–103.
78. E. Gorbunov, *Skhvatka s chernym drakonom: Tainaya voina na Dal'nem Vostoke* (Moscow: 2002), p. 99.
79. *Lubyanka. Stalin i VChK-GPU-OGPU-NKVD. January 1922–December 1936* (Moscow: Materik, 2003).
80. E. Gorbunov, "Bezosnovatel'naya trevoga. Voennaya razvedka dokladyvala sovetskomu rukovodstvu, chto napadenie na SSSR maloveroyatno," *Nezavisimoe voennoe obozrenie*, March 21, 2008; E. Gorbunov, *Stalin i GRU* (Moscow: Eksmo, 2010), p. 72.
81. V. Danilov, ed. *Tragediya sovetskoi derevni. Kollektivizatsiya i raskulachivanie 1927–1939: Dokumenty i materialy*, vol. 1 (Moscow: Rosspen, 1999), p. 23.
82. Ibid.

83. Ciphered telegram from Stalin to Menzhinsky, June 23, 1927: *Lubyanka. Dokumenty*, doc. 157.

84. Mitrokhin Archive, MITN 2/10.

85. "V chem sostoit oshibochnost' segodnyashnei politiki germanskoi kompartii," December 8, 1931, *Byulleten' oppozitsii* 27 (March 1932).

2. But Who Was the Main Enemy?

1. Artuzov, "Memorandum," in Zdanovich, *Organy gosudarstvennoi*, doc. 33.

2. Voitsekhovskii, *Trest*, p. 11.

3. Ibid., p. 3.

4. *Ocherki istorii Rossiiskoi vneshnei razvedki*, vol. 2, pp. 179–80.

5. T. Weingartner, *Stalin und der Aufstieg Hitlers: Die Deutschlandpolitik der Sowjetunion und der Kommunistischen Internationale 1929–1934* (Berlin: De Gruyter, 1970), p. 139.

6. *Ocherki istorii Rossiiskoi vneshnei razvedki*, vol. 2, p. 181.

7. "Pravitel'stvennyi krizis v Germanii," *Pravda*, June 3, 1932.

8. E. Carr, *Twilight of Comintern, 1930–1935* (London: Macmillan, 1982), chaps. 3 and 4; Haslam, *Soviet Foreign Policy 1930–33*, pp. 102–4.

9. Gladkov, *Nagrada na vernost'*, pp. 345–46.

10. The Mitrokhin Archive, MITN 1/6/8.

11. The Mitrokhin Archive, MITN 1/6/2.

12. The Mitrokhin Archive, MITN 1/7.

13. Artuzov's letter to Yezhov, March 2, 1937, reprinted in M. Tumshis and A. Papchinskii, *1937: Bol'shaya Chistka. NKVD protiv ChK* (Moscow: Eksmo, 2009), pp. 445–51.

14. Khaustov et al., eds., *Lubyanka, Stalin i VChK-GPU-OGPU-NKVD*, p. 801.

15. V. Antonov, "Fedor i Marta: neromanticheskaya istoriya razvedchika i ego istochnika informatsii," *Nezavisimoe voennoe obozrenie*, November 15, 2013, *passim*.

16. V. Peshcherskii, *"Krasnaya Kapella": Sovetskaya razvedka protiv Abvera i Gestapo* (Moscow: Tsentrpoligraf, 2000), p. 16; Sergei Vladimirov, "Syn shveitsartsa i latyshki schital sebya sebya russkim," *Nezavisimoe voennoe obozrenie*, January 28, 2011.

17. Poretsky, *Our Own People*, p. 145.

18. A. Feklisov, *The Man Behind the Rosenbergs* (New York: Enigma Books, 2004), p. 45.

19. V. Antonov, "Vasilii Zarubin—razvedchik ot boga," *Nezavisimoe voennoe obozrenie*, February 20, 2009.

20. V. Pavlov, *Tragedii sovetskoi razvedki* (Moscow: Olma Press, 2000), p. 362. Pavlov knew them both.

21. P. Sudoplatov, *Spetsoperatsii. Lubyanka i Kreml' 1930–1950 gody* (Moscow: Olma Press, 1998), pp. 300–301; also V. Denisov and P. Matveev, "Tainstvennaya Erna," *Nezavisimoe voennoe obozrenie*, January 19, 2001.

22. "Pokazaniya Ya. G. Blyumkina," October 20, 1929, *Voenno-istoricheskii arkhiv*, No. 6, 2002. Previous accounts have been based on hearsay.

294 • NOTES TO PAGES 49-57

23. V. Abramov, *Evrei v KGB. Palachi i zhertvy* (Moscow: Eksmo, 2005), p. 128, and pp. 197–99 (for Zarubina). Trotsky refers to this in L. Trotsky, "Mill as a Stalinist Agent," October 1932, *Writings of Leon Trotsky 1932* (New York: 1973), p. 237.
24. V. Antonov and V. Karpov, *Tainye informatory Kremlya: Vollenberg, Artuzov i drugie* (Moscow: Geia Iterum, 2001), p. 31.
25. N. West and O. Tsarev, *Triplex: Secrets from the Cambridge Spies* (New Haven, CT: Yale University Press, 2009), p. 337.
26. M. Smith, *Six: The Real James Bonds 1909–1939* (London: Biteback, 2010), p. 337.
27. West and Tsarev, *Triplex*, pp. 336–37.
28. Decision (not for publication) by the Politburo and the Council of People's Commissars, "On the Relief of Prisons," May 10, 1933, Khaustov et al., eds., *Lubyanka. Stalin i VChK-GPU-OGPU-NKVD 1922–1936*, doc. 366.
29. Abramov, *Evrei*, pp. 299–300.
30. Poretsky, *Our Own People*, pp. 110 and 149.
31. Abramov, *Kontrrazvedka*, p. 15.
32. *New York Times*, March 31, 1933. Contrast this with the declassified documents from the secret police archives on the famine in the Ukraine: L. Aubra et al., eds., *Golodomor 1932–1933 rokiv v Ukraini Za dokumentami GDA SBU: anatovanü dovidnik* (L'viv: Tsentr doslidzhen' vizvol'nogo rukhu, 2010). The attempt to withdraw the prize posthumously was defeated.
33. Jeffery, *MI6: The History of the Secret Intelligence Service 1909–1949*, p. 313.
34. Note in E. Woodward and R. Butler, eds., *Documents on British Foreign Policy 1919–1939*, 2nd series, vol. 7, 1929–1934 (London: HMSO, 1958), doc. 219.
35. T. Gladkov and M. Smirnov, *Menzhinskii* (Moscow: Molodaya gvardiia, 1969), pp. 322–23.
36. Quoted in West, *Triplex*, p. 123. See also *Documents on British Foreign Policy*, docs. 212, 219, 302, 398, 409, and appendixes 3 and 4; and Smith, *Six*, pp. 338–40, for an excellent summary of the events in 1933. Unfortunately MI6 did not see fit to share this information with Jeffery.
37. I. Akhmedov, *In and Out of Stalin's GRU* (Frederick, MD: University Publications of America, 1984), p. 152.
38. For the family, see M-K. Wilmers, *The Eitingons* (London: Faber and Faber, 2009).
39. S. Vladimirov, "Naum Eitingon—general-razvedchik osobogo naznacheniya," *Nezavisimoe voennoe obozrenie*, December 4, 2009.
40. Quoted in Artuzov's letter to Yezhov, March 22, 1937, reprinted in Tumshis and Papchinskii, *1937*, pp. 445–51.
41. Haslam, *The Soviet Union and the Struggle for Collective Security in Europe, 1933–39* (London: Macmillan, 1984), pp. 14, 20–21.
42. Krivitsky, "Iz vospominanii sovetskogo kommunista," *Sotsialisticheskii vestnik* 7 (April 15, 1938); further elaborated a year later with the help of the journalist Isaac Don Levine, his minder: Krivitsky, *In Stalin's Secret Service*, pp. 11–13; also Kolpakidi and Prokhorov, *Imperiya GRU*, pp. 205–7.
43. Gorbunov, *Stalin i GRU*, p. 168; I. Winarow, *Kämpfer der lautlosen Front: Erinnerungen eines Kundschafters* (Berlin: Militärverlag, 1969).

44. From the record: V. Kochik, *Svobodnaya mysl'* 8, no. 1477 (1998): 72.
45. Alekseev, *"Vash Ramzai,"* p. 748; Kolpakidi and Prokhorov, *Imperiya GRU*, vol. 1, p. 195.
46. Kolpakidi and Pokhorov, *Imperiya GRU*, pp. 195-204; Gorbunov, *Stalin i GRU*, pp. 248-49; and Damaskin, *Stalin i razvedka*, p. 164.
47. Chambers, *Witness* (London: A. Deutsch, 1952), pp. 212-13.
48. Alekseev, *"Vash Ramzai,"* pp. 160-72.
49. Collected and published as a book: Captain E. Pik, *China in the Grip of the Reds* (Shanghai: North China Daily News and Herald, 1927).
50. Alekseev, *"Vash Ramzai,"* pp. 208-26; also KV 2/1895 (London: National Archives).
51. "Zapiska V. A. Balitskogo I. V.: Stalinu s prilozheniem perevoda yaponskikh do-kumentov, kasayushchikhsya voiny s SSSR," December 19, 1931, in Khaustov et al., eds., *Lubyanka. Stalin i VChK-GPU-OGPU-NKVD*, doc. 293. The information came in from military counterespionage, the Osoby Otdel (special departments).
52. Poretsky, *Our Own People*, pp. 62-63.
53. Alekseev, *"Vash Ramzai,"* p. 257.
54. Ibid., p. 346.
55. Ibid., p. 361.
56. For the British, Jeffery, *MI6: The History of the Secret Intelligence Service 1909-1949*, p. 260; Smith, *Six*, pp. 344-45.
57. Alekseev, *"Vash Ramzai,"* p. 366.
58. Ibid., pp. 397-98.
59. Ibid., p. 522.
60. Sorge to Pyatnitsky, May 1932, M. Titarenko, ed., *VKP(b), Komintern i Kitai. Dokumenty*, vol. 4 (Moscow: In-t Dal'nego, Vostoka RAN, 2003), doc. 52.
61. Alekseev, *"Vash Ramzai,"* p. 633.
62. Ibid., p. 604.
63. *Na prieme u Stalina: zapisei lits, priniatykh I. V. Stalinym (1924-1953 gg.)*, ed. A. Chernobaev (Moscow: Rossiiskii fond ku'ltury, 2008), p. 127.
64. Ibid., p. 130.
65. Gorbunov, *Stalin i GRU*, chap. 6.
66. Krivitsky debriefing in London, March 1940, KV/2/804.
67. In a letter to Yezhov, *Ocherki istorii Rossiiskoi vneshnei razvedki*, vol. 2, p. 63.
68. For a more rosy view of Mink, see V. Pedersen, "George Mink, the Marine Workers Industrial Union, and the Comintern in America," *Labor History* 41, no. 3 (2000): 307-20.
69. The Mink story can also be found in KV 2/2067.
70. Quoted in *Ocherki istorii Rossiiskoi vneshnei razvedki*, vol. 3 (Moscow: Mezhdunarodnye Otnosheniya, 1997), p. 11.
71. Kolpakidi and Prokhorov, *Imperiya GRU*, pp. 121-22.
72. *Ocherki istorii Rossiiskoi vneshnei razvedki*, vol. 2, pp. 62-63.
73. One defector claims it was an INO department, but here he is unusually misinformed, since no such existed. A. Orlov, "The Theory and Practice of Soviet Intelligence," www.cia.gov/library/center-for-the-study-of-intelligence/kent-csi/vol7no2/html/v0.

74. Abramov, *Kontrrazvedka*, p. 40; D. Abakumov, "Legendy razvedki: velikii kombinator spetssluzhb," *Bratishka ru*, June 17, 2007.

75. F. Moravec, *Master of Spies* (London: Sphere, 1981), p. 50.

76. Ibid., p. 56.

77. For this, the memoirs of his oldest friend: T. Milne, *Kim Philby: The Unknown Story of the KGB's Master Spy* (London: Biteback, 2014), pp. 2–13.

78. Recollections of Philby's former wife in her daughter's memoir: B. Honigmann, *Ein Kapitel aus meinem Leben* (Munich: C. Hanser, 2004), p. 60.

79. For new information on the young Mály from Austrian archives, see W. Duff, *A Time for Spies* (Nashville, TN: Vanderbilt University Press, 1999).

80. Tsarev, *KGB v Anglii*, p. 47.

81. V. Mironov and M. Shchipanov, "Krestnyi otets 'kembridzhskoi pyaterki,'" *Rossiiskaya gazeta*, October 9, 1999. For more on Mály, see Poretsky, *Our Own People*, p. 128; and MI5 files KV2/1008 and KV2/1009, National Archives, London.

82. For his autobiographical sketch, see N. West and O. Tsarev, *The Crown Jewels: The British Secrets at the Heart of the KGB Archives* (New Haven, CT: Yale University Press, 1998), pp. 104–7; also Abramov, *Evrei v KGB*, pp. 182–84.

83. From Deutsch's most complete autobiographical note for the files, see West and Tsarev, *KGB v Anglii*, pp. 44–45.

84. KV2/804 and KV2/1008, National Archives, London.

85. Tsarev, *KGB v Anglii*, p. 45.

86. Ibid.

87. For Edith's recruitment, see the Mitrokhin Archive, MITN 1/7. On the bookshop and flight, personal information from a shop assistant who, having experienced the raid, was then shocked to see Edith settled in London.

88. J. Costello and O. Tsarev, *Deadly Illusions* (New York: Crown 1993), p. 448n48 and p. 449n65.

89. Ibid., p. 114; for the date of Deutsch's arrival, see *Ocherki istorii Rossiiskoi vneshnei razvedki*, vol. 3, p. 20.

90. KV 2/1898.

91. Poretsky, *Our Own People*, pp. 72–85.

92. Note by Reiss: Costello and Tsarev, *Deadly Illusions*, p. 448n50.

93. S. Golubev, "Nash Tovarishch Kim Filbi," *Krasnaya zvezda*, August 9–11, 2006.

94. Noel Annan Papers, NGA 7/4/1, Archive Centre, King's College, Cambridge, UK.

95. V. Popov, *Sovetnik korolevy—superagent Kremlya* (Moscow: Too Novina, 1995), p. 55.

96. Philby's own account retained by his widow: R. Philby, M. Lyubimov, and H. Peake, *The Private Life of Kim Philby: The Moscow Years* (London: Fromm International, 1999), pp. 220–21.

97. Deutsch's own history of events quoted in *Ocherki istorii Rossiiskoi vneshnei razvedki*, vol. 3, p. 41.

98. Haslam, "The Comintern and the Origins of the Popular Front, 1934–35," *Historical Journal* 22, no. 3 (1979): 673–91; also, for the full story, see Carr, *Twilight of Comintern, 1930–35*.

99. Orlov's comments to Edward Gazur, last of Orlov's FBI minders: E. Gazur, *Secret Assignment: The FBI's KGB General* (London: St. Ermin's, 2001), p. 15.
100. Abramov, *Evrei v KGB*, p. 253.
101. Golubev, "Nash tovarishch"; Costello and Tsarev, *Deadly Illusions*, p. 445n3.
102. Costello and Tsarev, *Deadly Illusions*, p. 462.
103. Ibid., p. 456n8.
104. West and Tsarev, *The Crown Jewels*, pp. 81–82.
105. Rothschild proceeded likewise. Statute BI, III, 3, *Ordinances of the University of Cambridge to October 1933*, Cambridge, UK, 1933.
106. Noel Annan Papers, NGA 7/4/1, Archive Centre, King's College, Cambridge, UK.
107. Popov, *Sovetnik korolevy*, p. 57. Popov was from 1980 to 1986 ambassador to London.
108. Costello and Tsarev, *Deadly Illusions*, p. 189.
109. Ibid., pp. 191–92.
110. Ibid., p. 225. Costello wrongly translates this as "little girl."
111. The Mitrokhin Archive, MITN 1/7.
112. Ibid., p. 228.
113. Jeffery, *MI6: The History of the Secret Intelligence Service 1909–1949*, pp. 267–71.
114. *Ocherki istorii Rossiiskoi vneshnei razvedki*, vol. 3, p. 45.
115. This was the so-called Syrtsov-Lominadze Affair. For a copy of his statement after interrogation, in which he is remarkably outspoken about the beatings he suffered and the confession he was offered in 1938, see October 5, 1953, http://istmat.info/node/22263.
116. V. Antonov, "Svyaznaya 'Kembridzhskoi pyaterki': Zhizn' po chuzhomu pasportu i zolotoi kulon na pamyat' o lyubvi," *Nezavisimoe voennoe obozrenie*, November 3, 2012.
117. The Mitrokhin Archive, MITN 1/7.
118. Tsarev, *KGB v Anglii*, p. 50.
119. Intelligence reaching Trotsky from Reiss in Moscow: "Zapiski Ignatiya Raissa," *Byulleten' Oppozitsii*, nos. 60–61, December 1937.
120. Y. Rybalkin, *Operatisya "Kh"* (Moscow: Airo-XX, 2000), pp. 28–29.
121. Abramov, *Kontrrazvedka*, p. 40.
122. Rybalkin, *Operatsiya*, p. 36.
123. Haslam, *The Soviet Union and the Struggle for Collective Security in Europe, 1933–39*, chap. 7.
124. Haslam, "Political Opposition to Stalin and the Origins of the Terror in Russia, 1932–1936," *Historical Journal* 29, no. 2 (1986): 395–418.
125. T. Gladkov, *Nash chelovek v Nyu-Iork. Sud'ba rezidenta* (Moscow: Eksmo, 2007), p. 105; Shvaryov, *Razvedchiki-Nelegaly*, p. 14; Vladimirov, "Naum Eitingon"; testimony of the defector Leon Helfand, July 1952, in KV/2/2681.
126. "In Franco's Spain . . . A War-Weary Land," *The Times* (Seville), May 24, 1936.
127. Quoted in *Ocherki istorii Rossiiskoi vneshnei razvedki*, vol. 3, p. 38; also I. McDonald, *The History of the Times*, vol. 5 (London: Times Books, 1984), p. 76.

128. Milne, *Kim Philby*, p. 52.

129. Quoted in McDonald, *The History*, p. 77.

130. Tsarev, *KGB v Anglii*, p. 46.

131. Ibid.

132. Abramov, *Evrei*, p. 254.

133. Vladimirov, "Naum Eitingon."

134. Abramov, *Evrei*, p. 343.

135. Obituary, *The Times*, September 30, 1982. On Philby's recruitment, see *Ocherki istorii Rossiiskoi vneshnei razvedki*, vol. 4 (Moscow: Mezhdunarodnye Otnosheniya, 1999), p. 170; also the manuscript from which it was taken: Philby, Lyubimov, and Peake, *The Private Life*, pp. 220-21.

136. Antonov, "Svyaznaya 'Kembridzhskoi pyaterki.'"

137. West and Tsarev, *The Crown Jewels*, p. 133.

138. Tsarev, *KGB v Anglii*, p. 53.

139. Ibid., p. 76.

140. Popov, *Sovetnik korolevy*, p. 71. Popov, formerly ambassador to London, received some assistance from the SVR archivists in writing his biography of Blunt.

141. M. Carter, *Anthony Blunt: His Lives* (London: Macmillan, 2001), pp. 262-63.

142. Y. Modin, *Sud'by razvedchikov: Moi kembridzhskie druz'ya* (Moscow: Olma Press, 1997), p. 36.

143. Assessment summing up work done in 1939, the Mitrokhin Archive, MITN 1/7.

144. Also in the Mitrokhin Archive, MITN 1/7.

145. S. Radó, *Dora meldet* (Berlin: Militärverlag, 1974), pp. 13-14.

146. As recalled by Pitovranov. Given the rarity of meeting Stalin, this is about as accurate an account as one is likely to find that is not contained in a document. It was so memorable that Pitovranov etched it into his memory on the way back to the office in order to write it down. It also fits in with Stalin's statement in 1952 highlighting the importance of ideologically motivated "friends" of the Soviet Union.

147. Poretsky, *Our Own People*, p. 150.

148. Originally in the Fourth, Krivitsky transferred to the INO under Artuzov in 1931.

149. A. Granovsky, *All Pity Choked: The Memoirs of a Soviet Secret Agent* (London: Kimber, 1955), p. 136.

150. Khaustov et al., eds., *Lubyanka. Stalin i VChK-GPU-OGPU-NKVD*, doc. 590.

151. Abramov, *Kontrrazvedka*, p. 46.

152. *Byulleten' Oppozitsii* 58-59 (September–October 1937).

153. Ibid.

154. Pieck testimony to MI5, April 12-16, 1950, KV2/1898, National Archives, London.

155. Abramov, *Kontrrazvedka*, p. 41.

156. Quoted in V. Lota, *"Al'ta" protiv "Barbarossy": Kak byli dobyty svedeniya o*

podgotovke Germani k napadeniyu na SSSR (Moscow: Molodaya Gvardiya, 2004), p. 53.

157. A. Bogomolov, "Kokain dlya tovarishcha Stalina," *Sovershenno sekretno* 3, no. 286 (February 25, 2013).
158. P. Gromushkin, *Razvedka: lyudi, portrety, sud'by* (Moscow: Dobrosovet, 2002), p. 47.
159. Abramov, *Evrei*, p. 343.
160. V. Myasnikov, "Kak unichtozhali vneshnyuyu razvedku," *Nezavisimoe voennoe obozrenie*, July 11, 2008.

3. Cryptography: Stunted by Neglect

1. M. Peterson, "Before BOURBON: American and British COMINT Efforts against Russia and the Soviet Union before 1945," *Cryptologic Quarterly* 12, no. 3–4 (Fall/Winter 1993): 4.
2. The original telegram was dated August 11: "Red Trickery," *The Times*, August 17, 1920.
3. *Brigadier John Tiltman: A Giant among Cryptanalysts*, Center for Cryptologic History, U.S. National Security Agency, 2007 (Fort Meade, MD), p. 7; also Peterson, "Before BOURBON," www. nsa.gov/public_info/_files/cryptologic_quarterly /before_bourbon.pdf.
4. Yuri Amiantov, ed., *V. I. Lenin: Neizvestnye dokumenty 1891–1922* (Moscow: Rosspen, 1999), p. 365.
5. Ibid., doc. 247.
6. "K istorii sozdaniya shifroval'noi sluzhby v MID Rossii," *Diplomaticheskii vestnik*, April 2001.
7. Peterson, "Before BOURBON."
8. *Brigadier John Tiltman*, p. 7.
9. Ibid.
10. Soboleva, *Istoriya shifroval'nogo dela v Rossii* (Moscow: Olma Press, 2002), pp. 414–15.
11. Agabekov, *Sekretnyi terror*, p. 14. Agabekov had headed the Eastern Department of the INO before defecting.
12. "Poslednyaya sluzhebnaya zapiska G.V. Chicherina."
13. Soboleva, "K voprosu ob izuchenii istorii kriptologicheskuyu sluzhby Rossii," "Ruskripto–99" conference, December 22–24, 1999, www.ruscrypto.org/sources /conference/rc1999/.
14. Evdokia Petrova, a former employee who defected in 1954: V. Petrov and E. Petrov, *Empire of Fear* (London: Andre Deutsch, 1955), pp. 126–27.
15. Recollections of a former employee, L. Razgon, quoted in Soboleva, *Istoriya*, pp. 418–19.
16. A. Babash and E. K. Baranov, "Kriptograficheskie metody obespecheniya informatsionnoi bezopasnosti do pervoi mirovoi voiny," http://agps-2006.narod .ru//ttb/2010–6/12–06–10.ttb.pdf.

17. V. Bondarenko, V. Andronenko, and M. Garanin, *50 Let Institutu Krip-tografii, Svyazi i Informatiki: Istoricheskii Ocherk* (Moscow: 1999); also www .vif2ne.ru.
18. Soboleva, *Istoriya*, p. 420.
19. Bondarenko, Andronenko, and Garanin, *50 Let*.
20. Petrov and Petrov, *Empire of Fear*, p. 127; L. Antonov, "Den' rozhdeniya Bo-kiya G. I. (1879)—pervogo rukovoditelya kriptograficheskoi sluzhby SSSR," June 22, 2013, www.securitylab.ru.
21. Ibid., pp. 130–31. This is hearsay, not direct evidence, however.
22. Quoted in S. Lekarev and V. Pork, "Radioelektronnyi shchit i mech," *Nezavisimoe voennoe obozrenie*, January 26, 2002.
23. Tsarev, *KGB v Anglii*, p. 42.
24. Bondarenko, Andronenko, and Garanin, *50 Let*.
25. O. Khlobustov, *Gosbezopasnost' ot Aleksandra I do Putina: 200 let tainoi voiny* (Moscow: Eksmo, 2006), p. 182.
26. Comment made in 1941 to be found in KV/2/2681.
27. The Russian economic historian V. Drobyzhev, formerly involved in war work, surprised me on one occasion with this admission.
28. Beria to Stalin, Molotov, and Voroshilov, January 13, 1940, *K 70–Letiyu Sovetsko-Finlyandskoi Voiny. Zinmnaya Voina 1939–1940gg. v rassekrechennykh dokumen-takh Tsentral'nogo arkhiva FSB Rossii i akhivov Finlyandii. Issledovaniya, Dokumenty, Kommentarii*, ed. A. Sakharov et al. (Moscow: Akademkniga, 2009), doc. 155.

4. What German Threat?

1. For details, see H. Roewer, *Die Rote Kapelle und andere Geheimdienst-Mythen: Spionage zwischen Deutschland und Russland im Zweiten Weltkrieg 1941–1945* (Graz: Ares, 2010). The book articulates the network perfectly. What it does not do, however, is explain what it produced and how valuable it actually was. The classic remains H. Höhne, *Kennwort: Direktor: Die Geschichte der Roten Kapelle* (Frankfurt a. Main: S. Fischer, 1970).
2. Granddaughter I. Davidovich, "V teni kembridzhskoi pyaterki," *Krugozor*, www .krugozormagazine.com, November 2007.
3. Modin, *Sud'by razvedchikov*, p. 45. This is the revised, Russian version of the original French edition (of which the English edition is a direct translation).
4. V. Antonov, "Anatoly Gorskii na peredovoi vneshnei razvedki," *Nezavisimoe voennoe obozrenie*, December 16, 2011; also *Ocherki istorii Rossiiskoi vneshnei razvedki*, vol 4, pp. 261–62.
5. Antonov, "Reanimator vneshnei razvedki," *Nezavisimoe voennoe obozrenie*, December 28, 2007.
6. Fitin's report on foreign intelligence for the years 1939–41 quoted in *Ocherki isto-rii Rossiiskoi vneshnei razvedki*, vol. 3, pp. 16–17.
7. His widow, Nora Tigranovna, has spoken of these years: *Noev-kovcheg.ru* 11, no. 194 (June 16–30, 2012).

8. Quoted in *Ocherki istorii Rossiiskoi vneshnei razvedki*, vol. 3, p. 55.
9. Antonov, "Anatoly Gorskii."
10. Ibid.
11. Blunt's testimony: Tsarev, *KGB v Anglii*, p. 67.
12. A. Shirokorad, *Velikii antrakt* (Moscow: AST, 2009), p. 99.
13. V. Antonov, "Razvedchik Den," *Voinskoe bratstvo* 2, no. 75 (February–March 2012).
14. Antonov, "Iz istorii Sluzhby vneshnei razvedki."
15. Note dated July 8, 1937, sent by special courier: *Ocherki istorii Rossiiskoi vneshnei razvedki*, vol. 3, p. 247.
16. The Mitrokhin Archive, MITN 2/28.
17. A. Feklisov, *Za okeanom i na ostrove* (Moscow: DEM, 1994), pp. 10 and 13.
18. V. Kirpichenko, *Razvedka: Litsa i lichnosti* (Moscow: Geia, 1998), p. 4. From 1943 it was called the Intelligence School (RaSh), then, from September 1948, the Higher Intelligence School (VRSh), also known as School 101. See P. Evdokimov, "Spetsrezerv KGB," *Spetsnaz Rossii* 3, no. 138 (March 2008); also "Al'ma-mater rossiiskikh razvedchikov," *Voinskoe Bratstvo* 8, no. 65 (November–December 2010): 86–87. "The woods" was later the sobriquet for the headquarters of the First Main Directorate at Yasenevo.
19. Feklisov, *Za okeanom*, p. 10.
20. Ibid., p. 11.
21. Ibid., p. 13.
22. Antonov, "Razvedchik Den."
23. *Ocherki istorii Rossiiskoi vneshnei razvedki*, vol. 4, p. 262.
24. Quoted from the Russian archives: *Istochnik* 5, no. 53 (2001).
25. Statement by Prime Minister Margaret Thatcher, *House of Commons Debates*, November 9, 1981, vol. 12, cc.40–2w.
26. Quoted in V. Antonov, "Na pol'skom napravlenii pered 22 iyunya," *Nezavisimoe voennoe obozrenie*, June 3, 2011. It is not entirely clear what date this information was sent. Antonov gives different dates in two separate articles, one in September 1940; elsewhere, March 1941.
27. V. Berezhkov, *Ryadom so Stalinym* (Moscow: Vagrius 1998), p. 226. Berezhkov, a diplomat, served with him in Berlin.
28. Evidence from the archives: Petrov, *Palachi*, p. 109.
29. *Ocherki istorii Rossiiskoi vneshnei razvedki*, vol. 3, p. 444.
30. Antonov, "Reanimator"; for the correct date of Korotkov's appointment under Kobulov, see N. Petrov, *Kto rukovodil organami gosbezopasnosti 1941-1954: Spravochnik* (Moscow: Zvenia Memorial, 2010), p. 491.
31. V. Pavlov, *Tragedii sovetskoi razvedki*, p. 363.
32. A. Pronin, "Legendy razvedki: Korol' nelegalov," *Bratishka.ru*, December 2002.
33. "Nelegal po familii Erdberg, on zhe Aleksandra," July 22, 2010, www.topwar.ru/760.
34. Pronin, "Legendy."
35. Petrov, *Kto rukovodil organami*, p. 491; also Pavlov, *Tragedii sovetskoi razvedki*, p. 364.

36. Pronin, "Legendy." The dates given, however, do not fit with Berezhkov's own account: V. Berezhkov, *Kak ya stal perevodchikom Stalina* (Moscow: DEM, 1993), chap. 4.

37. Roewer, *Die Rote Kapelle*, p. 62. Recruitment was reported to Moscow ten days later: *Ocherki istorii Rossiiskoi vneshnei razvedki*, vol. 4, p. 445.

38. Ibid., p. 446.

39. Petrov, *Palachi*, pp. 94–103.

40. From Müller's interrogation: *Ocherki istorii Rossiiskoi vneshnei razvedki*, vol. 4, p. 447.

41. Ibid., p. 448.

42. Enclosed in Merkulov to Stalin, Molotov, and Beria, May 25, 1941: A. P. Belozerov, *Sekrety Gitlera na stole u Stalina: razvedka i kontrrazvedka germanskoi agressii protiv SSSR, mart-iyun' 1941g.: dokumenty iz tsentral'nogo arkhiva FSB Rossii* (Moscow: Mosgorarkhiv, 1995), p. 125.

43. Akhmedov, *In and Out of Stalin's GRU*, p. 127.

44. F. Golikov, "Sovetskaya Voennaya Razvedka pered Gitlerovskim Nashestviem na SSSR," *Voenno-istoricheskii zhurnal* 12 (2007): 28.

45. L. E. Reshin, *1941 God*, vol. 2 (Moscow: Mezhdunarodnyi fond Demokratiya 1998), doc. 437.

46. May 19, 1941: *Na prieme u Stalina. Tetradi (zhurnaly) zapisei lits, prinyatykh I. V. Stalina (1924–1953gg.)* (Moscow: Novyi khronoagraf, 2008); V. Anfilov, "'Razgovor zakonchilsya ugrozoi Stalina.' Desyat' neizvestnykh besed s marshalom G. K. Zhukovym v mae-iyune 1965 goda," *Voenno-istoricheskii zhurnal* 3 (May–June 1995): 41.

47. "Zapiska NKGB SSSR v TsK VKP(b)—I. V. Stalinu, SNK SSSR—V. M. Molotovu i NKVD SSSR—L. P. Beriya s preprovozhdeniem telegramm angliiskogo posla v SSSR S. Krippsa," in Reshin, *1941 God*, doc. 434. This was the Cripps telegram of April 23.

48. "Spravka vneshnei razvedki NKGB SSSR," May 14, 1941, in Reshin, *1941 God*, doc. 467. The frantic haste is evident in the unusually careless listing of rezidentury: Berlin, London, Stockholm, America (*sic*), Rome.

49. "Spravka vneshnei razvedki NKGB SSSR," May 22, 1941, Reshin, *1941 God*, doc. 485.

50. "Zapiska starshego pomoshchnika Narkoma Inostrannykh Del SSSR v TsK VKP (b)—A.H. Poskrebyshevu s prepovozhdenie pis'ma V. G. Dekanozova," in Reshin, *1941 God*, doc. 494.

51. Belozerov, ed., *Sekrety Gitlera*, p. 116.

52. F. Hinsley, *British Intelligence in the Second World War*, vol. 1 (London: Stationary Office Books, 1979), pp. 470–71.

53. Antonov, "Anatoly Gorskii."

54. V. Karpov, "Vo glave Komiteta informatsii," *Voinskoe bratstvo*, special edition, 2005, p. 53.

55. Comment by Sargent, May 30, on Cripps (Moscow) to London, May 27, 1941: FO 371/29481, National Archives, London. The truly fatuous comment from R. A. Butler, parliamentary undersecretary of state for foreign affairs, is illustrative of

the deplorable state of ignorance, among those who mattered, of Stalin's Russia: "I have always thought that the Hess affair would reassure the Soviet" (*sic*): ibid.

56. JIC (41) 251 (Final), June 13, 1941: FO 371/29484, National Archives, London.
57. The Mitrokhin Archive, MITN 2/14/1.
58. Citing Ivashutin: E. Murphy, *What Stalin Knew: The Enigma of Barbarossa* (New Haven, CT: Yale University Press, 2005), p. 149.

5. The Test of War

1. A. Myasnikov, *Ya lechil Stalina* (Moscow: Eksmo, 2011), p. 183.
2. From the archives: S. Tyulyakov, "Istoricheskii anekdot kak zerkalo ideologii," *Nezavisimoe voennoe obozrenie*, July 27, 2012.
3. O. Renier and V. Rubinstein, *Assigned to Listen: The Evesham Experience 1939–43* (London: BBC Books, 1986), p. 104.
4. The words of the main historian of Soviet cryptography: Soboleva, "K voprosu."
5. L. Kuz'min, "Stanovlenie kafedry kriptografii," www.iso27000.ru/chitalnyi-zal /kriptografiya/; and D. Larin, "O vklade sovetskikh kriptografov v pobedu pod Moskvoi," www.pvti.ru/data/file/bit/bit_4_2011_8.pdf. The British at this point found the Russians unusually open: their confidence no doubt boosted by this success. See F. Hinsley et al., *British Intelligence in the Second World War*, vol. 2 (London: Stationery Office Books, 1981), p. 108.
6. Kuz'min, "Ne zabyvat' svoikh geroev," *Zashchita informatsii: Konfident*, No. 1, 1998, pp. 83–85.
7. *Istoriya kriptograficheskoi sluzhby i radiorazvedki organov gozbesopasnosti*, vif2ne.ru/nvk/forum/arhprint/61105.
8. See J. Haslam, *Russia's Cold War* (New Haven, CT: Yale University Press, 2011), p. 13.
9. D. Larin, "O vklade sovetskikh kriptografov v pobedu pod Moskvoi," *Bezopasnost' informatsionnykh tekhnologii* 4 (2011).
10. Soboleva, "K voprosu."
11. V. Lota, "Stalingradskaya bitva voennoi razvedki," *Voennoe obozrenie*, December 1, 2012.
12. Detailed from Soviet archives: I. Fedyushin, "V telefil'me 'semnadtsat' mgnovenii vesny' ispol'zovany podlinnye razvedyvatel'nye syuzhety," *Voenno-promyshlennyi kur'er*, January 25, 2006.
13. Ibid.
14. The definitive work is still Weingartner, *Stalin und der Aufstieg Hitlers*; also Carr, *Twilight of Comintern*, and Haslam, *Soviet Foreign Policy 1930–33*.
15. V. Lulechnik, "Pokushenie na Gitlera 20 iyulya 1944g. Novye dokumenty i fakty," *Rakus istorii*, www.russian-globe.com/N106/Lulechnik.PokushenieNaGitlera .htm.
16. For the memoirs of a defector who worked under him, see N. Khokhlov, *Pravo na sovest'* (Frankfurt: no pub., 1957), pp. 40–41. One can also see him interviewed by his son at www.youtube.com/watch?v-vGL6BDyzpns.

17. S. Voitovich, "'Sudoplatov pobeditel,' Banderovshchiny s nevidimogo fronta," *Mankurty* (blog), May 18, 2013.
18. *Tainy razvedki* No. 4, "Likvidatsiya Evgena Konoval'tsa," 2012, TV documentary, www.youtube.com/watch?v=qkjx30xVmPl.
19. "'Utka' dlya L'va Trotskogo," *Nezavisimoe voennoe obozrenie*, April 13, 2012; *Tainy razvedki*, No. 6, "Operatisya 'Utka'," 2012, www.youtube.com/watch?v=XeBqh cxpxL8; also "Naum eitingon poslednii rytsar sovetskoi razvedki," January 28, 2013, www.youtube.com/watch?v=egCi5wlMwx4.
20. I. Atamenko, "Bili, bili—ne dobili," *Nezavisimoe voennoe obozrenie*, April 2, 2010.
21. A. Bondarenko, "Smert' shpionam," *Krasnaya zvezda*, April 17, 2012.
22. "Naiti i obezvredit'," *Voenno-promyshlennyi kur'er*, April 9–15, 2008.
23. S. Pyatovskii and A. Kramarenko, "Londonskii rezident rodilsya v Kurske," *Kurskaya pravda*, December 7, 2012.
24. V. Antonov, "Rabotali pod gradom bomb, snaryadov i raket s nemetskikh samo-letov," *Nezavisimoe voennoe obozrenie*, December 2, 2011.
25. F. Ladygin and V. Lota, "Obrechennaya 'Tsitadel,'" *Rossiiskoe voennoe obozrenie*, May 2013, p. 52.
26. Antonov, "Zvezdnyi chas Dzhona Kernkrossa," *Nezavisimoe voennoe obozrenie*, October 18, 2013.
27. V. Lota, "Obrechennaya 'Tsitadel,'" *Krasnaya zvezda*, May 6, 2013.
28. Antonov, "Zvezdnyi chas Dzhona Kernkrossa," *Nezavisimoe voennoe obozrenie*, October 18, 2013.
29. Tsarev, *KGB v Anglii*, p. 79.
30. Antonov, "Zvezdnyi chas."
31. West and Tsarev, *The Crown Jewels*, pp. 149–50.
32. S. Lekarev, "Na kogo rabotala 'kembridzhskaya pyaterka'?" *Argumenty nedeli* 8, no. 94 (February 21, 2008). The comment on Liddell by Sir Maurice Oldfield, one-time head of MI6, towards the end of his life was "best forgotten and soonest mended," which was taken to mean that Oldfield believed Liddell could have worked for the Russians: R. Deacon, *"C." A Biography of Sir Maurice Oldfield, Head of MI6* (London: Futura, 1984), p. 86. Deacon was the journalist Donald McCormick.
33. Such as Sudoplatov: Lekarev, "Na kogo rabotala 'kembridzhskaya pyaterka'?"
34. Reprinted in West, *Triplex*, pp. 317–34.
35. The story is well told in detail: West and Tsarev, *The Crown Jewels*, pp. 159–71. Sudoplatov had been deputy head of the fifth department of the GUGB from May 10, 1939, to February 26, 1941, then renamed the First Main Directorate of the NKGB, where he also acted as deputy head until January 18, 1942. After a break through most of the year, he resumed his post on November 21, and held it until May 14, 1943. Stalin liked to have those charged with the most serious responsi-bilities at loggerheads with one another. It allowed him to hear cases argued out before a final decision was reached.
36. Lekarev, "Konets 'kembridzhskoi pyaterki,'" Part 4: *Argumenty nedeli* 10, no. 96 (March 7, 2008).

37. A. Tsipko, "Istoriya IEMSS glazami 'nevyezdnogo,'" in I. Orlik and T. Sokolova, eds., *"Eto bylo nedavno, eto bylo davno": Vospominaniya* (Moscow: IE RAN, 2010), p. 132.

38. J. Haslam, *The Soviet Union and the Threat from the East, 1933–41* (London: Macmillan, 1992), pp. 31–34.

39. V. Lota, "Morris," *Rossiiskoe voennoe obozrenie* 9, no. 68 (September 2009).

40. Poretsky, *Our Own People*, pp. 122–23.

41. Ibid., p. 148.

42. V. Sergeev, "Da Vinchi sovetskoi vneshnei razvedki," *Nezavisimoe voennoe obozrenie*, October 6, 2006.

43. V. Antonov, "7 aprelya ispolnyaetsya 105 let so dnya rozhdeniya vydayushchegosya sovetskogo razvedchika-nelegala Iskhaka Akhmerova," *Nezavisimoe voennoe obozrenie*, April 7, 2006.

44. Feklisov, *Za okeanom*, p. 51.

45. "'Pust' ukhodit. Zhelet' ne budem!," *Nezavisimoe voennoe obozrenie*, February 29, 2008.

46. *Ocherki istorii Rossiiskoi vneshnei razvedki*, vol. 4, p. 276.

47. Antonov, "Vasilii Zarubin—razvedchik ot boga."

48. *Ocherki istorii Rossiiskoi vneshnei razvedki*, vol. 4, p. 276.

49. The agent was Pavel Pastelnyak: A. Weinstein and A. Vassiliev, *The Haunted Wood: Soviet Espionage in America—the Stalin Era* (New York: Modern Library, 2000), p. 91.

50. *Ocherki istorii Rossiiskoi vneshnei razvedki*, vol. 4, pp. 224–25.

51. Gladkov, *Nash chelovek*, pp. 93, 97–99.

52. Weinstein and Vassiliev, *Haunted Wood*, p. 90; and B. Steil, *The Battle of Bretton Woods: John Maynard Keynes, Harry Dexter White, and the Making of a New World Order* (Princeton, NJ: Princeton University Press, 2013).

53. Feklisov, *Za okeanom*, p. 31.

54. A letter of entreaty written to Duggan by his handler, Norman Borodin ("Granite"), on November 25, 1942, for example, is almost embarrassing in its abject arguments: from the archives, Vassiliev Yellow Notebook 2, Russian transcript, p. 30, Wilson Center Digital Archive, Library of Congress, Washington, D.C., digitalarchive.wilsoncenter.org/collection/86/Vassiliev-Notebooks. The stories of Straight and Duggan receive detailed coverage in Weinstein and Vassiliev, *The Haunted Wood*, pp. 72–83 and 9–20, respectively.

55. The Mitrokhin Archive, MITN 1/6/2.

56. Andrew is utterly mistaken in suggesting that *Umnitsa* means "good girl." It means "a very clever person." Not patronising at all; indeed, rather the opposite—Andrew and Mitrokhin, *The Mitrokhin Archive*, p. 145.

57. Antonov, "Vasilii Zarubin—razvedchik ot boga."

58. Feklisov, *Za okeanom*, p. 53; also Feklisov and Kostov, *The Man behind the Rosenbergs*, pp. 45–46. But the attacks by a member of the embassy staff who denounced him to the FBI as a Japanese spy surely should be discounted.

59. Lota, "Omega," *Rossiiskoe voennoe obozrenie* 10, no. 69 (October 2009).

60. M. Narinskii, *Sovetskaya vneshnyaya politika i proiskhozhdenie kholodnoi*

voiny—Sovetskaya vneshnyaya politika v retrospesktive 1917–1991 (Moscow: privately printed, 1993), p. 122.

61. V. Korotkov, "On otkryval tainu yadernoi bomby," *Krasnaya zvezda*, May 30, 2013.
62. Unpublished memoir by Kremer, quoted by Barkovskii: "Eto byla uvlekatel'naya rabota . . ." V. B. Barkovskii interview in *Rol' razvedki v sozdanii yadernogo oruzhiya*, p. 101.
63. The date can be found in a communication from General Ilychyov, GRU director, to the head of the First Directorate of the NKGB, Fitin, November 29, 1943: Vassiliev Yellow Notebook 1, Russian transcript, p. 67; also, for Maisky and Gorsky: Sudoplatov, *Spetsoperatsii*, p. 307.
64. Lota, *GRU i atomnaya bomba* (Moscow: Kuchkovo Pole, 2002), p. 79. The director was Alexei Panfilov.
65. Barkovskii interviewed by K. Volkov, "Legenda razvedki," *Rossiya*, January 11, 2001.
66. Ciphered telegram 7073 and 1081/1096: www.shieldandsword.mozohin.ru/library /problem1_3.htm.
67. V. Antonov, "Leonid Kvasnikov i atomnaya bomba," *Nezavisimoe voennoe obozrenie*, August 24, 2008.
68. "Luka" (New York) to the Centre, November 24, 1941: from the archives, Vassiliev Yellow Notebook 1, Russian transcript, p. 125.
69. "Vadim" (London) to the Centre, December 17, 1941, ibid.
70. Volkov, *"Legenda."*
71. Kremer to Moscow, "Kratkaya zapiska o sovremennom polozhenii v Velikobritanii," August 17, 1942: RGASPI, Arkhiv Kominterna, f. 495, op. 74, d. 52.
72. Panfilov and Il'ichyov to Comintern's executive committee, eyes only, March 22, 1942: in ibid.
73. Fitin to Comintern's executive committee and Dimitrov, April 15, 1943: in ibid.
74. F. Hinsley and C. Simkins, *British Intelligence in the Second World War*, vol. 4 (London: Stationery Office Books, 1990), pp. 285–86.
75. Feklisov, *Za okeanom*, p. 144n.
76. Y. Yarukhin, ed., *Voennye razvedchiki 1918–1945gg.: Biograficheskii spravochnik* (Kiev: Voennaya Razvedka, 2010).
77. V. Chikov, "'Razvedka'—eto moya glavnaya zhizn," *Voenno-promyshlennyi kur'er*, September 15, 2004.
78. V. Antonov, "Odisseya vselogo Odessita," *Nezavisimoe voennoe obozrenie*, November 22, 2013.
79. Antonov, "Leonid Kvasnikov i atomnaya bomba."
80. A. Foote, *Handbook for Spies* (New York: Doubleday, 1953), p. 157.
81. For instance, on March 5, 1939, he wrote to Mekhlis, head of the armed forces political directorate: "Personally I consider that the purge of the Directorate is not finished. No one from the Directorate leadership is essentially engaged in this question. As before, Orlov looks at this question through his fingers. It is evident that he is misinforming the People's Commissar." Quoted in Zalesskaya, *Oni rukovodili GRU*, p. 200.

82. www.shieldandsword.mozohin.ru/library/problem1_3.htm.
83. Plan for measures with respect to "Enormoz" sanctioned by Fitin, November 5, 1944: from Vassiliev Yellow Notebook 1, Russian transcript, p. 223.
84. Antonov, "Rabotali pod gradom bomb."
85. B. Nikolaev, "V tumannom al'bione," *Novosti razvedki i kontrrazvedki*, March 22, 2006.

6. Postwar Advantage

1. For the evidence: Haslam, *Russia's Cold War*, pp. 34–40.
2. Ibid., pp. 87–94.
3. C. Fenyvesi and V. Pope, "The Angel Was a Spy: New Evidence: Sweden's Raoul Wallenberg Was a U.S. Espionage Asset," *US News and World Report*, May 5, 1996. See also V. Birstein and S. Berger, "The Fate of Raoul Wallenberg: Gaps in Our Current Knowledge," paper, Moscow, 2012; and C. McKay, "Excerpts from McKay's Notes on the Case of Raoul Wallenberg," January 2011.
4. Operation Sparrow: B. Rubin, *Istanbul Intrigues* (New York: Pharos, 1992), pp. 189 and 197.
5. For the visit testified to by Marcus Wallenberg, see Swedish Ministry of Foreign Affairs, Raoul Wallenberg: *Report of the Swedish-Russian Working Group, Stockholm*, 2000, p. 38. The secret negotiations: Lyubomir Valev, *Sovetskii Soyuz i bor'ba narodov Tsentral'noi i Yugo-vostochnoi Evropy za svobodu i nezavisimost' 1941–1945gg.* (Moscow: Nauka, 1978), p. 368.
6. S. Thorsell, *I Hans Majestäts tjänst* (Stockholm: Albert Bonniers, 2009), pp. 168 and 176.
7. L. Bezymensky, *Budapeshtskaya missiya: Raul' Vallenberg* (Moscow: Kollektsiya "Sovershenno Sekretno," 2001), pp. 97–99. Bezymensky, whom I knew, had been a GRU officer during the war. He was sufficiently familiar with how the "organs" operated, counting senior intelligence officers, usually Germanists, among his friends. At the archives he was shown the sizeable file on Kutuzov-Tolstoi, but even he was not allowed to examine it. However, the archivist, who had given him files of those captured by SMERSH, said laconically but helpfully, "Such a person is not among them ...": Bezymensky, *Budapeshtskaya*, p. 97. That is to say, Kutuzov-Tolstoi was actually an agent, but this could not be openly acknowledged.
8. Swedish Ministry of Foreign Affairs, Raoul Wallenberg: report, p. 35.
9. Deputy Foreign Minister Andrei Vyshinsky expressed sympathy for the Zionist assassins of Britain's resident minister Lord Moyne in Palestine that November: Haslam, *Russia's Cold War*, pp. 49–50. Vyshinsky did nothing, of course, without Stalin's express consent.
10. Swedish Ministry of Foreign Affairs, Raoul Wallenberg: Report, p. 93.
11. V. Erofeev, *Diplomat* (Moscow: Zebra E., 2005), pp. 176–77. Erofeev knew Vyshinsky well enough.
12. Bezymensky, *Budapeshtskaya*, pp. 100–114.
13. Swedish Ministry of Foreign Affairs, Raoul Wallenberg: Report, p. 97.

14. Recollections written for Khrushchev in July 1953 reprinted in "Beria stal boyat'sya Abakumova kak ogna," *Kommersant vlast'* 25, no. 779 (June 30, 2008).

15. Pavlov, *Tragedii sovetskoi razvedki*, pp. 349–54.

16. Ibid., pp. 356–57.

17. Mil'shtein, *Skvoz' gody voin i nishchety*, chap. 4.

18. For the memoirs of one who trained with him, see Galina Erofeeva, *Skuchnyi Sad: Zametki o nediplomaticheskoi zhizni* (Moscow: Podkova, 1998), p. 21.

19. Vassiliev Black Notebook, Russian transcript, pp. 58–59.

20. Ibid., p. 61.

21. Entry for October 5, 1945: KV4/466, pp. 255–56.

22. "Otroshchenko, Andrei Marakovich," *Sluzhba vneshnei razvedki rossiiskoi federatsii, 2000,* www.svr.gov.ru.

23. Tsarev, *KGB v Anglii*, pp. 80–81.

24. Modin, *My Five Cambridge Friends* (London: Headline, 1994), p. 205.

25. Ibid., pp. 178 and 158–59.

26. Report to the Chairman of the Committee of Information (KI), December 25, 1948, in Vassiliev Black Notebook, p. 76.

27. Orientation from the Centre, in ibid.

28. Ibid., pp. 76–77.

29. Pavlov, *Tragedii sovetskoi razvedki*, p. 339.

30. Information from the Main Directorate of the Border Forces, July 1949: Solov'ev, *Pogranichnye voiska SSSR 1945–1950*, doc. 158.

31. Haslam, *Russia's Cold War*, p. 109.

32. Kislitsyn, December 27, 1949, "Spravka po rabochemu delu No 5581 'S' o realizatsii dokumental'nykh materialov, poluchennykh iz Londona s pochtami 1949 goda," reprinted in full: N. Dolgopolov, *Kim Filbi* (Moscow: Molodaya Gvardiya, 2012), pp. 244–45.

33. Haslam, *Russia's Cold War*, p. 110.

34. A. Shirokorad, *Rossiya i Ukraina. Kogda zagovoryat pushki* (Moscow: AST, 2007), p. 332.

35. Mariya Karikh, "Komitet informatsii—nash otvet TsRU," *Voenno-promyshlennyi kur'ier* 14, no. 280 (April 15, 2009).

36. Pavlov, *Tragedii sovetskoi razvedki*, p. 339.

37. Feklisov, *Za okeanom*, p. 181. Pavlov considered Savchenko "weak," however.

38. Interview with Cecil Philips: www.pbs.org/redfiles/kgb/deep/kgb_deep_inter_frm .htm.

39. W. Friedman, *The Index of Coincidence* (Geneva, Ill., Riverbank Laboratories, 1922).

40. G. Zipf, *The Psycho-Biology of Language* (Boston: Houghton Mifflin, 1935).

41. B. Mandelbrot, "Structure formelle des textes et communications: deux études," *Word*, April 10, 1954, pp. 1–27; and L. Apostel, B. Mandelbrot, and A. Morf, *Logique, Langage et Théorie de l'Information* (Paris: Presses Universitaires de France, 1957).

42. Zipf, *The Psycho-Biology of Language*, p. 48.

43. www.nsa.gov/about/cryptologic_heritage/hall_of_honor/2006/Phillips.shtml.

44. Colin Burke, *It Wasn't All Magic: The Early Struggle to Automate Cryptanalysis, 1930s–1960s* (Meade, MD: NSA, 2000), p. 226.
45. Thomas Johnson, *American Cryptology during the Cold War, 1945–1989*, Book 1 (Meade, MD: NSA), p. 161.
46. www.nsa.gov/about/cryptologic_heritage/hall_of_honor/2004/gardner.shtml.
47. Burke, *It Wasn't All Magic*, p. 227.
48. The best summary is T. Sale, *Colossus 1943–1996* (Kidderminster, UK: privately published, 1998). The late Tony Sale not only created the Bletchley museum but also rebuilt the Colossus. The earlier models ceased operations by the early 1960s and had been destroyed along with their plans. Sale was Peter Wright's assistant on the technological side of MI5.
49. Burke, *It Wasn't All Magic*, p. 224.
50. Ibid., p. 225.
51. The NSA historians refer to "Longfellow" beginning in 1943: ibid., p. 267.
52. "Kozlov, Mikhail Stepanovich," http://crypto-volga.narod.ru/Text/KOZ.doc.
53. Johnson, *American Cryptology during the Cold War*, p. 160; Burke, *It Wasn't All Magic*, p. 265.
54. Ibid., p. 211.
55. Ibid., p. 207.
56. Ibid., p. 265.
57. N. Webster, *Cribs for Victory: The Untold Story of Bletchley Park's Secret Room* (Clifton-Upon-Teme, UK: privately published, 2011).
58. The Mitrokhin Archive, MITN 1/7.
59. "Biografiya I. Ya. Verchenko," *Mezhregional'naya olimpiarda shkol'nikov po matematike i kriptografii*, September 12, 2012.
60. Feklisov, *Za okeanom*, pp. 102–105. The identification of "Rupert" can be found in B. Syrkov, *Proslushka predtechi Snoudena* (Moscow: Algoritm, 2013), p. 49. Syrkov—whose real name is Anin—was a lieutenant colonel in the Soviet special service (codes and ciphers), later called FAPSI.
61. Vassiliev Black Notebook, Russian transcript, p. 75.
62. Burke, *It Wasn't All Magic*, p. 282.
63. Ibid., pp. 213–14.
64. V. Sosnovskii and A. Orlov, *Sovetskie kompyutery: predannye i zabytye*, December 10, 2002, nnm.ru/blog/dusty74/istoriya_razvitiya_otechestvennogo_komyuterostroeniya_2.
65. "Istoriya sozdaniya MESM—pervoi sovetskoi EVM," December 12, 2010, state history.ru/1305/Istoriya-sozdaniya-mesm-pervoy-sovetskoiEVM.
66. www.pseudology.org/Eneida/LesechkoMA.htm.
67. Sosnovskii and Orlov, *Sovetskie kompyutery*.
68. "Biografiya I. Ya."
69. Kuz'min, "Stanovlenie kafedry kriptografii."
70. RGASPI, f. 17. op. 162. d. 42. l. 76–81: reproduced at http://shieldandsword.mozohin.ru/documents/191049appendix1.html.

71. For Andreev's interview, see G. Ovcharenko, "V svyataya svyatykh bezopasnosti: Vpervye zhurnalist pereshagnul porog 8–go Glavnogo upravleniya KGB SSSR," *Pravda*, September 16, 1990.
72. "In the past there has been too much emphasis on theoretical mathematics vis-à-vis applied mathematics. Nowadays one sees references to their shortage of mathematicians to work on applications." J. Griffith, *Foreign vs. U.S. Computers: An Appraisal* (Meade, MD: National Security Agency, 1972).
73. *Doklady AN SSSR*, 1940, vol. 27, pp. 38–42.
74. A copy of the original document with Stalin's annotations and corrections was found. K. Rossiyanov, "Stalin as Lysenko's Editor: Reshaping Political Discourse in Soviet Science," http://cyber.eserver.org/stalin.text.
75. Kuz'min, "Stanovlenie kafedry kriptografii."
76. Chikov, " 'Razvedka.' "

7. Breakdown

1. Haslam, *Russia's Cold War*, chap. 4.
2. Ibid., pp. 119–20.
3. Ibid., pp. 119–30.
4. Quoted in N. Petrov, "Stalin i organy NKVD-MGB v sovetizatsii stran Tsentral'noi i Vostochnoi Evropy 1945–1953gg.," PhD, University of Amsterdam, 2008, p. 192.
5. The Mitrokhin Archive, MITN 1/6/2.
6. Andrew and Mitrokhin, *The Mitrokhin Archive*, pp. 205–206.
7. Private communication from the son of said attaché.
8. Dolgopolov, *Kim Filbi*, p. 145.
9. N. West, *VENONA: The Greatest Secret of the Cold War* (London: HarperCollins, 1999), pp. 134–35.
10. The Mitrokhin Archive, MITN 1/6/2.
11. At Claridges, Liddell was told by "Victor" and "Tess" (Rothschild) that they "felt that there were a certain number of people whom they knew who had had a considerable Left Wing past at the University, and who should in present circumstances come forward and assist the authorities. They were considering the desirability of going to these people and urging them to do their duty; failing which they would have to take the matter into their own hands." Liddell agreed. But there is no evidence this was ever done in the manner described. It was the gesture that counted. Entry, June 26, 1951, Liddell Diary, KV4/473.
12. Diary entry, August 20, 1951, KV4/473.
13. Diary entry, June 14, 1951, KV4/473.
14. Diary entry, October 1, 1951, KV4/473.
15. G. Corera, *The Art of Betrayal* (London: Pegasus, 2011), p. 76.
16. Elliott to John le Carré, May 1986: "Afterword" in B. Mcintyre, *A Spy Among Friends: Kim Philby and the Great Betrayal* (London: Bloomsbury, 2014), p. 292.
17. *Daily Telegraph*, January 6, 2014.
18. Elliott to le Carré, May 1986: "Afterword," in Mcintyre, *A Spy Among Friends*, p. 291.

19. Diary entry, July 13, 1951, Liddell Diary.
20. Khaustov et al., eds., *Lubyanka. Stalin i MGB SSSR, mart 1946–mart 1953*, doc. 171.
21. V. Chikov, "Shpion—Nakhodka dlya shpiona: Geroi Rossii rodom iz SShA," *Novaya gazeta*, April 10, 2000.
22. Vassiliev Black Notebook, p. 145.
23. The Mitrokhin Archive, MITN 1/7.
24. West and Tsarev, *The Crown Jewels*, p. 256.
25. FBI, U.S. Department of Justice, "Exposé of Soviet Espionage May 1960," U.S. Government Printing Office, Washington, D.C., 1960, p. 14.
26. Explanatory memorandum by head of the Third Directorate of the MVD, S. A. Gogilidze to Minister Beria, March 26, 1953, reprinted in Petrov, *Palachi*, p. 288.
27. Ignat'ev's memorandum in ibid., p. 302.
28. Myasnikov, *Ya lechil Stalina*, pp. 292–93.
29. Kuz'min, "Stanovlenie kafedry kriptografii."
30. "Na sluzhbe Rodine, matematike i kriptografii. Zhizn' i sud'ba V. Ya. Kozlova—odnogo iz osnovopolozhnikov otechestvennoi shifroval'noi nauki," *BIS Journal* 1, no. 8 (June 28, 2013).
31. Kirpichenko, *Razvedchik*, p. 156.
32. "Protokol No. 50a. Zasedanie 8 fevralya 1954 g.," in A. Fursenko, ed., *Prezidium TsK KPSS 1954–1964*, vol. 1 (Moscow: Rosspen, 2003), doc. 1.
33. Valerii Prokof'ev, *Aleksandr Sakharovskii: Nachal'nik vneshnei razvedka* (Moscow: Yauza, 2005), p. 88; West and Tsarev, *The Crown Jewels*, p. 269.

8. The German Theatre

1. For the evidence: Haslam, *Russia's Cold War*, chap. 2.
2. Addressing a committee on the reorganisation of the intelligence services, November–December 1952: *Istochnik* 5 (2001): 132.
3. Prokof'ev, *Aleksandr Sakharovskii*, p. 96.
4. Kirpichenko, *Razvedka*, pp. 271 and 159.
5. Titles change through the period—from head of "1-B" Directorate of the MGB to head of the Special Directorate of the KGB—though the underlying functions remained: N. Petrov, *Kto rukovodil organami*, p. 491.
6. N. Petrov, *Pervyi predsedatel' KGB Ivan Serov* (Moscow: Materik, 2005), p. 153.
7. Khokhlov, *Pravo na sovest'*, p. 410.
8. "Information on the MVD/MGB obtained from Captain Nikolai Evgenievich KHOKHLOV," July 27, 1954, KV 5/107.
9. Khokhlov, *Pravo na sovest'*, p. 183.
10. From the Soviet Party archive, reproduced photographically in the Bukovsky Archive at www.bukovsky-archive.net, doc. 1014.
11. Interview with Nikolai Khokhlov (1922–2007), "Nezhdu zheleznym zanavesom," *Spetsnaz*, October 1, 2011.
12. The Mitrokhin Archive, MITN 1/5.
13. "Biography of Ivan Aleksandrovich Serov," in Arneson (INR) to Dulles (CIA),

September 30, 1958, CIA Electronic Archive, www.foia.cia.gov. Much personal material evidently came from Berlin Tunnel intercepts.

14. See Haslam, *Russia's Cold War*, p. 46.

15. Mil'shtein, *Skvoz' gody voin i nishchety'*, p. 50.

16. "Biography of Ivan Aleksandrovich Serov."

17. Protokol No. 50, February 8, 1954: Fursenko, ed., *Prezidium TsK KPSS 1954–1964*, vol. 1, doc. 1.

18. T. Gladkov, *Lift v Razvedku: "Korol" nelegalov' Aleksandr Korotkov* (Moscow: Olma Press, 2002), p. 467.

19. A. Rostovtsev, "Nashi nemetskie druz'ya rodilis' agentami," *Nezavisimoe voennoe obozrenie*, April 5, 2013.

20. His titles changed over time, though the responsibilities remain unaltered: plenipotentiary until May 18, 1954; deputy supreme commissar and head of security inspection in the GDR until November 16, 1955; and with the creation of the Warsaw Pact, he was officially KGB advisor to the GDR's Ministry of State Security until March 23, 1957.

21. Khokhlov, *Pravo na sovest'*, p. 274.

22. Evgenii Zhirnov, "Chekist iz firmy," *Kommersant vlast'*, April 12, 2004.

23. From telephone calls intercepted via the Berlin Tunnel: "Soviet Intelligence and Security, Lieutenant General E. P. Pitovranov," CIA Electronic Archive, www.foia .cia.gov.

24. "Vol'f—odinochka," *Kommersant vlast'* 3, no. 506 (January 27, 2003); A. Kiselev, *Stalinskii favorit s Lubyanki* (St. Petersburg: Neva, 2003), p. 89.

25. G. Bohnsack, *Hauptverwaltung Aufklärung: Die Legende stirbt* (Berlin: Edition Ost, 1997), p. 64.

26. KV 5/83.

27. Letter on April 6, 1977: L. Mosley, *Dulles: A Biography of Eleanor, Allen and John Foster Dulles and Their Family Network* (London: Hodder and Stoughton, 1978), p. 494.

28. Testimony of Colonel Vitalii Chernyavskii, then head of secret intelligence under Pitovranov: Abramov, *Kontrrazvedka*, pp. 30–31.

29. Television documentary: *Tainy razvedki—Delo podpolkovnika Popova*, broadcast September 5, 2012, www.youtube.com/watch?v=dKoiDtirPNO. This online serial is "based on genuine documents from the archives of the FSB and the foreign intelligence service"—allserials.tv/serial-4740-tainy-razvedki-dokumental nyy-1-sezon.html. Parts of these documents can frequently be seen on-screen. Much is also based on interviews with those who have access to archives and, at times, those who were operationally active at the time of events described. Frequently some new information can be gained when treated with necessary caution.

30. I. Atamanenko, "Pervyi krot v Glavnom razvedyvatel'nom upravlenii," *Nezavisimoe voennoe obozrenie*, March 23, 2012; *Tainy razvedki*.

31. Speaking at "U.S. Intelligence and the End of the Cold War," November 18–20, 1999, conference at Texas A and M University, College Station, transcript,

pp. 8–9, CIA electronic reading room, www.foia.cia.gov/docs/DOC_0001445139 /DOC_00014445139.pdf.

32. *Tainy razvedki.*

33. V. Sobolev et al., eds., *Lubyanka 2* (Moscow: Glavarkhiv, 1999), pp. 264–71; also *The Victoria Advocate*, October 27, 1959.

34. For example, in R. Kasil'nikov, *KGB protiv MI-6: Okhotniki za shpionam* (Moscow: Tsentrpoligraf, 2000); also, personal acquaintance with Baroness Park.

35. *Novosti Vladivostoka*, April 5, 2014; *Trud*, December 1, 1998. On the Web: www .proshan.ru/6/68.

36. Antonov and Karpov, *Tainye informatory Kremlya*, pp. 196–97; Peter Lunn obituary, *Daily Telegraph*, February 6, 2011. Though otherwise informative, Murphy, Kondrashyov, and Bailey, *Battleground Berlin* (New Haven, CT: Yale University Press, 1997), are misleadingly Americocentric in attributing to CIA initiative the origins of the tunnel. Its true history has inevitably been distorted by the fact that at the time, no written record was to be kept, for reasons of secrecy. As is the case with the true history of MI6 operations against the USSR, it may well be the case that the best documentation is to be found under secure lock and key in Moscow.

37. Interview with Blake: www.pbs.org/redfiles/kgb/deep/interv/k_int_george _blake.htm.

38. R. Hermiston, *The Greatest Traitor: The Secret Lives of Agent George Blake* (London: Aurum Press, 2013), pp. 159–67 (scrupulously researched despite the lack of notes); on Kondrashyov's character, personal acquaintance.

39. Interview with Blake.

40. Antonov and Karpov, *Tainye informatory Kremlya*, p. 198.

41. From a memorandum by Lieutenant General Georgii Tsinyov, head of the KGB Directorate of Special Departments at the Soviet Group of Forces Germany: "Delo 'Vesna,'" *Krasnaya zvezda*, March 3, 2010.

42. *Clandestine Services History: The Berlin Tunnel Operation 1952–1956* (Langley, VA: CIA, June 1968), pp. 25–26.

43. A. Kornilkov, *Berlin: Tainaya voina po obe storony granitsy: Zapiski voennogo kontrrazvedchika* (Moscow: Kuchkovo Pole, 2009), p. 252.

44. Interview with Semichastny: www.pbs.org/redfiles/kgb/ddep/interv/k_in_vladimir _semichastny.htm.

45. B. Krotkov, "Ya prinimal u agenta prisyagu na vernost' fyureru," *Rossiiskaya gazeta*, August 31, 2007.

46. R. Friedman, "A Stone for Willy Fisher," *Studies in Intelligence* (Fall 2000): 137–48.

47. N. Dolgopolov, *Abel'-Fisher* (Moscow: Molodaya Gvardiya, 2010), p. 47.

48. V. Antonov, "Kak Vil'yam Fisher stal Rudol'om Abelem," *Voenno-promyshelennyi kur'er*, August 1, 2007.

49. Abakumov, "Legendy razvedki."

50. Dolgopolov, *Abel'-Fisher*, pp. 49–50 and 104.

51. Friedman, "A Stone."

52. W. Rocafort, "Colonel Abel's Assistant," *Studies in Intelligence* 3 (Fall 1959): 1.

53. Friedman, "A Stone."

54. J. Kahn, "The Case of Colonel Abel," *Journal of National Security Law and Policy* 5 (2011): 263–64.

55. Friedman, "A Stone."

56. Serov memorandum to the Party Prezidium (Politburo), November 19, 1964: Petrov, *Pervyi predsedatel' KGB Ivan Serov*, doc. 48, p. 338.

57. *Lubyanka 1917–1991: Spravochnik*, p. 156.

58. A point made by Semichastny at a summit with Mielke on November 30–December 1, 1964: "Bericht über die Besprechungen im Komitee für Staatssicherheit der UdSSR am 30. November/1. Dezember 1964": MfS. Sekr. D. Min., Nr 576, www .bstu.bund.de/DE/Wissen/MfS_Dokumente/Downloads/KGB-Projekt/64–11–30 _Gespraeche_.Mielke_Semichastny.pdf.

59. V. Semichastny, *Bespokoinoe serdtse* (Moscow: Vagrius, 2002).

60. E. Zhirnov, "Lubyanskii komsomolets," *Kommersant vlast'*, April 10, 2001.

61. West and Tsarev, *The Crown Jewels*, p. 257.

62. Feklisov, *Za okeanom*, pp. 154–61.

63. Ibid., p. 262; Tsarev, *KGB v Anglii*, chap. 15.

64. This occurred on May 25, 1959: West and Tsarev, *The Crown Jewels*, pp. 268–69.

65. Pavlov, *Tragedii sovetskoi razvedki*, pp. 281–82.

66. West and Tsarev, *The Crown Jewels*, p. 269.

67. "Fil'm 'Mertvyi sezon'–eto o nem," *Nezavisimoe voennoe obozrenie*, March 8, 2013; and A. Vitkovskii, "Legenda i zhizn' razvedchika—nelegala Konona Molodogo," *Parlamentskaya gazeta*, January 19, 2002.

68. West and Tsarev, *The Crown Jewels*, p. 269.

69. This was a direct consequence of persistent sexual harassment of local girls, for whom this was an abiding memory. For a detailed study of these issues: D. Reynolds, *Rich Relations: The American Occupation of Britain, 1942–1945* (New York: HarperCollins, 1995).

70. Feklisov, *Za okeanom*, pp. 138–39.

71. Vitkovskii, "Legenda."

72. N. Pushkaryov, *GRU: vymysly i real'nost'* (Moscow: Eksmo, 2004), p. 17. Pushkaryov was prosecuted for publishing the book but eventually rehabilitated.

73. Letters 2 and 3 written by Serov: A. Khinshtein, *Tayny Lubyanki* (Moscow: Olma Press, 2008), p. 92. For more on Chisholm's role: "Reflections on Handling Penkovsky," Document 0006122519-CIA FOIA.

74. "Kak Faina Ranevskaya obvela vokrug pal'tsa KGB," Ekabu.ru, May 25, 2013.

75. I. Atamanenko, "Operatsiya 'Sezam, otkroisya!,'" *Nezavisimoe voennoe obozrenie*, January 18, 2013.

76. *GRU: Tainy voennoi razvedki*, TV documentary produced by Sergei Ivanov, Series 9, www.onlineru.net/seriale/gru_tainy#socnets.

77. L. Gul'ev, *Missiya Meisi: Dokumental'naya povest'* (Moscow: Russkaya Razvedka, 2003), pp. 31–104.

78. Ibid., pp. 123 and 172.

79. F. Ladygin and V. Lota, "U kraya Karibskoi propasti," *Krasnaya zvezda*, October 18, 2012. Ladygin headed the GRU from August 1992 to June 1997.

80. Haslam, *Russia's Cold War*, pp. 199–209.
81. Testimony of General Nikolai Andreev: interview written up by Emel'yanov, Larin, and Butyrskii, "Prevrashchenie kriptologii v fundamental'nuyu nauku. N. N. Andreev: put' ot inzhenera do prezidenta Akademii kriptografii RF," *BIS Journal* 3, no. 10 (2013).
82. Gul'ev, *Missia Meisi*, p. 150.
83. F. Ladygin and V. Lota, *GRU i karibskii krizis* (Moscow: Kuchkovo Pole, 2012), pp. 94–95.
84. Ibid.
85. F. Ladygin and V. Lota, "U kraya Karibskoi propasti," part 2, *Krasnaya zvezda*, October 25, 2012.
86. Interview with former head of the Eighth Main Directorate of the KGB, Andreev, vif2ne.ru.
87. Haslam, *Russia's Cold War*, p. 209.
88. Revealed by FAPSI in a television documentary on the programme, *Sovershenno Sekretno*, broadcast October 25, 1997, RTA. See Kuz'min, "GUSS—etap v razvitii sovetskoi kriptografii," *Zashchita informatsii. Konfident* 22 (1998), reproduced online at iso2700.ru.
89. I. Atamanenko, "I poslali nichto chelovecheskoe ne chuzhdo," *Nezavisimoe voennoe obozrenie*, March 20, 2009. The defector Yuri Korotkov told MI6 of this. The Russians countered by spreading the rumour that this was merely a British attempt to discredit the ambassador.
90. Atamanenko, "Izmennik-neudachnik," *Nezavisimoe voennoe obozrenie*, June 28, 2013.
91. "Interv'yu Viktora Martynova v rubrike 'nevidimyi front,'" *Voinskoe bratstvo* 4 (2005).
92. The scriptwriters O. Shmelev and V. Vostokov, *Oshibka Rezidenta*, followed by *Sud'ba rezidenta, vozvrashchenie rezidenta, konets operatsii "Rezident,"* all put on screen. See *Oshibka*, at www.youtube.com/watch?v=mROspsexYKs.
93. E. Ivanov and G. Sokolov, *Golyi shpion: Russkaya redaktsiya. Vospominaniya agenta GRU* (Moscow: Kuchkovo Pole, 2009), p. 166. This is an amplified version of the English edition that appeared soon after the collapse of the Soviet Union.
94. House of Commons Debates, December 16, 1963, *Hansard*, vol. 686, col. 872.
95. Quoted in *Lord Denning's Report* (London: Her Majesty's Stationery Office, 1963), pp. 82–83.
96. Meeting of June 12, 1963, CC 37(63), National Archives, Kew, UK.
97. *Lord Denning's Report*, p. 83.
98. Meeting of June 13, 1963, CC (63) 38th conclusion.
99. Quoted in the authorised history: Andrew, *The Defence of the Realm*, p. 499. Andrew ignores the evidence presented in Cabinet and goes so far as to claim KGB personnel could not have overheard such a conversation from within the GRU. He appears ignorant of the fact that the KGB had its own people under deep cover in the GRU.
100. Ivanov, *Golyi shpion*, pp. 271–72.
101. Ibid., p. 287.

102. Ibid., p. 278. See C. Tuschhoff, *MC 70 und die Einführung Nuklearer Trägersysteme in die Bundeswehr 1956-1959* (Ebenhausen: Stiftung Wissenschaft und Politik, 1990).
103. Ivanov, *Golyi shpion*, p. 288.
104. Minutes of the first meeting, January 23, 1963; the fifth meeting, February 9, 1963; and the sixth meeting, May 3, 1963: D. (63), CAB 131/28.
105. D. Brennan to W. Sullivan, June 11, 1963: "Bowtie," File 65-68218, FBI Archives.
106. N. Pushkarev, *GRU: dela i sud'by* (Moscow: Eksmo, 2013), pp. 72-74.
107. N. Veryuzhskii, *Ofitserskaya sluzhba*, flot.com/blog/historyofNVMU/3316.php, chap. 13.
108. E. Zhirnov, interviewing a former senior officer: "U nas byla samaya legal'naya razvedka v mire," *Kommersant vlast'*, April 23, 2002.
109. "Razvedchik Petr Ivashutin: on postroil 'Akvarium,'" *Ukraina kriminal'naya*, July 7, 2006.
110. See T. Bower, *Red Web* (London: Mandarin, 1993).
111. Zalesskaya, *Oni rukovodili GRU*, p. 265.
112. A. Tereshchenko and A. Vdovin, *Iz SMERSHA do GRU: "Imperator Sptessluzhb"* (Moscow: Eksmo, 2013).
113. Ibid.; and V. Lota, "Marshal voennoi razvedki," *Krasnaya zvezda*, September 2, 2009; also an interview with Popov: N. Poroskov, "Ad"yutant ego prevoskhodi-tel'stva'," www.vremya.ru/2004/203/13/111454.html.

9. Loss of Faith

1. The Mitrokhin Archive, MITN 2/10.
2. Haslam, *Russia's Cold War*, p. 217.
3. Statement to Brezhnev "On the results of the work of the Committee of State Security under the Council of Ministers and its organs in place for 1967," May 6, 1968: A. Yakovlev, ed., *Lubyanka 1917-1991: Spravochnik* (Moscow: Demokra-tiya, 2003), doc. 181.
4. V. Malevannyi, "Inspektsiya Yuriya Andropova," *Nezavisimoe voennoe obozre-nie*, April 24, 1998. The author retired as a major general in the KGB.
5. O. Kalugin, *Spymaster: My Thirty-Two Years in Intelligence and Espionage* (New York: Basic Books, 2009), p. 168.
6. Former senior officer interviewed by Evgenii Zhirnov, "U nas byla samaya legal'naya razvedka v mire," *Kommersant vlast'*, April 23, 2002.
7. The Mitrokhin Archive, MITN 2/10.
8. Nikolai Koshkin ("Tokyo"): in H. Womack, ed., *Undercover Lives: Soviet Spies in the Cities of the World* (London: Phoenix, 1998), p. 107.
9. Zhirnov, "U nas byla samaya legal'naya razvedka v mire."
10. L. Mlechin, "Sluzhba vneshnei razvedki: Proval s bol'shimi posledstviyami," September 29, 2009, www.onlainkniga.ru/x4/x400/677-proval-s-bolshimi -posledstvijami.html.
11. Ibid.
12. For the detail: Haslam, *Russia's Cold War*, chap. 8.

13. S. Lekarev and A. Sudoplatov, "Londonskii proval sovetskoi razvedki," *Nezavisimoe voennoe obozrenie*, October 18, 2002. This can be considered the official Russian account of events.

14. For the authorised British account, see Andrew, *The Defence of the Realm*, pp. 567–74.

15. Lekarev and Sudoplatov, "Londonskii proval." Lyalin died of cancer in 1994.

16. Andrew, *The Defence of the Realm*, p. 578.

17. For a recent history: R. Aldrich, *GCHQ: The Uncensored Story of Britain's Most Secret Intelligence Agency* (London: Harper Press, 2010).

18. Andrew and Mitrokhin, *The Mitrokhin Archive*, pp. 492–93.

19. E. Zhirnov, "Pri nashem sodeistvii."

20. I. Pacepa, "The Arafat I Knew," *Wall Street Journal*, January 12, 2002.

21. Andrew and Mitrokhin, *The Mitrokhin Archive II*, pp. 246–49.

22. Haslam, *Russia's Cold War*, pp. 232–33.

23. Andrew and Mitrokhin, *The Mitrokhin Archive II*, pp. 251–52.

24. I. Pacepa, "The Arafat I Knew."

25. A. Selvatici, *Chi Spiava i Terroristi: KGB, Stasi—BR, RAF* (Bologna: Pendragon, 2010), pp. 27–28.

26. "Spetssluzhby Rossii v dele Rona Arada," *My zdes'* 143 (January 18–24, 2008), newswe.com.

27. Mil'shtein, *Skvoz' gody voin i nishchety*, p. 50.

28. V. Galaiko, "Shpion, za Kotorym okhotilis' chetvert' veka," *Gazeta.* zn.ua, March 23, 2001.

29. Gul'ev, *Missiya Meisi*, pp. 154–65.

30. A. Tereshchenko, *"Oborotny" iz voennoi razvedki. Devyat' predatel'stv sotrudnikov GRU* (Moscow: Zvonnitsa, 2004), pp. 242–43.

31. S. Grimes and J. Vertefeuille, *Circle of Treason* (Annapolis, MD: Naval Institute Press, 2012), chaps. 4–6; the Mitrokhin Archive, MITN 1/6/8.

32. E. Epstein, "The Spy Wars," *New York Times Magazine*, September 28, 1980. Epstein identified his informants as "former CIA executives and a staff member of the Senate Select Committee on Intelligence." This was an extraordinary act of irresponsibility on their part.

33. "General GRU—amerikanskii agent," June 19, 2012: vse-war.ru/video/istorija /general-gru-amerikanskij-agent.html; Sandy Grimes testimony, January 30, 1998: National Security Archive oral history of the Cold War, interview 21; "'Krot' v GRU: predatel' v general'skikh pogonakh," *NTV Film 8*, aired December 20, 2011; www .ntv.ru/video/575353.

34. Andrew and Mitrokhin, *The Mitrokhin Archive*, p. 265.

35. Kalugin, *Spymaster*, p. 93.

36. I. Latunskii, "Boi s ten'yu: iz istorii protivosostoyaniya TsRU i KGB," *Pravda*, June 5, 2006.

37. P. Earley, interview with Solomatin, *Washington Post Magazine*, April 23, 1995, pp. 18–21, 28–29.

38. Kalugin, *Spymaster*, p. 74.

39. Earley interview with Solomatin.

40. Andropov to Brezhnev, May 21, 1970. Brezhnev agreed four days later. The Mitrokhin Archive, MITN 4/1/4.
41. Kalugin, *Spymaster*, p. 75.
42. V. Antonov, "Virtuoz verbovki," *Nezavisimoe voennoe obozrenie*, June 2, 2006.
43. B. Krotkov, "Ya prinimal u agenta prisyagu na vernost' fyureru"; also the Mitrokhin Archive, MITN 2/18.
44. The Mitrokhin Archive, MITN 1/6/7.
45. The Mitrokhin Archive, MITN 1/6/8.
46. The Mitrokhin Archive, MITN 1/6/1.
47. The Mitrokhin Archive, MITN 1/6/8.
48. Ibid.
49. Y. Drozdov, "SShA, N'yu-Iork (1975–1979gg.)," vatanym.ru/?=vs307_mem1. This also forms chapter 6 of Drozdov, *Zapiski nachal'nika nelegal'noi razvedki*. This can be found at www.lib.ru/MEMUARY/DROZDOW/nelegal.txt_Ascii.txt.
50. Latunskii, "Boi s ten'yu."

10. The Computer Gap

1. "After Words with Pete Earley and Sergei Tretyakov," January 28, 2008, C-SPAN Video Library, www.c-span.org/video/?c3962664/clie_words-pete-earley-sergei-tretyakov.
2. M. Boltunov, *"Zolotoe Ukho" voennoi razvedki* (Moscow: Veche, 2011), chap. 34.
3. "Radiotekhnicheskaya razvedka spetssluzhb SSSR," October 9, 2011, Istoricheskii forum . . . iz istorii organov gosudarstvennoi bezopasnosti, www.forum.mozohin.ru; and information off the record.
4. Boltunov, *"Zolotoe Ukho,"* chap. 37; also "Nebo smotrit na tebya," *Okno v Rossiyu*, March 28, 2012.
5. I. Afanas'ev and D. Vorontsov, "Lyubopytnyi vzglyad iz Kosmosa: fotoshpionazh," *Populyarnaya mekhanika*, April 2009.
6. Pavlov, *Tragedii sovetskoi razvedki*, p. 238.
7. U.S. Senate, Final Report of the Select Committee to Study Governmental Operations with Respect to Intelligence Activities, 94th Congr., 2nd Sess., Washington, D.C., 1976, Appendix 3: "Soviet Intelligence Collection and Operations Against the United States," p. 561.
8. G. Nekhoroshev, "Sekretnyi kod Martina i Mitchella," *Sovershenno sekretno*, August 2, 2012.
9. Feklisov, *Za okeanom*, p. 209.
10. "Biografiya I. Ya. Verchenko"; also www.ovvkus.ru/kgb5491/school/highschool/4.htm.
11. Pavlov, *Tragedii sovetskoi razvedki*, p. 249.
12. V. Dvinin, "Operatsiya 'Karfagen' ili tainye seifovoi komnaty," *Rossiiskaya gazeta*, March 3 and 9, 2006.
13. L. Maksimenkov, "Do Snoudena byl Gamil'ton," *Ogonyok* 26, no. 5286 (July 8, 2013).
14. Emel'yanov, Larin, and Butyrskii, "Prevrashchenie kriptologii."
15. www.kitov-anatoly.ru/biografia/polnaa-biografia.

16. V. Tuchkov, "Anatolii Ivanovich Kitov. Sovsekretnyi podpolkovnik," *Super-kompyutery*, September 15, 2012.
17. Sheymov, *Tower of Secrets*, p. 212.
18. "Lampovye dinozavry pervogo pokoleniya," *Vokrug sveta* 8, no. 2875 (August 2013).
19. Statement by Lopatin (KGB), November 11, 1969, "Notiz über Besprechungen beim Genossen Sacharowski zu fragen der wissenschaftlich-technischen Aufklärung am 11.11.69," Berlin, November 21, 1969, www.bstu.bund.de/DE/Wissen/MfS_Dokumente/Downloads/KGB-Projekt/.
20. "Na sluzhbe Rodine, matematika i kriptografii," *BIS Journal* 1, no. 8 (2013).
21. Emel'yanov, Larin, and Butyrskii, "Prevrashchenie kriptologii."
22. V. Marchetti and J. Marks, *The CIA and the Cult of Intelligence* (New York: Knopf, 1974), pp. 220–21. The CIA wanted this section excised from Marchetti and Marks. Marchetti resigned from the agency in 1969.
23. Emel'yanov, Larin, and Butyrskii, "Prevrashchenie kriptologii."
24. Sheymov, *Tower of Secrets*, p. 12.
25. Emel'yanov, Larin, and Butyrskii, "Prevrashchenie kriptologii."
26. M. Maslennikov, *Kriptografiya i svoboda*, available at mikhailmas.livejournal.com., p. 48.
27. V. Uspenskii, "Soveshchanie po statistike rechi," Leningrad, October 1–10, 1957; in *Trudy po nematematike* (Moscow: OGI, 2002), p. 313.
28. Quoted in S. Singh, *The Code Book* (New York: Anchor, 2000), p. 286.
29. Uspenskii, "Soveshchanie."
30. Quoted in Haslam, *Russia's Cold War*, p. 318.
31. B. Malinovsky, ed., A. Fitzpatrick, *Pioneers of Soviet Computing*, e-book, www.sigcis.org/files/SIGCISMC2010_001.pdf, p. 91.
32. Maslennikov, *Kriptografiya i svoboda*, p. 50. The Vesna was originally produced under Polin (1959–1964). This was certainly not the last word in homegrown computers. It is quite possible Maslennikov was mistaking this for the Sneg, which appeared later.
33. Haslam, *Russia's Cold War*, pp. 319–27.
34. Confirmed by a knowledgeable source.
35. Interview, "Nas podtolknuli k vvodu voisk," February 15, 2007, www.Afghanistan.ru.
36. www.cvni.net/radio/e2k/e2k005/e2k05article.html.
37. S. Lekarev, "Eksfil'tratsiya shifroval'shchika Andropova," *Argumenty nedeli*, May 24, 2007.
38. "Ubiistvo pod grifom 'sekretno,'" www.1tv.ru/documentary/fi=6399.
39. S. Lekarev, "Shpionskie skandaly XX veka ne ostalis' v proshlom," *Moskovskii komsomolets*, June 9, 2002.

II. Pride Before the Fall

1. Haslam, *Russia's Cold War*, chap. 10.
2. "Razvedchik Pyotr Ivashutin: on postroil 'Akvarium,'" *Ukraina kriminal'naya*, July 7, 2006.

3. There is a lot of popular writing on this, but the most reliable in Russian are Evdokimov, "Spetsrezerv KGB" and "Kuos bez grifa 'sekretno,'" *Voenno-Promyshlennyi kur'er*, April 1, 2009.
4. I. Atamanenko, "Groza shpionov: K sorokaletiyu obrazovaniya gruppy 'ALFA,'" *Nezavisimoe voennoe obozrenie*, July 25, 2014.
5. Ibid.
6. "'Shtorm-333': Shtorm dvortsa Amina," January 3, 2014, Bratishka.ru.
7. "'Shtorm-333': Shtorm dvortsa Amina," December 29, 2013, Bratishka.ru; and T. Skorikov's interview with Major General Drozdov in August 2005, "Legendy Spetsnaz: Yurii Drozdov: 'Vympelovtsy'—razvedchiki spetsial'nogo naznacheniya," www.bratishka.ru/archiv/2005/8/2005_8_5.php. Also V. Udmantsev's interview with Col. Oleg Shvets (GRU), "Ofitseram GRU khvatilo pyati mesyatsev, chtoby podgotovit' elitnyi spetsnaz," December 29, 2004.
8. Quoted, off-guard in conversation after dinner in my college, by the chief military assistant William ("Bill") Odom, later head of the NSA: Haslam, *Russia's Cold War*, p. 326. General Varennikov has since echoed this interpretation in an interview published on February 15, 2007: "they [the Americans] nudged us in . . . they had more interest in the entry of our forces than we ourselves had"—www.afghanistan.ru/doc/8049.html.
9. The Mitrokhin Archive, MITN 2/2 and 1/6/1.
10. "Kak odin poltavchanin Gimmlera obmanul," *Poltavshchina*, February 23, 2010; "Umer genii rossiiskoi kontrrazvedki," *Argumenty nedeli*, June 1, 2007; an interview with Grigorenko recorded for Zvezda TV in 2001: "95 let so dnya rozhdeniya generala Grigorii Grigorenko," August 16, 2013, tvzvezda.ru/news/forces/ . . . /201308161737-3mbs.htm or www.youtube.com/watch?v=uhFRnaDBpOo; also www.a-lubyanka.ru; "Chelovek-legenda: Grigorenko Grigorii Fyodorovich," Okhrana.ru, January 23, 2008. He died on May 19, 2007.
11. This request came from Tokyo: V. Malevanny, "'Yaponskii Goroskop' dlya TsRU," *Nezavisimoe voennoe obozrenie*, March 31, 2000.
12. J. Fellows, "Murder by the Book," *Washington Monthly*, April 1976, p. 23.
13. The Mitrokhin Archive, MITN 2/28.
14. J. Marks, "How to Spot a Spook," *Washington Monthly*, November 1974, reprinted in http://cryptome.org/dirty-work/spot-spook.htm.
15. The Mitrokhin Archive, MITN 1/6/1.
16. The Mitrokhin Archive, MITN 1/6/8.
17. Ibid.; also by V. Malevanny, "Sensei iz Yaseneva," *Nezavisimoe voennoe obozrenie*, September 28, 2000. *Sensei* is the Japanese word for "teacher."
18. Kalugin, *Spymaster*, p. 288.
19. H. Hristov, *Ubiite "Skitnik"* (Sofia: Siela, 2006). This is based on files, but all those relating to the KGB were purposefully destroyed.
20. F. Corley, "Soviet Reactions to the Election of Pope John Paul II," *Religion, State and Society* 22, no. 1 (1994): 37–64.
21. Sheymov, *Tower of Secrets*, p. 125.

22. John Paul II, *Memory and Identity: Personal Reflections* (London: Wiedenfeld and Nicolson, 2005), p. 184.
23. Kirpichenko, *Razvedka*, p. 58.
24. Kalugin, *Spymaster*, p. 201; the Mitrokhin Archive, MITN 1/6/8.
25. V. Udilov, *Zapiski kontrrazvedchika. Vzglyad iznutri* (Moscow: Iaguar, 1994), p. 100.
26. E. Zhirnov, "Propushchennye cherez Tito," *Kommersant vlast'*, April 3, 2001.
27. Commissione Parlamentare d'Inchiesta Concernente il *"Dossier* Mitrokhin" e l'Attività d'*Intelligence* Italiana: Documento Conclusivo sull'Attività Svolta e sui Risultati dell'Inchiesta, Rome, 2006, p. 268.
28. F. Imposimato and S. Provissionato, *Attentato al Papa* (Milan: Chiare Lettere, 2011), p. 104.
29. Commissione Parlamentare, p. 267.
30. Ibid., p. 268.
31. *Avvenire*, April 19, 2005.
32. Commissione Parlamentare, pp. 262–63.
33. Reported by Ağca in a handwritten letter to Imposimato only in 1997: ibid., p. 123. CBS journalists for *60 Minutes* obtained a copy of the letter, reported on May 29, 2001.
34. Commissione Parlamentare, p. 255.
35. The Mitrokhin Archive, MITN 1/6/9.
36. "Notiz über Besprechungen beim Genossen Sacharowski zu fragen der wissenschaftlich-technischen Aufklärung am 11.11.69," Berlin, November 21, 1969, www.bstu.bund.de.
37. S. Kostine and E. Raynaud, *Adieu Farewell* (Paris: Robert Laffont, 2009), p. 158.
38. E. Merlen and F. Ploquin, *Carnets intimes de la DST: 30 ans au coeur du contre-espionnage français* (Paris: Fayard, 2003), p. 53. The figures are from the DST, which ran Vetrov. Also A. Khinshtein, "Oboroten' s Lubyanki," *Moskovskii komsomolets*, September 13, 1998. This includes extracts from Vetrov's letters.
39. Sheymov, *Tower of Secrets*, p. 19.
40. V. Kalashnikov, "Porozhdenie vzaimnogo strakha," *Nezavisimoe voennoe obozrenie*, October 20, 2006.
41. "Analitika v organakh gosbezopasnosti," *Voinskoe bratstvo*, special edition, 2005.
42. V. Shlykov, "Chto pogubilo Sovetskii Soyuz?," www.mfit.ru/defensive/vestnik/vestnik9_8.html#s-up. For the impact of SALT, see Haslam, *Russia's Cold War*, pp. 261–64.
43. Shlykov, "Chto pogubilo."
44. Haslam, *Russia's Cold War*, pp. 264–68.
45. U.S. Senate. Select Committee on Intelligence, 94th Cong., 2nd Sess., Final Report of the Select Committee to Study Government Operations with Respect to Intelligence Activities, U.S. Senate 1976, Appendix III: "Soviet Intelligence Collection and Operations Against the United States," p. 557.

46. "US Intelligence and the End of the Cold War," conference, November 18–20, 1999, foia.cia.gov/docs/Doc_0001445139/Doc_0001445139.pdf.

47. Malevanny, "Sensei iz Yasenevo."

48. I. Atamanenko, "Okhota na 'krotov': kontrrazvedka KGB protiv agentura TsRU i MI-6," *Pravdinform*, January 6, 2013. Atamanenko is a lieutenant colonel in the FSB reserves.

49. Solomatin interviewed by P. Earley: www.trutv.com/library/crime/terrorists _spies/spies/solomatin.

50. Krasil'nikov, *Novye krestnonostsy: TsRU i perestroika*, p. 224.

51. "US Intelligence and the End of the Cold War," conference transcript, p. 12.

52. C. Lynch, *The C.I. Desk: FBI and CIA Counterintelligence as Seen from My Cubicle* (Indianapolis, IN: Dog Ear Pub., 2009), p. 91. For more on this, Haslam, *Russia's Cold War*, p. 333. See also "The 1983 War Scare," posted on the website of the National Security Archive, May 16, 2013, www.2.gwu.edu.

53. Grimes and Vertefeuille, *Circle of Treason*, p. 200.

54. Ibid., p. 133.

55. The fullest account is V. Cherkashin, *Spy Handler: Memoir of a KGB Officer* (New York: Basic Books, 2005).

Conclusion: Out from the Shadows

1. Solomatin interviewed by P. Earley, www.trutv.com/library/crime/terrorists _spies/spies/solomatin.

2. V. Lota, "Marshal voennoi razvedki," *Krasnaya zvezda*, September 2, 2009.

3. "Kremlin's Corporate Seizure as a War of Elites," *Christian Science Monitor*, October 31, 2003.

4. "Russia under Putin—The Making of a Neo-KGB State," *Economist*, August 23, 2007.

5. A. Soldatov and I. Borogan, *The New Nobility: The Restoration of Russia's Security State and the Enduring Legacy of the KGB* (New York: PublicAffairs 2011), p. 5.

6. "Russia under Putin . . ."

7. I. Borogan and A. Soldatov, "Za pyat' let rossiyan stali proslushivat' v dva raza bol'she," *Ezhednevnyi zhurnal*, June 4, 2012.

8. "'Goryachie tochki' vblizi nashikh granits," www.vz.ru/society/2013/1/26/617599 .html.

9. S. Smirnov, "Shoigu usiliyat boevymi generalami," *Gazeta.ru*, November 8, 2012.

BIBLIOGRAPHY

Archival Material and Official Publications

Adibekov, Grant, ed. *Politburo TsK RKP (b)—VKP (b) i Evropa: resheniya 'Osoboi papki' 1923–1939.* Moscow: Rosspen, 2001.

Amiantov, Yuri, ed. *V. I. Lenin. Neizvestnye dokumenty 1891–1922.* Moscow: Rosspen, 1999.

Belozerov, A. P., ed. *Sekrety Gitlera na stole u Stalina: razvedka i kontrrazvedka germanskoi agressii protiv SSSR, mart-iyun' 1941g.: dokumenty iz tsentral'nogo arkhiva FSB Rossii.* Moscow: Mosgorarkhiv, 1995.

BStU (Stasi) archives. www.bstu.bund.de/DE/Archive/_node.html.

Chernobaev, Anatoly, ed. *Na prieme u Stalina: zapisei lits, priniatykh I. V. Stalinym (1924–1953 gg.).* Moscow: Rossiiskii fond Kultury, 2008.

Chicherin, G. Memorandum for successor. *Kommersant vlast'* 4 (February 1, 2010); Russian Foreign Ministry archives. Also at www.mid.ru/bdomp/ns-arch.nsf/88ff23e 5441b5caa43256b05004bc . . .

CIA Electronic Archive. www.foia.cia.gov/.

Commissione Parlamentare d'Inchiesta Concernente il *"Dossier* Mitrokhin" e l'Attività d'Intelligenza Italiana. Documento Conclusivo sull'Attività Svolta e sui Risultati dell'Inchiesta. Rome, 2006. parlamento.it.

FBI. U.S. Department of Justice. *Exposé of Soviet Espionage May 1960.* U.S. Government Printing Office, Washington, D.C., 1960.

FBI Files. "Profumo Affair" (Bowtie). CD-ROM, Washington, D.C.

Fel'shtinskii, Yuri, ed. *VChK-GPU: Dokumenty i Materialy.* Moscow: Gumanitarnaya Literatura, 1995.

Fesyun, Andrei, ed. *Delo Rikhard Zorge. Neizvestnye dokumenty.* Moscow: Letnii Sad, 2000.

FO 371 series. National Archives, London.

Fursenko, Aleksandr, ed. *Prezidium TsK KPSS 1954–1964.* Vol. 1. Moscow: Rosspen, 2003.

House of Commons. Intelligence and Security Committee. *Cm. 4764. The Mitrokhin Enquiry Report.* London: HMSO, June 2000.

Khaustov, Vladimir, ed. *Lubyanka. Stalin i VChK-GPU-OGPU-NKVD Yanvar' 1922—dekabr' 1936. Dokumenty.* Moscow: Mezhdunarodnyi fond "Demokratiya," 2003.

K-70-Letiyu Sovetsko-Finlyandskoi Voiny. Zimnaya Voina 1939–1940gg. Zassek-rechennykh dokumentakh Tsentral'nogo arkhiva FSB Rossii i arkhivov Fin-lyandii. Issledovaniya, Dokumenty, Kommentarii, ed. A. Sakharov et al. (Moscow: Akadem-kniga, 2009).

Kvashonkin, A. V. ed. *Bol'shevistskoe rukovodstvo. Perepiska. 1912–1927.* Moscow: Rosspen, 1996.

KV2 series. National Archives, London.

Lord Denning's Report. HMSO, London, 1963.

Lubyanka. Stalin i MGB SSSR, mart 1946–mart 1953. Dokumenty. Moscow: Materik, 1953.

The Mitrokhin Archive, Churchill College, Cambridge, UK.

Nevezhin, Vladimir, ed. *Stalin o voine: Zastol'nye rechi 1933–1945gg.* Moscow: Eksmo, 2007.

Noel Annan Papers. NGA 7/4/1. Archive Centre, King's College, Cambridge, UK.

Petrov, Nikita, ed. *Kto rukovodil organami gosbezopasnosti 1941–1945. Spravochnik.* Moscow: Memorial, 2010.

Pick, Eugene. *China in the Grip of the Reds.* Shanghai: North China Daily News and Herald, 1927.

"Pokazaniya Ya. G. Blyumkina," October 20, 1929. *Istoricheskii arkhiv,* no. 6, 2002.

Reshin, L. E., ed. *1941 God.* Vol. 2. Moscow: Mezhdunarodnyi fond Demokratiya, 1998.

RGASPI. Arkhiv Kominterna, Moscow.

Sakharov, Andrei, ed. *Zimnaya Voina 1939–1940gg. v rassekrechennykh dokumentakh Tsentral'nogo arkhiva FSB Rossii i akhivov Finlyandii. Issledovaniya, Dokumenty, Kommentarii.* Moscow: Akademkniga, 2009.

Senate Select Committee on Intelligence. 94th Congress, 2nd Session. *Final Report of the Select Committee to Study Government Operations with Respect to Intelligence Activities,* U.S. Senate 1976, Appendix III. "Soviet Intelligence Collection and Operations Against the United States." U.S. Government Printing Office, Washington, D.C., 1976.

Solov'ev, E. D., ed. *Pogranichnye Voiska SSSR 1918–1928: Sbornik dokumentov i mate-rialov.* Moscow: Nauka, 1973.

———. *Pogranichnye Voiska SSSR 1945–1950: Sbornik dokumentov i materialov.* Moscow: Nauka, 1975.

Stalin. "Pravil'naya politika pravitel'stva reshaet uspekh armii." *Istochnik* 3 (2002): 72–76.

———. "Razvedka—svyatoe, ideal'noe dlya nas delo." In "Zapiska Yu. Andropova L. Brezhnevu," April 15, 1973. *Istochnik* 5 (2001).

Stalin to Minister Ignat'ev, August 1952. *Novaya Gazeta*, Moscow, 2011, pp. 299–300.

Stepashin, S. V., ed., *Organy Gosudarstvennoi bezopasnosti SSSR v velikoi otechestvennoi voine.* Moscow: Kniga i biznes, 1995.

Swedish Ministry of Foreign Affairs. *Raoul Wallenberg: Report of the Swedish-Russian Working Group.* Stockholm, 2000. www.government.se/sb/d/574/a/41137.

Titarenko, M. L., ed. *VKP(b), Komintern i Kitai. Dokumenty.* Vol. 4. Moscow: In-t Dal'nego Vostoka RAN, 2003.

Tragediya sovetskoi derevni. Kollektivizatsiya i raskulachivanie 1927–1939. Dokumenty i materialy. Vol. 1. Moscow, 1999.

Valeva, L. B., ed. *Sovetskii Soyuz i bor'ba narodov Tsentral'noi i Yugo-vostochnoi Evropy za svobodu i nezavisimost', 1941–1945.* Moscow: Nauka, 1978.

Vassiliev (Aleksandr Vasil'ev) Notebooks. Library of Congress. Cold War International History Project website. www.digitalarchive.wilsoncenter.org/collection/86/Vassiliev-Notebooks.

Yarukhin, Yuri, ed. *Voennye razvedchiki 1918–1945gg.: Biograficheskii spravochnik.* Kiev: Voennaya Razvedka, 2010.

"Zapiski Ignatiya Raissa." *Byulleten' Oppozitsii* 60–61 (December 1937).

Zdanovich, Aleksandr, ed. *Organy gosudarstvennoi bezopasnosti i Krasnaya armiya. Deyatel'nost' organov VChK-OGPU po obespecheniyu bezopasnosti RKKA (1921–1934).* Moscow: Kuchkovo Pole, 2008.

Memoirs

Agabekov, Georgii. *Sekretnyi terror: Zapiski razvedchika.* Moscow: Sovremennik, 1996.

Akhmedov, Ismail. *In and Out of Stalin's GRU.* Frederick, MD.: University Publications of America, 1984.

Berezhkov, Valentin. *Kak ya stal perevodchikom Stalina.* Moscow: DEM, 1993.

———. *Ryadom so Stalinym.* Moscow: Vagrius, 1998.

Bohnsack, Günter. *Hauptverwaltung Aufklärung: Die Legende stirbt.* Berlin: Edition Ost, 1997.

Chambers, Whittaker. *Witness.* London: A. Deutsch, 1952.

Cherkashin, Viktor. *Spy Handler: Memoirs of a KGB Officer.* New York: Basic Books, 2005.

Ciliga, Anton. *The Russian Enigma.* London: Routledge, 1940.

Dmitrievskii, Sergei. *Sovetskie Portrety.* Berlin: Strela, 1932.

Drozdov, Y. *Vymysel isklyuchen: Zapiski nachal'nika nelegal'noi razvedki.* Moscow: Al'manakh Vympel, 1996.

Erofeeva, Galina. *Skuchnyi Sad. Zametki o nediplomaticheskoi zhizni.* Moscow: Podkova, 1998.

Feklisov, Aleksandr. *The Man Behind the Rosenbergs*. New York: Enigma Books, 2004.

———. *Za okeanom i na ostrove*. Moscow: DEM, 1994.

Foote, Alexander. *Handbook for Spies*. New York: Doubleday, 1949.

Gazur, Edward. *Secret Assignment: The FBI's KGB General*. London: St Ermin's, 2001.

Grimes, Sandy, and Jeanne Vertefeuille. *Circle of Treason*. Annapolis, MD: Naval Institute Press, 2012.

Gromushkin, Pavel. *Razvedka: lyudi, portrety, sud'by*. Moscow: Dobrosovet, 2002.

Honigmann, Barbara. *Ein Kapitel aus meinem Leben*. Munich: C. Hanser, 2004.

Kalugin, Oleg. *Spymaster: My Thirty-Two Years in Intelligence and Espionage*. New York: Basic Books, 2009.

Khokhlov, N. *Pravo na sovest'*. Frankfurt/Main: no publisher, 1957.

Krasil'nikov, R. *KGB protiv MI-6: okhotniki za shpionami*. Moscow: Tsentrpoligraf, 2000.

———. *Konets "Krota."* Moscow: Veche, 2001.

Krivitsky, Walter. *In Stalin's Secret Service*. New York: Enigma Books, 2000.

———. "Iz vospominaniya sovetskogo kommunista," *Sotsialisticheskii vestnik* 7, no. 411 (April 15, 1938), and 8, no. 412 (April 29, 1938).

Leonov, Nikolai. *Likholet'e*. Moscow: Mezhdunarodnye Otnosheniya, 1995.

Marchetti, Victor, and John Marks. *The CIA and the Cult of Intelligence*. New York: Knopf, 1974.

Maslennikov, Mikhail. *Kriptografiya i svoboda*. Moscow, 2008. Available only online, at www.mikhailmas.livejournal.com.

Merlen, Eric, and Frédéric Ploquin. *Carnets intimes de la DST: 30 ans au coeur du contre-espionnage français*. Paris: Fayard, 2003.

Milne, Tim. *Kim Philby: The Unknown Story of the KGB's Master Spy*. London: Biteback, 2014.

Mil'shtein, Mikhail. *Skvoz' gody voin i nishchety*. Moscow: Itar-TASS, 2000.

Modin, Yuri. *My Five Cambridge Friends*. London: Headline, 1994.

———. *Sud'by razvedchikov. Moi kembridzhskie druz'ya*. Moscow: Olma Press, 1997.

Myasnikov, Aleksandr. *Ya lechil Stalina*. Moscow: Eksmo, 2011.

Novye krestonostsy: TsRU o perestroika. Moscow: Olma Press Obrazovanie, 2003.

Pavlov, Vitalii. *Tragedii sovetskoi razvedki*. Moscow: Olma Press, 2000.

Petrov, Vladimir, and Evdokia Petrov. *Empire of Fear*. London: Andre Deutsch, 1955.

Philby, Rufina, Mikhail Lyubimov, and Hayden Peake. *The Private Life of Kim Philby: The Moscow Years*. London: Fromm International, 1999.

Pushkaryov, Nikolai. *GRU: vymysli i real'nost'*. Moscow: Eksmo, 2004.

Poretsky, Elizabeth. *Our Own People*. London: Oxford University Press, 1969.

Radó, Sandor. *Dora meldet . . .* Berlin: Militärverlag, 1974.

Semichastny, Vladimir. *Bespokoinoe serdtse*. Moscow: Vagrius, 2002.

Sheymov, Viktor. *Tower of Secrets*. Annapolis, MD: Naval Institute Press, 1993.

Sudoplatov, Pavel. *Pobeda v taine voine 1941–1945 gody*. Moscow: Olma Press, 2005.

———. *Spetsoperatsii. Lubyanka i Kreml' 1930–1950 gody*. Moscow: Olma Press, 1998.

Trepper, Leopold. *Le Grand Jeu*. Paris: A. Michel, 1975.

Udilov, Vadim. *Zapiski kontrrazvedchika: Vzglyad iznutri*. Moscow: Iaguar, 1994.

Voitsekhovskii, Sergei. *Trest*. Ontario: Zaria, 1974.

Webster, Nigel. *Cribs for Victory: The Untold Story of Bletchley Park's Secret Room.* Clifton-upon-Teme, UK: privately published, 2011.

Winarow, Iwan. *Kämpfer der lautlosen Front: Erinnerungen eines Kundschafters.* Berlin: Militärverlag, 1969.

Womack, Helen, ed. *Undercover Lives: Soviet Spies in the Cities of the World.* London: Weidenfeld and Nicolson, 1998.

Monographs

Abramov, Vadim. *Evrei v KGB. Palachi i zhertvy.* Moscow: Eksmo, 2005.

———. *Kontrrazvedka. Shchit i mech protiv Abvera i Tsru.* Moscow: Eksmo, 2006.

Aldrich, Richard. *GCHQ: The Uncensored Story of Britain's Most Secret Intelligence Agency.* London: HarperPress, 2010.

Alekseev, Mikhail. *Leksika russkoi razvedki.* Moscow: Mezhdunarodnye Otnosheniya, 1996.

———. *Sovetskaya voennaya razvedka v Kitae i khronika "kitaiskoi smuty" (1922–1929).* Moscow: Kuchkovo Pole, 2010.

———. *"Vash Ramzai": Rikhard Zorge i sovetskaya voennaya razvedka v Kitae 1930–1933gg.* Moscow: Kuchkovo Pole, 2010.

Andrew, Christopher. *The Defence of the Realm: The Authorised History of MI5.* London: Allen Lane, 2009.

Andrew, Christopher, and Oleg Gordievsky. *KGB: The Inside Story.* London: Hodder and Stroughton, 1990.

Andrew, Christopher, and Vasili, Mitrokhin. *The Mitrokhin Archive: The KGB in Europe and the West.* London and New York: Allen Lane, 2000.

———. *The Mitrokhin Archive II: The KGB and the World.* London and New York: Allen Lane, 2005.

Antonov, Vladimir, and Vladimir Karpov. *Tainye informatory Kremlya: Vollenberg, Artuzov i drugie.* Moscow: Geia Iterum, 2001.

Apostel, Léo, Benoît Mandelbrôt, and Albert Morf. *Logique, Langage et Théorie de l'Information.* Paris: Presses Universitaires de France, 1957.

Benson, Robert. *The Venona Story.* Meade, MD: NSA, 2000.

Bezymensky, Lev. *Budapeshtskaya missiya: Raul' Vallenberg.* Moscow: Kollektsiya "Sovershenno Sekretno," 2001.

Boltunov, Mikhail. *"Zolotoe Ukho" voennoi razvedki.* Moscow: Veche, 2011.

Bondarenko, V. I., V. V. Andronenko, and M. V. Garanin. *50 Let Institutu Kriptografii, Svyazi i Informatiki: Istoricheskii Ocherk.* Moscow: publisher unknown, 1999; also www.vif2ne.ru.

Bower, Tom. *Red Web.* London: Mandarin, 1993.

Brigadier John Tiltman: A Giant among Cryptanalysts. Meade, MD: NSA, 2007.

Burke, Colin. *It Wasn't All Magic: The Early Struggle to Automate Cryptanalysis, 1930s–1960s.* Meade, MD: NSA, 2000.

Carr, Edward. *Twilight of Comintern, 1930–1935.* London: Macmillan, 1982.

Carter, Miranda. *Anthony Blunt: His Lives*. London: Macmillan, 2001.

Clandestine Services History: The Berlin Tunnel Operation 1952–1956. Langley, VA: CIA, 1968.

Corera, Gordon. *The Art of Betrayal*. London: Pegasus, 2011.

Costello, John, and Oleg Tsarev. *Deadly Illusions*. New York: Crown, 1993.

Damaskin, Igor. *Semnadtsat' imyon Kitti Kharris*. Moscow: Geia Iterum, 1999.

———. *Stalin i Razvedka*. Moscow: Veche, 2004.

Danilov, Viktor, ed. *Tragediya sovetskoi derevni. Kollektivizatsiya i raskulachivanie 1927–1939. Dokumenty i Materialy*. Vol. 1. Moscow: Rosspen, 1999.

Dolgopolov, Nikolai. *Abel'-Fisher*. Moscow: Molodaya Gvardiya, 2010.

Duff, William, *A Time for Spies*. Nashville, TN: Vanderbilt University Press, 1999.

Erofeev, Vladimir. *Diplomat*. Moscow: Zebra E., 2005.

Firsov, Friedrich. *Sekretnye kody istorii Kominterna 1919–1943*. Moscow: Airo-XXI, 2007.

Galvazin, Sergei. *Okhrannye struktury Rossiiskoi Imperii: Formirovanie apparata, analiz operativnoi praktiki*. Moscow: Kollektsiya "Sovershenno Sekretno," 2001.

Gasparyan, Armen. *Operatsiya "Trest": Sovetskaya razvedka protiv russkoi emigratsii 1921–1937*. Moscow: Veche, 2008.

Gladkov, Teodor. *Lift v Razvedku: "Korol" nelegalov Aleksandr Korotkov*. Moscow: Olma Press, 2002.

———. *Nagrada na vernost'—Kazn'*. Moscow: Tsentrpoligraf, 2000.

———. *Nash chelovek v Nyu-Iork: Sud'ba rezidenta*. Moscow: Eksmo, 2007.

Gladkov, Teodor, and Nikolai Zaitsev. *I ya emu ne mogu ne verit'*. . . Moscow: Politizdat, 1983.

Gorchakov, Ovidii. *Skhvatka s chernym drakonom: Tainaya voina na Dal'nem Vostoke*. Moscow: Veche, 2002.

———. *Stalin i GRU*. Moscow: Eksmo, 2010.

———. *Yan Berzin—komandarm GRU*. Moscow: Neva, 2004.

Granovsky, Anatoly. *All Pity Choked: The Memoirs of a Soviet Secret Agent*. London: W. Kimber, 1955.

Grey, Muriel. *Le Général Meurt à Minuit: l'enlèvement des généraux Koutiepov (1930) et Miller (1937)*. Paris: Plon, 1981.

Griffith, John. *Foreign vs. U.S. Computers: An Appraisal*. Meade, MD: NSA, 1972.

Gul'ev, Leonid. *Missiya Meisi. Dokumental'naya povest'*. Moscow: Russkaya Razvedka, 2003.

Haslam, Jonathan. *Russia's Cold War*. New Haven, CT: Yale University Press, 2011.

———. *Soviet Foreign Policy 1930–33: The Impact of the Depression*. London: Macmillan, 1983.

———. *The Soviet Union and the Politics of Nuclear Weapons in Europe 1969–87*. Ithaca, NY: Cornell University Press, 1989.

———. *The Soviet Union and the Struggle for Collective Security in Europe, 1933–39*. London: Macmillan, 1984.

———. *The Soviet Union and the Threat from the East, 1933–41*. London: Macmillan, 1992.

Haslam, Jonathan, and Karina Urbach, eds. *Secret Intelligence in the European States System 1918–1989*. Stanford, CA: Stanford University Press, 2013.

Hermiston, Roger. *The Greatest Traitor: The Secret Lives of Agent George Blake*. London: Aurum Press, 2013.

Hinsley, Francis, et al. *British Intelligence in the Second World War*. Vol. 1. London: Stationery Office Books, 1979.

———. *British Intelligence in the Second World War*. Vol. 2. London: Stationery Office Books, 1981.

———. *British Intelligence in the Second World War*. Vol. 4. London: Stationery Office Books, 1990.

Höhne, Heinz. *Kennwort: Direktor. Die Geschichte der Roten Kapelle*. Frankfurt/Main: S. Fischer, 1970.

Horne, Alistair. *Macmillan: The Official Biography*. London: Macmillan, 2008.

Hristov, Hristo. *Ubiite "Skitnik."* Sofia: Siela, 2006.

Imposimato, Ferdinando, and Sandro Provissionato. *Attentato al Papa*. Milan: Chiare Lettere, 2011.

Ivanov, Evgenii, and Gennadii Sokolov. *Golyi shpion. Russkaya readktsiya. Vospominaniya agenta GRU*. Moscow: Kuchkovo Pole, 2009.

Jeffery, Keith. *MI6: The History of the Secret Intelligence Service 1909–1949*. London: Bloomsbury, 2011.

John Paul II. *Memory and Identity: Personal Reflections*. London: Weidenfeld and Nicolson, 2005.

Johnson, Thomas. *American Cryptology During the Cold War, 1945–1989*, Book 1. Meade, MD: NSA, 1995.

Khinshtein, Aleksandr. *Tayny Lubyanki*. Moscow: Olma Press, 2008.

Khlobustov, Oleg. *Gosbezopasnost' ot Aleksandra I do Putina: 200 let tainoi voiny*. Moscow: Eksmo, 2006.

Kirpichenko, Vadim. *Razvedka: Litsa i lichnosti*. Moscow: Geia, 1998.

Kiselev, Aleksandr. *Stalinskii favorit s Lubyanki*. St. Petersburg: Neva, 2003.

Knight, Amy. *The KGB: Police and Politics in the Soviet Union*. London: Unwin Hyman, 1990.

Kolpakidi, Aleksandsr, and Dmitrii Prokhorov. *Imperiya GRU*. Moscow: Olma Press, 2000.

Kornilkov, Arkadii. *Berlin: Tainaya voina po obe storony granitsy: Zapiski voennogo kontrrazvedchika*. Moscow: Kuchkovo Pole, 2009.

Kostine, Sergei, and Éric Raynaud. *Adieu Farewell*. Paris: Robert Laffont, 2009.

Ladygin, Fyodor, and Vladimir Lota. *GRU i karibskii krizis*. Moscow: Kuchkovo Pole, 2012.

Leonard, Raymond. *Secret Soldiers of the Revolution*. London: Greenwood Press, 1999.

Lota, Vladimir. *"Al'ta" protiv "Barbarossy": Kak byli dobyty svedeniya o podgotovke Germani k napadeniyu na SSSR*. Moscow: Molodaya Gvardiya, 2004.

———. *GRU i atomnaya bomba*. Moscow: Olma Press, 2002.

Macintyre, Ben. *A Spy among Friends: Kim Philby and the Great Betrayal*. London: Bloomsbury, 2014.

MacKinnon, Janice, and Stephen MacKinnon. *Agnes Smedley: The Life and Times of an American Radical.* Berkeley: University of California Press, 1998.

Malinovsky, Boris. *Pioneers of Soviet Computing.* www.sigcis.org/files/SIG CISMC2010_001.pdf.

McDonald, Iverach. *The History of the Times.* Vol. 5. London: Times Books, 1984.

Moravec, František. *Master of Spies.* London: Sphere, 1981.

Mosley, Leonard. *Dulles: A Biography of Eleanor, Allen, and John Foster Dulles and Their Family Network.* London: Hodder and Stoughton, 1978.

Mozohin, Oleg. *Bor'ba sovetskikh organov gosudarstvennoi bezopasnosti s terrorizmom.* Moscow: Kuchkovo Pole, 2011.

Murphy, David, Sergei Kondrashev, and George Bailey. *Battleground Berlin.* New Haven, CT: Yale University Press, 1997.

Narinskii, Mikhail. *Sovetskaya vneshnyaya politika i proiskhozhdenie kholodnoi voiny—Sovetskaya vneshnyaya politika v retrospesktive 1917–1991.* Moscow: privately printed, 1993.

Nevezhin, Vladimir, ed. *Stalin o Voine: Zastol'nye rechi 1933–1945gg.* Moscow: Eksmo, 2007.

Nikonov, Vyacheslav. *Molotov: Molodost'.* Moscow: Vagrius, 2005.

Ocherki istorii Rossiiskoi vneshnei razvedki. Vol. 2. Moscow: Mezhdunarodnye Otnosheniya, 1996.

Ocherki istorii Rossiiskoi vneshnei razvedki. Vol. 3. Moscow: Mezhdunarodnye Otnosheniya, 1997.

Ocherki istorii Rossiiskoi vneshnei razvedki. Vol. 4. Moscow: Mezhdunarodnye Otnosheniya, 1999.

Ostrjakow, Sergei. *Militär-Tschekisten.* Berlin: Militär Verlag, 1984.

Ovcharenko, G. "V svyatay svyatykh bezopasnosti: Vpervye zhurnalist pereshagnul porog 8-go Glavnogo upravleniya KGB SSSR," *Pravda,* September 16, 1990.

Peregudova, Zinaida. *Politicheskii sysk Rossii (1880–1917).* Moscow: Rosspen, 2000.

——, ed. *"Okhranka": Vospominaniya rukovoditelei okhrannykh otdelenii.* Vol. 2. Moscow: Novoe literaturnoe obozrenie, 2004.

Peshcherskii, Vladimir. *"Krasnaya Kapella": Sovetskaya razvedka protiv Abvera i Gestapo.* Moscow: Tsentrpoligraf, 2000.

Petrov, Nikita. *Kto rukovodil organami gosbezopasnosti 1941–1954: Spravochnik.* Moscow: Zvenia, Memorial, 2010.

——. *Palachi: Oni vypolnyali zakazy Stalina.* Moscow: Novaya Gazeta, 2011.

——. *Pervyi predsedatel' KGB Ivan Serov.* Moscow: Materik, 2005.

Plekhanov, Aleksandr. *Dzerzhinskii: Pervyi chekist Rossii.* Moscow: Olma Media Group, 2007.

Popov, Viktor. *Sovetnik korolevy—Superagent Kremlya.* Moscow: TOO "Novina," 1995.

Prokof'ev, Valerii. *Aleksandr Sakharovskii: Nachal'nik vneshnei razvedki.* Moscow: Yauza, 2005.

Pushkaryov, Nikolai. *GRU: dela i sud'by.* Moscow: Eksmo, 2013.

Roewer, Helmut. *Die Rote Kapelle und andere Geheimdienst-Mythen: Spionage zwischen Deutschland und Russland im Zweiten Weltkrieg 1941–1945*. Graz: Ares, 2010.

Rubin, Barry. *Istanbul Intrigues*. New York: Pharos, 1992.

Rybalkin, Yuri. *Operatsiya "Kh."* Moscow: Airo XX, 2000.

Sale, Tony. *COLOSSUS 1943–1996*. Kidderminster: privately published, 1998.

Schwarz, Paul. *This Man Ribbentrop: His Life and Times*. New York: Messner, 1943.

Selvatici, Antonio. *Chi spiava i terroristi: KGB, Stasi-BR, RAF. I documenti negli archivi dei servizi segreti dell'Europa "comunista."* Bologna: Pendragon, 2010.

Shirokorad, Aleksandr. *Rossiya i Ukraina: Kogda zagovoryat pushki . . .* Moscow: AST, 2007.

———. *Velikii antrakt*. Moscow: AST, 2009.

Shvaryov, Nikolai. *Razvedchiki-Nelegaly SSSR i Rossii*. Moscow: Veche, 2011.

Simbirtsev, Igor. *Spetssluzhby pervykh let SSSR 1923–1939*. Moscow: Tsentrpoligraf, 2008.

Singh, Simon. *The Code Book*. New York: Anchor, 2000.

Smith, Michael. *Six*. London: Biteback, 2011.

Sobolev, Vasilii, ed. *Lubyanka 2*. Moscow: Glavarkhiv, 1999.

Soboleva, Tatyana. *Istoriya shifroval'nogo dela v Rossii*. Moscow: Olma Press, 2002.

Steil, Benn. *The Battle of Bretton Woods: John Maynard Keynes, Harry Dexter White, and the Making of a New World Order*. Princeton, NJ: Princeton University Press, 2013.

Syrkov, Boris. *Proslushka predtechi Snoudena*. Moscow: Algoritm, 2013.

Taylor, Sally. *Stalin's Apologist: Walter Duranty, the New York Times's Man in Moscow*. New York: Oxford University Press, 1990.

Tereshchenko, Anatolii. *"Oborotny" iz voennoi razvedki: Devyat' predatel'stv sotrudnikov GRU*. Moscow: Zvonnitsa M-G, 2004.

Tereshchenko, Anatolii, and Aleksandr Vdovin. *Iz SMERSHA do GRU: "Imperator Spetssluzhb."* Moscow: Eksmo, 2013.

Thorsell, Staffan. *I Hans Majestäts tjänst*. Stockholm: Albert Bonniers, 2009.

Tinchenko, Yaroslav. *Golgofa russkogo ofitserstva v SSSR 1930–1931 gody*. Moscow: Moskovskii obshchestvennyi fond, 2000.

The Trust. Security and Intelligence Foundation Reprint Series. Langley, VA: CIA, July 1989.

Tsarev, Oleg, *KGB v Anglii*. Moscow: Tsentrpoligraf, 1999.

Tumshis, Mikhail, and Aleksandr Papchinskii. *1937: Bol'shaya chistka: NKVD protiv ChK*. Moscow: Eksmo, 2009.

Tuschhoff, Christian. *MC 70 und die Einführung Nuklearer Trägersysteme in die Bundeswehr 1956–1959*. Ebenhausen: Stiftung Wissenschaft und Politik, 1990.

Ulanovskie, Nadezhda and Maya. *Istoriya odnoi sem'i*. New York: Chalidze, 1982.

Uspenskii, Vladimir. *Trudy po nematematike*. Moscow: OGI, 2002.

Valev, Lyubomir. *Sovetskii Soyuz i bor'ba narodov Tsentral'noi i Yugo-vostochnoi Evropy za svobodu i nezavisimost' 1941–1945gg*. Moscow: Nauka, 1978.

Veryuzhskii, Nikolai. *Ofitserskaya sluzhba*. www.navy.ru/blog/historyofNVMU.

Viktorov, Ivan. *Podpol'shchik, voin, chekist*. Moscow: Politicheskaya Literatura, 1963.

Weingartner, Thomas. *Stalin und der Aufstieg Hitlers: Die Deutschlandpolitik der Sowjetunion und der Kommunistischen Internationale 1929–1934.* Berlin: De Gruyter, 1970.

Weinstein, Allen, and Alexander Vassiliev. *The Haunted Wood.* New York: Modern Library, 1999.

West, Nigel. *VENONA: The Greatest Secret of the Cold War.* London: HarperCollins, 1999.

West, Nigel, ed. *The Guy Liddell Diaries.* Vol. 1. London: Routledge, 2005.

West, Nigel, and Oleg Tsarev. *The Crown Jewels.* New Haven, CT: Yale University Press, 1999.

Wilmers, Mary-Kay. *The Eitingons.* London: Faber & Faber, 2009.

Yarukhin, Yuri, ed. *Voennye Razvedchiki 1918–1945gg.: Biograficheskii spravochnik.* Kiev: Voennaya Razvedka, 2010.

Zalesskaya, M. K., ed. *Oni rukovodili GRU:* Moscow: Veche, 2010.

Zdanovich, Aleksandr. *Organy gosudarstvennoi bezopasnosti i Krasnaya armiya: Deyatel'nost' organov VChK-OGPU po obespecheniyu bezopasnosti RKKA (1921–1934).* Moscow: Kuchkovo Pole, 2008.

Zipf, George. *The Psycho-Biology of Language.* Boston: Houghton Mifflin, 1935.

Periodicals

Argumenti ru
Avvenire
Bezopasnost' informatsionnykh tekhnologii
B.I.S. Journal
Bratishka ru
Byulleten' oppozitsii
Christian Science Monitor
Cryptologic Quarterly
Daily Mail
Daily Telegraph
Diplomaticheskii vestnik
Economist
Ekabu ru
Ezhednevnyi zhurnal
Gazeta ru
Gazeta Wyborcza
Historical Journal
Istochnik
Kommersant vlast'
Komsomol'skaya pravda
Krasnaya zvezda
Krugozor
Kurskaya pravda

Labor History
Lyudi
Moskovskii komsomolets
My zdes'
New York Times
Nezavisimoe voennoe obozrenie
Novosti razvedki i kontrrazvedki
Novosti Vladivostoka
Ogonek
Okhrana ru
Okno v Rossiyu
Parlamentskaya gazeta
Poltavshchina
Populyarnaya mekhanika
Pravda
Pravdinform
Rakus istorii
Religion, State and Society
Rossiiskaya gazeta
Rossiiskoe voennoe obozrenie
Rossiya
Sotsialisticheskii vestnik
Sovershenno sekretno
Spetsnaz Rossii
Sunday Times (London)
Superkomyutery
Svobodnaya mysl'
Times (London)
Trud
Ukraina kriminal'naya
US News and World Report
Victoria Advocate
Voennoe obozrenie
Voenno-istoricheskii arkhiv
Voenno-istoricheskii zhurnal
Voenno-promyshlennyi kur'er
Voinskoe bratstvo (voin-brat.ru)
Vokrug sveta
Voprosy istorii
Wall Street Journal
Washington Monthly
Washington Post
Zashchita informatsii. Konfident
Zavtra

Articles

Abakumov, Dmitrii. "Legendy razvedki: velikii kombinator spetssluzhb." www
.bratishka.ru/archiv/2007/6/2007_6_17.php.

———. "Legendy razvedki: Vybor polkovnika Abelya." www.bratishka.ru/archiv
/2006/12/2006_12_12.php.

Afanas'ev, Igor', and Dmitrii Vorontsov. "Lyubopytnyi vzglyad iz Kosmosa:
fotoshpionazh." www.popmech.ru/ . . . /8999-lyubopytnyy-vzglyad-iz-kozmosa:
fotoshpionazh.

"Al'ma-mater rossiiskikh razvedchikov." *Voinskoe Bratstvo* 8, no. 65 (November–
December 2010).

Anfilov, Viktor. "'Razgovor zakonchilsya ugrozoi Stalina': Desyat' neizvestnykh
besed s marshalom G. K. Zhukovym v mae-iyune 1965 goda." *Voenno-istoricheskii
zhurnal* 3 (May–June 1995).

Antonov, Vladimir. "Anatoly Gorskii na peredovoi vneshnei razvedki." *Nezavisimoe
voennoe obozrenie*, December 16, 2011.

———. "Den' rozhdeniya Bokiya G. I. (1879)—pervogo rukovoditelya kriptograficheskoi sluzhby SSSR." June 22, 2013. www.securityliba.ru.

———. "Iskusstvo vybirat' druzei i vragov." *Nezavisimoe voennoe obozrenie*, October 31, 2013.

———. "Iz istorii Sluzhby vneshnei razvedki . . .' *Nezavisimoe voennoe obozrenie*, December 28, 2007.

———. "Kak Vil'yam Fisher stal Rudol'om Abelem." *Voenno-promyshelennyi kur'er*,
August 1, 2007.

———. "Leonid Kvasnikov i atomnaya bomba." *Nezavisimoe voennoe obozrenie*, August 24, 2008.

———. "Na pol'skom napravlenii pered 22 iyunya." *Nezavisimoe voennoe obozrenie*,
June 3, 2011.

———. "Odisseya vselogo Odessita." *Nezavisimoe voennoe obozrenie*, November 22,
2013.

———. "Razgrom belogvardeiskogo gnezda." *Nezavisimoe voennoe obozrenie*, October 19, 2012.

———. "Razvedchik Den." *Voenskoe bratstvo* 2, no. 75 (February–March 2012).

———. "Reanimator vneshnei razvedki." *Nezavisimoe voennoe obozrenie*, December 28, 2007.

———. "7 aprelya ispolnyaetsya 105 let so dnya rozhdeniya vydayushchegosya
sovetskogo razvedchika-nelegala Ishaka Akhmerova." *Nezavisimoe voennoe obozrenie*, April 7, 2006.

———. "Svyaznaya 'Kembridzhskoi pyaterki.' Zhizn' po chuzhomu pasportu i zolotoi
kulon na pamyat' o lyubvi." *Nezavisimoe voennoe obozrenie*, November 3, 2012.

———. "Vasilii Zarubin—razvedchik ot boga." *Novoe voennoe obozrenie*, February
20, 2009.

———. "Virtuoz verbovki." *Nezavisimoe voennoe obozrenie*, June 2, 2006.

———. "Vladimir Bustrem—revolyutsioner, katorzhanin, rezident: Vklad berlinskoi rezidentury v stanovlenie sovetskoi vneshnei razvedki." *Nezavisimoe voennoe obozrenie*, September 9, 2011.

———. "Yakov Serebryanskii—trizhdy uznik Lubyanki." *Voenno-promyshlennyi kur'er*, November 1, 2006.

———. "Zvezdnyi chas Dzhona Kernkrossa." *Nezavisimoe voennoe obozrenie*, October 18, 2013.

Atamanenko, Igor. "Bili, bili—ne dobili." *Nezavisimoe voennoe obozrenie*, April 2, 2010.

———. "I poslali nichto chelovecheskoe ne chuzhdo . . ." *Nezavisimoe voennoe obozrenie*, March 20, 2009.

———. "Izmennik-neudachnik." *Nezavisimoe voennoe obozrenie*, June 28, 2013.

———. "Okhota na 'krotov'; kontrrazvedka KGB protiv agentura TsRU i M16," *Pravdainform*, January 6, 2013.

———. "Operatisiya 'Sezam, otkroisya!'" *Nezavisimoe voennoe obozrenie*, January 18, 2013.

———. "Pervyi krot v Glavnom razvedyvatel'nom upravlenii." *Nezavisimoe voennoe obozrenie*, March 23, 2012.

Babash, Aleksandr, and Elena Baranov. "Kriptograficheskie metody obespecheniya informatsionnoi bezopasnosti do pervoi mirovoi voiny." publications.hse.ru.

Berezin, Aleksandr. "Legendy Razvedki: 'Tarantella' dlya Dzhentl'menov." www.brati shka.ru/archiv/2008/4/2008_4_13.php.

"Beria stal boyat'sya Abakumova kak ogna." *Kommersant vlast'*, June 30, 2008.

"Biografiya I. Ya. Verchenko." *Mezhregional'naya olimpiarda shkol'nikov po matematike i kriptografii*, September 12, 2012.

Bogomolov, Aleksei. "Kokain dlya tovarishcha Stalina." *Sovershenno sekretno* 3, no. 286 (February 25, 2013).

Bondarenko, Aleksandr. "Smert' shpionam." *Krasnaya zvezda*, April 17, 2012.

Borogan, Irina, and Andrei Soldatov. "Za pyat' let rossiyan stali proslushivat' v dva raza bol'she." *Ezhednevnyi zhurnal*, June 4, 2012.

"Chelovek-legenda. Grigorenko Grigorii Fyodorovich." *Okhrana.ru*, January 23, 2008.

Chikov, Vladimir, " 'Razvedka—eto moya glavnaya zhizn'." *Voenno-promyshlennyi kur'er*, September 15, 2004.

Corley, Felix. "Soviet Reactions to the Election of Pope John Paul II." *Religion, State and Society* 22, no. 1 (1994).

Davidovich, Inna. "V teni kembridzhskoi pyaterki." November 2007, www.krugozor magazine.com.

"Delo 'Vesna'." *Krasnaya zvezda*, March 3, 2010.

Denisov, Vladimir, and Pavel Matveev. "Tainstvennaya Erna." *Nezavisimoe voennoe obozrenie*, January 19, 2001.

Drozdov, Yuri. "SShA, N'yu-Iork (1975–1979gg.)." www.vatanym.ru/?=vs307_mem1.

Dvinin, Valentin. "Operatsiya 'Karfagen' ili Tainye seifovoi komnaty." *Rossiiskaya gazeta*, March 3 and 9, 2006.

Earley, Pete. Interview with Solomatin. *Washington Post Magazine*, April 23, 1995.

Emelyanov, Gennadii, Dmitrii Larin, and Leonid Butyrskii. "Prevrashchenie kriptologii v fundamental'nuyu nauku. N. N. Andreev: put' ot inzhenera do prezidenta Akademii kriptografii RF." *BIS Journal* 3, no. 10 (2013).

Epstein, Edward. "The Spy Wars." *New York Times Magazine*, September 28, 1980.

Evdokimov, Pavel. "Spetsrezerv KGB." *Spetsnaz Rossii* 3, no. 138 (March 2008).

Fedyushin, Il'ya. "V telefil'me 'semnadtsat' mgnovenii vesny' ispol'zovany podlinnye razvedyvatel'nye syuzhety." *Voenno-promyshlennyi kur'er*, January 25, 2006.

Fenyvesi, Charles, and Victoria Pope. "The Angel Was a Spy. New Evidence: Sweden's Raoul Wallenberg Was a U.S. Espionage Asset." *US News and World Report*, May 5, 1996.

"Fil'm 'Mertvyi sezon'—eto o nem." *Nezavisimoe voennoe obozrenie*, March 8, 2013.

Friedman, Richard. "A Stone for Willy Fisher." *Studies in Intelligence* (Fall 2000).

Galaiko, Vladimir. "Shpion, za kotorym okhotilis' chetvert' Veka." *Gazeta.zn.ua*, March 23, 2001.

"General GRU—amerikanskii agent." June 19, 2012. www.vse-war.ru/video/istorija /general-gru-amerikanskij-agent.html.

Golikov, Filipp. "Sovetskaya Voennaya Razvedka pered Gitlerovskim Nashestviem na SSSR." *Voenno-istoricheskii zhurnal* 12 (2007).

Golubev, Sergei. "Nash Tovarishch Kim Filbi." *Krasnaya zvezda*, August 9–11, 2006.

Gorbunov, Evgenii. "Aktivnaya razvedka, perekhodyashchaya v banditizm." *Nezavisimoe voennoe obozrenie*, September 9, 2005.

———. "Bezosnovatel'naya trevoga. Voennaya razvedka dokladyvala sovetskomu rukovodstvu, chto napadenie na SSSR maloveroyatno." *Nezavisimoe voennoe obozrenie*, March 21, 2008.

"Govorit Aleksandr Gusak." *Zavtra*, September 10, 2001.

Gudz', Boris. "Ya videl, kak Dzerzhinskii tseloval dame ruku." *Trud*, December 20, 2002.

Haslam, Jonathan. "The Comintern and the Origins of the Popular Front, 1934–35." *Historical Journal* 22, no. 3 (1979): 673–91.

———. "Political Opposition to Stalin and the Origins of the Terror in Russia, 1932–1936." *Historical Journal* 29, no. 2 (1986): 395–418.

Holloway, David. "Barbarossa and the Bomb: Two Cases of Soviet Intelligence in World War II." In J. Haslam and K. Urbach, eds. *Secret Intelligence in the European States System 1918–1989*. Stanford, CA: Stanford University Press, 2013.

"Interv'yu Viktora Martynova v rubrike 'nevidimyi front.'" *Voinskoe bratstvo* 4 (2005).

Kahn, Jeffrey. "The Case of Colonel Abel." *Journal of National Security Law and Policy* 5 (2011): 263–301.

"Kak Faina Ranevskaya obvela vokrug pal'tsa KGB." *Ekabu.ru*, May 25, 2013.

"Kak odin poltavchanin Gimmlera obmanul." *Poltavshchina*, February 23, 2010.

Kalashnikov, Viktor. "Porozhdenie vzaimnogo strakha." *Nezavisimoe voennoe obozrenie*, October 20, 2006.

Karikh, Mariya. "Komitet informatsii—nash otvet TsRU." *Voenno-promyshlennyi kur'ier* 14, no. 280 (April 15, 2009).

Karpov, Igor'. "Vo glave Komiteta informatsii." *Voinskoe bratstvo*, special edition, 2005.

Khinshtein, Aleksandr. "Oboroten' s Lubyanki." *Moskovskii komsomolets*, September 13, 1998.

"K istorii sozdaniya shifroval'noi sluzhby v MID Rossii." *Diplomaticheskii vestnik*, April 2001.

Kochik, Valerii. "Sovetskaya voennaya razvedka: struktura i kadry." *Svobodnaya mysl'* 6, no. 1475 (June 1998).

———. "Sovetskaya voennaya razvedka: struktura i kadry." *Svobodnaya mysl'* 7, no. 1476 (July 1998).

"Kozlov, Mikhail Stepanovich." http://crypto-volga.narod.ru/Text/KOZ.doc.

Krivitskii, Valter. "Iz vospominanii sovetskogo kommunista." *Sotsialisticheskii vestnik* 7 (April 15, 1938).

Krotkov, Boris. "Ya prinimal u agenta prisyagu na vernost' fyureru." *Rossiiskaya Gazeta*, August 31, 2007.

Kuz'min, Leonid. "GUSS—etap v razvitii sovetskoi kriptografii." *Zashchita informatsii: Konfident* 22 (1997).

———. "Ne zabyvat' svoikh geroev." *Zashchita informatsii: Konfident* 1 (1998).

———. "Stanovlenie kafedry kriptografii." www.iso27000.ru/chitalnyi-zai/kripto grafiya/.

Ladygin, Fyodor, and Vladimir Lota. "Obrechennaya 'Tsitadel.'" *Rossiiskoe voennoe obozrenie*, May 2013.

———. "U kraya Karibskoi propasti." *Krasnaya zvezda*, October 18, 2012.

———. "U kraya Karibskoi propasti," part 2. *Krasnaya zvezda*, October 25, 2012.

———. "Zvezdnyi chas Dzhona Kernkrossa." *Nezavisimoe voennoe obozrenie*, October 18, 2013.

"Lampovye dinozavry pervogo pokoleniya." *Vokrug sveta* 8, no. 2875 (August 2013).

Larin, Dmitrii. "O vklade sovetskikh kriptografov v pobedu pod Moskvoi." www .pvti.ru/data/file/bit/bit_4_2011_8.pdf.

Latunskii, Il'ya. "Boi s ten'yu: iz istorii protivosostoyaniya TsRU i KGB." *Pravda*, June 5, 2006.

Lekarev, Stanislav. "Eksfil'tratsiya shifroval'shika Andropova." *Argumenty nedeli*, May 24, 2007.

———. "Konets 'kembridzhskoi pyaterki'," part 4. *Argumenty nedeli* 10, no. 96 (March 7, 2008).

———. "Na kogo rabotala 'kembridzhskaya pyaterka?" part 2. *Argumenty nedeli* 8, no. 94 (February 21, 2008).

———. "Shpionskie skandaly XX veka ne ostalis' v proshlom." *Moskovskii komsomolets*, June 9, 2002.

———. "Umer genii rossiiskoi kontrrazvedki." *Argumenty nedeli*, June 1, 2007.

Lekarev, Stanislav, and Valerii Pork. "Radioelektronnyi shchit i mech." *Nezavisimoe voennoe obozrenie*, January 26, 2002.

Lekarev, Stanislav, and Anatolii Sudoplatov. "Londonskii proval sovetskoi razvedki." *Nezavisimoe voennoe obozrenie*, October 18, 2002.

Lota, Vladimir. "Marshal voennoi razvedki." *Krasnaya zvezda*, September 2, 2009.

———. "Morris." *Rossiiskoe voennoe obozrenie* 9, no. 68 (September 2009).

———. "Obrechennaya 'Tsitadel.'" *Krasnaya zvezda*, May 6, 2013.

———. "Omega." *Rossiiskoe voennoe obozrenie* 10 no. 69 (October 2009).

———. "Stalingradskaya bitva voennoi razvedki." *Voennoe obozrenie*, December 1, 2012.

Lyulechnik, Vilen. "Pokushenie na Gitlera 20 iyulya 1944g.: Novye dokumenty i fakty." *Rakus istorii*. www.russian-globe.com/N106/Lulechnik.PokushenieNaGitlera.htm.

Makarenko, Pavel. "'Nemetskii Oktyabr' 1923 g. i sovetskaya vneshnyaya politika." *Voprosy Istorii* 3 (March 2012): 36–55.

Maksimenkov, Leonid. "Do Snoudena byl Gamil'ton." *Ogonyok* 26, no. 5286, July 8, 2013.

Malevanny, Valerii. "Inspektsiya Yuriya Andropova." *Nezavisimoe voennoe obozrenie*, April 24, 1998.

———. "Sensei iz Yasenevo." *Nezavisimoe voennoe obozrenie*, September 28, 2000.

———. "'Yaponskii goroskop' dlya TsRU." *Nezavisimoe voennoe obozrenie*, March 31, 2000.

Matveev, Oleg, and Vladimir Merzlyakov. "Azbuka Kontrrazvedka." *Nezavisimoe voennoe obozrenie*, March 3, 2000.

"Mezhdu zheleznym zanavesom." *Spetsnaz*, October 1, 2011.

Mironov, Viktor, and Mikhail Shchipanov. "Krestnyi otets 'kembridzhskoi pyaterki.'" *Rossiiskaya gazeta*, 1999.

Mlechin, Leonid. "Sluzhba vneshnei razvedki: Proval s bol'shimi posledstviyami." September 29, 2009. www.onlainkniga.ru/x4/x400/677-proval-s-bolshimi-posledstvijami.html.

Myasnikov, Viktor. "Kak unichtozhali vneshnyuyu razvedku." *Nezavisimoe voennoe obozrenie*, July 11, 2008.

"Na sluzhbe Rodine, matematike i kriptografii: Zhizn' i sud'ba V. Ya. Kozlova—odnogo iz osnovopolozhnikov otechestvennoi shifroval'noi nauki." *BIS Journal* 1, no. 8 (June 28, 2013).

"Nebo smotrit na tebya." *Okno v Rossiyu*, March 28, 2012.

Nekhoroshev, Grigorii. "Sekretnyi kod Martina i Mitchella." *Sovershenno sekretno*, August 2, 2012.

"Nelegal po familii Erdberg, on zhe Aleksandr Korotkov." July 22, 2010. www.topwar.ru/760.

Nowik, Grzegorz. "Znaczenie i zakres deszyfracij depesz bolszewickich w latach 1919–1920." *Gazeta wyborcza*, August 7, 2005.

Orlov, Alexander. "The Theory and Practice of Soviet Intelligence." www.cia.gov/library/center-for-the-study-of-intelligence/kent-csi/vol7no2/html/v0.

"Ostroshchenko, Andrei Marakovich." Sluzhba vneshnei razvedki rossiiskoi federatsii, 2000. www.svr.gov.ru.

Pacepa, Ion. "The Arafat I Knew." *Wall Street Journal*, January 12, 2002.

Pedersen, Vernon. "George Mink, the Marine Workers Industrial Union, and the Comintern in America." *Labor History* 3, no. 41 (2000): 307–20.

Peterson, Michael. "Before BOURBON: American and British COMINT Efforts Against Russia and the Soviet Union before 1945." *Cryptologic Quarterly* 12 (Fall/ Winter 1993): 3–4.

Pronin, Aleksandr. "Legendy razvedki: Korol' nelegalov." *Bratishka.ru*, December 2002.

"Pust' ukhodit. Zhelet' ne budem!" *Nezavisimoe voennoe obozrenie*, February 29, 2008.

Pyatovskii, S., and A. Kramarenko. "Londonskii rezident rodilsya v Kurske." *Kurskaya pravda*, December 7, 2012.

"Razvedchik Petr Ivashutin: on postroil 'Akvarium.'" *Ukraina kriminal'naya*, July 7, 2006.

"Red Trickery." *The Times* (London), August 17, 1920.

Rocafort, W. W. "Colonel Abel's Assistant." *Studies in Intelligence* 3 (Fall 1959).

Rostovtsev, Aleksei. "Nashi nemetskie druz'ya rodilis' agentami." *Nezavisimoe voennoe obozrenie*, April 5, 2013.

Sergeev, Vladimir. "Da Vinchi sovetskoi vneshnei razvedki." *Nezavisimoe voennoe obozrenie*, October 6, 2006.

Shlykov, Vitalii. "Chto pogubilo Sovetskii Soyuz?" www.mfit.ru/defensive/vestnik /vestnik9_8.html#s-up.

Smirnov, Sergei. "Shoigu usilyat boevymi generalami." *Gazeta.ru*, November 8, 2012.

Soboleva, Tat'yana. "K voprosu ob izuchenii istorii kriptologicheskuyu sluzhby Rossii." Ruskripto-99 conference, December 22–24, 1999. sfinxclub.ru.

Solov'ev, Vladimir, and Vladislav Trifonov. "Svezho predatel'stvo." *Kommersant*, November 11, 2010.

Trotsky, Lev. "Jakob Blumkin Shot by the Stalinists, January 4, 1930." *Writings of Leon Trotsky.* 1930 repr. New York: Pathfinder, 1975.

Tsipko, Aleksandr. "Istoriya IEMSS glazami 'nevyezdnogo.'" In I. Orlik and T. Sokolova, eds. *"Eto bylo nedavno, eto bylo davno":* Vospominaniya. Moscow: I. E. RAN, 2010.

Tuchkov, Vladimir. "Anatolii Ivanovich Kitov: Sovsekretnyi podpolkovnik." *Super-kompyutery,* September 15, 2012.

Tyulyakov, Sergei. "Istoricheskii anekdot kak zerkalo ideologii." *Nezavisimoe voennoe obozrenie*, July 27, 2012.

"Ukhodit Epokha." *Spetsnaz* 5, no. 187 (June 2012).

Vitkovskii, Aleksandr. "Legenda i zhizn' razvedchika—nelegala Konona Molodogo." *Parlamentskaya gazeta*, January 19, 2002.

Vladimirov, Sergei. "Naum Eitingon—general-razvedchik osobogo nasnacheniya." *Nezavisimoe voennoe obozrenie*, December 4, 2009.

———. "Syn shveitsartsa i latyshki schital sebya sebya russkim." *Nezavisimoe voennoe obozrenie*, January 28, 2011.

"Vol'f—odinochka." *Kommersant vlast'* 3, no. 506 (January 27, 2003).

"Zdes' lezhit Chicherin, zhertva sokrashchenii i chistok." *Kommersant vlast'* 4, no. 858 (February 1, 2010).

Zhirnov, Evgenii. "Chekist iz firmy." *Kommersant vlast'*, April 12, 2004.

———. "Lubyanskii komsomolets." *Kommersant vlast'*, April 10, 2001.

———. "Pri nashem sodeistvii rabotayut bandy za kordonom." *Kommersant vlast'*, August 23, 2004.

———. "Propushchennye cherez Tito." *Kommersant vlast'*, April 3, 2001.

———. "U nas byla samaya legal'naya razvedka v mire." *Kommersant vlast'*, April 23, 2002.

INDEX

Manuilskii, Dmitrii, 63
Mao Tse-tung, 167, 225–26
Maritime Workers Industrial Union, 65
Markin, Yuri, 129
Markov, Georgi, 259, 260
Marling, Melinda, 81
Marsden-Smedley, Hester Harriot, 81
Marshall Plan, 152, 166, 268
"Marshall Plan of the Mind," 268
"Marta," 46–48
Martella, Ilario, 261–62
Martin, William, 236
Martynov, Valerii, 270, 271
Martynov, Viktor, 206
Marx, Karl, 8
Marxism, 68–69, 72–73, 75
Marxist-Leninism, 43, 173
Maslennikov, Mikhail, 242–43, 245, 319n32
Maslov, Colonel, 224, 242–43
mathematics, 236–37, 240, 241–43, 245
Matvieiko, Miron, 155
Maxse, Marjorie, 81
Mayor, Tessa, 83, 170, 310n11
MC-70 plans, 209
McCarthyism, 169
McNamara, Robert, 203–204, 209–10
McNeil, Hector, 151
Meiklejohn, Ronald, 33
Mein Kampf (Hitler), 40
Mekhmata department, 163–64
Melkishev, Pavel, 140–41
Mendel, Gregor, 164
Menshikov Mikhail, 202
Menzhinsky, Vyacheslav, 6, 7, 16, 18, 19, 21, 22, 37, 39, 45, 53, 85
Menzies, Stewart, 170
Mercader, Ramón, 3, 123
Merkulov, Vsevolod, 111, 114, 124–25, 140, 148, 179
Metropolitan-Vickers Electrical Co. (Metrovick), 52–53
MGB, 145–46, 153–54, 155, 159, 163, 171, 173, 174, 180–81, 187, 205

MGIMO, xxiii, 228, 253
MI5, xvii, xix, xx, 4, 35, 73, 82–83, 88, 127, 138, 139, 170–71, 196–99, 207–208, 219
Soviet infiltration of, 82–83, 88, 138, 171, 207–208
MI6, xvi, xx, xxii, 4, 19, 21, 32–39, 49–53, 62, 74, 77, 81, 94, 103–106, 115, 126, 127, 151, 154, 169, 170, 183, 188, 195, 197, 219–20, 251, 273, 313n36
MI14, 107
microdots, 196
microelectronics, 244
Middle East, 221–22
Miedziński, Bogusław, 56
Mielke, Erich, 263
Miklashevskii, Igor', 123–24
Mikron factory, 244
Military-Diplomatic Academy, Soviet, 210, 225
Miller, Peter, 34
Milne, Tim, 170
Mil'shtein, Mikhail, 179
Mil'shtein, Vladimir, 179
Ministry of Defence, Soviet, 267
Ministry of Internal Affairs, Soviet, 174–75
Ministry of State Security, Soviet, 263
Mink, George (Minkovsky), 65–66
Minsker, Yakov, 55
"missile gap," 233
Mitchell, Bernon, 236
Mitrokhin, Vasili, xvi–xviii
Mitrokhin Archive, xvi–xvii
Mitskevich, Evgenii, 124
Modrzhinskaya, Yelena, 126–28
Moisenko-Velikaya, Tat'yana, 61
mokrie dela (wet jobs), 123
Molody, Konon, 194, 195–97
Molotov, Vyacheslav, 10, 39, 63, 99, 106, 112, 114, 124, 128, 146, 154–55
Monarchist Organisation of Central Russia (MOTsR), 20
Monkhouse, Allan, 53